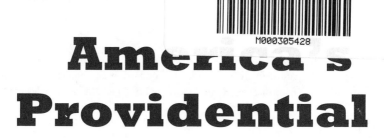

America's Providential History

Including

Biblical Principles of Education, Government, Politics, Economics, and Family Life

Revised and Expanded Edition

Mark A. Beliles and Stephen K. McDowell

PROVIDENCE FOUNDATION

America's Providential History
© 1989 by Mark A. Beliles & Stephen K. McDowell

First printing, 1989
Second edition, 1991
Third edition, 2010
Fourth revised and expanded edition, 2020

Published by: The Providence Foundation
                     PO Box 6759
                     Charlottesville, VA 22906
                     434-978-4535
                     Email: info@providencefoundation.com
                     www.providencefoundation.com

The Providence Foundation is a Christian educational organization whose purpose is to train and network leaders of education, business, and politics to transform their culture for Christ.

Printed in the United States of America

ISBN13: 978-1-887456-59-3

Cover Painting:

The Prayer at Valley Forge

Valley Forge itself inspired this splendid masterpiece of patriotic art. Biblical painter Arnold Friberg has created a monumental and sacred scene, capturing what many Americans feel are the deep spiritual roots of our country. We are grateful to Mr. Friberg for permission to use his painting on our cover.

"The most sublime picture in American history is of George Washington on his knees in the snow at Valley Forge. That image personifies a people who know that it is not enough to depend on our own courage and goodness; we must also seek help from God, our Father and Preserver."

President Ronald Reagan, National Day of Prayer Proclamation, May 6, 1982

Smaller pictures (from left): Frances Willard (educator), George Washington Carver (scientist), John Robinson (pastor) – Christians who were providentially used by God to transform various spheres of American life.

Acknowledgements

Both of the authors were initially inspired to study and teach the material in this book through two sources: 1) the book *The Light and the Glory* by Peter Marshall and David Manuel and 2) the ministry and encouragement of Bob and Rose Weiner. Our ideas were then dramatically influenced by scholarly writings and loving personal training of Miss Rosalie Slater and Miss Verna Hall. Many other individuals have contributed to our development, and their writings are cited in this book. Our wives, Nancy Beliles and Beth McDowell, have contributed the greatest amount in our lives and work. Their names will not be found in the footnotes or credits of this book, but if you could read our hearts there you would find them above all other names except that of our Lord Jesus Christ.

America's Providential History

Table of Contents

Introduction

In *America's Providential History* we examine the history of America from a Christian perspective. Since God is the author of history, and He is carrying out His plan in the earth through history, any view of the history of America, or any country, that ignores God is not true history. He is Sovereign over His creation and "His Story" in the earth, and is at work in significant, and seemingly insignificant, events to accomplish His purposes for mankind. This is a providential view of history and was held by the vast majority of those people who founded this nation.

While we do not look at all the events in America's birth and growth, we do highlight the providence and purposes of God, and the faith of our founders. Understanding this will provide a proper framework in which other historical information can be properly placed.

We begin the history of America with Creation, and Adam and Eve, because if one does not understand God's plan and purpose for man from the beginning, he will not be able to understand how America fits into His overall plan. The history of America, or any country, cannot be studied as an isolated event.

We have designed the book to be easily studied and digested, yet we have included many excerpts from original sources (for example, numerous pages of Bradford's *History of Plymouth Plantation* and shorter excerpts of various sermons of the colonial clergy) to introduce modern Americans to the ideas, character, and literacy level of early Americans. Colonial Americans were educated far better by the home, church, and private sector than our youth today are by modern state schools, and at a fraction of the cost.

America's Providential History teaches more than just historical Christian facts. Biblical principles of education, law, government, and economics, the Christian idea of man and government, the Chain of Liberty moving westward—in short, a biblical worldview—are imparted through this book. While all of America's founders were not Christians (though a great majority were), almost everyone had a biblical worldview, even the non-Christians.

Most of our founders were Christians, but this does not mean they were without fault. Providential history does not mean "sinless" or "sugarcoated" history. Like the Bible, it introduces people God has used for His purposes, even though they had short-comings and sins not to be emulated. God is glorified even more when we see fallible, finite men used by Him. Since most modern secular texts tend to provide plenty of criticism of America's leaders (much of which is unfounded), we generally present their positive contributions, which are becoming harder to find in modern writings. America's early leaders did sin, like all men, but their heart was to obey God. Today, most of our leaders have a much different heart and mind.

Most Americans today, including most Christians, have a humanistic (man-centered) worldview. This is one great difference in early and present-day America and is a primary reason why our nation is experiencing great problems. Ideas have consequences. The internal beliefs and ideas of a people are expressed in their external actions. Today, we are experiencing the fruit of secularism. To see godly transformation in America, we must renew our minds to view the world from God's perspective as revealed in the Bible—we must infuse the faith of our Fathers into the life of our country.

In other words, we as Christians must learn what it means to disciple a nation. The study of America's history provides the best example of this, because colonial Christians discipled their nation. Part of the goal of the Providence Foundation, and our vision as its founders, is to accomplish this task. This book is one resource to assist in this endeavor (some other books and resources are listed in the back, and many more can be found on our website, providencefoundation.com). We have not only worked to train Americans to think and act from a biblical perspective, but also people from scores of other nations; after all, we are to make disciples of all the nations.

Providence is a word that signifies the Bible doctrine of the overruling power of God that governs in the affairs of men. The Providence Foundation is working to establish such an understanding in the hearts and minds of all people. We urge pastors, Christian leaders, Christian schools, and homeschoolers to use this book as a text for a regular class to help disciple people in a biblical worldview. Many already do so.

The people of a free nation must have a foundation that will support liberty, for without it, that nation will surely fall. The great nineteenth century statesman and politician Daniel Webster declared:

If we and our posterity shall be true to the Christian religion, if we and they shall live always in the fear of God and shall respect His Commandments,...we may have the highest hopes of the future fortunes of our country;...But if we and our posterity neglect religious instruction and authority, violate the rules of eternal justice, trifle with the injunctions of morality, and recklessly destroy the political constitution which holds us together, no man can tell how sudden a catastrophe may overwhelm us that shall bury all our glory in profound obscurity.[1]

Daniel Webster

To bring God's liberty to the nations and secure their future fortunes is the goal of the Providence Foundation. We start Chapter One with a quote by Benjamin Franklin: "He who shall introduce into public affairs the principles of primitive Christianity shall change the face of the world." We are working in this way to change the face of America and the world.

Chapter 1

God's Plan for the Nations

"He who shall introduce into public affairs the principles of primitive Christianity will change the face of the world."[2] — Benjamin Franklin

The goal *of America's Providential History* is to equip Christians to be able to introduce biblical principles into the public affairs of America and every nation in the world, and in so doing bring godly change throughout the world. We will be learning how to establish a biblical power and form of government in America, and we will see how our present governmental structures must be changed. Since the principles we will

Benjamin Franklin

be learning are valid in every society and in any time in history, they will be able to be applied throughout the world and not just in America. As we learn to operate nations on biblical principles, we will be bringing liberty to the nations of the world and hence fulfilling part of God's plan for the nations.

The Need for World Reformation

The Bible reveals to us that the world longs for liberation. Romans 8:19, 21 says that "creation eagerly waits for the revealing of the sons of God…because creation itself also will be delivered from the bondage of corruption into the glorious liberty of the children of God" (NKJV). The following statistics show the desperate need for real answers to world problems.

The Need for World Reformation

(1) **Megapoverty**—The World Bank estimates that 1.4 billion people in the developing world (one in four) live on less than U.S. $1.25 a day (international line for poverty) in 2005. Over 3 billion people live on less than $2.50/day, and at least 80% of humanity live on less than $10/day. 1.1 billion people in developing countries have inadequate access to water, and 2.6 billion lack basic sanitation. 1.6 billion people live without electricity; nearly a billion people are unable to read a book or sign their names. Of the 2.2 billion children in the world, 1 billion are in poverty; 25,000 children die each day due to poverty; 1.4 million die each year from lack of access to safe drinking water and adequate sanitation. Of the 1.9 billion children from the developing world there are: 640 million without adequate shelter (1 in 3), 400 million with no access to safe water (1 in 5) and 270 million with no access to health services (1 in 7). In 2003, 10.6 million died before the age of 5.[3]

(2) **Human Trafficking** —The number of people held in slavery worldwide is estimated to be between 12-27 million, more than at any time in world history. Between 700,000 and 900,000 people are bought and sold across international borders each year. Between 14,500 and 17,500 victims are trafficked into the United States annually and nearly 250,000 children are considered at risk of child sexual exploitation in America. Human trafficking exists in at least 127 countries and has become the second most lucrative business after drug trafficking.[4]

(3) **STD's and Sexual Activity** —Nearly half (46%) of all 15-19 year-olds in the United States have had sex at least once. One in three teen girls is estimated to get pregnant at least once before the age of 20. Of the 750,000 pregnancies among teens, around 200,000 ended in abortion (in 2006). The Center for Disease Control estimates that there are approximately 19 million new sexually transmitted disease infections each year—almost half of them among young people 15 to 24 years of age. 1 in 4 teenage girls (3 million) have a STD.[5]

(4) **Abortion** —Over 60 million abortions have been performed in the U.S since 1973. 50% of women obtaining abortions are under the age of 25. Worldwide each year about 35 of every 1,000 women of childbearing age have an induced abortion. About 26 million women have legal abortions each year, and an estimated 20 million have illegal abortions. 22% of all pregnancies end in abortion.[6]

(5) **Crime** —Nearly one-half million homicides were committed worldwide in 2004. Over 10 million crimes are committed every year in America with a total annual cost of $675 billion. Every 3 seconds a crime occurs against someone's

property; a violent crime occurs every 35 seconds (America ranks 24th in the world for murders per capita and 8th worldwide for all crimes). More than 1 in 100 Americans are in jail or prison (2.3 million behind bars), an all-time high that is costing federal, state, and local governments about $62 billion a year. The U.S. spends over $30,000 per year per inmate.[7]

(6) **Refugees**—Total refugees worldwide reached 21 million in 2005.[8]

(7) **Arms**—Worldwide annual military expenditure rises from $2 billion in 1969 to $650 billion in 1982, to $940 billion in 1985, reaching $1.46 trillion in 2008.[9]

(8) **Totalitarian Governments**—The number of citizens killed by totalitarian or extreme authoritarian governments is greater than 130 million since 1900 (1918-54, USSR killed 40 million citizens, China under Mao 45 million, 1975-79 Cambodia 2 million), far greater than 36 million combatants killed in wars since 1900; absolutist governments are now mankind's deadliest scourge, with attacks against other nations and their own citizens (for example North Korea, Iran, Sudan). Internal civil conflict killed millions in various nations in the past few decades.[10]

(9) **Statism and Debt**—In 2000 developing nations owed industrialized nations over $1.3 trillion; for developing nations the average debt is 71% of the gross domestic product; loan defaults and forgiveness have resulted in large redistribution of wealth. Big government is a great threat to liberty and economic growth with ever increasing regulations and debt. With decades of deficit spending by 2020, the U.S. federal government amassed a $22 trillion national debt (over $65,000 per person), saddling future generations with a massive debt burden. While 70% of Americans favor "smaller government with fewer services and lower taxes," current leaders borrow and spend with reckless abandon (with many recent budget deficits around $1 trillion); only 21% of voters nationwide say the U.S. Government has consent of the governed.

(10) **Global Terrorism**—International terrorism proliferates around the world: Muslim terrorists, bombings, kidnappings, blackmail. Almost every nation is affected.

The Answers Are Found in the Bible

The truth of the Bible (John 8:32) provides mankind with a theology of liberty that brings real freedom to those individuals and nations who are oppressed. From the beginning of time, God created the earth and made man responsible to rule over it. Genesis 1:28 says: "And God blessed them; and God said to them, 'Be fruitful and multiply, and fill the earth and subdue it; and rule over…the earth.'" When man rejected God's Law and lost the ability to not only govern himself, but also to govern society, public tyranny and oppression reigned through sinful men.

Through the ministry and death of Jesus Christ, however, the power for both self and civil government was restored to mankind. Though internal liberty was a primary focus of Jesus Christ, it must not be overlooked that His inaugural and farewell sermons both emphasized external civil liberty. In Luke 4:18, Christ's first public message focused on "liberty" for "the poor…the captives…[and] those who are oppressed." It is safe to assume that poverty, slavery, tyranny and injustice were on the Lord's mind when, in His final sermon, He commissioned His followers to "Go therefore and make disciples of all the nations" (Matt.

Jesus commissioned us to disciple the nations.

28:19). Matthew Henry, the great Bible commentator studied by our Founding Fathers, explains that "the principal intention of this commission" is clear. It is to "do your utmost to make the nations Christian nations."[11] This is God's plan for the nations.

The apostle Paul understood this plan very well and sought to communicate it to the Christians of the first century. In 1 Corinthians 6:2 Paul asks a vital question: "Do you not know that the Christians will one day judge and govern the world?" (Amplified Bible) If this is true, Paul says, then they ought to at least be competent to hold public offices such as the local judgeships in Greece. To those Christians in Corinth, as well as in America today, who incorrectly assume that Paul means we should rule **only** in the next age after the second coming of Christ, the next question and answer of the apostle is aimed: "Do you not know that we shall judge angels? How much more the matters of this life?" (vs. 3). Paul then rebukes the Christians for their apathy and irresponsibility that allowed non-Christians to be in control: "If then you have law courts dealing with matters of this life, do you appoint them as judges who are of no account in the church. I say this to your shame" (vs. 4-5).

This shameful situation has become the reality in America. The battle for God's earth (Psalm 24:1) is being lost today mainly because Christians have thought that God does not really care about such things. They fail to see that Christ taught us to focus our prayers, not on heaven, but upon His kingdom coming "on earth as it is in heaven" (Matthew 6:9-10). The results of such ignorance and neglect of duty

has been costly in the 20th century. America has experienced great revival since 1900, leading to over 60 million people claiming to be "Christian," yet simultaneously our nation has plummeted into debauchery and corruption at a rate unparalleled in our history. In 1900, Africa was about 1% Christian. By 1988 the Christian populace of that continent had grown to about 35%! However, in that same year, 85% of Africa lived under Communist and totalitarian regimes. Historically, the gospel has liberated nations, but why not in Africa? One primary reason is that Christian missionaries have offered African nations a truncated Gospel message devoid of biblical answers to anything not strictly of a pietistic or personal nature.

As a result, these and other nations have not been presented with a true biblical theology of liberty and so are being increasingly deceived by Satan's counterfeit. The devil's "Liberation Theology" incorrectly identifies the root of public evil as the socio-economic environment, and claims that liberation comes through violent revolution, followed by the people's dependency on a government they can trust. Christ, in contrast, says the root of evil is the heart of man, and therefore, external liberty is possible only when it flows from the internal to the external. Revival, therefore, must precede reformation.

Jesus Christ spoke of this "cause and effect" principle in Luke 6:43-45:

> For there is no good tree which produces bad fruit; nor, on the other hand, a bad tree which produces good fruit. For each tree is known by its own fruit; ... The good man out of the good treasure of his heart brings forth what is good; and the evil man out of the evil treasure of his heart brings forth what is evil.

Every effect has a cause. The fruit is determined by the root. Man's conduct is determined by man's heart. The external is determined by the internal. All external "forms" or structures come from some internal "power." We will call this the Principle of Power and Form. The Christian religion is the essential power needed to create and preserve a form of government that is free and just.

History Is Shaped by the Heart of Man under the Providence of God

The external affairs of a nation are a reflection of the condition of the hearts of the people. Historian Charles Rollin presents the view of most eighteenth century writers in stating that God is sovereign over history, but deals with nations dependent upon the heart and action of the people. He wrote:

> Nothing gives history a greater superiority to many branches of literature, than to see in a manner imprinted, in almost every page of it, the precious footsteps and shining proofs of this great truth, viz. that God disposes all events as Supreme Lord and Sovereign; that He alone determines the fate of kings and the duration of empires; and that he transfers the government of kingdoms from one nation to another because of the unrighteous dealings and wickedness committed therein.[12]

George Bancroft

You cannot understand history without understanding Divine Providence. George Bancroft, eminent historian of American history in the nineteenth century said, "Providence is the light of history and the soul of the world. God is in history and all history has a unity because God is in it." Providential history is true history. Many modern educators deny the providential view of history and would have us believe that their promotion of one of several "secular" views of history is simply the recounting of undeniable facts. They fail to tell their students that their own humanistic presuppositions and religious doctrines determine their choice of people, places, principles, and events. They fail to communicate that neutrality is not possible in the teaching of history, for the historian's worldview will dictate his perspective. Even as there are not many interpretations of Scripture (2 Pet. 1:20-21), neither are there of history. There is really only one correct view — that which is the Author's interpretation and perspective. God is the Author of Scripture and History.

Reverend S.W. Foljambe, in 1876, defined history as "the autobiography of Him 'who worketh all things after the counsel of His will' (Eph. 1:11) and who is graciously timing all events after the counsel of His Christ, and the Kingdom of God on earth. It is His-Story."[13]

The Bible overwhelmingly affirms this truth. Consider these few Scriptures:

Acts 17:24-26 — "The God who made the world...gives to all life and breath and all things; and He made...every nation...having determined their appointed times, and the boundaries of their habitation."

1 Timothy 6:15-16 — "He is the blessed and only Sovereign, the King of Kings and Lord of lords;... To Him be honor and eternal dominion! Amen."

Proverbs 16:9-10 — "The mind of man plans his way, but the Lord directs his steps. A divine decision is in the lips of the king."

Job 12:23 — "He makes the nations great, then destroys them; He enlarges the nations, then leads them away."

Psalms 22:28 — "For the kingdom is the Lord's, and He rules over the nations."

Daniel 2:21 — "It is He who changes the times and the epochs; He removes kings and establishes kings."

Daniel 4:17, 26 — "The Most High is ruler over the realm of mankind;... Your kingdom will be assured to you after you recognize it is Heaven that rules."

The Founders of the United States of America Believed in the Providential View of History

Webster's 1828 Dictionary defines *Providence* as "the care and superintendence which God exercises over His creatures. By 'Divine Providence' is understood 'God Himself.'"[14] This definition, written in the times in which our Founders lived, is significant, for it helps us to see what they meant when they used this term in their writings (and they used it often). In addition to *Providence*, they used many other names for God, not just referring to Him as *God, Lord,* or *Jesus.* George Washington used at least 54 different titles for God in his writings, Abraham Lincoln used 49, and Robert E. Lee used 45. This reflects the depth of understanding our Founding Fathers had of God and His involvement in human affairs.

Here are some statements that reveal how America's Founders recognized God's hand in history:

William Bradford, Governor of the Pilgrims

"But these things did not dismay them...for their desires were set on the ways of God, and to enjoy His ordinances; but they rested on His Providence and knew whom they had believed."[15]

Declaration of Independence, 1776

"And for the support of this Declaration, with a firm reliance on the Protection of Divine Providence, we mutually pledge to each other our Lives, our Fortunes and our Sacred Honor."

Benjamin Franklin Addressing the Constitutional Convention, 1787

"How has it happened, Sir, that we have not hitherto once thought of humbly appealing to the Father of lights to illuminate our understandings? In the beginning of the contest with Great Britain, when we were sensible to danger, we had daily prayers in this room for Divine protection. Our prayers, Sir, were heard and they were graciously answered. ... I have lived, Sir, a long time and the longer I live, the more convincing proofs I see

Benjamin Franklin

of this truth—that God governs in the affairs of men.—And if a sparrow cannot fall to the ground without His notice, is it probable that an empire can rise without His aid? We have been assured, Sir, in the sacred writings that 'except the Lord build the house, they labor in vain that build it.'... I firmly believe this."[16]

The United States House of Representatives in 1854

"The people of these United States, from their earliest history to the present time, have been led by the hand of a Kind Providence, and are indebted for the countless blessings of the past and present, and dependent for continued prosperity in the future upon Almighty God. ... The great vital and conservative element in our system is the belief of our people in the pure doctrines and divine truths of the gospel of Jesus Christ."[17]

George Washington's Thanksgiving Proclamation, 1789

"It is the duty of all nations to acknowledge the Providence of Almighty God, to obey His will, to be grateful for His benefits, and humbly to implore His protection and favor."[18]

George Washington

Everyone must learn the providential history of America. Rev. A.W. Foljambe warns that, "The more thoroughly a nation deals with its history, the more decidedly will it recognize and own an overruling Providence therein, and the more religious a nation it will become; while the more superficially it deals with its history, seeing only secondary causes and human agencies, the more irreligious will it be."[19]

A lack of providential education contributes more than any other factor to the rise of secularism in a nation—a separation of history from God as the Author of history.

Chapter 2

Providential Geography

God's plan for the nations has been unfolding in a specific geographic direction. This geographical march of history is called the **Chain of Christianity** or the **Chain of Liberty.** Another way to define the Chain of Liberty is the sequence of events in the lives of men and nations that are links or stepping stones in history which result in bringing forth internal and external liberty.

The Bible attests to this geographical march of the Gospel:

> And they passed through the Phrygian and Galatian region, having been forbidden by the Holy Spirit to speak the word in Asia; and when they had come to Mysia, they were trying to go into Bithynia, and the Spirit of Jesus did not permit them; and passing by Mysia, they came down to Troas. And a vision appeared to Paul in the night: a certain man of Macedonia was standing and appealing to him and saying, "Come over to Macedonia and help us." And when he had seen the vision, immediately we sought to go into Macedonia, concluding that God had called us to preach the gospel to them. (Acts 16:6-10)

Why did God forbid Paul to speak the word in Asia? It is because He had other plans for the spread of the gospel. Paul and his companions were trying to go into Bithynia (northeast of where they were in Mysia) to preach the word, but God called them west into Europe. This was not by chance, but by God's choice in accordance with His plan for reaching the world with the gospel. From the beginning, God has had a systematic plan for filling the earth with his glory.

We know from later biblical events (see for example Romans 15:19, 28— Illyricum is the Baltic region of Europe) and world history that the spread of

Christianity (and hence civilization) has occurred in a westward direction. It is true that early disciples carried the gospel into northern Africa and in much of Asia, but it was in Europe where Christianity firmly took root and affected the entire society. As we will see, Christianity produced internal and external liberty in a westward direction. This is why we speak of the westward move of the Chain of Christianity.

It seems as if God's direction is westward. Even as the sun rises in the east and travels to the west, so His Son rose in the east and has traveled to the west. It is interesting that the children of Israel entered the Promised Land, not traveling the shortest route, northeast, but traveling from east to west. In the tabernacle in the wilderness, the priests moved from east to west as they approached the presence of God in the Holy of Holies. Matthew 24:27 states that "just as the lightning comes from the east, and flashes even to the west, so shall the coming of the Son of Man be." Some manuscripts add this verse at the end of the book of Mark: "Jesus Himself sent out through them from east to west the sacred and imperishable proclamation of eternal salvation."

God had prepared Europe in many ways to enable it to fulfill its part in God's plan for the world. One, He formed Europe with a geographic individuality — with a unique placement on the earth in relation to the other continents, with a unique geographic structure, coastline, and climate, and with unique people groups. Studying these, in conjunction with history, reveals the sovereignty of God over the nations.

The Individuality of the Continents

Like Europe, God has prepared all the continents for a specific purpose. Insight into the purpose of a continent or nation can be revealed by studying its geographic structure.

What is geography? The word *geography* is derived from two Greek words meaning "the earth" and "to write." We could figuratively say that geography is God's handwriting on the earth. (He is the only one that I know who is big enough to write on the earth!)

"Christian" geography (which is true geography) is the view that the earth's origin, end, purposes, and physiography (physical structure, climate, plant and animal distribution) are for Christ and His glory.

Shakespeare was correct in saying that "all the world's a stage." God is the One who has created the props, placing the mountains, oceans, rivers, seas, deserts, islands, and continents just where He wanted them in order that they might assist in carrying out His plan for mankind on the earth.

God's Principle of Individuality

All of God's creation is a reflection of His infinity, diversity, and individuality. God does not create carbon-copy entities, but distinct and unique individualities, be they animals, plants, humans, planets, stars, etc. While a unity exists among all creation, since all is created by God, there also exists a great diversity, since God himself is three, yet one. God displays the principle of individuality, and his creation does as well.

People display the principle of individuality.

There are certain characteristics that all humans have (unity), yet no two people are alike (diversity):

- Each person has a unique purpose and call from God.
- Each person also has unique characteristics, both internal and external.

One external characteristic that you possess that no one else has are your fingerprints. Of the seven billion people on the earth today, no two have the same fingerprints. You also have a unique profile, voiceprints, and nerve pattern on the inside of your eye. Internal characteristics that are uniquely yours include your thoughts, attitudes, and emotions. These are just a few characteristics you possess that reveal that God made you "the one and only you."

God gives us certain internal and external characteristics that enable us to fulfill our God-given purpose and call. (As an example, God made Eric Liddell physically fast so that he could win races and bring God glory through it.)

Nations also display God's principle of individuality.

Like individuals, nations have a unique purpose. As an example, Babylon was used by God to bring his judgment upon Israel by taking them into captivity. We will see throughout this book how God has raised up and put down nations of the world for his purposes.

Nations also have unique characteristics, such as their time of existence in history, their power, national spirit, geographic location, boundaries, and structure. As with people, God gives nations unique characteristics in order that they can fulfill their divine purposes in history.

Continents reflect the principle of design.

Arnold Guyot, a nineteenth century scientist and professor of geography at Princeton University, was an expert in the providential view of geography. In his book *The Earth and Man,* Guyot wrote:

> We must elevate ourselves to the moral world to understand the physical world: the physical world has no meaning except by and for the moral world...
>
> [I]t is correct to say that inorganic nature is made for organized nature, and the whole globe for man, as both are made for God, the origin and end of all things. ... Science may attempt to comprehend the purpose of God, as to the destinies of nations, by examining with care the theatre, seemingly arranged by Him for the realization of the new social order, towards which humanity is tending."[20]

Contrasting the Southern and Northern Continents

In his book *Physical Geography,* 1873, Guyot summarizes the distinction of the northern and southern continents and concludes the "the southern continents...may be designated the continents of nature" and "the northern continents, may properly be designated the continents of history."[21]

In *The Earth and Man,* Guyot gives these distinctions:

> The continents of the North are more indented, more articulated; their contours are more varied. Gulfs and inland seas cut very deep into the mass of their lands, and detach from the principal trunk a multitude of peninsulas. ... A great number of continental islands are scattered along their shores, and are a new source of wealth to them...
>
> The southern continents, on the other hand, are massive, entire, without indentations, without inland seas or deep inlets, scanty in articulations of every kind and in islands...
>
> The continents of the North are more open to maritime life, to the life of commerce; they are more richly organized; they are better made to stimulate improvement.
>
> The northern continents are brought nearer together, more consolidated...whence the others appear to radiate in all directions, losing themselves as they taper off in the ocean. ... Owing to this greater nearness, to the facility of communication between one continent and another...the three northern continents have a mutual relationship not to be mistaken...

The continents of the South are more remote from each other than the foregoing. Broad oceans separate them even to isolation.[22]

The Southern Continents — The Continents of Nature

Guyot calls the southern continents, the "continents of nature." These reflect the glory of God in various ways. As Guyot writes in the conclusion of *Physical Geography,* "the fullness of nature's life is typified by Africa, with its superabundant wealth and power of animal life; South America, with its exuberance of vegetation; and Australia, with its antiquated forms of plants and animals."[23]

Australian Animals

The Northern Continents — The Continents of History

He refers to the northern continents as the "continents of history," for it is in the northern continents that man has progressed and developed throughout history. The southern continents are just beginning to enter into the historical development of mankind. This has not happened by chance, but by God's choice. He has even positioned and structured the continents so as to assist in the westward move of the *Chain of Christianity.*

The Climate Affects the Development of Mankind.

The climate, as well, has assisted in the progress of mankind. While the northern continents lie primarily in a temperate climate zone, the Southern Continents lie primarily in the tropical zone. This tropical climate is conducive for plant and animal life to flourish. Yet with man it is otherwise. Guyot writes:

> Here is the reason, gentlemen, that the Creator has placed the cradle of mankind in the midst of the continents of the North, so well made, by their forms, by their structure, by their climate, as we shall soon see, to stimulate and hasten individual development and that of human societies; and not at the centre of the tropical regions, whose balmy but innervating and treacherous atmosphere would perhaps have lulled him to sleep the sleep of death in his very cradle.[24]

The temperate climate incites man to action and challenges him to labor, which assists in his development and growth. Guyot continues:

> The man of the temperate regions is the…most favored. Invited to labor by everything around him, he soon finds, in the exercise of all his faculties, at once progress and well-being…[25]
>
> In the temperate climates all is activity, movement. The alternations of heat and cold, the changes of the seasons, a fresher and more bracing air, incite man to a constant struggle, to forethought, to the vigorous employment of all his faculties.[26]

The Purpose of the Continents of History

Asia, the Continent of Origins

In his conclusion to *Physical Geography,* Arnold Guyot summarizes the characteristics and functions of the continents of history:

Asia is the largest of the continents, the most central, the only one with which all the others are closely connected; and the one whose different physical regions show the greatest contrasts, and are separated by the greatest barriers. This great and strongly marked continent is the continent of origins. The human family, its races and civilizations, and the systems of religion which rule the most enlightened nations, all had their beginning here. By the great diversity of its physical features and climate, and the strong barriers isolating them one from another, Asia was admirably fitted to promote the formation of a diversity of races; while its close connection with the other continents facilitated their dispersion throughout the earth.[27]

Europe, the Continent of Development

Europe shows a diversity of structure even greater than that of Asia; but with smaller areas, more moderate forms of relief, less extreme contrasts of climate, a more generally fertile soil, and everywhere an abundance of the most useful minerals; while the relative extent of its coast line—its maritime zone—is greater than that of any other continent. This continent is especially fitted, by its diversity, to foster the formation of distinct nationalities, each developing in an especial direction. Moreover, the proximity of these nations one to another, the greater facility of communication between them, and, above all, the common

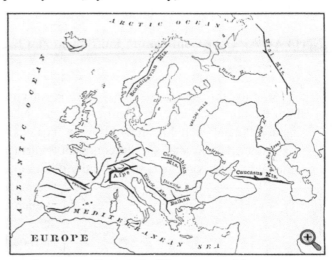

highway to the sea, nowhere very distant, facilitates mutual intercourse, the lack of which arrested the progress of the civilization of Asia. Though not the continent of origins, Europe is emphatically the continent of development. The Indo-European race—the people of progress—find their fullest expansion and activity, not in their original seat in Iran, but in Europe, whence they are spreading over all the quarters of the globe. The arts and learning of antiquity attained their highest development, not in western Asia and Egypt, the places of their origin, but in Greece and Rome. Christianity, also, only germinated in western Asia. Transplanted to Europe, it gradually attained its full development, and became the foundation on which is reared the vast and noble edifice of modern civilization.[28]

As Guyot has noted, Asia (and particularly the Middle East) has been the center for the origins, from science, math, and languages, to Christianity, religions, and mankind.

While these things, and more, originated in Asia, they did not develop there, but in Europe. God had arranged the structure of the earth to assure that the *Chain of Christianity* would move, not south into Africa or east into Asia, but westward into Europe. Great physical barriers lie both in Africa (the Sahara Desert) and Asia that prohibited civilization from spreading into the heart of these continents.

When Paul was called westward into Europe, he had no problem getting there, for the Mediterranean Sea provided easy access to the European Continent. It would have been quite different had he attempted to go into central Africa or Asia. The physical structure of the continents has helped to assure that Europe would be the continent of development.

North America, the Continent of Fulfillment and Propagation

Guyot writes:

America, different in position, structure, and climatic conditions, from both the other northern continents, seems destined to play a part in the history of mankind unlike that of Europe and Asia, though not less noble than either. The structure of this continent is characterized by a unity and simplicity as striking as is the diversity of Europe. In its climate, those contrasts in temperature which are so violent in Asia, and still prevail in Europe, are obliterated. Nowhere do we find in America those local centres, each having a strongly marked individuality, which fostered the progress of the race in its infancy and its youth; but everywhere provision is made for mutual intercourse, a common life, and the blending of the entire population into one. Evidently this continent was not designed to give birth and

development to a new civilization; but to receive one ready-made, and to furnish to the cultivated race of the Old World the scene most worthy of their activity. Its vast plains, overflowing with natural wealth, are turned towards Europe, and its largest rivers discharge into the Atlantic; while its lofty mountains, and less fertile lands, are removed far towards its western shores. Thus it seems to invite the Indo-European race, the people of progress, to new fields of action; to encourage their expansion throughout its entire territory, and their fusion into one nation; while it opens for them a pathway to all the nations of the earth. America, therefore, with her cultured and progressive people, and her social organization, founded upon the principle of the equality and brotherhood of all mankind, seems destined to furnish the most complete expression of the Christian civilization; and to become the fountain of a new and higher life for all the races of men.[29]

That which originated in Asia and developed in Europe has had its greatest fulfillment in America. In addition, America has served as a propagator of those areas of fulfillment, from the Gospel and ideas of civil and religious freedom to scientific ideas and technological advancements. All the continents of the world have in recent history been affected by the things America has propagated.

America is the only nation in the world that is made up of people from every nation in the world. It is truly a melting pot. The physical geography of America promotes the blending together of all the peoples who came and settled this land.

Many historians have acknowledged the providential preparation of America. Emma Willard stated: "In observing the United States, there is much to convince us, that an Almighty, Overruling Providence, designed from the first, to place here a great, united people."[30]

Alexis de Tocqueville wrote:

Although the vast country which we have been describing was inhabited by many indigenous tribes, it may justly be said, at the time of its discovery by Europeans, to have formed one great desert. The Indians occupied, without possessing it. ... Those coasts, so admirably adapted for commerce and industry; those wide and deep rivers; that inexhaustible valley of the Mississippi; the whole continent, in short, seemed prepared to be the abode of a great nation, yet unborn.

In that land the great experiment was to be made by civilized man, of the attempt to construct society upon a new basis; and it was there, for the first time, that theories hitherto unknown, or deemed impracticable, were to exhibit a spectacle for which the world had not been prepared by the history of the past.[31]

Conclusion—the Earth Manifests God's Glory

Guyot concludes his *Physical Geography* with these words:

Each continent has, therefore, a well-defined individuality, which fits it for an especial function. The fullness of nature's life is typified by Africa, with its superabundant wealth and power of animal life; South America, with its exuberance of vegetation; and Australia, with its antiquated forms of plants and animals.

In the grand drama of man's life and development, Asia, Europe, and America play distinct parts, for which each seems to have been admirably prepared. Truly no blind force gave our Earth the forms so well adapted to perform these functions. The conclusion is irresistible—that the entire globe is a grand organism, every feature of which is the outgrowth of a definite plan of the all-wise Creator for the education of the human family, and the manifestation of his own glory.[32]

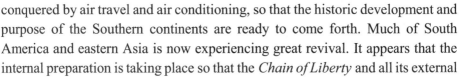

Now, in the 20th and 21st centuries, the travel and climactic barriers are being conquered by air travel and air conditioning, so that the historic development and purpose of the Southern continents are ready to come forth. Much of South America and eastern Asia is now experiencing great revival. It appears that the internal preparation is taking place so that the *Chain of Liberty* and all its external blessings might continue its westward march from America around the globe.

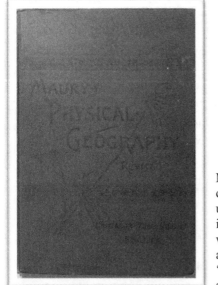

Matthew Maury's *Physical Geography* (1873) concludes: "the science of Physical Geography unfolds to us this grand view of our planet, that in all its arrangements there is proof of All-wise and beneficent design. The study leads to a deeper understanding of the Psalmist's words, 'The earth is full of the goodness of the Lord; so is the great and wide sea also.'"

Chapter 3

The Chain of Liberty: Origins

Self-Government and the Dominion Mandate

The history of government begins in the Garden of Eden with the first man. God placed man in the Garden and gave him a Dominion Mandate to subdue and rule all creatures including himself (Genesis 1:26-28). The test of man's self-government was his ability to resist eating of the forbidden tree without any type of external restraints. He had to internally govern himself to succeed (Genesis 2:16-17), but he did not. Through Adam's failure, sin entered into the world and made it difficult for any man to govern himself. At this time no civil government had been established. The Dominion Mandate did not include the responsibility for ruling over other men. Therefore, when Cain did not control his anger and jealousy, and violently slew his brother, who took responsibility for justice and protection? God Himself. (Genesis 4:1-16)

Civil Government for Protection

After a period of time, the prevalence of sin and lack of self-government led to so much violence that God saw the end result would be all men destroying one another (Genesis 6:5-13). Therefore, God decided to intervene and bring a flood to destroy all but one righteous family. When God brought Noah through the flood to a new earth, He re-established the Dominion Mandate, but added to man the responsibility for governing other men in order to protect human life (Genesis 9:5-7). This authorization included instituting capital punishment—the backbone of civil government.

Civil government, then, is just as much a divine institution as the family and the church. All were established by God with clear purposes and principles of operation revealed in the Bible. Some scriptures defining the purpose of civil government include:

When Cain killed Abel, God took responsibility for justice.

> Submit yourselves for the Lord's sake to every human institution, whether to a king as the one in authority, or to governors as sent by him for the punishment of evildoers and the praise of those who do right. (1 Peter 2:13-14)

> Let every person be in subjection to the governing authorities;…for rulers are not a cause of fear for good behavior, but for evil;…for it is a minister of God to you for good. But if you do what is evil, be afraid;…for it is a minister of God, an avenger who brings wrath upon the one who practices evil. (Romans 13:1, 3-4)

The purpose of government is, therefore, to protect the life, liberty, and property of all individuals by punishing evildoers and encouraging the righteous. When governing rulers fail to do this, then they themselves are resisting the ordinances of God and are illegitimate authorities who should be resisted and replaced. The main functions of the family, church, and civil government are procreation, propagation, and protection respectively. Most Christians today know much (or at least some) about the first two divine institutions, but very little about the latter. Most churches avoid teaching about government, although the Bible deals with it abundantly.

The Origin of Nations

In Genesis 10:4, 20, 31-32 we find the first reference to *nations* arising from family groups. We also find the rise of pagan monarchy (kingdoms) as the form of civil government in these nations. Centralization of power is a pagan tendency and is also seen in the rise of the first cities such as at Nineveh (Gen. 10:11) and Babel (Gen. 11:1). Egypt with its *Pharaohs* are mentioned in Genesis 12:10, 15 and nine kings are mentioned in Genesis 14:1-2.

Centralization of Civil Government at Babel — c. 2300 B.C.

Nowhere in Scripture is civil government said to have responsibility to be provider or savior for men by the centralization of its powers; yet between 2300-2400 B.C. men began to pervert the purpose of civil government in this way. The men at Babel began to congregate together rather than spread out and "fill the earth." They wanted to make a name for themselves and save themselves through the state as their *counterfeit* Messiah. This was the first public expression of humanism, where sovereignty was placed in a man or a collection of men rather than God (Genesis 11:1-8). In order to prevent centralized, one-world government, God made diverse languages which are an effective deterrent to this day.

The Hebrew Republic with Biblical Civil Laws — c. 1500 B.C.

God called Abraham to establish a unique "nation" among the other pagan nations around 2000 B.C. (Genesis 12:2 and 17:6, 10). Abraham becomes the "prince" (Genesis 23:6) or ruler of the nation and negotiates and battles with Pharaoh (Genesis 12:18), kings of Sodom and Salem (Genesis 14:17, 18), and King of Gerar (Genesis 20:2 and 21:27).

When God gave Moses the Law around 1300-1500 B.C. to be interpreted by judges and prophets in Israel, the first representative republic on earth was established. From the beginning, God's purpose was not limited to Israel, but he desired that these laws and their blessings might be exported to all nations on earth who had perverted God's plan of civil government into pagan centralized monarchy. God established in Israel a decentralized, representative government where every group of 10, 50, 100 and 1,000 families could choose or elect someone to be their judge or ruler. All of their civil laws were based upon God's higher fixed law, and not majorities. This makes it a republic, not a democracy.

The Hebrew Republic also had an unelected civil body known as the "Sanhedrin" which was the 70 "elders" of the Republic. These elders were civil, not religious offices. There was a separation of "church and state." The clergy of the land were the priests and the Levites and the judges were civil rulers. It is important to note that the prophets were primarily social reformers and statesmen among the people and included both clergy and non-clergy in their ranks. All

Babel was the beginning of the pagan tendency toward centralization.

civil rulers in Israel, even kings, did not rule unless they obtained the consent of the governed by a covenant.[33]

By 1120 B.C., however, as Israel backslid from God and their self and family government, there arose very poor and corrupt leadership under their judges (1 Samuel 8:19-20). Pagan monarchy was effective in keeping order but

God delivered His Law to mankind through Moses.

at the high price of oppression, taxation, and the loss of much liberty (1 Samuel 8:10-20). Unfortunately, Israel conformed to this pagan form of civil government where dominion was turned into domination. From this point forward until the landing of the Pilgrims at Plymouth—almost 3000 years—the entire world would know little to nothing of full external liberty for the individual man.

Greece and Rome's Pagan Attempts at Civil Liberty — c. 500 B.C.

The second major attempt at democratic government in history was in the Greek city-state of the sixth century before Christ. The Athenian lawgiver, Solon, drew up a legal system that would allow the people to make their own laws. Plato and Aristotle emphasized that a just society was one where every man is moved by concern for the common good. These concepts were also embraced by Roman statesmen such as Cicero and Seneca in the second century before Christ. They proposed an impartial system of laws based on Natural Law which, Cicero said, comes from God and originated before "any written law existed or any state had been established."

The Greek and Roman theories were never as democratic as the Hebrew, however, because of their belief in inequality of men. The ideas of democracy and freedom were only extended to certain classes and all others were denied basic rights. Such tyranny eventually produced conflicts in society that led to chaos and disorder. Cicero was murdered, and they reverted to complete totalitarianism to restore order. Greek and Roman contributions to democratic ideas were therefore more theoretical than actual, but nonetheless were helpful to later generations who learned from their mistakes.

The fundamental flaws of their attempts at democracy were rooted in their belief that man was naturally unequal and that only one or a privileged few were competent to govern the rest.

The pagan and Christian ideas of man and government are contrasted well by historian Richard Frothingham. Of this pagan view that dominated the world at this time in history, he wrote:

> At that time, social order rested on the assumed natural inequality of men. The individual was regarded as of value only as he formed a part of the political fabric, and was able to contribute to its uses, as though it were the end of his being to aggrandize the State. This was the pagan idea of man. The wisest philosophers of antiquity could not rise above it. Its influence imbued the pagan world;...especially the idea that man was made for the State, the office of which, or of a divine right vested in one, or in a privileged few, was to fashion the thought and control the action of the many.[34]

The Gospel of Jesus Christ Introduces the Christian Idea of Man and Government

With the coming of Jesus Christ and His death on the cross for the sins of the world, man's ability to govern himself internally was restored. The Law of God was no longer an external thing, but now could be written on men's hearts and interpreted not by prophets and judges, but by the Spirit within them.

In addition to this internal liberty, Christ also proposed principles for external civil liberty. As the church propagated these principles throughout the pagan world, the Christian idea of man and government became clear. As Frothingham states:

> Christianity then appeared with its central doctrine...that man was created in the Divine image, and destined for immortality; pronouncing that, in the eye of God, all men are equal. This asserted for the individual an independent value. It occasioned the great inference, that man is superior to the State, which ought to be fashioned for his use;...that the

state ought to exist for man; that justice, protection, and the common good, ought to be the aim of government.[35]

The Declaration of Independence states these Christian ideas this way:

> We hold these Truths to be self-evident, that all Men are created equal, that they are endowed by their Creator with certain unalienable Rights, that among these are Life, Liberty, and the Pursuit of Happiness—That to secure these Rights, Governments are instituted by Men, deriving their just powers from the Consent of the Governed.

Few nations today operate their governments based on the Christian idea of man and government. However, the pagan ideas are gradually being overcome.

Jesus Christ and Civil Government

Why did Jesus come into the world? There are many answers to this question. He came to seek and to save those who are lost, He came to destroy the works of the devil, and He came to establish the Kingdom of God, to name a few.

We have seen how man lost his ability to be self-governed when he disobeyed God. This led to external governmental tyranny. Christ also came to restore to man the potential of being self-governing under God. As man begins to be self-governed, it will affect the external governments operating on his life. Jesus came to not only bring internal salvation, but also external political freedom.

After Jesus had risen from the dead and before He ascended into heaven, He gathered His disciples together. Acts 1:6-8 explains,

> And so when they had come together, they were asking Him saying, "Lord, is it at this time You are restoring the kingdom to Israel?" He said to them, "It is not for you to know times or epochs which the Father has fixed by His own authority; but you shall receive power when the Holy Spirit has come upon you; and you shall be My witnesses both in Jerusalem, and in all Judea and Samaria, and even to the remotest part of the earth."

Of what type of kingdom were Jesus' disciples speaking? They were speaking of an external kingdom. For centuries the Hebrew people had read the prophecies of Scripture declaring a Messiah would come and set up His throne and deliver the people from bondage.

While Jesus walked on the earth, many of His followers thought He would set up His reign at any time. They even tried to make Him King. His disciples did not understand how His Kingdom was going to come. While they had not seen it established during Jesus' ministry on earth, surely now that He had risen from the dead, He would restore the Kingdom. That's why they asked Him this question.

Jesus did not deny that an external expression of the Kingdom would come. In fact, He said that times and epochs would follow (which we can look back upon today) that would contribute to the establishment of the Kingdom and the extension of external and internal liberty "to the remotest part of the earth."

Jesus giving one of His teachings on civil government.

The "power" for this external establishment of liberty is the "Spirit of the Lord;" therefore, Jesus emphasized the receiving of this power through the baptism of the Holy Spirit. He knew the inevitable result of internal liberty would be external liberty.

God's Pathway to Liberty

God's pathway to liberty is from the internal to the external. God's desire is for an external expression of His Kingdom on earth. Yet it must first begin in the heart of man, and then it will naturally express itself externally in all aspects of society.

The Bible reveals that "where the Spirit of the Lord is, there is liberty" (2 Corinthians 3:17). When the Spirit of the Lord comes into the heart of a man, that man is liberated. Likewise, when the Spirit of the Lord comes into a nation, that nation is liberated. The degree to which the Spirit of the Lord is infused into a society (through its people, laws, and institutions), is the degree to which that society will experience liberty in every realm (civil, religious, economic, etc.)

Christ came to set us free (Gal. 5:1, 3). Spiritual freedom or liberty ultimately produces political freedom. External political slavery reflects internal spiritual bondage.

Gradual Leavening Principle

Christianity's method of change is the same for nations as it is for individuals. As Christians, we are gradually transformed as we apply the truth of His word to our lives.

Dr. Augustus Neander reveals in his 1871 book, *General History of the Christian Religion,* how Christianity has historically brought about change in various nations of the world. Neander writes:

> Again, Christianity, from its nature, must pronounce sentence of condemnation against all ungodliness, but at the same time appropriate to itself all purely human relations and arrangements, consecrating and ennobling, instead of annihilating them. ... That religion which aimed nowhere to produce violent and convulsive changes from without, but led to reforms by beginning in the first place within,—whose peculiar character it was to operate positively rather than negatively,—to displace and destroy no faster than it substituted something better."[36]

Christian reforms within a nation do not begin with external or violent means (quite a contrast to Marxist/Communist "reforms" we see today), but they begin within.

In dealing with unbiblical situations in the nations today, we must remember that reform begins within, and as we remove the bad, we must simultaneously substitute something good. A government-controlled and funded welfare system is unbiblical, yet the solution is not to pass a law that immediately eliminates civil government support of the needy. Individuals and churches must begin to fulfill their God-given responsibility in this area (substitute the good) as we remove the role of our civil government.

Neander goes on to say:

> Yet Christianity nowhere began with outward revolutions and changes, which, in all cases where they have not been prepared from within, and are not based upon conviction, fail of their salutary ends. The

new creation to which Christianity gave birth, was in all respects an inward one, from which the outward effects gradually and therefore more surely and healthfully, unfolded themselves to their full extent.[37]

Civil Authority Comes through Service and Work, Not Imposition

External liberty, then, must come gradually, not immediately. It was this mindset of immediate civil change that Christ sought to change in His parable found in Luke 19:11-17. The "nobleman" in the parable, who is a type of Christ, emphasizes to his servants that their responsibility is to "occupy" or "do business" with their earthly finances, time, and talents until He returned. The reward for the faithful was that they would be given "authority over cities."

In other words, Jesus was giving a clue to Christians as to how to gain control of civil government. It is not by obtaining a position of power and then imposing a "Christian agenda" upon people, but by consistent hard work and service to meet the needs of society around us. It comes about through democratic process, not by usurpation of power.

Through Christ, God releases the "Law of liberty" into society through the cleansed hearts of men (James 1:25; 2:12). The self-governing Christian is governed by the internal law written on his heart interpreted by the Holy Spirit.

This does not mean that the Old Testament moral law is done away with, but that man can now carry out the law, for God has empowered us to do so. The more a nation applies His law, the more that nation will prosper and walk in liberty. The degree which a people apply the law personally will be reflected through their governmental institutions, for the law flows from the heart of man out to the nation.

Christ's Teachings on Politics and Government

Jesus did not specifically lay out external plans for setting up a godly civil government. He more importantly dealt with the "spirit" or "power" by giving certain principles and knew that a godly "form" would follow.

Knowing that internal liberty would move outward, Jesus provided some principles and guidelines on civil government. These include:

1. The Lord is sovereign in human history and government.

In answer to Pilate, Jesus said, "You would have no authority over Me, unless it had been given you from above" (John. 19:11). Here Jesus asserts that civil authority is delegated and controlled by God. Paul states this in Romans 13:1 by saying, "there is no authority except from God, and those which exist are established by God."

2. The individual has inherent value because he is made in the image of God (Matthew 22:17-21).

This contradicted the pagan idea that an individual was regarded as valuable only if he could contribute something to the state or he belonged to a certain social class or race.

3. Government exists to serve the common good of every individual.

Jesus taught much about civil affairs.

When we read the familiar passage of Matthew 20:25-28 in context, we receive a broader view of what Jesus meant. "But Jesus called them to Himself, and said, 'You know that the rulers of the Gentiles lord it over them, and their great men exercise authority over them. It is not so among you, but whoever wishes to become great [a governor (NKJV); a ruler (NIV)] among you shall be your servant." (Matt. 20:25-26; see also Luke 22:26).

Jesus is making reference to civil authorities and is declaring that they are to be public servants. Therefore, the purpose of civil government is to serve people. This was a radical new idea, and it contrasted greatly with the pagan idea of rulers dominating the people, an idea which existed throughout the entire world at this time.

As we will see, this idea gradually leavened many nations of the world, especially the United States. Today we call our civil leaders "public servants." That the civil government is the servant of man is a Christian idea.

4. Civil government and the church have separate jurisdictions.

While God cannot be separated from government, the Bible does speak of limits of jurisdiction of the state and church. Jesus taught that we are to render "to Caesar [the state] the things that are Caesar's, and to God the things that are God's" (Matt. 22:17-21).

We have already seen that one thing that belongs to the state and not the church is the use of the sword to protect the citizenry (Rom. 13:1-4). Some things that belong to God and not the state include our worship of God, our children, and our own consciences and lives. In these matters, the state has no authority and should not interfere.

Three views of this "church/state" issue exist today. They can be summed up by the following:

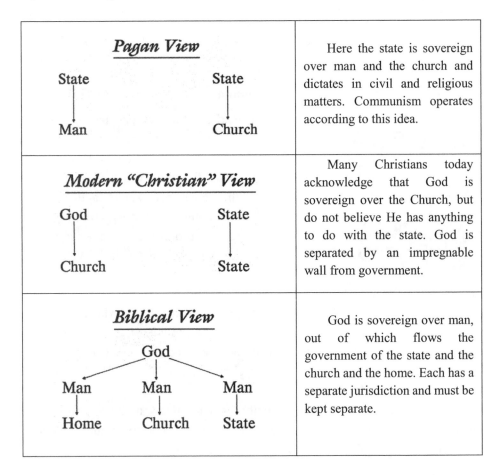

Pagan View State State Man Church	Here the state is sovereign over man and the church and dictates in civil and religious matters. Communism operates according to this idea.
Modern "Christian" View God State Church State	Many Christians today acknowledge that God is sovereign over the Church, but do not believe He has anything to do with the state. God is separated by an impregnable wall from government.
Biblical View God Man Man Man Home Church State	God is sovereign over man, out of which flows the government of the state and the church and the home. Each has a separate jurisdiction and must be kept separate.

Jesus also taught that taxation is an appropriate function of civil government (Matthew 17:24-27), that people should try to settle disputes before going to court (Luke 12:58), and that when a government ruler acts in a tyrannical manner, he must be resisted (Acts 5:29).

Christ's Guidelines for Resistance to Tyranny

There may come a time when we must resist unlawful authority. If so, we must be prepared to suffer the consequences, but we must also recognize that there are steps we should take in our resistance. A tyrant is one who exercises unlawful authority. We should observe the following guidelines in resisting tyranny.

1. Protest or Legal Action

Our first means of recourse should be to protest and/or to take all legal action possible. Jesus protested when He remained silent before Pilate and refused to cooperate (Mt. 27:14) and when He publicly censured Herod for his death threats (Luke 13:31-32).

He also instructed His disciples to publicly protest if city officials denied them their inalienable right to religious speech. He told them to go out into the streets and say, "Even the dust of your city which clings to our feet, we wipe off in protest against you" (Luke 10:11). "Wiping off the dust" is equivalent to boycotting.

The free nations of the world generally have more means of legal recourse and of protesting ungodly action than do others. Examples of protesting include picketing abortion chambers, boycotting stores that sell pornography, and removing our children from public schools that deny God. We who live in free nations not only have the right to do this but are obligated to God to do so to keep our consciences clean.

The Apostles also protested and took legal action. When Paul and Barnabas were driven out of Antioch by the city officials, "they shook off the dust of their feet in protest against them" (Acts 13:51) as Jesus had instructed them.

Protesting unlawful action is a Christian idea. "Protestants" originally received this title due to their protesting action by authorities (civil and ecclesiastical) that God declared was wrong.

In Acts 16 we see how Paul and Silas were unlawfully thrown into jail. When the chief magistrates tried to cover this up, Paul, recognizing his civil liberties were a sacred cause, demanded restitution to be made. "Paul said to them, 'They have beaten us in public without trial, men who are Romans, and have thrown us into prison; and now are they sending us away secretly? No indeed! But let them come themselves and bring us out.'" (Acts 16:37). The chief magistrates did come and bring them out themselves.

The reason Paul appealed to Caesar in Acts 24-26 was because his civil rights had been violated. He was being a good steward of the civil liberties God gave to him. The whole course of Paul's life was changed due to his exerting his rights as a citizen. He saw this action as part of the Great Commission. Even when non-Christians apply biblical methods for resisting tyranny, they find some measure of success. An example is Gandhi in India.

2. Flight

If all avenues of protest or legal action are expended to right unlawful acts of civil authorities, then flight, if possible, is the next appropriate measure to take.

Jesus told His disciples that "whenever they persecute you in this city, flee to the next" (Matt. 10:23). He also warned them to flee the destruction that was to come upon Jerusalem (Matt. 24:15-18). The early church also took flight as persecution rose against them (Acts 8:1-4). This is not to say that we are to hide out in mountains, but that sometimes flight to other places will more surely allow us to fulfill God's will.

Paul being taken away from prison to Rome. His appeal to Caesar was a result of his civil rights being violated.

Many people who came to settle in America were fleeing civil and religious tyranny. After exhausting all means of protest and legal action, they saw that flight was the best means of accomplishing God's purpose. This principle is the basis of the Constitutional right of emigration.

3. Force in Self-Defense

As a last recourse in resisting tyranny, force is a legitimate biblical means. The Old Testament contains many examples of the children of Israel using force to defend themselves. We will examine in a later chapter how a defensive war in a just cause is sinless, but for now we want to show that Jesus considered force legitimate at certain times in resisting tyranny.

At the conclusion of the Last Supper, Jesus finished His instructions He had begun earlier with the seventy by instructing His disciples to prepare themselves militarily: "'Let him who has no sword sell his robe and buy one.' And they said, 'Lord, look, here are two swords.' And He said to them, 'It is enough'" (Luke 22:36, 38), implying the legitimacy of using force at certain times. John Jay, the first Supreme Court Chief Justice, commented on this incident in a letter written in 1818:

> Although just war is not forbidden by the gospel in express terms, yet you think an implied prohibition of all war, without exception, is deducible from the answer of our Lord to Pilate, viz: "If my kingdom were of this world, then would my servants fight, etc."
>
> At the conclusion of the Last Supper, our Lord said to his disciples: "He that hath no sword, let him now sell his garment and buy one." They answered: "Lord, here are two swords." He replied: "It is enough."

John Jay

> It is not to be presumed that our Lord would have ordered swords to be provided, but for some purpose for which a sword was requisite...
>
> When the officers and their band arrived, with swords and with staves, to take Jesus, they who were about him saw what would follow. "They said unto him: Lord, shall we smite with the sword?" [Luke 22:49]. It does not appear that any of the eleven disciples who were with him, except one, made the least attempt to defend him. But, Peter, probably inferring from the other swords, that they were now to be used, proceeded to "smite a servant of the high-priest, and cut off his right ear" [vs. 50]. Jesus (perhaps, among other reasons, to abate inducements to prosecute Peter for that violent attack) healed the ear.
>
> He ordered Peter to put his sword into its sheath, and gave two reasons for it. The *first* related to himself, and amounted to this, that he would

make no opposition, saying: "The cup which my Father hath given me, shall I not drink?" The *second* related to Peter, viz., they who take the sword, shall perish by the sword; doubtless meaning that they who take and use a sword, as Peter had just done, without lawful authority, and against lawful authority, incur the penalty and risk of perishing by the sword. This meaning seems to be attached to those words by the occasion and circumstances which prompted them. If understood in their unlimited

Jesus taught that the use of force in resisting tyranny was legitimate at certain times. Before His betrayal, Jesus told His disciples that if they owned no swords to purchase them (Luke 22:36).

latitude, they would contradict the experience and testimony of all ages, it being manifest that many military men die peaceably in their beds.[38]

As Jay noted, Christ's mission precluded the use of force in this particular instance, nonetheless, Jesus taught the legitimacy of using the legal sword to restrain the illegal sword of an aggressor (Mt. 26:52).

The authority and responsibility of using the sword to punish evil or protect the righteous (either from within a nation or from aggression by an outside enemy) resides with the civil government (Rom. 13:1-4). That is why anytime we reach the step where force is necessary in resisting tyranny, we must go through legitimate governing officials. A lower representative must be convinced to ignore a higher decree in obedience to God's higher law. Those who disobey an ungodly law or ruler must be prepared to pay the price for such an action.

We will see that the American colonists were not in rebellion (from God's perspective) in their struggle for independence from Britain but were acting in accordance with the biblical guidelines for resisting tyranny. They followed the above three steps in order. If we do not follow these steps in order, we will bring undue harm to ourselves, to others, and to God's cause.

Chapter 4

The Chain of Liberty: Development

The Chain of Liberty Moves Westward to Europe

Primitive Churches in the Roman Empire — 33-312 A.D.

As the early Church applied the political principles that Jesus taught, they not only affected multitudes of lives, but also turned the world upside down. Paganism was being overthrown throughout Europe as Christianity rapidly spread. By 500 A.D. about 25% of the known world had become Christian and over 40% had been evangelized.

In the previous chapter we documented the frequent instances in the New Testament where the apostles resisted tyranny by various forms of civil protest and legal action (Acts 13, 16, 24, 25, 26). In Chapter 1 we mentioned how the apostle Paul rebuked the Christians in Greece for their apathy and irresponsibility regarding politics that allowed non-Christians to be in control (1 Corinthians 6:2-5). He urged them to seek public office such as in the local court system of Corinth. When the Christians found it difficult to make inroads in the Roman legal system, they began to form their own alternative courts, which were binding only upon those who voluntarily accepted the outcome by covenant agreement. Over time, the pagans began to reject the arbitrary Roman system and seek for real justice through the Christian courts. By the time of Constantine, in the early fourth century, half of the empire's population had been converted to

Origins and Development of Civil Government

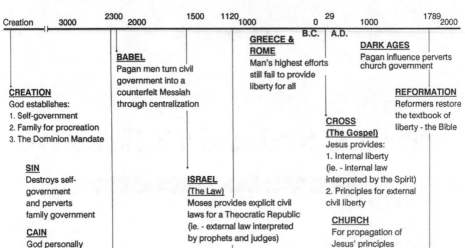

Christianity and consequently were involved in the "Christian" court system. When Constantine made Christianity the official established religion of the empire, the Christian judges were given legal status and required to wear the official dark robe or gown worn by all civil magistrates. The modern practice of mainline denominational clergymen wearing "pulpit gowns" traces its origins to this act, because most of these "Christian judges" were clergymen. The "pulpit gown" therefore is a testimony and memorial of the primitive churches being involved in politics.

Paul's exhortation to these Christians in Corinth was so strong that one of Paul's own staff—a man named Erastus—eventually switched from being a gospel minister to become a civil "minister" (Romans 13:4, 6 — "Rulers are servants of God...a minister of God to you for good."). Erastus had been a full-time apostolic assistant to Paul, just like Timothy, until he sent by Paul over to Greece (Acts 19:22). While ministering to the churches there, Erastus began to feel God's calling into political office. Paul tells us what happened to him when, in the close of his letter to the Romans (written from Corinth), Paul says: "Erastus, the city treasurer greets you" (Romans 16:23). Archaeology has uncovered in Corinth a first-century tablet that reads: "Erastus, the Commissioner of Public Works, laid this pavement at his own expense." This is believed to be the Erastus of the Bible.[39]

What an exciting illustration of obedience to Christ's command to his disciples to be public servants once they gain positions in government! Here Erastus does something unprecedented in pagan Roman government—he personally pays for the project instead of raising taxes—and is honored with a special tablet. Here we have an example in the New Testament of Christians not just protesting evil government but taking the initiative to provide good government by seeking civil office—and it's sanctioned by the greatest apostle!

Besides all this, the primitive churches provided a model of self-government with union among their congregations. Although church government on the local level was predominantly self-governing, nonetheless, there were certain limited powers in the hands of the apostles and elders of the churches at large who met in council at Jerusalem (Acts 15:2, 4, 6 and 16:4) and approved special ministries, such as a poor fund which was administered out of Jerusalem (Gal. 2:1-2, 9 and 2 Cor. 8:19, 23). The relationship between the mother church in Jerusalem and all the other new churches was the first example of federalism, or dual governments working both at once in defined spheres of jurisdiction (local and national).

As the centuries went on, the church gradually lost its virtue and biblical knowledge and began to embrace a pagan philosophy of government and education. This caused church leaders to think that only they could understand God's Word and, therefore, they must tell the people what God required of them, instead of allowing every person to be self-governing and learn for themselves.

Instead of sowing the truth in the hearts of the people and allowing the inevitable fruit to grow, the clergy simply tried to externally dictate to the people what they thought God commanded (and what they thought was often quite contrary to the Bible). The first pagan king to be converted was the king of Armenia in 295 A.D. He declared his nation to be "Christian," although it was not genuine in that it continued to have a pagan form of monarchical government.

Constantine also attempted to accomplish God's will with pagan methods. After Constantine was converted (about 312 A.D.) he desired to make his empire Christian. However, not understanding God's method of gradualism, he superficially united the church and state and set up a national church declaring all citizens in his empire must become Christians. His attempt at accomplishing that which was good without utilizing biblical methods actually hindered the work of God in the centuries that followed. Constantine's actions contributed to the stagnation of society that marked the "Dark Ages," a period of about 1000 years that followed the fall of the Roman Empire in 410 A.D.

Patrick, Alfred, and the Law of Moses in Britain

Christianity was introduced in Britain in the first century, possibly by Joseph of Arimathea. As the Celts were converted, they established decentralized churches, unlike those that developed in the Roman and Byzantine Empires. By 150 A.D. the pastors of the Celtic churches preached in the common language from interlinear Bible translations called glosses.

The greatest of the pastors was Patrick who left England and went to evangelize Ireland. He influenced King Loeghaire, who made Patrick his counselor (termed *Anmchara*), and as such introduced biblical law into the civil realm. In 432 Patrick wrote *Liber Ex Lege Moisi* (*Book of the Law of Moses*) which was applied by local chieftains or kings throughout Ireland (not yet a united political arrangement, only a biblical/religious unity). It emphasized the rule of law and local self-government.

Patrick greatly influenced government through writing the *Book of the Law of Moses.*

The Anglo-Saxons first came to Britain around 428 A.D. when two brothers, Hengist and Horsa, were invited to bring their relatives and help the king of Kent fight off his enemies. They stayed in Britain, and after some time eventually took the island over and named it Anglo-land, or Engel-land (today England).

Initially the Anglo-Saxons turned on the Celts, killing many of them. One time they killed 1200 Celtic pastors in prayer. However, while the Saxons conquered the Celts militarily, the Celts conquered the Saxons spiritually. The Saxons were thus converted to Celtic Christianity. Catholicism did not come to Britain until 597. After its introduction, the church in Britain, due to the Celtic influence, still emphasized the Bible above Papal authority.

Around 565 a follower of Patrick, named Columba, left his home in Ireland and evangelized the king of the Picts (who lived in what is today Scotland). Columba also translated Patrick's *Liber* into the Scottish language.

The first king who was revered enough to unite all of England into one nation was Alfred the Great, who ruled from 871 to 899. Just before Alfred became king, most of England had been conquered by the Vikings from Denmark through a long series of fierce battles. Wessex, in the southwest portion of England, was the only region that remained for Alfred to rule. Almost immediately, and for years to follow, Alfred found himself in thick battle with the Danes. David Chilton writes of this struggle:

> In 876 the Danish chieftain Guthrum attacked Wessex in earnest with a powerful host, aiming to break Alfred's hold on the country once and for all. The Vikings succeeded: in the winter of early 878, Guthrum pushed Alfred into the marshes, where the king and a small group of loyal followers were forced to hide out on the Isle of Athelney. Historians have called this time of testing Alfred's "Valley Forge," where he had to bide his time while virtually all England was overrun with pagan enemies of the faith who sacked churches and monasteries, wiping out the tattered remains of a Christian past. The legends say, however, that the bold and daring Alfred entered the Viking camp disguised as a minstrel and actually performed for Guthrum and his chiefs—getting a chance to listen to their plans and plotting his own strategy. When spring came, Alfred rallied the English army for a final push against the invader's vastly superior forces. This time Alfred was victorious. As the *Anglo-Saxon Chronicle* puts it, "he fought against the entire host, and put it to flight." The Vikings agreed never to attack Wessex again, and they submitted to the terms of peace.
>
> Alfred did not banish Guthrum and his men. He didn't have them executed, either. His solution to the problem of the Vikings seems incredible to us, but it worked. The peace treaty he imposed on them included this provision: that Guthrum and "thirty of the most honorable men in the host" become Christians! Guthrum accepted the conditions, and he was baptized into the Christian faith, Alfred standing as his godfather. At the conclusion of the ceremony, Alfred embraced his newborn brother in Christ and threw a twelve-day feast for him and his men. And then, as if this weren't enough already, Alfred made the strangest political move of all. He said to Guthrum, in effect: "My

brother, this land is much too big for me to rule all by myself; and the important thing isn't who's in charge. The real issue is a Christian England. So don't go back to Denmark. Stay here and rule this land with me, under the lordship of Jesus Christ."

That's exactly what Guthrum did. In fact, when later groups of Danes tried to launch invasions against England, Guthrum and Alfred stood together as Christian kings, united in defense of a Christian land. As the first Viking leader to become a Christian, Guthrum foreshadowed the conversion of all the Norse peoples and their incorporation into the civilizations of Christendom.[40]

Alfred the Great

With the coming of peace, Alfred instituted Christian reforms in many areas including establishing a government that served the people. Alfred was taught how to read by a Celtic Christian scholar named Asser and studied Patrick's *Liber*. He established the Ten Commandments as the basis of law and adopted many other patterns of government from the Hebrew Republic. The nation was organized into units of tens, fifties, hundreds, and thousands and had an elected assembly known as the "Witen." These representatives were called respectively: a tithingman (over ten families), a vilman (over 50), a hundredman, and an earl. The territory which the earl oversaw was called a "shire," and his assistant was the "shire-reef," from which we get our word *sheriff* today. England's government also had an unelected body made up of nobleman. The king, however, was elected; he was not a hereditary king. The nation's laws were established by the consent of the people. Alfred's uniform Code of Laws (890) recognized common law and had provisions for individual rights, such as trial by jury and habeas corpus. Alfred's Code was derived from Mosaic Law and Jesus' golden rule.

Thomas Jefferson said that the Anglo-Saxon laws were "the sources of the Common Law...[and] the wisest and most perfect ever yet devised by the wit of man, as it stood before the 8th century." The National Seal proposed by Jefferson in 1776 was to have on one side "the children of Israel in the wilderness, led by a cloud by day, and a pillar of fire by the night." But on the other side Jefferson proposed images of "Hengist and Horsa, the Saxon chiefs...whose political principles and form of government we have

One side of Jefferson's proposal for the National Seal.

assumed."[41] This is true because of the Saxons' contact with the Celtic Christians (British natives); the Saxon culture in Germany from which they originated provided no constitutionalism whatsoever. In the 800s the clergy began to serve as judges in England and build common law on the Bible.

Reaching its height in the late 800s under the Christian King Alfred, Anglo-Saxon law was eroding at the time of the Norman Conquest in 1066. The Normans, under William the Conqueror, established a royal dynasty—a system which destroyed the rights of the people yet increased efficiency by centralization of common law under Henry II.

Meanwhile, in 1016, Iceland became a Christian nation by genuine democratic process. The "Holy Roman Empire," founded by Otto I, King of Germany, in 962 A.D., launched a series of eight crusades to "liberate" the Holy Land from the Muslims (1095 -1272). At the apex of the Medieval Papacy under Pope Innocent III, a significant step toward liberty occurred in England.

Magna Carta — 1215

In England, the Norman system of government removed the rights of the people. Consequently, the kings abused the people, barons as well as commoners.

Things worsened to the point under King John that the English barons drew up a contract that addressed the abuses and guaranteed the barons certain rights and privileges as contained in biblical law. King John, needing the help of the barons to raise money, reluctantly signed the Magna Carta in 1215. It is interesting to note (but not surprising) that a clergyman, Stephen Langton, is likely the chief architect of the document. The Pope said it was illegal but the English Catholic Church, still influenced by its Celtic origins, ignored the Pope and helped preserve the

In 1215 King John signed the Magna Carta, which was written by Rev. Langton.

document in various ways, including encouraging the application of its principles in the government.

The Magna Carta embodied the principle that both sovereign and people are beneath the law and subject to it. Later, both Englishmen and American colonists cited the Magna Carta as a source of their freedom.

Monument at Runnymede, site of signing: "To Commemorate Magna Carta Symbol of Freedom Under Law

It is also notable that in England around the year 1200, a Catholic monk named Dominque instituted the first example of representative government on a national level in his Order of Monks. This was in great contrast to most of Catholicism. Around 1300 Parliament was created, reflecting the representative principle. In 1231 the Pope initiated the first phase of the Inquisition to identify and punish "heretics."

John Wycliffe in England — 1382

The time period from approximately 500 -1500 A.D. has been termed the Dark Ages due to the fact that mankind generally was stagnant — there was little or no advancement in civil liberty, scientific discoveries, technology, and most other areas of life. This lack of advancement was primarily a result of the light of the Word of God being hidden from the common people. The Word of God was completed by the apostles in the first century and canonized in the following few centuries; yet as the church backslid from God, His Word was further removed from the people. Nevertheless, "the textbook of Liberty" was providentially being preserved by various scribes and monks who painstakingly spent their entire lives hand-copying the Bible.

John Wycliffe translating the Bible

The lack of access to the truth of the Bible kept the common people ignorant during the Dark Ages. Around 1348, the bubonic plague killed about one third of the population of Europe. Shortly after this the Catholic clergyman John Wycliffe, who did have access to the truth, began to see that "Scripture must become the common property of all" that there might be a "government of the people, by the people, and for the people."[42] To accomplish this goal, he translated the whole Bible from Latin into English. This was completed around 1382, one hundred fifty years before the Reformation occurred.

He not only translated the Bible but set out to implant the truth of the Scriptures in the hearts of all men. This was accomplished by distributing Bibles, books of the Bible, and tracts throughout all England.

His followers, called *Lollards* (a derogatory term meaning *idle babblers*), would travel to towns and villages passing out Bibles and tracts and preaching and teaching on street corners, in chapels, gardens, assembly halls, and everywhere else they had an opportunity. As most people were uneducated, the Lollards taught many how to read, including many nobles.

In the words of Prof. G. V. Lechler, the Lollards "were, above all, characterized by a striving after holiness, a zeal for the spread of Scriptural truth, for the uprooting of prevalent error, and for Church reform. Even the common people among them were men who believed; and they communicated, as by a sacred contagion, their convictions to those around them. Thus they became mighty."[43]

The translation of the Bible in the hands of the Lollards became such a power, that at the close of the century, "according to the testimony of opponents, at least half the population had ranged themselves on the side of the Lollards."[44]

As prevalent error in the church began to be addressed, the church leaders showed their appreciation by trying to eradicate this *heretical* movement. Over the decades, they were able to stomp out most of the effects of Wycliffe's work and drive his followers underground, but the seeds of truth had been planted and would later spring forth and produce a Reformation that no man could stop.

In 1425, hoping to remove all the traces of Wycliffe's *treachery,* the church ordered his bones exhumed and burned along with some 200 books he had written. His ashes were then cast into the little river Swift, "the little river conveyed Wycliffe's remains into the Avon, the Avon into the Severn, the Severn into the narrow seas, they to the main ocean. And thus the ashes of Wycliffe are the emblem of his doctrine, which now is dispersed all the world over."[45]

With John Wycliffe, the "Morning Star of the Reformation," the first rays of the light of God's Word began to shine forth in the darkness. This coincided with the beginning of the "Renaissance" (1340 to 1540), or revival of Greek and Roman art and learning.

The Printing Press in Germany — 1455

An event occurred in the 15th century that assured that the light of the truth would never be put out by any civil or ecclesiastical government. That event was the invention of moveable type and the modern printing press by Johannes Gutenberg around the year 1455.

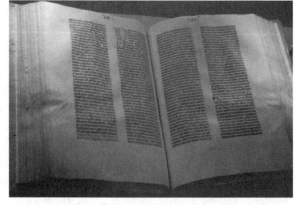

A Gutenberg Bible on display in the Library of Congress.

The first book printed by Gutenberg was the Bible. Before this time, the only means of recording was by hand. It would take scribes over a year to hand copy one Bible. It's no wonder Bibles were scarce and expensive.

The first book printed on Gutenberg's press was the Bible.

In the next century as the Reformation broke forth, the use of the printing press was instrumental in spreading the knowledge of liberty. Within 10 years of the invention of the press the total number of books increased from 50,000 to 10 million. Historian Charles Coffin wrote:

> Through the energizing influence of the printing press, emperors, kings, and despots have seen their power gradually waning, and the people becoming their masters.[46]

Christopher Columbus in Spain — 1492

The Catholic monarchs of Spain came under the influence of a man (whose name meant the "Christ-bearer") who believed that it would be possible to reach the east by sailing west. With the help of Spanish funds, Christopher Columbus sailed across the Atlantic Ocean hoping to reach Asia, but ended up "discovering" the New World when he landed on an island in October 1492 that he named San Salvador (*San Salvador* means *Holy Savior*; it is part of modern-day Bahamas).

We all know of this event, but do we know what motivated Columbus to embark on such an arduous and dangerous journey? The following excerpts from a letter he wrote to King Ferdinand and Queen Isabella of Spain tell us:

Columbus said the Lord inspired him to make his voyage.

It was the Lord who put it into my mind (I could feel His hand upon me) to sail from here to the Indies. All who heard of my project rejected it with laughter, ridiculing me. There is no question that the inspiration was from the Holy Spirit, because He comforted me with rays of marvelous illumination from the Holy Scriptures...

For the execution of the journey to the Indies I did not make use of intelligence, mathematics, or maps. It is simply the fulfillment of what Isaiah had prophesied...

No one should fear to undertake a task in the name of our Savior, if it is just and if the intention is purely for His Service. ... The fact that the Gospel must still be preached to so many lands in such a short time — this is what convinces me.[47]

While Columbus discovered the New World (more precisely, he opened the New World to European colonization and western civilization[48]), God did not allow Spain, the country from which he sailed, to colonize the territory which originally comprised the United States. Columbus and other explorers carried with them seeds of religious tyranny, and God had plans for America to be planted with seeds of liberty. Historian Daniel Dorchester writes:

While thirst for gold, lust of power, and love of daring adventure served the Providential purpose of opening the New World to papal Europe, and Roman Catholic colonies were successfully planted in some portions, the territory originally comprised within the United States was mysteriously guarded and reserved for another—a prepared people.[49]

During the century following the discovery of the New World, colonization occurred in much of South and Central America. In 1493 the Pope gave much of Africa, Asia, and eastern South America to Portugal, and the rest of Latin America to Spain. This is reflected in the colonization that followed. Every attempt to colonize the territory comprising the original United States met with failure. God was preserving this land for a people who He had yet to prepare.

In 1497, John Cabot, landing near the St. Lawrence River, laid claim to America for England. At this time, England, as all of Europe, lived under civil and religious tyranny; yet, God would be at work in the sixteenth century to assure that this changed. B.F. Morris writes of God's providential hand at work during this era:

> No era in history is more signally and sublimely marked than that of the discovery and Christian colonization of the North American continent.
>
> The intervening century was in many respects the most important period of the world; certainly the most important in modern times. More marked and decided changes, affecting science, religion, and liberty, occurred in that period than had occurred in centuries before; and all these changes were just such as to determine the Christian character of this country. Meantime, God held this vast land in reserve, as the great field on which the experiment was to be made in favor of a civil and religious liberty. He suffered not the foot of Spaniard, or Portuguese, or Frenchman, or Englishman to come upon it until the changes had been wrought in Europe which would make it certain that it would always be a land of religious freedom.[50]

The Spanish Inquisition — 1478

The Inquisition was a movement started by Pope Gregory IX (1227-1241) in the thirteenth century to eliminate heretics. Led by Dominicans, the Inquisition was, in essence, a "Christian Holy War" against splinter groups and dissenters who did not embrace Catholic doctrine. Many of these heretics were people who thought for themselves, read the Bible, and taught ideas contrary to the established church.

There were three phases to the Inquisition. The first phase, from about 1200-1300, was marked by strong persecution. Then for the next two centuries (about

1300-1500) the movement largely went into hibernation, although some people were still persecuted, like the Czech reformer Jan Hus who was burned at the stake in 1415.

Then in 1478, the Papacy revived the Spanish Inquisition which wiped out virtually all Protestants in Spain by 1558 and persecuted heretics all over Europe. Dominican friar Torquemada (1420-1498) was appointed to lead the Office for the Propagation of the Faith, later assuming the position of Grand Inquisitor.

During this third phase (1480-1820), the Catholic state religion used force to attempt to produce "orthodox" belief. When biblical methods of transformation are ignored, the consequences are not good. Such was the case with the Spanish Inquisition. Millions were forced to flee their country. Hundreds of thousands and were falsely accused, arrested, held without knowledge of charges, tortured, burnt at the stake, stretched on racks, buried alive, brutally killed via "iron maidens" and other items invented for torture. In addition, the property of many of these heretics was confiscated, which may have increased the coffers of the church and state but only contributed to the economic demise of society at large. During the 300 years of the Spanish Inquisition, over 300,000 people were arrested and 32,000 burnt at the stake in Spain alone. Many more suffered throughout Europe.

Martin Luther in Germany — 1482-1546

Martin Luther was God's instrument to awaken the conscience of man. His act of nailing his 95 theses on the church door at Wittenberg in 1517 is often referred to as a beginning point of the Protestant Reformation. Yet seeds of the Reformation had been planted many years before. About 100 years before, Jan Hus was burned at the stake for stressing Scripture authority instead of corrupt papal authority. He was directly influenced by Wycliffe's works. Hus influenced Luther by his example.

Luther's defense at the Diet of Worms in 1521 reveals that which characterized his life:

> "I am," he pleaded, "but a mere man, and not God; I shall therefore defend myself as Christ did," who said, 'If I have spoken evil, bear witness of the evil.'… For this reason, by the mercy of God I conjure you,

most serene Emperor, and you, most illustrious electors and princes, and all men of every degree, to prove from the writings of the prophets and apostles that I have erred. As soon as I am convinced of this, I will retract every error, and will be the first to lay hold of my books, and throw them into the fire. ... I cannot submit my faith either to the Pope or to the councils, because it is clear as the day that they have frequently erred and contradicted each other. Unless, therefore, I am convinced by the testimony of Scripture, or by clear reasoning, unless I am persuaded by means of the passages I have quoted, and unless my conscience is thus bound by the Word of God, I cannot and will not retract; for it is unsafe and injurious to act against one's own conscience. Here I stand, I can do no other: may God help me! Amen."[51]

His life, and those of the reformers, can be summed up in the Latin phrase, *sola scriptura,* "Scripture alone." He translated the first German Bible in 1534. That was to be the basis of the reformers' thoughts and actions, rather than the decree of pope or king. It was Luther who brought forth out of darkness the great truth that we are justified by faith. His biblical teachings spread rapidly to many nations. In 1540 Denmark, Norway, and Sweden became Lutheran nations.

Luther at the Diet of Worms

John Calvin and Switzerland – 1509-1564

After the French lawyer John Calvin was converted to the evangelical faith in his early 20s, he left the Roman church around 1534, for which he was briefly imprisoned. After his release, he lived in hiding in Paris for a short time, where he was forced to worship secretly in various homes and in the woods. At the end of 1534, he fled to Germany and then to Geneva, Switzerland. This city had officially voted to be Protestant as a result of seeds planted by Ulrich Zwingli, who was killed in battle in 1531 while serving as chaplain in the Swiss army.

John Calvin said that the Bible is the scepter by which God rules His universe.

Calvin first published his famous *Institutes of Christian Religion* in 1536. Two years later the Council of Geneva ordered Calvin to do something that he felt conscience bound to disobey. As a result, he was banished from Geneva and went to Strasbourg, where he pastored a French refugee congregation for three years. During that time, he married a French refugee named Idelette. In 1541 Calvin was invited back to Geneva by the Council. Over the years that followed he was instrumental in bringing biblical reforms through his teachings and actions to every sphere of life. One of his writings was *Ecclesiastical Ordinances,* which included policies for jails, education, and the physical health and safety of citizens, such as sanitation requirements.

The writings of John Calvin have probably had more impact upon the modern world than any book except the Bible. "No writing of the Reformation era was more feared by Roman Catholics, more zealously fought against and more hostilely pursued, than Calvin's Institutes."[52] In his history of the Reformation, J. H. Merle D'Aubigne writes:

> The renovation of the individual, of the Church, and of the human race, is his theme...

The reformation of the sixteenth century restored to the human race what the middle ages had stolen from them; it delivered them from the traditions, laws, and despotism of the papacy; it put an end to the minority and tutelage in which Rome claimed to keep mankind forever; and by calling upon man to establish his faith not on the words of a priest, but on the infallible Word of God, and by announcing to every one free access to the Father through the new and saving way—Christ Jesus, it proclaimed and brought about the hour of Christian manhood.

An explanation is, however, necessary. There are philosophers in our days who regard Christ as simply the apostle of political liberty. These men should learn that, if they desire liberty outwardly, they must first possess it inwardly...

There are, no doubt, many countries, especially among those which the sun of Christianity has not yet illumined, that are without civil liberty, and that groan under the arbitrary rule of powerful masters. But, in order to become free outwardly, man must first succeed in being free inwardly...

The liberty which the Truth brings is not for individuals only: it affects the whole of society. Calvin's work of renovation, in particular, which was doubtless first of all an internal work, was afterwards destined to exercise a great influence over nations.[53]

D'Aubigne explains how Calvin added to the work of Luther:

What chiefly distinguishes the Reformation of Calvin from that of Luther is, that wherever it was established, it brought with it not only truth but liberty.[54]

John Calvin and other reformers, Reformation Wall, Geneva

Calvin worked hard to make Geneva a model of biblical government. He established the first Protestant university in history—the Geneva Academy whose rector was Theodore Beza. Geneva became a center of reform for not only Huguenot but also Protestant refugees from all over Europe. Puritan leaders of England, as well as John Knox of Scotland, studied under Calvin at Geneva.

The nation of the United States of America has been influenced greatly by Calvin, as D'Aubigne observed:

Lastly, Calvin was the founder of the greatest of republics. The *pilgrims* who left their country in the reign of James I and, landing on the barren shores of New England, founded populous and mighty colonies, are his sons, his direct and legitimate sons; and that American nation which we have seen growing so rapidly boasts as its father the humble reformer on the shores of the Leman.[55]

John Knox was largely responsible for directing the Reformation in Scotland. Mary Queen of Scots said of him, "I fear the prayers of John Knox more than an army of ten thousand men!"

The Huguenots: The Protestants in France — 1523-1598

In 1523, just one year after Luther's New Testament translation into the German language and two years prior to Tyndale's English translation, Jacques Lefevre d'Etaples published the New Testament in French. The whole Bible, known as the *Antwerp Bible,* was available in 1530. Another translation by Pierre Robert Olivetan was published in 1535.

Olivetan's cousin, John Calvin, fled persecution in France and settled in Geneva where he established a training center for many French Protestants. These Protestants became known as *Huguenots,* which is a term from a German word meaning *confederates.* Despite severe oppression, the Huguenots grew until in 1553 five were publicly burned at the stake. This event, instead of quenching the movement, fueled it so that four years later one third of all Frenchmen were Protestants!

In 1557 in Paris, a national synod convened and wrote the *Confession of Faith of the Reformed Churches*. The Pope responded by making the reading of the Bible illegal. Within three years the number of Reformed churches in France grew from 300 to 2000, and because of severe violations of their religious freedom they formed a political alliance to protect it. This plunged the nation into civil war between Protestant and Catholic powers which lasted until the *Edict of Toleration of 1598,* which guaranteed religious and political freedom in certain partitioned areas of the country.

In 1572, up to 30,000 Protestants were massacred while worshipping on St. Bartholomew's Day. The Huguenots became convinced of the necessity of using force in self-defense and articulated their biblical reasoning of this in their *Vindicae Contra Tyrannos (A Defense of Liberty Against Tyrants)* in 1579. This document, drafted by Philippe DuPlessis Mornay, drawing from reasoning found in Calvin's writings, became a precedent for the American Colonists at the

Tens of thousands of Huguenots were persecuted and martyred by civil and religious tyrants.

time of their Revolution in 1776. An old Huguenot song said: "Spirit who made them live, awaken their children, so that they will know how to follow them."

LEX, REX,

OR

THE LAW AND THE PRINCE;

A DISPUTE FOR

THE JUST PREROGATIVE OF KING AND PEOPLE:

CONTAINING

THE REASONS AND CAUSES OF THE MOST NECESSARY DEFENSIVE WARS OF THE KINGDOM OF SCOTLAND,

AND OF THEIR

EXPEDITION FOR THE AID AND HELP OF THEIR DEAR BRETHREN OF ENGLAND;

IN WHICH THEIR INNOCENCY IS ASSERTED, AND A FULL ANSWER IS GIVEN TO A SEDITIOUS PAMPHLET,

ENTITULED,

"SACRO-SANCTA REGUM MAJESTAS,"

OR

THE SACRED AND ROYAL PREROGATIVE OF CHRISTIAN KINGS;

UNDER THE NAME OF J. A., BUT PENNED BY

JOHN MAXWELL, THE EXCOMMUNICATE POPISH PRELATE;

WITH A SCRIPTURAL CONFUTATION OF THE RUINOUS GROUNDS OF W. BARCLAY, H. GROTIUS, H. ARNISÆUS, ANT. DE DOMI. POPISH BISHOP OF SPALATO, AND OF OTHER LATE ANTI-MAGISTRATICAL ROYALISTS, AS THE AUTHOR OF OSSORIANUM, DR FERNE, E. SYMMONS, THE DOCTORS OF ABERDEEN, ETC.

IN FORTY-FOUR QUESTIONS.

BY THE

REV. SAMUEL RUTHERFORD.

SOMETIME PROFESSOR OF DIVINITY IN THE UNIVERSITY OF ST. ANDREWS.

"But if you shall still do wickedly, ye shall be consumed, both ye and your king."—1 SAM. xii. 25.

The Scottish Reformation, begun by John Knox, gave rise to writings on Christian resistance to tyranny, such as *Lex Rex*, written by Rev. Samuel Rutherford in 1644.

Chapter 5

The Chain of Liberty: Preparation for America

Puritans and Separatists in England

God not only prepares people to shape history, but He also shapes history to prepare people so that they may fulfill their destiny and accomplish God's purposes in the earth. This latter aspect of God's principle of preparation is evident in English history of the sixteenth century. We will see God using various leaders and events to help prepare those people who would become the "Parents of the Republic of the United States of America."

William Tyndale — 1494-1536

God's chief instrument in bringing about the Reformation in England was William Tyndale. Much of Tyndale's life was spent fulfilling his vision: "If God preserves my life, I will cause a boy that driveth a plow to know more of the Scriptures than the pope."[56] Tyndale's dream was accomplished, but only at a great cost.

He spent over twelve years in exile from his native country, all the time facing the possibility of being captured and put to death. During this time, he translated the Bible from the original languages with

William Tyndale

the idea of making it available for the common man. His New Testament was published in 1525. So scholarly was Tyndale's work that is has been estimated that our present English Bibles retain eighty percent of his original work in the Old Testament, and ninety percent in the New.

In 1536 Tyndale was betrayed, arrested, and killed as a heretic. On the day of his death, Tyndale calmly stated: "I call God to record that I have never altered, against the voice of my conscience, one syllable of his Word. Nor would I this day, if all the pleasures, honors, and riches of the earth might be given to me."[57]

Before he was strangled and burned at the stake, he prayed for King Henry VIII who had persecuted and put to death many reformers and caused Tyndale to flee his country. As he was being fastened to the stake he cried out with these final words: "Lord, open the king of England's eyes!"[58] Although his life was extinguished, the flames of liberty would burn brighter than ever, for the Word of God would be spread to all people throughout England.

During Tyndale's life many copies of his New Testament were circulated throughout England, but only undercover for the king had banned Tyndale's work. Shortly after Tyndale's death, Henry VIII "authorized the sale and the reading of the Bible throughout the kingdom," for he wanted "to emancipate England from Romish domination," and saw the "Holy Scriptures as the most powerful engine to destroy the papal system."[59] Ironically, the king put his approval on the Matthew Bible (the revised to be called the Great Bible promoted by Henry VIII in 1539), which was in reality Tyndale's work under another name.

As the Word of God spread throughout the land, many people cried out with Tyndale, "We know that this Word is from God, as we know that fire burns; not because anyone has told us, but because a Divine fire consumes our hearts."[60]

These men and events all contribute to the movement of the Chain of Christianity and the beginning of liberty upon the earth. We will continue to trace the hand of God in history and see various links in the Chain of Christianity. As we do, "We should never forget that the prison, the scaffold, and the stake were stages in the march of civil and religious liberty which our forefathers had to travel in order that we might attain our present liberty."[61]

Tyndale being burned at the stake.

Henry VIII — 1534

When Henry VIII became king of England in 1509, Roman Catholicism was the established religion, not only in England, but in all of Western Europe. The government of the church reached beyond its biblical sphere of jurisdiction by exercising control in all areas of life.

Henry VIII

Most people, when they hear of Henry VIII, think of his many wives. His first wife, Catherine of Aragon, had borne him no sons, plus he had acquired a particular fondness for Anne Boleyn, so he decided to divorce Catherine. Such action required permission from the pope, so Henry sent a petition asking for approval for the divorce. When he was denied approval, Henry, not being the submissive type, decided he would not only go on and divorce Catherine, but he would also divorce himself (and take England with him) from the Catholic Church.

Henry, with England, thus split from the Roman Catholic Church, and around 1534 he set up the Church of England in its place. At the time, the only difference in the two was that Henry was the pope over the Church of England instead of the Pope in Rome. However, this event would prove to be very important in the advancement of religious and civil liberty in England and throughout the world.

God was using Henry, who was not a godly man, to fulfill His purposes. Henry's actions toward Tyndale and other reformers—his policies led to Tyndale's and many others' deaths—reveal that his split from Rome had nothing to do with godly reform, but only selfish desires; yet, God who governs in the affairs of men, was using this historical event to accomplish His will. We saw earlier how God even used Henry to distribute Bibles that Tyndale had translated. While Henry broke from Roman Catholicism, there was still no freedom for individuals to worship God. Due to Tyndale's translation of the Bible, people throughout England were being awakened, yet the climate of Henry's England did not permit reform to flourish. Many saw that the Church of England needed reform as much as the Catholic Church, but little external reform occurred under Henry.

Edward VI — 1547

When Henry VIII died in 1547, he left the throne in the hands of his son, Edward VI, and Edward's protectorates. They favored those who wanted further reform in the Church of England. Under Edward the Puritan movement was born. Those people desiring to purify the Church of its errors and ungodliness were called "purifiers" or "puritans."

These reformers were overjoyed when Edward assumed power, for they could now begin to freely carry out their desired reform. Yet, they learned that one righteous ruler is not enough to ensure reform within a nation.

"Bloody" Mary — 1553

Edward died in 1553, having reigned only six years. His half-sister and Henry's daughter, Mary, succeeded him to the throne. She has earned the title *Bloody Mary* because she put to death hundreds of reformers including the "first Puritan," John Hooper. It was Hooper who first denied the right of the state to interfere with religion in 1553.

Mary not only detested the church reforms that occurred under Edward, but also never liked the fact that her father had separated from the Catholic Church. She set about to make amends with the Pope and purge England of the Puritan movement. She caused 286 Reformed Anglican leaders, including Thomas Cranmer, Nicholas Ridley, and Hugh Latimer, to be burned at the stake.

Consequently, thousands of Puritans fled England to places in Europe that harbored reformers, in particular Geneva. Due to the influence of Calvin, Geneva was one of the most free and advanced cities in the world. Internal liberty, resulting from biblical truth, was affecting all aspects of society in Geneva— from religious and civil freedom to education for the general populace and the best sanitation system in all of Europe.

It was in Geneva that the English Puritans were taught much biblical truth that they were lacking, in particular ideas on civil liberty. God made sure that the people He was preparing were equipped in every way. He even used Bloody Mary to help accomplish His purposes.

Elizabeth I — 1558

Mary died in 1558, after reigning only five years, and was succeeded by her half-sister, Elizabeth. This began the Elizabethan Era. Elizabeth did not want England to return to Catholicism, but she also was not interested in promoting the needed reforms within the Church of England. She did promise religious toleration which caused many Puritans to return to England who had fled during Mary's reign.

As the Puritans returned, they brought with them fuller ideas of civil and religious liberty, plus the Geneva Bible. While in exile in Geneva, a number of reformers translated and published a relatively compact and affordable Bible. The Geneva Bible would become the Bible of the masses. Since it was also the first English Bible to be divided into chapter and verse, it proved to be a good study Bible.

Queen Elizabeth I

After a few years, Elizabeth saw her tolerance of reformers was causing many to cry out for more reform than she desired, so in 1562 she issued her *Articles of Religion* which prohibited further reform. At this, some of the Puritans gave up hope of ever seeing the needed church reform and separated themselves from the Church of England. Thus, the "Separatist" movement was born around 1580. The Pilgrims who first sailed to America in 1620 were English separatists. The Separatist movement continued to grow throughout Elizabeth's long reign, although there were attempts from within England and from other nations to stop it.

The Miraculous Defeat of the Spanish Armada — 1588

Satan hates revival and will use any means to try to stop it. The Catholic monarchs of France initiated the massacre of 30,000 Protestants (Huguenots) on St. Bartholomew's Day in 1572. Finding that persecution only strengthened the movement in England, Satan attempted to stamp it out by war.

In 1588, Philip II of Spain sent the Spanish Armada to bring England and the Low Countries (the Netherlands) again under the domination of the Holy Roman Empire. One-half century before, under Henry VIII, England had split from Rome and established her own church, the Church of England. Holland had also separated from Catholic control and had already been engaged with the Spanish in many battles. Those faithful to Rome had not appreciated the direction these two countries were taking and had sought for ways to bring them back into the fold of the Catholic religion. With the rise of Puritanism and Separatism in

England and Holland, these renegades were straying even further from the established religion. With the build-up of the massive Spanish fleet, there was now a way to bring these nations back to Catholicism — the "true faith." King Philip had amassed a mighty navy "as never the like had before that time sailed upon the Ocean sea."[62] It was comprised of 134 ships and about 30,000 men; Spain considered it invincible.

When the English learned that the Armada was being assembled to be sent against them, they began to prepare as best as they could, but they had fewer ships that were smaller and not nearly as well armed. Their only hope was for a miracle to occur. People gathered throughout England to pray for such a miracle — especially those of the reformed faith because the Spanish specifically mentioned them as a target of their attack, for they knew these reformers were the major threat to the re-establishment of the Catholic religion in England. Contemporary historian Richard Hakluyt[63] records:

> [I]t is most apparant, that God miraculously preserved the English nation. For the L. Admirall wrote unto her Majestie that in all humane reason, and according to the judgement of all men (every circumstance being duly considered) the English men were not of any such force, whereby they might, without a miracle, dare once to approch within sight

The Spanish Armada

of the Spanish Fleet: insomuch that they freely ascribed all the honour of their victory unto God, who had confounded the enemy, and had brought his counsels to none effect...[64]

While this woonderfull and puissant Navie was sayling along the English coastes, and all men did now plainely see and heare that which before they would not be perswaded of, all people thorowout England prostrated themselves with humble prayers and supplications unto God: but especially the outlandish Churches (who had greatest cause to feare, and against whom by name, the Spaniards had threatened most grievous torments) enjoyned to their people continuall fastings and supplications, that they might turne away Gods wrath and fury now imminent upon them for their sinnes: knowing right well, that prayer was the onely refuge against all enemies, calamities, and necessities, and that it was the onely solace and reliefe for mankinde, being visited with affliction and misery. Likewise such solemne dayes of supplication were observed thorowout the united Provinces.[65]

As the Spanish fleet sailed up the English Channel, they were met by the much smaller English and Dutch navies. In the natural, the English had little hope, yet England and Holland had been fasting and praying. A series of storms caused many of the Armada ships to sink, disease wiped out many of the Spanish troops, and other providential occurrences resulted in a resounding defeat of the invincible Armada. Of the original force only 53 ships returned to Spain with less than half of the original 30,000 men. It seemed apparent to those delivered that "God...fought for them in many places with his owne arme."[66]

After this miraculous defeat, Holland minted coins as a perpetual memory. Of one coin Hakluyt recorded: "on the one side contained the armes of Zeland, with this inscription: GLORY TO GOD ONELY: and on the other side, the pictures of certeine great ships, with these words: THE SPANISH FLEET: and in the circumference about the ships: IT CAME, WENT, AND WAS. Anno 1588. That is to say, the Spanish fleet came, went, and was vanquished this yere; for which, glory be given to God onely." They minted another coin that "upon the one side whereof was represented a ship fleeing, and a ship sincking: on the other side foure men making prayers and giving thanks unto God upon their knees; with this sentence: Man purposeth; God disposeth. 1588."[67]

England and Holland marked the victory with public days of fasting and prayer. Hakluyt writes:

Also a while after the Spanish Fleet was departed, there was in England, by the commandement of her Majestie [Elizabeth], and in the united Provinces, by the direction of the States, a solemne festivall day publikely appointed, wherein all persons were enjoyned to resort unto the Church, and there to render thanks and praises unto God: and the Preachers were commanded to exhort the people thereunto. The foresayd solemnity was observed upon the 29 of November; which day was wholly spent in fasting, prayer, and giving of thanks.[68]

Elizabeth traveling to church to observe a Day of Prayer and Thanksgiving she had proclaimed after the defeat of the Spanish Armada.

The Queen rode into London in great triumph and fanfare and all the people turned out with banners and ensigns heralding the event.

Her Majestie being entered into the Church, together with her Clergie and Nobles gave thanks unto God, and caused a publike Sermon to be preached before her at Pauls crosse; wherein none other argument was handled, but that praise, honour, and glory might be rendered unto God, and that Gods name might be extolled by thanksgiving.[69]

James I — 1603

At Elizabeth's death in 1603, James I came to the throne. Intense persecution of Separatists under James' policies caused many of them to flee the country, this time to Holland. As we shall see, this was another providential event that helped prepare those people who were to be "stepping-stones" for the founding of a new nation—one birthed by God.

These events in 16th century England had a direct effect upon the advancement of liberty in history and the birth of the United States. God in His providence was governing in the affairs of men to accomplish His purposes.

Chapter 6

The Pilgrims: A Model of Christian Character

The Separatist Movement began in England in the latter part of the sixteenth century as people began to embrace the idea of "reformation without tarrying for any." The many Separatists in and around the little town of Scrooby in the north of England were destined to have a great impact upon the world, for it was here that many of the Pilgrims had their roots. At Scrooby, these Christians wrote a church covenant—the first of its kind affirming church self-government—in 1606.

Three of the most prominent leaders of the Pilgrims started on their great pilgrimage from Scrooby. As we briefly look at their lives, we will begin to understand the heart of the Pilgrims.

William Brewster

William Brewster was one of the only Pilgrims to have position in English society, and that was by no means an exalted one. After serving as a confidential secretary to a prominent member of Queen Elizabeth's court, he returned to Scrooby where he became Postmaster and the overseer of a gentleman's estate in the area. Authors Marshall Foster and Mary-Elaine Swanson write:

He set about trying to reform the Church of England from within by getting good Scriptural preachers for the local churches and paying for them out of his own pocket. (Many churches went without preaching for years on end, since Queen Elizabeth plainly preferred the reading of government-approved "homilies" to sermons that reflected individual interpretation of Scripture.) When the Church of England demanded more rigid conformity to its rituals and rejected the right of individuals to hear "unauthorized" preachers, Brewster finally decided to separate from the Church and to covenant with other Christians in his area to form a Scriptural congregation.[70]

William Brewster

Brewster later served as an elder in the congregation in England, Holland, and America. During the first year in America, the Pilgrims had no pastor, so Brewster effectively served in that capacity. According to Bradford, he was also a highly effective evangelist — "He did more in this behalf in a year than many...do in all their lives."[71]

John Robinson

More than anyone else, John Robinson prepared the Pilgrims to accomplish the great task of preparing the way for the settlement of a new nation. It was he who served as the Pilgrims pastor in England and Holland.

Robinson was trained as a clergyman in the Church of England, but was "dismissed from his first pastoral assignment for failure to conform to the Church of England's requirements regarding the wearing of priestly vestments."[72] Afterwards he took much time in considering whether he should remain in the Church of England. While he witnessed much that was unscriptural in the Church, he hesitated for there were many godly men who still remained in the

John Robinson

Church. Yet the truth of God burned in his heart. Robinson said,

> had not the truth been in my heart as a burning fire shut up in my bones, Jer. 20:9, I had never broken those bonds…wherein I was so straitly tied, but had suffered the light of God to have been put out in mine own unthankful heart by other men's darkness.[73]

The truth did prevail, and the light within him burned brighter as he left the Church of England and joined the Separatist congregation that met in William Brewster's home in Scrooby. Foster and Swanson write:

> Though often neglected by historians, John Robinson should be known as one of the great Christian philosophers who propounded religious toleration in an intolerant age and representative government in an age of absolute monarchy. For twenty years, he taught these principles in depth to his persecuted and beloved Pilgrim church. More than any other man, John Robinson prepared a people to take dominion over the wilderness to the glory of God. Through his godly wisdom, he taught the Pilgrims individual Christian unity.
>
> "His love was great towards them, and his care was all ways bente for their best good, both for soule and body; for besids his singuler abilities in devine things (wherein he excelled), he was also very able to give directions in civill affaires, and to foresee dangers & inconveniences; by which means he was very helpful to their outward estats, and so was every way as a commone father unto them."[74]

William Bradford

One of the best-known Pilgrim Fathers was William Bradford. He served as governor of Plymouth for 33 years and also wrote the *History of Plymouth Plantation,* the first great literary work of America.

As a young teenager, Bradford reasoned that the Church of England was unbiblical and so removed himself from it. He had such insight because a few years earlier, while confined to the bed with a long illness, he had read the Bible continuously. He attended the Church of

William Bradford

England in Bobworth for some time simply because he was impressed by the Scriptural preaching of Rev. Richard Clyfton. When Clyfton withdrew and joined the Scrooby Congregation, Bradford followed, even though he faced enormous pressure. He decided

> to withdraw from the communion of the parish-assemblies, and engage with some society of the faithful that should keep close unto the written word of God, as the rule of their worship…although the provoked rage of his friends tried all the ways imaginable to reclaim him from it, unto all…his answer was. … "Nevertheless, to keep a good conscience, and walk in such a way as God has prescribed in his word, is a thing which I must prefer before you all, and above life itself."[75]

It was 1602 when Bradford started attending the Separatist Church in Scrooby. Six years later he would travel with part of this church to Holland, and twelve years after that with a smaller number to America.

History *Of Plymouth Plantation*

A book which every American and Christian should read, but whose title (not to mention the content) is rarely even mentioned in our schools today, is William Bradford's *Of Plymouth Plantation.* This history plainly reveals God's hand in the Pilgrims' lives and in the events they went through to settle in the north parts of America. We can see no greater human example of Christian character than in the lives of the Pilgrims.

To appreciate the price paid for liberty and to introduce you to one of America's greatest historical and literary writings, there follows many excerpts from Bradford's original manuscript, written in 1647. (The text is from *Bradford's History "Of Plimoth Plantation," from the Original Manuscript,* printed by order of the General Court of Massachusetts by Wright & Potter Printing Co., State Printers, in 1898. The spelling and some punctuation have been modernized.) The story starts in the early 1600s in England when many people who had been converted began to be persecuted as they lived out their new-found faith.

"Of Plimoth Plantation" by William Bradford

When as by the travail and diligence of some godly and zealous preachers, and God's blessing on their labors, as in other places of the land, so in the North parts, many became enlightened by the Word of God, and had their ignorance and sins discovered unto them, and began by His grace to reform their lives, and make conscience of their ways, the work of God was no sooner manifest in them, but presently they were both scoffed and scorned by the profane multitude; and the ministers urged with the yoke of subscription, or else must be silenced...

So many, therefore, of these professors as saw the evil of these things in these parts, and whose hearts the Lord had touched with heavenly zeal for His truth, they shook off this yoke of antichristian bondage, and as the Lord's free people joined themselves (by a covenant of the Lord) into a church estate, in the fellowship of the gospel, to walk in all His ways made known, or to be made known unto them, according to their best endeavors, whatsoever it should cost them, the Lord assisting them. And that it cost them something this ensuing history will declare...

Of their Departure into Holland and their Troubles thereabout, with some of the many difficulties they found and met withal. Anno 1608

Being thus constrained to leave their native soil and country, their lands and livings, and all their friends and familiar acquaintance, it was much, and thought marvelous by many. But to go into a country they knew not (but by hearsay), where they must learn a new language and get their livings they knew not how, it being a dear place and subject to the miseries of war, it was by many thought an adventure almost desperate; a case intolerable and a misery worse than death. Especially seeing they were not acquainted with trades nor traffic (by which that country doth subsist) but had only been used to a plain country life and the innocent trade of husbandry. But these things did not dismay them (though they did sometimes trouble them) for their desires were set on the ways of God and to enjoy His ordinances; but they rested on His providence, and knew Whom they had believed. Yet this was not all, for though they could not stay, yet were they not suffered to go; but the ports and havens were shut against them, so as they were fain to seek secret means of conveyance, and to bribe and fee the mariners, and give extraordinary rates for their passages. And yet were they often times betrayed (many of them), and both they and their goods intercepted and surprised, and thereby put to great trouble and charge, of which I will give an instance or two and omit the rest.

There was a large company of them purposed to get passage at Boston in Lincolnshire, and for that end had hired a ship wholly to themselves and made agreement with the master to be ready at a certain day, and take them and their goods in at a convenient place, where they accordingly would all attend in readiness. So after long waiting and large expenses, though he kept not day with them, yet he came at length and took them in, in the night. But when he had them and their goods aboard, he betrayed them, having beforehand complotted with the searchers and other officers so to do; who took them, and put them into open boats, and there rifled and ransacked them, searching to their shirts for money, yea even the women further than became modesty; and then carried them back into the town and made them a spectacle and wonder to the multitude which came flocking on all sides to behold them. Being thus first, by the catchpoll officers rifled and stripped of their money, books and much other goods, they were presented to the magistrates, and messengers sent to inform the Lords of the Council of them; and so they were committed to ward. Indeed the magistrates used them courteously and showed them what favor they could; but could not deliver them till order came from the Council table. But the issue was that after a month's imprisonment the greatest part were dismissed and sent to the places from whence they came; but 7 of the principal were still kept in prison and bound over to the Assizes.

The next spring after, there was another attempt made by some of these and others to get over at another place. And it so fell out that they light of a Dutchman at Hull, having a ship of his own belonging to Zealand; they made agreement with him, and acquainted him with their condition, hoping to find more faithfulness in him than in the former of their own nation. He bade them not fear, for he would do well enough. He was by appointment to take them in between Grimsby and Hull, where was a large common a good way distant from any town. Now against the prefixed time, the women and children, with the goods, were sent to the place in a small bark which they had hired for that end; and the men were to meet them by land. But it so fell out that they were there a day before the ship came, and the sea being rough and the women very sick, prevailed with the seamen to put into a creek hard by, where they lay on ground at low water. The next morning the ship came but they were fast and could not stir until about noon. In the meantime, the shipmaster, perceiving how the matter was, sent his boat to be getting the men aboard whom he saw ready, walking about the shore. But after the first boatful was got aboard and she was ready to go for more, the master espied a great company, both horse and foot, with bills and guns and other weapons; for the country was raised to take them. The Dutchman seeing that, swore his country's oath, "sacremente," and having the wind fair, weighed his anchor, hoisted sails, and away.

But the poor men which were got aboard were in great distress for their wives and children which they saw thus to be taken, and were left destitute of their helps; and themselves also, not having a cloth to shift them with, more than they had on their backs, and some scarce a penny about them, all they had being aboard the bark. It drew tears from their eyes, and anything they had they would have given to have been ashore again; but all in vain, there was no remedy, they must thus sadly part. And afterward endured a fearful storm at sea, being 14 days or more before they arrived at their port; in 7 whereof they neither saw sun, moon nor stars, and were driven near the coast of Norway; the mariners themselves often despairing of life, and once with shrieks and cries gave over all, as if the

A Dutch Ship

ship had been foundered in the sea, and they sinking without recovery. But when man's hope and help wholly failed, the Lord's power and mercy appeared in their recovery; for the ship rose again and gave the mariners courage again to manage her. And if modesty would suffer me, I might declare with what fervent prayers they cried unto the Lord in this great distress (especially some of them) even without any great distraction, when the water ran into their mouths and ears and the mariners cried out, "We sink, we sink!" they cried (if not with miraculous, yet with a great height or degree of divine faith), "Yet Lord Thou canst save! Yet Lord Thou canst save!" with such other expressions as I will forbear. Upon which the ship did not only recover, but shortly after the violence of the storm began to abate, and the Lord filled their afflicted minds with such comforts as everyone cannot understand, and in the end brought them to their desired haven, where the people came flocking, admiring their deliverance; the storm having been so long and sore, in which much hurt had been done, as the master's friends related unto him in their congratulations.

But to return to the others where we left. The rest of the men that were in greatest danger made shift to escape away before the troop could surprise them; those only staying that best might to be assistant unto the women. But pitiful it was to see the heavy case of these poor women in this distress; what weeping and crying on every side, some for their husbands that were carried away in the ship as is before related; others not knowing what should become of them and their little ones; others again melted in tears, seeing their poor little ones hanging about them, crying for fear and quaking with cold. Being thus apprehended, they were hurried from one place to another and from one justice to another, till in the end they knew not what to do with them; for to imprison so many women and innocent children for no other cause (many of them) but that they must go with their husbands, seemed to be unreasonable and all would cry out of them; and to send them home again was as difficult, for they alleged, as the truth was, they had no homes to go to, for they had either sold or otherwise disposed of their houses and livings. To be short, after they had been thus turmoiled a good while and conveyed from one constable to another, they were glad to be rid of them in the end upon any terms, for all were wearied and tired with them. Though in the meantime they (poor souls) endured misery enough; and thus in the end necessity forced a way for them.

But that I be not tedious in these things, I will omit the rest, though I might relate many other notable passages and troubles which they endured and underwent in these their wanderings and travels both at land and sea; but I haste to other things. Yet I may not omit the fruit that came hereby, for by these so public troubles in so many eminent places their cause became famous and occasioned many to look into the same; and their godly carriage and Christian behavior was such as left a deep impression in the minds of many. And though some few shrunk at these first conflicts and sharp beginnings (as it was no marvel) yet many more came on with fresh courage and greatly animated others. And in the end, notwithstanding all these storms of opposition, they all got over at length, some at one time and some at another, and some in one place and some in another, and met together again according to their desires, with no small rejoicing.

Of their settling in Holland, and their manner of living, and entertainment there

Being now come into the Low Countries, they saw many goodly and fortified cities, strongly walled and guarded with troops of armed men. Also, they heard a strange and uncouth language, and beheld the different manners and customs of the people, with their strange fashions and attires; all so far differing from that of their plain country villages (wherein they were bred and had so long lived) as it seemed they were come into a new world. But these were not the things they much looked on, or long took up their thoughts, for they had other work in hand and another kind of war to wage and maintain. For although they saw fair and beautiful cities, flowing with abundance of all sorts of wealth and riches, yet it was not long before they saw the grim and grisly face of poverty coming upon them like an armed man, with whom they must buckle and encounter, and from whom they could not fly. But they were armed with faith and patience against him and all his encounters; and though they were sometimes foiled, yet by God's assistance they prevailed and got the victory...

Leyden, Holland

And when they had lived at Amsterdam about a year... they removed to Leyden, a fair and beautiful city and of a sweet situation, but made more famous by the university wherewith it is adorned, in which of late had been so many learned men. ... And first, though many of them were poor, yet there was none so poor but if they were known to be of that congregation the Dutch (either bakers or others) would trust them in any reasonable matter when they wanted money. Because they had found by experience how careful they were to keep their word, and saw them so painful and diligent in their callings; yea, they would strive to get their custom and to employ them above others in their work, for their honesty and diligence...

Showing the reasons and causes of their removal

After they had lived in this city about some 11 or 12 years (which is the more observable being the whole time of that famous truce between that state and the Spaniards) and sundry of them were taken away by death and many others began to be well stricken in years (the grave mistress of Experience having taught them many things), those prudent governors with sundry of the sagest members began both deeply to apprehend their present dangers and wisely to foresee the future and think of timely remedy. In the agitation of their thoughts, and much discourse of things hereabout, at length they began to incline to this conclusion, of removal to some other place. Not out of any newfangledness or other such like giddy humor by which men are oftentimes transported to their great hurt and danger, but for sundry weighty and solid reasons, some of the chief of which I will here briefly touch.

And first, they saw and found by experience the hardness of the place and country to be such as few in comparison would come to them, and fewer that would bide it out, and continue with them. ... Yea, some preferred and chose the prisons in England rather than this liberty in Holland with these afflictions. But it was thought that if a better and easier place of living could be had, it would draw many and take away these discouragements...

Secondly, they saw that though the people generally bore all these difficulties very cheerfully, and with a resolute courage, being in the best and strength of their years; yet old age began to steal on many of them, (and their great and continual labors, with other crosses and sorrows, hastened it before the time)...

Thirdly;...many of their children, by these occasions and the great licentiousness of youth in that country, and the manifold temptations of the place, were drawn away by evil examples into extravagant and dangerous courses, getting the reins off their necks and departing from their parents. Some became

The Pilgrims consistently sought God in prayer.

soldiers, others took upon them far voyages by sea, and others some worse courses tending to dissoluteness and the danger of their souls, to the great grief of their parents and dishonor of God. So that they saw their posterity would be in danger to degenerate and be corrupted.

Lastly (and which was not least), a great hope and inward zeal they had of laying some good foundation, or at least to make some way thereunto, for the propagating and advancing the gospel of the kingdom of Christ in those remote parts of the world; yea, though they should he but even as stepping-stones unto others for the performing of so great a work.

These and some other like reasons moved them to undertake this resolution of their removal; the which they afterward prosecuted with so great difficulties, as by the sequel will appear.

The place they had thoughts on was some of those vast and unpeopled countries of America, which are fruitful and fit for habitation, being devoid of all civil inhabitants, where there are only savage and brutish men which range up and down, little otherwise than the wild beasts of the same. This proposition being made public and coming to the scanning of all, it raised many variable opinions amongst men and caused many fears and doubts amongst themselves. ... For there they should be liable to famine and nakedness and the want, in a manner, of all things. The change of air, diet and drinking of water would infect their bodies with sore sicknesses and grievous diseases. And also those which should escape or overcome these difficulties should yet be in continual danger of the savage people, who are cruel, barbarous and most treacherous, being most furious in their rage and merciless where they overcome; not being content only to kill and take away life, but delight to torment men in the most bloody manner that may be; flaying some alive with the shells of fishes, cutting off the members and joints of others by piecemeal and broiling on the coals, eat the collops of their flesh in their sight whilst they live, with other cruelties horrible to be related.

And surely it could not be thought but the very hearing of these things could not but move the very bowels of men to grate within them and make the weak to quake and tremble. It was further objected that it would require greater sums of money to furnish such a voyage and to fit them with necessaries, than their consumed estates would amount to; and yet they must as well look to be seconded with supplies as presently to be transported.

Also many precedents of ill success and lamentable miseries befallen others in the like designs were easy to be found, and not forgotten to be alleged; besides their own experience, in their former troubles and hardships in their removal into Holland, and how hard a thing it was for them to live in that strange place, though it was a neighbor country and a civil and rich commonwealth.

It was answered, that all great and honorable actions are accompanied with great difficulties and must be both enterprised and overcome with answerable courages. It was granted the dangers were great, but not desperate. The difficulties were many, but not invincible. For though there were many of them likely, yet they were not certain. It might be sundry of the things feared might never befall; others by provident care and the use of good means might in a great measure be prevented; and all of them, through the help of God, by fortitude and patience, might either be borne or overcome...

[Next are two chapters dealing with their difficult legal and economic preparation. Then Bradford continues:]

Of their departure from Leyden

At length, after much travail and these debates, all things were got ready and provided ... So being ready to depart, they had a day of solemn humiliation, their pastor taking his text from Ezra 8.21: "And there at the river, by Ahava, I proclaimed a fast, that we might humble ourselves before our God, and seek of him a right way for us, and for our children, and for all our substance." Upon which he spent a good part of the day very profitably and suitable to their present occasion. The rest of the time was spent in powering [pouring] out prayers to the Lord with great fervency, mixed with abundance of tears...

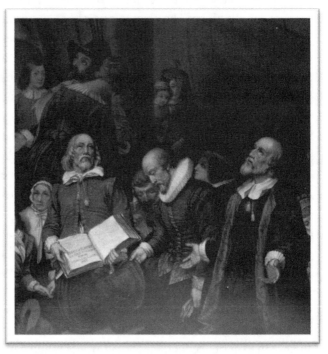

John Robinson (at right) prays with the Pilgrims as they leave Holland in 1620.

So they left that goodly and pleasant city which had been their resting place near 12 years; but they knew they were pilgrims [Heb. 11], and looked not much on those things, but lift up their eyes to the heavens, their dearest country, and quieted their spirits...

At their parting Mr. Robinson write a letter to the whole company; which though it hath already been printed, yet I thought good here likewise to insert it...

> Loving Christian friends, I do heartily and in the Lord salute you all. ... And first, as we are daily to renew our repentance with our God, especially for our sins known, and generally for our unknown trespasses ... sin being taken away by earnest repentance and the pardon thereof from the Lord, sealed up unto a man's conscience by His Spirit, great shall be his security and peace in all dangers, sweet his comforts in all

distresses, with happy deliverance from all evil, whether in life or in death...

Lastly, whereas you are become a body politic, using amongst yourselves civil government, and are not furnished with any persons of special eminency above the rest, to be chosen by you into office, of government; let your wisdom and godliness appear, not only in choosing such persons as do entirely love and will promote the common good, but also in yielding unto them all due honor and obedience in their lawful administrations, not beholding in them the ordinariness of their persons, but God's ordinance for your good; not being like the foolish multitude who more honor the gay coat than either the virtuous mind of the man, or glorious ordinance of the Lord...

I do earnestly commend unto your care and conscience, joining therewith my daily incessant prayers unto the Lord, that He who hath made the heavens and the earth, the sea and all rivers of waters, and whose providence is over all His works, especially over all His dear children for good, would so guide and guard you in your ways. ... John Robinson...

Of their voyage...and...safe arrival at Cape Cod

[After 66 days at sea, in a space no larger than a volleyball court, these 102 passengers aboard the Mayflower finally reached America. The Pilgrims intended to settle just north of the Virginia Colony but were providentially blown off course and out from under the jurisdiction of the Virginia Land Company. Being unable to sail southward due to the weather, they put ashore at Cape Cod. Had they arrived here some years earlier they would have been met by Patuxet Indians and would have found no place to settle. These Indians had murdered many white men who landed on their shores, but in 1617 a plague had mysteriously wiped them out (all except one, Squanto) and now neighboring tribes were afraid to come near the place for fear that some great supernatural spirit had destroyed them. Bradford writes of their voyage and arrival in the new world:]

The Mayflower

Sept. 6 … and now all being compact together in one ship, they put to sea again with a prosperous wind, which continued diverse days together, which was some encouragement unto them; yet according to the usual manner many were afflicted with sea-sickness. And I may not omit here a special work of God's providence. There was a proud and very profane young man, one of the sea-men, of a lusty, able body, which made him the more haughty. He would always be contemning the poor people in their sickness, and cursing them daily with grievous execrations, and did not let [hesitate] to tell them, that he hoped to help to cast half of them over board before they came to their journey's end, and to make merry with what they had; and if he were by any gently reproved, he would curse and swear most bitterly. But it pleased God before they came half seas over, to smite this young man with a grievous disease, of which he died in a desperate manner, and so was himself the first that was thrown overboard. Thus his curses light on his own head; and it was an astonishment to all his fellows, for they noted it to be the just hand of God upon him.

After they had enjoyed fair winds and weather for a season, they were encountered many times with cross winds, and met with many fierce storms, with which the ship was shroudly [much] shaken, and her upper works made very leaky. … In sundry of these storms the winds were so fierce, and the seas so high, as they could not bear a knot of sail, but were forced to hull, for diverse days together. … [A]fter long beating at sea they fell with that land which is called Cape Cod; the which being made and certainly known to be it, they were not a little joyful…

Being thus arrived in a good harbor and brought safe to land, they fell upon their knees and blessed the God of heaven, who had brought them over the vast and furious ocean, and delivered them from all the perils and miseries thereof,

When the Pilgrims arrived at shore "they fell upon their knees and blessed the God of heaven, who had brought them over the vast and furious ocean and delivered them from all the perils and miseries thereof."

again to set their feet on the firm and stable earth, their proper element. And no marvel if they were thus joyful...

But here I cannot but stay and make a pause, and stand half amazed at this poor peoples present condition; and so I think will the reader too, when he well considers the same. Being thus passed the vast ocean, and a sea of troubles before in their preparation (as may be remembered by that which went before), they had now no friends to welcome them, nor inns to entertain or refresh their weatherbeaten bodies; no houses or much less towns to repair to, to seek for succour. It is recorded in Scripture [Acts 28] as a mercy to the Apostle and his shipwrecked company, that the barbarians showed them no small kindness in refreshing them, but these savage barbarians, when they met with them (as after will appear) were readier to fill their sides full of arrows than otherwise. And for the season it was winter, and they that know the winters of that country know them to be sharp and violent, and subject to cruel and fierce storms, dangerous to travel to known places, much more to search an unknown coast.

Besides, what could they see but a hideous and desolate wilderness, full of wild beasts and wild men – and what multitudes there might be of them they knew not. Neither could they, as it were, go up to the top of Pisgah to view from this wilderness a more goodly country to feed their hopes; for which way soever they turned their eyes (save upward to the heavens) they could have little solace or content in respect of any outward objects. For summer being done, all things stand upon them with a weatherbeaten face, and the whole country, full of woods and thickets, represented a wild and savage hue. If they looked behind them, there was the mighty ocean which they had passed and was now as a main bar and gulf to separate them from all the civil parts of the world. If it be said they had a ship to succour them, it is true; but what heard they daily from the master and company? But that with speed they should look out a place with their shallop, where they would be at some near distance; for the season was such as he would not stir from thence till a safe harbor was discovered by them, where they would be, and he might go without danger; and that victuals consumed apace but he must and would keep sufficient for themselves and their return. Yea, it was muttered by some that if they got not a place in time, they would turn them and their goods ashore and leave them. Let it also be considered what weak hopes of supply and succour they left behind them, that might bear up their minds in this sad condition and trials they were under; and they could not but be very small. It is true, indeed, the affections and love of their brethren at Leyden was cordial and entire towards them, but they had little power to help them or themselves; and how the case stood between them and the merchants at their coming away hath already been declared.

What could now sustain them but the Spirit of God and His grace? May not and ought not the children of these fathers rightly say: Our fathers were

The signing of the Mayflower Compact

Englishmen which came over this great ocean, and were ready to perish in this wilderness; they cried unto the Lord, and He heard their voice and looked on their adversity, etc. Let them therefore praise the Lord, because He is good: and His mercies endure forever [Psa. 107: 1, 2, 4, 5, 8]. Yea, let them which have been redeemed of the Lord, show how He hath delivered them from the hand of the oppressor. When they wandered in the desert wilderness out of the way, and found no city to dwell in, both hungry and thirsty, their soul was overwhelmed in them. Let them confess before the Lord His lovingkindness, and His wonderful works before the sons of men...

[The Mayflower Compact and Their First Winter]

I shall a little return back and begin with a combination made by them before they came ashore, being the first foundation of their government in this place; occasioned partly by the discontented and mutinous speeches that some of the strangers amongst them had let fall from them in the ship — That when they came ashore they would use their own liberty; for none had power to command them, the patent they had being for Virginia and not for New England, which belonged to another government, with which the Virginia Company had nothing to do. And partly that such an act by them done, this their condition considered, might be as firm as any patent, and in some respects more sure.

The form was as followeth.

In the name of God, Amen. We whose names are underwritten, the loyal subjects of our dread Sovereign Lord, King James, by the Grace of God, of Great Britain, France, and Ireland king, defender of the faith, etc., having undertaken, for the glory of God and advancement of the Christian faith and honour of our king and country, a voyage to plant the first colony in the Northern parts of Virginia, do by these presents solemnly and mutually in the presence of God, and one of another, covenant and combine ourselves together into a civil body politic, for our better ordering and preservation and furtherance of the ends aforesaid; and by virtue hereof to enact, constitute and frame such just and equal laws, ordinances, acts, constitutions and offices, from time to time, as shall be thought most meet and convenient for the general good of the Colony, unto which we promise all due submission and obedience. In witness whereof we have hereunder subscribed our names at Cape Cod, the 11th of November, in the year of the reign of our sovereign lord, King James, of England, France and Ireland the eighteenth, and of Scotland the fifty-fourth. Anno Domini 1620.

After this they chose, or rather confirmed, Mr. John Carver (a man godly and well approved amongst them) their Governor for that year. And after they had provided a place for their goods, or common store (which were

The Mayflower Compact in Bradford's handwriting

long in unlading for want of boats, foulness of the winter weather and sickness of diverse) and begun some small cottages for their habitation; as time would admit, they met and consulted of laws and orders, both for their civil and military government as the necessity of their condition did require, still adding thereunto as urgent occasion in several times, and as cases did require.

In these hard and difficult beginnings they found some discontents and murmurings arise amongst some, and mutinous speeches and carriages in other; but they were soon quelled and overcome by the wisdom, patience, and just and equal carriage of things, by the Governor and better part, which clave faithfully together in the main.

[The Starving Time]

But that which was most sad and lamentable was, that in 2 or 3 months' time half of their company died, especially in January and February, being the depth of winter, and wanting houses and other comforts; being infected with the scurvy and other diseases which this long voyage and their inaccommodate condition had brought upon them. So as there died some times 2 or 3 of a day in the foresaid time; that of 100 and odd persons, scarce 50 remained. And of these, in the time of most distress, there was but 6 or 7 sound persons, who, to their great commendations be it spoken, spared no pains, night nor day, but with abundance of toil and hazard of their own health, fetched them wood, made them fires, dressed them meat, made their beds, washed their loathsome clothes, clothed and unclothed them; in a word, did all the homely and necessary offices for them which dainty and queasy stomachs cannot endure to hear named; and all this willingly and cheerfully, without any grudging in the least, showing herein their true love unto their friends and brethren; a rare example and worthy to be remembered...

[Squanto: a special instrument sent of God]

But about the 16. of March a certain Indian came boldly amongst them, and spoke to them in broken English, which they could well understand but marveled

The Pilgrims thanked God for a safe Voyage.

at it. ... His name was Samaset; he told them also of another Indian whose name was Squanto, a native of this place, who had been in England and could speak better English than himself. Being, after some time of entertainment and gifts, dismissed, a while after he came again, and 5 more with him...and made way for the coming of their great Sachem, called Massosoyt; who, about 4 or 5 days after, came with...the aforesaid Squanto. With whom, after friendly entertainment, and some gifts given him, they made a peace with him, which hath now continued this 24 years...

After these things he returned to his place...but Squanto continued with them, and was their interpreter, and was a special instrument sent of God for their good beyond their expectation. He directed them how to set their corn, where to fish, and to procure other commodities, and was their pilot to bring them to unknown places for their profit, and never left them till he died...

Afterwards they (as many as were able) began to plant their corn, in which service Squanto stood them in great stead, showing them both the manner how to set it, and after how to dress and tend it. Also he told them, except they got fish and set with it (in these old grounds) it would come to nothing. And he showed them that in the middle of April they should have store enough come up the brook, by which they began to build, and taught them how to take it, and where to get other provisions necessary for them. All which they found true by trial and experience...

And thus they found the Lord to be with them in all their ways, and to bless their outgoings and incomings, for which let His holy name have the praise forever, to all posterity.[76]

The Pilgrims in prayer.

———

(Various editions of *Bradford's History* are available at libraries and used bookstores if you wish to read more.)

The First Thanksgiving

Squanto not only taught the Pilgrims how to plant corn and catch fish, he also taught them to stalk deer, plant pumpkins, find berries, and catch beaver, whose pelts proved to be their economic deliverance. He was also helpful in securing a peace treaty between the Pilgrims and surrounding Indian tribes, which lasted over fifty years. In the words of William Bradford, "Squanto ...was a special instrument sent of God for their good beyond their expectation."[77] His life story is amazing in itself.

The Pilgrims at church

In 1605, Squanto, a member of the Patuxet Indian tribe, was captured by an English explorer and taken to England. He remained there nine years, during which time he learned to speak English. In 1614, Captain John Smith took him back to New England, but shortly after this he was again taken captive and sold into slavery at a port in Spain. Providentially, some local friars bought and rescued him.

From Spain, he eventually went to England where he remained until 1619, when he obtained passage back to his home in New England. As Squanto went ashore at what was to become Plymouth, he found his entire tribe had been killed by a plague. He was the only survivor of the Patuxet tribe. Joining himself to a nearby tribe, he remained there until the spring of 1621 when he joined himself with the Pilgrims, determining to see them survive at the place where his tribe had not.[78]

Thanks to God, His instrument Squanto, and the character and determination of the Pilgrims, half of them had survived an unimaginably difficult first year. Moreover, they harvested a sufficient food supply for their second winter at Plymouth. Even though there was no surplus food, things looked much better than the preceding winter.

Governor Bradford appointed a day of thanksgiving and invited the nearby Wampanoag Indians (Squanto's adopted tribe) to celebrate and give thanks unto God with them. Chief Massasoit and ninety of his men came and feasted with the Pilgrims. They ate deer, turkey, fish, lobster, eels, vegetables, corn bread, herbs, berries, and pies, and the Indians even taught the Pilgrims how to make popcorn. The Pilgrims and Indians also competed in running, wrestling, and shooting games. Massasoit enjoyed himself so much that he and his men stayed for three days.[79] It is easy to see where the American tradition of feasting at Thanksgiving began.

While many people today follow the Pilgrim's example of feasting at Thanksgiving, they too often ignore the entire reason that the Pilgrims set aside a special day – that was to give thanks to Almighty God and acknowledge their utter dependence upon Him for their existence. While many today take ease in having plenty, never seeing a need to cry out to God, the Pilgrims relied upon God in their lack and thanked Him in their abundance. Their trust was in God and not in their abundant provisions.

The Pilgrims — An Example to All

As you have seen reading through the excerpts of *Bradford's History*, we can learn so much from the example of the Pilgrims. Following are only a few lessons we should learn:

1. The Pilgrims give us an excellent example of the Principle of Christian Character.
2. God will providentially prepare us to accomplish His destiny for our lives.
3. God will supernaturally protect and care for us as we walk in the way He has set before us.
4. Freedom of worship and liberty for ourselves and our descendants is worth any price we must pay.
5. The Pilgrims knew how to apply biblical truth to civil affairs as seen in the Mayflower Compact, which was the first expression of civil government that recognized the Christian idea of man and government.

In the life of the Pilgrims, God had prepared those of humble beginnings to be a light of liberty to an entire nation. In the words of Bradford:

Thus out of small beginnings greater things have been produced by His hand that made all things of nothing, and gives being to all things that are; and as one small candle may light a thousand, so the light here kindled hath shone to many, yea in some sort to our whole nation; let the glorious name of Jehovah have all the praise.

Sunday at Plymouth

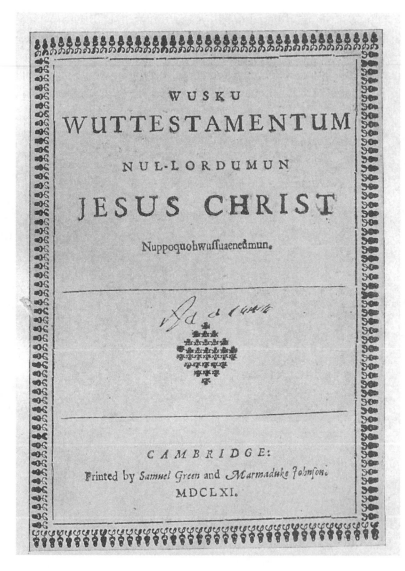

Title page of the New Testament in the Algonquin Indian language. A primary reason the early settlers came to America was to propagate the Gospel to the Native Americans. As a means of accomplishing this mission, Rev. John Eliot learned to speak in the Algonquin tongue, developed a written language, and then worked 12 years to translate the Bible into the Algonquin language. This Bible was first published in 1661-1663.

Chapter 7

The Colonies: Seeds of a Nation

There is a direct causal relationship between the dispersion of the Bible in the hands of the people and the rise of civil liberty. A survey of civil government from the time of Christ to the present reveals a sudden profusion of documents such as the Mayflower Compact, English Bill of Rights, and the Constitution beginning in 1620. Before this, pagan monarchies were ubiquitous.

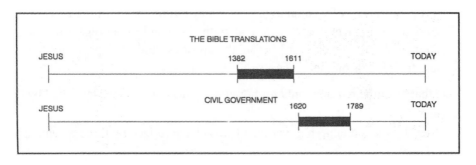

What produced these changes in ideas of government? How does one explain this? For two centuries prior to these changes, the Bible began to be translated and disseminated in the common language. It all began with John Wycliffe in 1382 who said of his new translation into English: "This Bible is for the government of the people, by the people, and for the people."[80]

As people began to read the Bible, three things occurred: People were converted; the church began to return to biblical Christianity; and society began to be reformed and enjoy civil liberty.

Restoration of Biblical Church Government

Christians in the religious system of the 16th century began to study the Scriptural model of church government. They found that governing authority in the church was placed in the hands of apostles and elders:

> The brethren determined that Paul and Barnabas and certain others of them should go up to Jerusalem to the apostles and elders concerning this issue. ... And the apostles and the elders came together to look into this matter. (Acts 15:2, 6; see also vs. 1-6, 23)

> Now while they were passing through the cities, they were delivering the decrees, which had been decided upon by the apostles and elders who were in Jerusalem, for them to observe. (Acts 16:4; see also Acts 2:42; 4:35; 14:23)

The entire congregation could be involved and consulted in directional matters, but even here the final approval or appointing power remained with the apostles and elders:

> The twelve summoned the congregation of the disciples and said, "It is not desirable for us to neglect the word of God in order to serve tables. But select from among you, brethren, seven men of good reputation, full of the Spirit and of wisdom, whom we may put in charge of the task."... And the statement found approval with the whole congregation; and they...brought [seven men] before the apostles; and after praying, they laid their hands on them." (Acts 6:2, 3, 5-6)

Note that even the requirements for nominating deacons were established by the apostles.

New Testament church government was characterized by three essentials in the original:

1. **Covenant Commitment** — A more general word for this was "love." It meant that every believer must do "his share" and participate in church activities. "Fellowship" meant partnership in the Gospel. The "body" of Christ is "held together by the joints and ligaments" (or "bonds") (Col. 2:19). The perfect "bond" or "ligament" of unity is "love" or covenant (Col. 3:14).

2. **Plurality of elders** — The government of the church is the responsibility of the elders. The Bible shows that these elders were appointed by God

through apostles. Never is there an example of an elder ruling a church by himself; a plurality was always required to prevent poor decisions.

"And when they [the apostles] had appointed elders for them in every church, having prayed with fasting, they commended them to the Lord." (Acts 14:23)

"For this reason I [Paul] left you in Crete, that you might set in order what remains, and appoint elders in every city as I directed you." (Tit. 1:5; see also 1 Tim. 3:1-5 and Prov. 11:14)

3. **"Senior" elders, apostles and prophets** — Strong, decisive leadership is necessary at times in the plurality of elders. Jerusalem, which was a model for other local churches, had James as the "senior" elder:

- James was the one to whom people reported (Acts 12:17).
- James moderated the council of elders (Acts 15:13, 19).
- James was the one that Paul consulted for advice (Acts 21:18).
- James was the one with whom the Jerusalem believers identified themselves (Gal. 2:12).

And there were also apostles and prophets who exercised authority in the Body of Christ at large:

"God has appointed these in the church: first apostles, second prophets" (1 Cor. 12:28).

"The household of God is built on the foundation of the apostles and prophets" (Eph. 2:20).

The Original Corrupted and Restored

These three New Testament elements of church government were corrupted over time as the church backslid. Fewer and fewer believers were willing to love or lay down their lives and serve in the church. As this covenant commitment waned, most church functions were being performed by leaders rather than all members. Laziness and unspirituality among common believers led to a clear clergy-laity distinction by the third century.

As time progressed, even the elders became less exemplary and therefore fewer. Authority became more centralized in the hands of the most prominent and spiritual elders known as "bishops." In the body of Christ at large, this same apostasy led to fewer qualified apostles, and therefore more centralization of apostolic authority. Within a few centuries it was all centralized in the hands of the "Popes."

After many centuries, the dispersion of the Bible produced a revival in Europe and a rejection of the papal centralization of power. Catholic Reformers known as "Protestants" sprang up within the Catholic Church throughout Europe. An ungodly king of England, Henry VIII, desired to divorce his wife but could not without being excommunicated by the Pope. Therefore in 1534, he decided to break off from Rome and start the Church of England. The centralized form of church government, however, was the same, and became known as the Episcopal form.

In 1553 Protestants reestablished the role of elders in plurality (Presbytery) ruling the church instead of popes. This became known as Presbyterian Church government. In 1570, Protestants known as "Separatists" began emphasizing the role of the whole congregation in participating and ministering in the church. They placed church authority in the hands of the people through elections.

These three truths produced three distinct movements:

1. Episcopalians (1534) — emphasizing strong apostolic leadership.
2. Presbyterians (1558) — emphasizing plurality of elders.
3. Congregationalists (1570) — emphasizing covenant participation of all members.

The Movements Planted in America

Each of these movements settled in the American colonies in three major geographical areas. This was significant because their views of church government determined their colonial forms of civil government. Let us examine how these Christian movements started America and gained dominance in three distinct regions.

The Southern Colonies — Stronghold of Episcopalianism

Virginia — 1607

Jamestown was the first permanent English settlement in America. After the future settlers of Jamestown reached Virginia in April of 1607, one of the first acts of Captain John Smith and his soldiers was to erect a wooden cross on the shore at Cape Henry. It was at the foot of this cross that Reverend Robert Hunt led the 149 men of the Virginia Company in public prayer, thanking God for their safe journey and recommitting themselves to God's plan and purpose for this New World. The Virginia Charter of 1606 reveals that part of their reason for coming to America was to propagate the "Christian Religion to such People, as yet live in Darkness and miserable Ignorance of the true Knowledge and Worship of God."[81] From 1609 to 1612, some of the leaders wrote America's first civil laws, and they were based upon God's higher law.[82] In 1611, the Rev. Alexander Whitaker built Virginia's second church in Henrico and preached a famous sermon entitled "Good News from Virginia" that encouraged Europeans to colonize America for the glory of God. He performed the celebrated marriage of John Rolfe and the Indian princess Pocahontas.

John Smith

When Pocahontas was a young teenager, she providentially saved Captain John Smith from being killed by members of her Indian tribe. Jamestown would have probably not survived as a settlement had it not been for Pocahontas, for without Smith's leadership the colony would have likely died. In addition, she brought much needed food to Jamestown. Smith also took part in preserving the Pilgrims from extinction by carrying the Indian Squanto from England to America. The first representative assembly in America began in the church in Jamestown with the Rev. Bucke leading the Burgesses in prayer, asking God to guide and sanctify their proceedings to His own glory

Pocahontas providentially saved John Smith's life.

and the good of the plantation. They issued laws requiring church attendance, believing that men's affairs cannot prosper where God's service is neglected. In that same year, 1619, they also observed the first American Day of Thanksgiving.[83]

The first representative assembly in the New World was held in the Jamestown Church in 1619.

North Carolina — 1653

Quakers and other religious dissenters from Virginia began to settle in North Carolina in 1653 and nine years later obtained a Charter which acknowledged that the settlement was constituted for "the propagation of the gospel...in the parts of America not yet cultivated and planted."[84]

South Carolina — 1662

The original charter which established North Carolina as a colony also applied to South Carolina, but seven years later their own Fundamental Constitution of Carolina was drawn up by the great Christian philosopher John Locke. It required people to: (1) believe that there is a God, (2) in court, recognize Divine justice and human responsibility, and (3) be a church member in order to be a freeman of the colony.[85]

Georgia – 1731

Dr. Thomas Bray and General James Oglethorpe teamed up in 1731 to establish "a colony...for instructing the Negroes and the poor of this kingdom [England's imprisoned debtors and unemployed], and for other good purposes."[86]

James Oglethorpe

The original 100 settlers were followed by Moravians and other persecuted Protestants in 1736 who, when they touched shore, kneeled in thanks to God. They said, "our end in leaving our native country is not to gain riches and honor, but singly this—to live wholly to the glory of God." The object of the devout Oglethorpe and others was "to make Georgia a religious colony" and so they laid out Savannah with numerous religious ceremonies and invited John and Charles Wesley and Rev. George Whitefield to come and serve as chaplains, oversee Indian affairs, and build orphanages. When Whitefield died, the legislature attempted to have him buried there at public cost in honor of his influence.[87]

Northern Colonies — Bastion of Congregationalism

Massachusetts — 1620

As we have seen, the Pilgrims established the first permanent settlement in New England at Plymouth in 1620. As was their desire, the Pilgrims were truly "stepping-stones" for those leaving Europe in search of religious and civil liberty. The Puritans soon followed their leading.

After decades of attempting to purify the Church of England with little result, many Puritans decided another plan was necessary. If they could not purify the Church from within, they would set up a model Church of England in America as an example of the true Church. They had not intended to break from the Church of England originally, as the Pilgrim Separatists had done, but after being some years in the new world they saw no other recourse if they desired to grow in God.

In the spring of 1630, some 1000 Puritans (which was more than the total inhabitants of the ten-year-old Plymouth Colony) sailed to America. They were led by John Winthrop, who served as the governor of Massachusetts Bay Colony for many years. Historian John Fiske writes of him:

> When his life shall have been adequately written...he will be recognized as one of the very noblest figures in American history.... From early youth he had the same power of winning confidence and commanding respect for which Washington was so remarkable; and when he was selected as the Moses of the great Puritan exodus, there was a widespread feeling that extraordinary results were likely to come of such an enterprise.[88]

John Winthrop

While at sea in passage to America, Winthrop wrote "A Model of Christian Charity" which contains their reasons for starting a new colony and the goals they wished to accomplish. Winthrop spoke of their desire to be "as a city upon a hill," which all the people of the earth could look upon and say of their own nation, "the Lord make it like that of New England."[89]

President Reagan often spoke of this vision for America that our Pilgrim and Puritan Fathers had. We have been an example to the people of the world of what a godly nation should be like. However, as we have forgotten that it was the Lord who made us a nation, we have also failed to be a "model of Christian Charity" in various ways. We must remember as Winthrop wrote, "that if we shall deal falsely with our God in this work we have undertaken and so cause Him to withdraw his present help from us, we shall be made a story and a byword through the world."[90]

The Separatists at Plymouth and the Puritans at Boston Complement Each Other

When the Puritans first came to America, they still held to a few pagan ideas of government, yet they also carried important scriptural truths. Over the years God would combine the strengths of both Puritan and Pilgrim as they began to populate New England.

The major Puritan weakness was their holding to the idea of a state church. They saw nothing wrong with a national church and compelled religion (as existed in Europe). The problem they had regarding affairs in England was that the church and state were corrupt and unbiblical in many aspects. In Massachusetts they would set up right government, in church and state.

Over time the Pilgrims, and certain Puritan ministers, would help leaven the thinking of the Puritans to allow more freedom of conscience and individual liberty. The advancement of biblical truth that had begun to be recovered during the Reformation was continuing during the settlement of America.

Governor Winthrop desired to make New England "as a city upon a hill."

The primary strength of the Puritans was their "spirit of dominion." They recognized the scriptural mandates requiring godly rule, and zealously set out to establish that in all aspects of society. New England would become a blend of the best of these two movements — Puritan mandates and Pilgrim principles of liberty. The Separatist influence brought about the gradual dominance of Congregational self-government throughout New England, and also greater liberty for everyone.

Some progressing ideas of civil liberty were seen in the Massachusetts Body of Liberties, written by Rev. Nathaniel Ward and adopted in 1641. This document, the first "bill of rights" in history, was the precursor of the 1789 Bill of Rights.

Settlement of New England

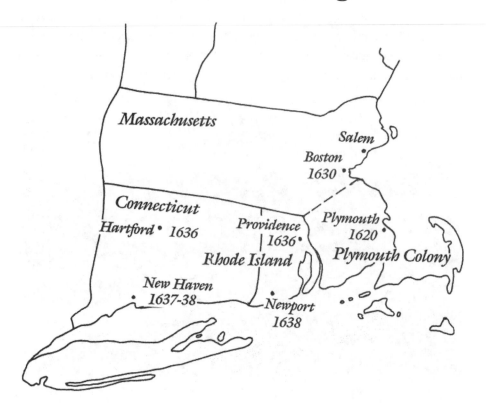

Massachusetts Colonies	1. Plymouth (1620)—Pilgrims—Separatists
	2. Bay Colonies (1628, 1629 – Charter)—Puritans
Connecticut Colonies	1. Connecticut Colony (1636)—Thomas Hooker—Puritan
	2. New Haven Colony (1637)—John Davenport—Puritan
Rhode Island	1. Providence (1636)—Roger Williams—Separatist
	2. Newport (1638)—John Clarke—Separatist

Connecticut — 1636

In 1633 Puritan Minister Thomas Hooker came to the Massachusetts Bay Colony. Rev. Hooker's eloquent and learned support of scriptural Christianity caused him to be driven from England. Shortly after arriving in the Bay Colony, Hooker became Pastor of the Church at Newtown (now Cambridge). After observing the governmental workings of the colony, he noticed the intolerance of the Puritans and attempted to correct some of their wrongs. When this resulted in little success, he petitioned the Bay Colony leaders and was granted the right to migrate to the Connecticut Valley.

In June 1636, Rev. Hooker and most of his Newtown congregation of about 100 people settled in what would become Connecticut Colony. Many others followed in the months to come. By May 1637, eight hundred people had settled

Rev. Thomas Hooker's Sermon in Connecticut in 1638 shaped the framing of the first constitution in history.

in the valley. In January 1639 the *Fundamental Orders of Connecticut* were adopted as the Constitution of Connecticut. Rev. Hooker chiefly formulated this document, "the first written constitution known to history."[91] This constitution, which contained many biblical rights and ideas expressed politically, would have a great influence on our nation. Historian John Fiske writes that "the government of the United States today is in lineal descent more nearly related to that of Connecticut than to any of the other thirteen colonies."[92]

In 1637 Puritan minister, John Davenport, led the colonization of New Haven Colony. His reasons for coming were similar to those which motivated Hooker to settle the Connecticut Colony. These two colonies would later unite to form Connecticut.

Rhode Island — 1636

In many ways Connecticut was a Puritan/Episcopal colony with Separatist/Pilgrim ideas, but Rhode Island was a Separatist colony through and through. A brilliant young Separatist minister, Roger Williams, came to the Bay Colony in 1631 as a refugee from the tyranny of Charles I. Williams served as minister in Plymouth for a time, and then by mutual agreement left to pastor in Salem.

State Seal of Rhode Island

His firm convictions regarding liberty of conscience and his outspoken manner brought him into conflict with the intolerant Puritan leaders of the Bay Colony. After he was warned of causing trouble by spreading heretical ideas and failing to comply with the civil leaders, he was tried and banished from the Massachusetts Bay Colony. In 1636 he purchased some land from the Indians and founded Providence. In Williams' words, this was "in a sense of God's merciful providence unto me in my distress."

His belief that the civil power has no jurisdiction over the conscience, was reflected in the laws of Providence and later in the colony of Rhode Island. Many others who had been persecuted for their religious convictions began settling in Rhode Island.

In 1638 Rev. John Clarke led a group to found Newport "in the presence of Jehovah" by agreeing to "incorporate ourselves in a Body Politic, and as He shall help us, will submit our persons, lives, and estate unto our Lord Jesus Christ, the King of Kings, the Lord of Lords."

Roger Williams

One excellent truth that Roger Williams helped to advance was that a free and prosperous civil state is dependent upon individuals and a church that are grounded in biblical truth and at liberty to worship God. This is revealed in the Royal Charter of Rhode Island of 1663:

...that they, pursueing, with peaceable and loyall minds, their sober, serious and religious intentions, of godlie edifying themselves, and one another, in the holie Christian faith and worship...together with gaineing over and conversion of the poore ignorant Indian natives...

A most flourishing civill state may stand and best be maintained...with a full libertie in religious concernements; and that true pietye rightly grounded upon gospell principles, will give the best and greatest security to sovereignetye, and will lay in the hearts of men the stongest obligations to true loyaltye.[93]

In Connecticut and Rhode Island, we see that God's people and God's ministers were involved in formulating every aspect of the public affairs of these colonies. We also see the principles of liberty of the Separatists and the spirit of dominion of the Puritans coming together. As a result of this excellent blend, these two colonies were the only ones to remain self-governing all the way up to the American Revolution.

Rev, John Clarke wrote in a 1661 petition that his earnest request was "to hold forth a lively experiment that a most flourishing civil state may stand ... and best be maintained ... with a full liberty in religious concernments," which was included in the Charter of Rhode Island (1663).

New Hampshire — 1639

The colonists of Exeter wrote in 1639:

...considering with ourselves the holy will of God and our own necessity, that we should not live without wholesome laws and government among us, of which we are altogether destitute, do, in the name of Christ and in the sight of God combine ourselves together, to erect and set up among us such government as shall be to our best discerning, agreeable to the will of God.[94]

Later, in 1680, they proposed their "glorious cause [to be]...the glory of God...and spreading the gospel among the heathen," so "a civil assembly was convened, and a solemn public fast proclaimed and observed to propitiate the favor of Heaven" as they established themselves as a province independent of Massachusetts.[95]

The Middle Colonies — Dominant Area of Presbyterianism

New York — 1628

New York was originally started as two colonies in 1628 — New Amsterdam and New Netherlands — by Rev. Jonas Michaelius and others of the Dutch Reformed Church.

The first entry in New Amsterdam's city records (present day New York City) is Rev. John Megapolensis' prayer opening the court in 1653: "Graciously incline our hearts, that we exercise the power which thou hast given us, to the general good of the community, and to the maintenance of the church, that we may be praised by them that do well, and a terror to evildoers."

In 1665, the legislature passed an act to uphold "the public worship of God" and instruction of "the people in the true religion."

Maryland — 1633

Maryland was started as a "reformed Catholic" colony but became Protestant within a couple of decades. The governor leading the expedition sent by Lord Baltimore took possession of the country "for our Lord Jesus Christ" and made "Christianity the established faith of the land."[96] One of the leaders wrote: "bearing on our shoulders a huge cross, which we had hewn from a tree, we moved in procession to a spot selected…and erected it as a trophy to Christ our

Savior; then humbly kneeling, we recited with deep emotion the Litany of the Holy Cross."

Father Andrew White wrote: "Behold the lands are white for the harvest, prepared for receiving the seed of the Gospel into a fruitful bosom;…who then can doubt that by one such glorious work as this, many thousands of souls will be brought to Christ?"

The beginnings of Maryland

In 1649, Maryland's "Act Concerning Religion" stated that: "No person professing to believe in Jesus Christ should be molested on account of their religion, or denied the free exercise of their particular modes of worship."[97]

Delaware — 1638

New Sweden was established along the Delaware River in 1638 due to the backing of the heroic King Gustavus Adolphus who envisioned such a Protestant "planting" in the New World. It was settled by Rev. John Campanius and others of the Lutheran Church of Sweden.

New Jersey — 1664

An association of church members from New Haven, Connecticut, settled New Jersey in order "to carry on their spiritual and town affairs according to godly government."[98] Leaders of the Dutch Reformed Church settled much of Eastern New Jersey in 1664.

Western New Jersey's constitution was developed by the Quakers. William Perm wrote: "There we lay a foundation for after ages to understand their liberty as men and Christians, that they may not be brought in bondage but by their own consent, for we put the power in the people."

In 1697, the governor made a proclamation "in obedience to the laws of God" to duly execute "all laws made and provided for the suppression of vice and encouraging of religion and virtue, particularly the observance of the Lord's day." The motto of New Jersey on their Provincial seal was Proverbs 14:34 — "Righteousness exalteth a nation."[99]

Pennsylvania — 1681

Quaker preacher William Penn was given the land between New York and Maryland in 1681. He said that "my God that has given it to me...will, I believe, bless and make it the seed of a nation."[100]

In 1682 the Great Law of Pennsylvania was enacted revealing the desire of Penn and the inhabitants of the colony to establish "laws as shall best preserve true Christian and civil liberty, in opposition to all unchristian, licentious, and unjust practices, whereby God may have his due, Caesar his due, and the people their due."[101]

William Penn

Thomas Jefferson called Penn "the greatest lawgiver the world has produced." Penn, whose wisdom was "derived from the book of the gospel statutes," recognized Christian character as the basis of good government. He states in the Frame of Government of Pennsylvania:

> Governments like clocks, go from the motion men give them; and as governments are made and moved by men, so by them they are ruined too. Wherefore governments rather depend upon men, than men upon governments. ... Let men be good, and the government cannot be bad; if it will be ill, they will cure it.[102]

At a later time William Penn told the Russian Czar, Peter the Great, that "if thou wouldst rule well, thou must rule for God, and to do that, thou must be ruled by him."[103] Penn also said that "those who will not be governed by God will be ruled by tyrants."[104]

When Penn received the Charter of Pennsylvania from Charles II, he believed that God would "bless and make it the seed of a nation."

Biblical Reformation of Civil Government

We can see a consistent Christian dominance in the settlement of every single colony. A joint statement made by all of the Northern Colonies in the *New England Confederation* of 1643 would just as well have been made by all 13 colonies. It stated: "We all came into these parts of America with one and the same end and aim, namely, to advance the kingdom of our Lord Jesus Christ, and to enjoy the liberties of the Gospel in purity with peace."[105]

Civil government is a reflection or a product of church government ideas. This relationship was clearly seen in the colonial civil governments. The three religious movements settled in America in three geographical groupings: The Northern Colonies were settled predominately by Congregationalists, the Southern Colonies by Episcopalians, and the Middle Colonies by Presbyterians.

Each of these colonies established civil government that coincided with their view of church government:

1. Northern Colonies were self-governing (Democratic).
2. Middle Colonies were proprietary governments (which tended to be Aristocratic).
3. Southern Colonies were royal provinces ruled by a Governor (Monarchial).[106]

Each colony developed its form of government (and thoroughly understood the strengths and weaknesses of each) for 150 years until the Revolutionary period when they were blended together under our Constitution. Elements of *all three* forms of government are seen in America today:

1. Episcopalian or monarchial elements found in our president and governors.
2. Presbyterian or aristocratic elements found in our judges and originally in our U.S. Senators.
3. Congregational or democratic elements found in our U.S. and State Representatives.

Even as none of the forms of church government alone constitutes the biblical model, so also the Christian form of civil government must be a composite of all three. Episcopalian, Presbyterian and Congregational forms *together* make biblical church government. Monarchy, aristocracy and democracy *together* make a biblical civil republic. This indeed was what God providentially arranged in the establishment of the United States of America.

The first brick church built in Jamestown
Scene of the 1st Free Representative Assembly in America

Chapter 8

Education in America: How the Principles Are Planted

The biblical principles upon which America was birthed were passed on to succeeding generations through education in the home, church, and school. Christian education assured a foundation of liberty. Our Founders understood that tyranny and bondage would result from ignorance of the truth. This truth was rooted in the Bible.

Benjamin Franklin said: "A nation of well informed men who have been taught to know and prize the rights which God has given them cannot be enslaved. It is in the region of ignorance that tyranny begins."

Rosalie Slater writes that "American Christian education was the foundation of our nation's great growth, progress, and success. ... The colonists brought with them a tradition of Biblical scholarship and the

Benjamin Franklin

fruition of the Reformation — the Scriptures in English. And with their Bibles they brought a determination to continue the individual study and practice of the Christian verities contained therein. Because of their sincere desire to teach their children to read the Scriptures they established schools. Their colleges were the culmination of the need for an enlightened ministry."[107]

Biblical Scholarship

What was this "Biblical scholarship" that formed the basis for all education in America for over two centuries? Simply stated, biblical scholarship is the ability to reason from biblical principles and relate it to all of life. Not only did early American Christians reason from the Bible, but even non-Christians were trained in this manner and held to a biblical worldview. This is quite the opposite of today because both non-Christians and even many Christians view life from a man-centered, humanistic worldview. Decades of humanistic teaching in schools and by the media has engrained this philosophy in a large majority of Americans.

What Is a Worldview?

Gary Demar writes that "a world view is simply the way you look at yourself and the world around you. It includes your beliefs about God, yourself, your neighbors, your family, civil government, art, music, history, morality, education, business, economics, and all other areas of life."[108]

Greg Anthony states: "Your world view, of course, is how you view the world. It is the set of presuppositions — that which is believed beforehand — which underlies all of our decisions and actions. These presuppositions (our world view) determine our thinking patterns, which in turn influence our actions. ... Our world view may be conscious or unconscious, but it determines our destiny and the destiny of the society we live in."[109]

The biblical worldview and scholarship of Colonial Americans provided the basis of a free and prosperous America. Miss Slater writes:

> The Pilgrims learned Biblical reasoning from Pastor John Robinson during their twelve years in Holland. Thus they were prepared to extend Christian principles into civil government and to deal with the problems that confronted them in the New World. Challenged on the Mayflower by rebellious "strangers," they wrote the Mayflower Compact, so that every man might voluntarily share in making and keeping the laws. Confronted with distrustful Indians, they made a mutual pact and maintained a long-lasting peace. Faced with starvation, William Bradford, Governor of Plymouth Plantation, "had the courage and wisdom" to shift from "labor in common" to the responsibility of individual enterprise and private property. For more than twenty years the Pilgrims labored to repay their original debt to venture capitalists in England who had financed the voyage of the Mayflower. There were many opportunities to escape from this responsibility but they held to the obligation as a matter of Christian

conscience. The Pilgrims were consistent because of their applications of Christian truths or principles.

The ability to reason from the Word of God and to relate its principles to every area of life was characteristic of the American clergy prior to the American Revolution. ... Their election and artillery sermons identified "the principles of civil government with the principles of Christianity."

The Pilgrims learned biblical reasoning from Pastor John Robinson.

At the time of the Declaration of Independence the quality of education had enabled the colonies to achieve a degree of literacy from "70% to virtually 100%." This was not education restricted to the few. Modern scholarship reports "the prevalence of schooling and its accessibility to most segments of the population." Moses Coit Tyler, historian of American Literature, indicates the colonist's "familiarity with history ... extensive legal learning ... lucid exposition of constitutional principles, showing, indeed, that somehow, out into that American wilderness had been carried the very accent of cosmopolitan thought and speech." When the American State Papers arrived in Europe they surprised and astonished the "enlightened men." Americans had been dismissed as "illiterate back-woodsmen" as, perhaps, "law-defying revolutionists." But when these papers were read they were found to contain "nearly every quality indicative of personal and national greatness."

Dr. Lawrence A. Cremin in his study of American Education from 1607 to 1789, credits the high quality of American education to the Bible, "the single most important cultural influence in the lives of Anglo-Americans."[110]

Christian Education

Colonial Americans exemplified qualities of "personal and national greatness" because of their Christian education. To restore liberty and greatness to America, we must restore Christian education to America. For education to be Christian, one's philosophy (why, who, when, and where), methodology (how), and curriculum (what) must be Christian, that is, be "Christ-like" or "pertain to Christ."

Christian Philosophy

It has been said, "the philosophy of the school room in one generation will be the philosophy of government in the next." Colossians 2:8 tells us that a worldly philosophy brings captivity:

> See to it that no one takes you captive through philosophy and empty deception, according to the tradition of men, according to the elementary principles of the world, rather than according to Christ.

A worldly, humanistic philosophy in the present educational system of many nations has produced bondage within individuals' lives. As an example of this, there are 30-40 million American adults today who are functionally illiterate. They cannot read a job application, a warning sign at work, or a label on a medicine bottle. That is bondage! This great illiteracy is the fruit of a humanistic method of teaching reading.

While a worldly philosophy brings captivity, the Bible tells us that a Christian philosophy brings liberty. In order to liberate our nation, individuals must be liberated first. True education is the primary means of imparting a Christian philosophy of life, and hence in bringing liberty to our nation.

A Christian philosophy of education brings liberty.

What is education?

In order to properly educate ourselves, we must first understand what true education is. If we were to define education from our experience in public schools, we would probably agree with most modern dictionary definitions of the word, which define it as teaching that primarily is concerned with imparting information. While education does involve imparting information, according to the Bible this is of secondary concern.

Noah Webster, in his original 1828 dictionary, reveals to us four minimal goals of education. He writes: "Education comprehends all that series of instruction and discipline which is intended to [1] enlighten the understanding, [2] correct the temper, [3] form the manners and habits of youth, and [4] fit them for usefulness in their future stations."[111]

We can see from his definition that education deals primarily with the inward man — with forming character. The formation of character is inevitable. Bad character, not good, is the result of the failure of public schools to discipline.

A Biblical Method of Education — The Principle Approach

Methods of education are not neutral. Colonial America had a biblical method of education. Noah Webster (1758-1843) helped to establish the Principle Approach as the standard method of education in the new Republic of America.

What is the Principle Approach?

One thing it is not, is another program. It is not a pre-packaged, daily lesson plan that a teacher follows in instructing her students, where each step is given each day for each class. Briefly stated, the Principle Approach to education inculcates in individuals the ability to reason from the Bible to every aspect of life. As Christians, we know we are supposed to do this, but do we? Do we really know how to reason from the Bible to geography, astronomy, mathematics, or history, not to mention national defense, foreign policy, or civil government?

The Principle Approach restores the art of biblical reasoning.

Many Christians of recent generations have read Romans 12:2 as follows: "Do not be conformed to this world, but be transformed by the *removal* of your mind." We know that we are transformed by the *renewing* of our mind and not by its *removal,* yet many Christians over-responded to the decay of the institutionalized church in past generations into a "mental religion only" by rejecting the use of our minds in following God, desiring only to be "led by the Spirit."

We must again realize that as Christians we have the potential to be the greatest thinkers in all the world. Historically, Christians have been the leaders in almost every area of life (Johann S. Bach in music, Isaac Newton in science, Rembrandt in art, Adam Smith in economics, John Locke in civil government, to name only a few[112]). Those men who founded America were only able to produce a free and prosperous society because they knew how to reason biblically to all areas of life.

We are in great need today of restoring the art of biblical reasoning to our educational system. We may have more facts taught in our schools today (even though in many fields, major facts are conspicuously missing), but we must teach more than just facts. We must teach how to arrive at those facts as well.

To more fully understand the Principle Approach, let's look at each of the words separately. A *principle*, according to Webster's 1828 dictionary, is: "1. the cause, source, or origin of anything; that from which a thing proceeds; 2) Element; constituent part."

A principle is like an element in chemistry. An element is the lowest form in which matter can exist naturally—it can be broken down no further. A principle is an absolute truth (and hence biblical) that is reduced to its most basic form. While the Bible contains thousands of truths, these can be broken down into a small number of principles from which the truths spring forth. If these principles are known, this provides parameters through which to view life, assuring that one truth is not forgotten while embracing a new one.

A *principle* and a *seed* are very similar in their meanings. A seed, being a plant in embryo, contains the entire plant—the whole thing is there, albeit in a condensed form. After a seed is planted, given some time, water, sunlight, and care, a huge tree can be produced. Likewise, principles are first given in seed form to children, yet these principles contain the potential of giant trees of truth

Principles are like seeds.

and application. God starts with a seed and produces a plant. Today most classes try to shove plants down children's throats.

The Principle Approach teaches seed principles over and over again in each subject and grade level with different illustrations, examples, assignments, educational methods, etc. This ensures that a child not only knows biblical principles, but that he lives them—that they are a part of his life.

Approach simply means "to come or go near, in place; to draw near." Therefore, the Principle Approach involves getting biblical principles so near someone that they become a part of their life.

A "Wholistic" Method

The Principle Approach is also a "wholistic" method of education, that is, it is instruction from the whole to the part. Take history, for example. Instead of teaching fragments of history throughout the various grade levels with seemingly no unifying factor among the different classes, a biblical approach would look at the whole of history first, and then look at the parts in more detail, and those always in relation to the whole.

The whole of history can be looked at from a biblical philosophy because there is an overall purpose in history which unifies all the specific events of history. From a humanistic viewpoint, there is no purpose in history and hence no unifying theme which ties events of history together.

A truly biblical approach to education involves much more than just taking various academic subjects and trying to squeeze the Bible into them. A Principle Approach to education reveals that the source, origin, and purpose of all knowledge revolves around God and His plan for man.

How Do We Implant Principles?

If we desire to have a Principle Approach education, we must restore the "4-R's" to teaching and learning:

1. **First R—RESEARCH:** We must research the subjects and topics of interest from the Bible and other resources to identify basic principles.

2. **Second R—REASON:** As we are researching a subject we must continually ask ourselves what is God's perspective and purpose for the subject and what does this information reveal to me of God and His purpose.

3. **Third R—RELATE:** As we are researching and reasoning we must also relate the truths uncovered to our own lives or to the situation at hand.

4. **Fourth R—RECORD:** The principles and truths uncovered and related must be recorded or written down to accurately and permanently preserve them.[113]

This process of researching, reasoning, relating, and recording ("4-Ring") is the best way to implant truth within our hearts — the best method by which to learn and be educated.

Children are to be brought up in the instruction of the Lord.

In most schools today students are seldom required to research, reason, relate, or record in their pursuit of being educated. This is true in the everyday study of subjects as well as the tests on the subjects. Most tests are fill-in-the-blank, matching, or true-false. (These type of tests were not used in our schools until the 1920's; before that, essays were the primary method of testing.) Students can take and pass these test for years and years without truly learning how to reason and think and be prepared for life after completion of school. Consequently, Americans today do not know how to reason and think.

Practical Ways to Implement the 4-R's in Our Educational Process

1) Essays

Writing essays is an excellent way to implant within the student the ability to research, reason, relate, and record. Writing essays enables students to truly express themselves—to communicate what they really know and believe. As one writes his ideas in complete sentences, he is forced to reason and think for himself. This personal expression brings liberty to the individual. He will not be dependent upon the media, teachers, or anyone else for his ideas, for he will have learned how to search out the truth for himself.

2) Notebooks

The compilation of notebooks by students on various subjects and topics is an excellent means of inculcating truth within them. Instead of being handed a textbook at the beginning of the year and memorizing pages of facts and information, in order to receive good grades, the student develops his own textbook by taking notes from the teacher and doing his own research and writing from various resources (which can include a textbook).

The notebook method not only assures that the student acquires knowledge, but it also builds character within the individual (which is the primary purpose of education). Self-government, industry, orderliness, discipline, and the ability to communicate and reason are only a few of the character qualities produced by the notebook method of education.

America's Founding Fathers were educated by the notebook method. Many of George Washington's early notebooks are still preserved in the Library of Congress. His lifetime habits of orderliness, neatness, and consistency are readily seen within the pages of his manuscripts. His father required this of him from his first years of being educated.

In a letter to his father on June 2, 1777, at age 10, John Quincy Adams wrote:

> P.S. — Sir, If you will be so good as to favor me with a blank-book I will transcribe the most remarkable occurrences I meet with in my reading, which will serve to fix them upon my mind.[114]

This is quite an amazing statement for a ten-year old, not only in that his literary level is beyond most college graduates today, but also in his educational insight. Our future sixth president was revealing the importance of a notebook approach to education.

John Quincy Adams

There are many other practical educational methods that can be used to restore the 4-R's. Some include:

1. Verbal reports and tests
2. Complete sentences answers to classroom and test questions
3. Practical outlets for expression of all that is learned
4. Apprenticeship programs
5. Doing useful projects within the various classes

You can begin to see that a principle approach to education requires much work. While true education will be exciting and challenging, and not boring (one reason for the many discipline problems in schools today is that students are extremely bored), it will also, as Noah Webster felt, require severe effort.

If you have not exercised in many years and then participate in strenuous activity, your body will hurt. Likewise, if you haven't exercised your mind for years and begin to use it strenuously, it will also hurt. But the more you use your mind, the better in shape you will be to think.

Your mind is more than just a computer—garbage in, garbage out. It is like a womb, for you can get more out of your mind than you put in it. This is part of true reasoning.

Three Essentials for Christian Education

To sum up what has been stated previously, these three elements are essential for an education to be truly Christian:

1. **Teacher** — A teacher who is a living witness or textbook (2 Cor. 3:3) is the most important aspect of education. When you teach, you impart more of who you are than what you know. Students will read you. Therefore, to be most effective as a teacher (we are all teachers, for we instruct all we come in contact with), you must master what you teach so that it is a living part of you.
2. **Content** — In the material we teach, the Bible must be our central text (as we have discussed, not in a superficial way). While the Bible doesn't contain all the facts on all the subjects, it does contain all the principles, and reveals God's purpose for each subject.
3. **Method** — In addition to a godly teacher and content, the educational method must also be Christian. This method should build godly character, impart a love of learning, and prepare individuals to take dominion over the earth.

Important Aspects of Education in Early America

Home Education

Almost every child in early America was educated. This was largely due to the colonists' desire for their children to be able to read the Scriptures. Parents saw it as their responsibility, and not that of the government, to provide education. They understood the biblical command of Deuteronomy 6:6-7 — "And these words, which I am commanding you today, shall be on your heart; and you shall teach them diligently to your sons." — and Ephesians 6:4 — "Fathers, do not provoke your children to anger; but bring them up in the discipline and instruction of the Lord."

For our first 200 years, America's education was primarily centered in the home. Home education was sometimes supplemented by tutors or schools, but even here the responsibility and bulk of a child's education rested in the home.

The model of education in Colonial America was very similar to the model used by ancient Israel. With both, education was centered in the home. This was solely the case until around the age of eight or nine. At this age some children had tutors to further instruct them, or an even smaller number attended a school. With the Israelites, the Levites and the Priests were the tutors; with colonial Americans, the ministers were generally the tutors. If there were too many children in the minister's community for him to go into each home to tutor, he would receive a group of children into his home. These were the first "grammar schools" and began in the late 1600s.

Education is the responsibility of the parents.

This would comprise a child's education until around age thirteen when they would enter an apprenticeship program or possibly enroll in a college.

First School – 1636

In 1636 Rev. John Cotton of Boston willed half his property to establish a school to provide education for children who were disadvantaged or had no parents. The Boston Latin School was the first school established in America outside the home.

The Christians of Colonial America not only recognized that God required them to educate their own children, but also saw it as their responsibility to educate the general public. The Great Commission of Matthew 28:19-20, to "disciple the nations," was to be accomplished by "teaching them to observe all that I commanded you." As we have looked at the *Chain of Christianity* we have seen that education always accompanies the spread of the Gospel. The Lollards are an excellent example. Remember that they educated the common people in order that they could read the Scriptures for themselves. Education of the common man also followed the preaching of Luther, Tyndale, Calvin, and other Reformation leaders.

The desire to educate every individual accompanied the Pilgrims, Puritans, Quakers, and most others who came to settle America. One reason the Puritans came to America was to escape the ungodly influence that education in Europe had upon their children. Cotton Mather said, "The schools of learning and religion (in Europe) are so corrupted as most children, even the best and wittiest, and of the fairest hopes, are perverted, corrupted, and utterly overthrown by the multitude of evil examples and licentious behavior in these seminaries."[115]

First Common Schools – 1647

The "Old Deluder Law" of 1647 established the first free common schools in America. Historian John Fiske writes:

> In 1647 the legislature of Massachusetts enacted a law with the following preamble: "It being one chief purpose of that old deluder, Satan, to keep men from the knowledge of the Scriptures," it was therefore ordered that every township containing fifty families or householders should set up a school in which children might be taught to read and write, and that every township containing one hundred families or householders should set up a school in which boys might be fitted for entering Harvard College.[116]

Wages for the teachers were paid by the parents or the general inhabitants. These "public" schools (public in that they were required by law, although this was not enforced) were not under the control of a state government board, such as Horace Mann set up in Massachusetts 200 years later. The teacher's curriculum, methodology, and administration were completely under local control.

Free schools were also established in other towns and cities of New England over the next number of decades, but these always involved a small percentage of those being educated. The home, church, and private sector educated the vast majority of pupils. Samuel Blumenfeld writes that "by 1720 Boston had far more private schools than public ones, and by the close of the American Revolution many towns had no common schools at all."[117] Pennsylvania and New York had public schools like New England early but only in the cities, not in rural areas. There were no public schools in the Southern colonies until 1730 and only five by 1776.

Although public and private schools were established, the home was still where the majority of Colonial Americans were educated, even up through the Revolution. Some of our greatest leaders and thinkers (not just of that era but including recent years) were primarily educated at home. This includes such men as George Washington, Thomas Jefferson, James Madison, Benjamin Franklin, Noah Webster, Abraham Lincoln, Thomas Edison, Alexander G. Bell, and many, many more.

Samuel L. Blumenfeld says: "Of the 117 men who signed the Declaration of Independence, the Articles of Confederation and the Constitution, one out of three had had only a few months of formal schooling, and only one in four had gone to college. They were educated by parents, church schools, tutors, academies, apprenticeship, and by themselves."[118]

The New England Primer – 1690

The Pilgrims' and Puritans' belief that all must seek the word of God in the Bible caused them to teach all boys and girls to read. For this purpose, *hornbooks* were made, usually consisting of the alphabet and a Bible text, mounted on a board and covered with a sheet of transparent animal horn. Later on, children used the New England Primer, first printed in Boston in 1690.

The Primer, known as the "Little Bible of New England," is considered the most influential schoolbook in the history of American education. The three by five inch, 88-page devotional was the primary schoolbook of America during most of the 18th century. Over three million copies were printed with the alphabet and some verse. Simply viewing how the alphabet was taught using biblical verse reveals the obvious Christian nature of this important book.

A page from a New England primer

Noah Webster's Blue-backed Speller – 1783

No single American has contributed as much to American education as has Noah Webster, the Founding Father of American Scholarship and Education. This expert in grammar and philology was known by more Americans than anyone except George Washington during the 19th century primarily due to his famous "blue-backed Speller" and his *American Dictionary of the English Language*. These, along with his self-teaching textbooks, were produced out of his desire to make America intellectually independent of England and Europe.

After America won her independence from Great Britain and established herself as a Constitutional Republic, Webster worked to see that our liberty and growth continued by providing educational tools that imparted the principles that originally gave birth to our nation. He recognized that the success of our system of government depended upon the quality of education. He saw this education as the responsibility of the parents and the individual, and that its basis must be upon Christianity. Webster stated:

> In my view, the Christian religion is the most important and one of the first things in which all children, under a free government, ought to be instructed. ... No truth is more evident to my mind than that the Christian religion must be the basis of any government intended to secure the rights and privileges of a free people.[119]

While Webster is most known for his dictionary, this is only one of his phenomenal accomplishments. In 1783, Webster wrote his famous "Blue-backed Speller," which did more for American education than any other single book, except the Bible. His Speller, which old over 100 million copies in a century, was written to instill into the minds of the youth "the first rudiments of the language and some just ideas of religion, morals, and domestic economy."[120]

Its premise is that "God's word, contained in the Bible, has furnished all necessary rules to direct our conduct." It includes a moral catechism, large portions of the Sermon on the Mount, a paraphrase of the Genesis account of creation and other statements such as: "He who came to save us, will wash us from all sin; I will be glad in his name."[121]

Webster's Dictionary – 1828

Noah Webster worked about twenty-six years on his *An American Dictionary of the English Language.* By the time of its completion and publication in 1828, Webster had mastered 28 languages. This colossal work reflects the diligence, scholarship, and Christian character of this great yet humble man.

His dictionary, which was the first American dictionary and the grandfather of all others, defines words biblically and generously uses scriptural references. The present-day dictionary that bears Webster's name is a good example of how education has been secularized. A comparison reveals that not only have thousands of Scriptures been removed in

Noah Webster

modern editions, but biblical definitions have been replaced by definitions reflecting humanistic thought.

Noah Webster's life can be characterized as prolific. In addition to his dictionary and textbooks — the "Blue-backed Speller," a *Grammar*, and a *Reader* — he wrote much more on many topics including religious, political, educational, musical, economic, commercial, medical, social, and scientific. He was also the first person to publicly promote the idea of a constitutional convention. His efforts brought about copyright legislation at state and national levels. He served in state government, published a magazine and newspaper, founded a college, and translated the first American revised version of the Bible. While doing all these things, his family was not neglected as he lovingly raised seven children.

In light of such an astoundingly productive life, Noah Webster's statement in the preface to his 1828 American Dictionary particularly reveals his Christian character. He said:

> And if the talent which (God) entrusted to my care, has not been put to the most profitable use in His service, I hope it has not been "kept laid up in a napkin," and that any misapplication of it may be graciously forgiven.[122]

It was men with character like Noah Webster who educated the generations of Americans that secured this country as the most free and prosperous nation the world has seen. The continuance of a positive course for our nation will only occur as men like Noah Webster reestablish our educational system upon the Bible, removing any dependence upon man's own intellect. This philosophy of education will produce leaders in all of life who will know how to properly guide our nation to secure life and liberty to all men.

McGuffey and His Readers – 1836

William Holmes McGuffey was another extremely influential educational reformer. This university professor and Presbyterian minister authored the *McGuffey Readers,* which earned him the right to be called "The Schoolmaster of the Nation." His textbooks, which were first published in 1836, were designed to "fit the child's education to the child's world" and to build character as well as vocabulary. One hundred and twenty-two million copies were sold in 75 years. Thousands of copies are still sold each year, and they continue to be used in many schools. His *Readers* promoted a theistic, Calvinist worldview and ideas of salvation, righteousness and piety that were found in the New England Primer the century before. The *Readers* "represent the most significant force in the framing of our national morals and tastes" other than the Bible. In the Preface to the *Fourth Reader*, he wrote:

Rev. William Holmes
McGuffey

> From no source has the author drawn more copiously, in his selections, than from the sacred Scriptures. For this, he certainly apprehends no censure. In a Christian country, that man is to be pitied, who at this day, can honestly object to imbuing the minds of youth with the language and spirit of the Word of God.[123]

John Westerhoff writes:

> From the *First* to the *Fourth Reader*, belief in the God of the Old and New Testaments is assumed. When not mentioned directly, God is implied: "You cannot steal the smallest pin...without being seen by the eye that never sleeps." More typically, however, lessons make direct references to the Almighty: "God makes the little lambs bring forth wool, that we may have clothes to keep us warm. ... All that live get life from God. ... The humble child went to God in penitence and prayer. ... All who take care of you and help you were sent by God. He sent his Son to show you his will, and to die for your sake."
>
> When we investigate the content of McGuffey's *Readers*, three dominant images of God emerge. God is creator, preserver, and governor.[124]

America's Christian Universities

As with the private and public schools, the universities of America were established by the Christian community. One hundred and six of the first one hundred and eight colleges in America were founded on the Christian faith. By the time of the Civil War non-religious universities could be counted on one hand. College presidents were almost always clergymen until around 1900. A study entitled *An Appraisal of Church and Four-year Colleges* (1955) stated that "nearly all of those institutions which have exerted a decided influence, even in our literary and political history, were established by evangelical Christians."[125]

The first universities, which were really seminaries (not like most modern seminaries though), were started for the central purpose of perpetuating a learned clergy. Harvard, established in 1636, was our first university.

Harvard — 1636

The Rev. John Harvard gave half of his property and his entire library to start this Congregational institution. "For Christ and the Church" was its official motto, which was written on its original seal. Ten of its twelve presidents up to the Revolution were clergymen. The governing rules required both the president and professors to "open and explain the Scriptures to his pupils with integrity and faithfulness, according to the best light God shall give him...so that, through the blessing of God it may be conducive to their establishment in the principles of the Christian Protestant religion."[126]

Seal of Harvard College

Students at Harvard College were "to consider well, the maine end of (their) life and studies is, to know...Jesus Christ."

The following report on Harvard College, from "New England's First Fruits" published in 1643, reveals the purpose for its establishment:

After God had carried us safe to New England, and wee had builded our houses, provided necessaries for our livelihood, rear'd convenient places for Gods worship, and settled the Civil Government: One of the next things we longed for, and looked after was to advance Learning, and perpetuate it to Posterity, dreading to leave an illiterate Ministry to the Churches, when our present Ministers shall lie in the Dust.[127]

Following are a few of the "rules and precepts" that were "observed in the College:"

> Let every Student be plainly instructed, and earnestly pressed to consider well, the maine end of his life and studies is, to know God and Jesus Christ which is eternall life, (John 17:3), and therefore to lay Christ in the bottome, as the only foundation of all sound knowledge and Learning.
>
> And seeing the Lord only giveth wisedome, Let every one seriously set himselfe by prayer in secret to seeke it of him (Prov. 2:3).[128]

Harvard was not unique in its beginning. The following brief look at other universities reveals the same Christian foundation.

College of William and Mary — 1693

The College of William and Mary was started mainly due to the efforts of Rev. James Blair in order, according to its charter, "that the Church of Virginia may be furnished with a seminary of ministers of the Gospel, and that the youth may be piously educated in good letters and manners, and that the Christian religion may be propagated among the Western Indians to the glory of Almighty God."[129] All presidents and professors were originally clergymen who taught the students and the Episcopal catechism.

Yale University — 1701

Rev. John Davenport began promoting the idea in 1652, and finally a plan and resources were provided by a synod of Congregational churches led by Rev. Pierport, Rev. Andrew, and Rev. Russell which led to an official Charter in 1701: "for the liberal and religious education of suitable youth…to propagate in this wilderness, the blessed reformed Protestant religion.[130]

Yale was started "to propagate…the blessed reformed Protestant religion."

Every president was a clergyman until 1898 and included such notables as Elisha Williams, Ezra Styles, and Timothy Dwight. *Yale's Rules* were modeled after Harvard's: "Seeing God is the giver of all wisdom, every scholar, besides private or secret prayer, where all we are bound to ask wisdom, shall be present morning and evening at public prayer in the hall at the accustomed hour."[131]

Princeton University — 1746

Princeton, founded by Presbyterians who called it the "Log College," was chartered in 1746. Rev. Jonathan Dickinson became its first president, declaring: "Cursed be all that learning that is contrary to the cross of Christ."[132] Every president was a clergyman until 1902 and included well-known men such as Jonathan Edwards, Samuel Davies, and John Witherspoon. The official motto is: "Under God's Power She Flourishes."

Princeton

Rutgers University — 1766

Through the efforts of Rev. Theodore Frelinghuysen, the Dutch Reformed Church established "Queen's College," "for the education of youth in the learned languages, liberal and useful arts and sciences, and especially in divinity, preparing them for the ministry and other good offices." The official motto was, "Son of Righteousness, Shine upon the West also."[133]

The Need for Christianity in Our Public Schools

A free nation must rest upon a Christian philosophy of education. This truth was recognized by the founders of our nation. Congress declared in the *Northwest Ordinance* of 1787 that, "Religion, morality, and knowledge, being necessary to good government and the happiness of mankind, schools and the means of education shall forever be encouraged."[134]

Congress recognized that the basis of happiness for mankind and good government was "religion, morality, and knowledge" and that these were to be taught in our schools. These schools were predominantly private and home-based, for this is the most effective way to educate our youth. Privatizing education would be a great step forward in correcting the problems of modern education. With God and morality being ignored in most public schools today, and true knowledge often "overlooked," it's no wonder Americans are losing their freedoms, government is becoming more corrupt, and the general state of happiness is declining.

Historian B.F. Morris writes:

> Education, next to the Christian religion, is an indispensable element of republican institutions, the basis upon which all free governments must rest. The state must rest upon the basis of religion, and it must preserve this basis, or itself must fall. But the support which religion gives to the state will obviously cease the moment religion loses its hold upon the popular mind. The very fact that the state must have religion as a support for its own authority demands that some means for teaching religion be employed. Better for it to give up all other instruction than that religion should be disregarded in its schools.[135]

Every civil government is based upon some religion or philosophy of life. Education in a nation will propagate the religion of that nation. In America the foundational religion was Christianity, and it was sown in the hearts of Americans through the home, church, and private and public schools for centuries. Our liberty, growth, and prosperity were the result of a biblical philosophy of life. Our continued freedom and success are dependent upon our educating the youth of America in the principles of the Christian religion.

Noah Webster understood this as he wrote:

> The foundation of all free government and of all social order must be laid in families and in the discipline of youth. ... The Education of youth, an employment of more consequence than making laws and preaching the gospel because it lays the foundation on which both law and gospel rest for success.[136]

How we educate our youth has immeasurable consequences for the future of our nation. This can be for great good or great evil. Samuel Adams said:

> Let divines and philosophers, statesmen and patriots, unite their endeavors to renovate the age, by impressing the minds of men with the importance of educating their little boys and girls, of inculcating in the minds of youth the fear and love of the Deity and universal philanthropy, and, in subordination to these

Samuel Adams

great principles, the love of their country; of instructing them in the art of self-government, without which they never can act a wise part in the government of societies, great or small; in short, of leading them in the study and practice of the exalted virtues of the Christian system.[137]

In *Provincial Congress*,

Cambridge, December 6, 1774.

RESOLVED, That the following Addrefs be prefented to the feveral Minifters of the Gofpel in this Province.

REVEREND SIR,

WHEN we contemplate the Friendfhip and Affift-ance, our Anceftors the firft Settlers of Province (while over-whelmed with Diftrei received from the pious Paftors of the Churches of CHRIST, who, to enjoy the Rights of Confcience, fled with them into this Land, then a favage Wildernefs, we find ourfelves fill'd with the moft grateful Senfa-tions.---And we cannot but acknowledge theGoodnefs of Heaven, in conftantly fupplying us with Preachers of the Gofpel, whofe Concern has been the temporal and fpiritual Happinefs of this People.

In a Day like this, when all the Friends of civil and religious Liberty are exerting themfelves to deli-ver this Country from its prefent Calamities, we can-not but place great Hopes in an Order of Men, who have ever diftinguifhed themfelves in their Country's Caufe ; and do therefore recommend to the Minifters of the Gofpel, in the feveral Towns and other Pla-ces in this Colony, that they affift us, in avoiding that dreadful Slavery with which we are now threatened, by advifing the People of their feveralCongregations, as they wifh their Profperity, to abide by and ftrictly adhere to the *Refolutions* of the *Continental Congrefs*, as the moft peaceable and probable Method of pre-venting Confufion and Bloodfhed, and of reftoring that Harmony between Great-Britain and thefe Colo-nies, on which we wifh might be eftablifhed not only the Rights and Liberties of America, but the Opulence and lafting Happinefs of the whole Britifh Empire.

Sign'd by Order of the Provincial Congrefs,

JOHN HANCOCK, Prefident.

A true Extract from the Minutes.

BENJAMIN LINCOLN, Secretary.

Proclamation by the government of Massachusetts honoring pastors for their important role in American history (see page 164).

Chapter 9

The Role of the Church and Clergy in the Cultivation of Liberty

The description of the early American Republic by historian David Gregg nicely summarizes the role of the church in a Christian nation: "The people made the laws, and the churches made the people."[138] The role of the church is not to directly hold power as an ecclesiastical body that makes civil law. The influence of the church on government is not by positional power, but by the influential power of its teachings.

This role was described by a French political philosopher, Alexis de Tocqueville, who came to the United States of America in the 1830s in search of her greatness. After a thorough examination he communicated in his book, *Democracy in America:*

> On my arrival in the United States the religious aspect of the country was the first thing that struck my attention; and the longer I stayed there, the more I perceived the great political consequences resulting from this new state of things.[139]

Elsewhere in his writings, de Tocqueville states:

> I sought for the greatness and genius of America in her commodious harbors and her ample rivers, and it was not there; in her fertile fields and boundless prairies, and it was not there; in her rich mines and her vast world commerce, and it was not there. Not until I went to the churches of America and heard her pulpits aflame with righteousness did I understand

the secret of her genius and power. America is great because she is good and if America ever ceases to be good, America will cease to be great.[140]

In other words, de Tocqueville said that our civil government will not work without the people being virtuous, which is the product of the religious influence of the church.

Ministers were involved in every aspect of the public affairs of America. They colonized and formed many of our states, they wrote our laws and constitutions, they served as judges and lawyers, they established schools and universities, and they participated directly in civil government.

The colonists considered that the greatest and most dreaded curse was for them to someday have impotent

According to John Adams, ministers were important Founding Fathers of America.

preachers who through ignorance of God's Word knew not how to make it relevant to any situation. In their thinking, this was the primary cause of the religious and civil tyranny of the Dark Ages.

In an election sermon of 1742, preaching before the governor of Massachusetts, Nathanial Appleton stated:

> As for you my Fathers and Brethren in the Ministry...surely it concerns us to be ready Scribes, well instructed in the Law of our God, and in the Gospel of his Son. ... Surely then, it is absolutely necessary for Ministers to be well acquainted with the holy Scriptures. Not only to have some certain Portions of Scripture by rote, to use upon all Occasions, but to understand the Meaning of Scripture, and to be able to give the Meaning of it to others—And it was a Concern for a learned as well as godly Ministry, that stirred up such an early Care in our Fathers, to encourage Schools, and to erect a College, which has now for a Century of Years, conferred academical Honour upon the learned Youth, that have been trained up in it. God forbid, that an ignorant, and unlearned Ministry should ever rise up in this Land, especially a Ministry that should be

ignorant of the Holy Scriptures; or that should think or speak disparagingly of them, or that should insinuate the Uselessness of them to unconverted Men; ... And no less dangerous is it to insinuate, as if the Bible was not very necessary for the Saints, by Reason of their having the Spirit to inlighten and direct them. ... Accordingly we who are the Ministers of Christ, and have the glorious Gospel committed to our Trust, should be upon the Watch-Tower, to spy out every Thing of such a dangerous Tendency, that we may give seasonable Warnings thereof.[141]

Pastors in Public Affairs in the 1600s

We have already looked at significant clergymen who were links on the Chain of Liberty in America's beginnings. Some of those pastors who participated directly in politics include:

- 1619—Clergy serving in Virginia's First General Assembly (Rev. William Wickham).
- 1620—John Robinson shaping the Mayflower Compact.
- 1636—John Cotton starting the first public school.
- 1636—Roger Williams and John Clarke founding the state of Rhode Island.
- 1636—John Harvard founding the first university.
- 1639—Thomas Hooker and John Davenport founding the state of Connecticut and writing the first Constitution.

Thomas Hooker

- 1641—Nathaniel Ward writing the Massachusetts Body of Liberties.
- 1681—William Penn founding Pennsylvania and writing its Frame of Government.

And there were many more ministers who influenced the nation in the 17th century.

Significant Preachers Who Cultivated Liberty in the 1700s

John Wise, Father of American Independence

In 1717 John Wise, who has been called a "Father of American Independence," wrote *The Law of Nature in Government,* which contained such important ideas that it was reprinted and studied by our Founders in 1772 and cited as legal authority by the Massachusetts Supreme Court. Sections of this work appear word for word in the Declaration of Independence.

Elisha Williams, Chaplain and Awakening Leader — 1744

Elisha Williams was a significant force during the First Great Awakening. He served as a schoolteacher, a state representative, President of Yale University, a judge, and an ambassador. He was a disciple of George Whitefield's and became chaplain of the New England forces in the French and Indian War. Whitefield blessed the troops as they marched off to battle, and Williams even became a colonel who led the troops a year later in 1746. Elisha Williams wrote a 66-page pamphlet in 1744 which should be studied by every American Christian. Called *The Essential Rights and Liberties of Protestants,* it was one of the clearest and fullest explanations of the principles of equality, liberty, and property. These ideas were influential in preparing people for the Revolution a few decades later.[142]

Elisha Williams

Samuel Davies, Ambassador from the South — 1755

Rev. Samuel Davies was a bold ambassador for Christ. In his desire to see the Kingdom of God come "on earth as it is in heaven" he also became a lawyer, an ambassador to England, and President of Princeton. E.L. Magoon writes that "he had made himself a thorough master of English law, civil and ecclesiastical, and always chose to meet every persecuting indictment in the highest courts with his own plea. ... He went to

Samuel Davies

England and obtained the explicit sanction of the highest authority with respect to the extension of the Toleration Law to Virginia. It was during this mission that…George II and many of his court were in the congregation of this" preacher. When his majesty spoke several times to those around him "Davies paused a moment, and then looking sternly at the king, exclaimed, 'When the lion roars, the beasts of the forest all tremble; and when King Jesus speaks, the princes of the earth should keep silence.'"[143] The boldness, eloquence and ideas of Davies had a great impact upon the life of his neighbor in Virginia, Patrick Henry.

Jonathan Mayhew, "Father of Civil Liberty" — 1766

Rev. Jonathan Mayhew has been called the Father of Civil Liberty in America for several reasons. He was the first clergyman to begin preaching resistance to England's tyranny in 1750. In his *Discourse Concerning Unlimited Submission* he said, "Although there be a sense…in which Christ's kingdom is not of this world, his inspired apostles have, nevertheless, laid down some general principles concerning the office of civil rulers, and the duty of subjects. …   It is the duty of all Christian people to inform themselves what it is which their religion teaches concerning that subjection which they owe to the higher powers."[144] After the passage of the Stamp Act, Mayhew became even more influential. George Bancroft wrote:

Rev. Jonathan Mayhew

Whoever repeats the story of the Revolution will rehearse the fame of Mayhew. He spent whole nights in prayer for the dangers of this country. Light dawned on his mind on a Sabbath morning of July, 1766, and he wrote to Otis saying, "You have heard of the communion [i.e. unity] of the churches; while I was thinking of this … [the] importance of the communion of the colonies appeared to me in a striking light. Would it not be decorous in our Assembly to send circulars to all the rest [of the colonies], expressing a desire to cement a union among ourselves? … It may be the only means of perpetuating our liberties." This suggestion of a "more perfect union" for the common defence, originating with Mayhew, was the first public expression of that future Union which has been the glory of the American republic; and it came from a clergyman, on a Sabbath morning, under the inspiration of Heaven."[145]

John Witherspoon, Signer of the Declaration of Independence — 1776

Rev. John Witherspoon typified the Colonial Clergy — he literally discipled the nation. Witherspoon was a minister, President of Princeton College, and a member of the Continental Congress, where he signed the Declaration of Independence and served on over 100 committees during our struggle for independence. He is said to have had more influence on the monetary policies found in the Constitution than any other man.

While President of Princeton he trained not only ministers but leaders in all areas of life. One man came to study theology, but biblical principles of law and government were so impressed upon him that he went on to become the chief architect of the Constitution and the fourth President of the United States — James Madison. Witherspoon's training enabled him to accomplish this.

Witherspoon also trained:

- 1 vice president
- 3 Supreme Court justices
- 10 Cabinet members
- 12 governors
- 60 Congressmen (21 Senators and 39 Congressmen)
- Plus, many members of the Constitutional Convention and many state congressmen[146]

John Witherspoon

The following is an excerpt from a sermon entitled "The Dominion of Providence Over the Affairs of Men," that Witherspoon preached on May 17, 1776, in observance of a Day of Fasting and Prayer called for by Congress:

> Upon the whole, I beseech you to make a wise improvement of the present threatening aspect of public affairs and to remember that your duty to God, to your country, to your families, and to yourselves is the same. True religion is nothing else but an inward temper and outward conduct suited to your state and circumstance in Providence at any time. And as peace with God and conformity to Him, adds to the sweetness of created comforts while we possess them, so in times of difficulty and trial,

it is in the man of piety and inward principle that we may expect to find the uncorrupted patriot, the useful citizen, and the invincible soldier,— God grant that in America true religion and civil liberty may be inseparable, and the unjust attempts to destroy the one, may in the issue tend to the support and establishment of both.[147]

Abraham Baldwin and Hugh Williamson, Delegates at the Constitutional Convention

Rev. Abraham Baldwin was a lawyer, a chaplain in the war, a member of the Georgia legislature, and a member of the Continental Congress before becoming Georgia's delegate to the Constitutional Convention. Afterwards, he was elected to the U.S. House of Representatives and the U.S. Senate. He also founded the University of Georgia.

North Carolina signatory of the United States Constitution Hugh Williamson was a licensed preacher of the Presbyterian Church who, in addition to conducting church services early in his career, also served as an educator, physician, legislator, merchant, and scientist.

Abraham Baldwin

Other Significant Clergy/Statesmen

Isaac Backus and John Leland were lobbyists for religious freedom in 1786. Manassas Cutler was the author of the Northwest Ordinance written in 1787. Approximately 50 clergy were part of the state ratifying conventions in 1788. William Provost was selected as the first chaplain to the United States Congress in 1789. Frederick A. C. Muhlenberg was the first Speaker of the United States House of Representatives, elected to that position by his colleagues in 1789.

Frederick A. C. Muhlenberg, first Speaker of the House of Representatives. His painting hangs in the U.S. Capitol just outside the House Chamber.

Clergy in Public Affairs in the 19th and 20th Centuries

The number of ministers holding public office and influencing public affairs in the 18th century is voluminous. (See Alice Baldwin's book, *The New England Clergy and the American Revolution*, for a partial list.) But this did not cease in the last 200 years. Clergy such as Charles Finney led the fight against slavery. Lyman Beecher, D.L. Moody, and Billy Sunday championed the movements for temperance and women's rights. Other ministers helped to build hospitals and establish charitable organizations such as the Salvation Army and the Red Cross. U.S. President James Garfield was a lay preacher before seeking public office. In recent times we have seen the political leadership of Martin Luther King, Jr. against discrimination and Jerry Falwell against abortion and pornography. In 1988, Pat Robertson and Jesse Jackson, although opposites in political philosophy, were both clergymen who ran for President of the United States.

Biblical Precedents

Were the American clergy following the biblical example? Indeed, they were. Clergy in the Old Testament who became politically active included Samuel, Jeremiah, Ezekiel, Zechariah, and Ezra. They were clergymen who became statesmen and social reformers, or in biblical terms, they were prophets. Many of God's people in the Bible not only influenced politics (like the prophets, Esther, and Mordecai), but actually served in public office (such as Joseph, Daniel, Moses, Samuel, and Erastus).

How the Clergy Discipled the Nation in Principles of Liberty

While schools were established to train new generations in a biblical worldview, the clergy continually clarified and applied that worldview to the present-day, relevant issues that the colonists faced. For 150 years leading up to the Revolution, the colonial pastors used every opportunity possible to educate the people in the principles of liberty. Various means included:

1. The Weekday Lecture — The most famous weekday class was held on Thursday in Boston and was copied by pastors in many colonies. Historian Jonathan Trumbull wrote that the clergy "were the principal instructors of those who received an education for public life. For many years they were consulted by the legislature in all affairs of importance, civil or religious. They were appointed on committees with the Governor and magistrates to assist them in the most delicate concerns of the Commonwealth. ... So influential and authoritative were their teachings, that it is said of one of the Puritan ministers, John Cotton, 'That what he preached on the Lord's day was followed by the synod, and that what he preached in the Thursday Lecture was followed by the General Court.'"[148]

John Cotton

2. The Election Sermon — An annual event begun in 1633 in Massachusetts, Election Sermons were the colonists' political textbooks. John Wingate Thornton writes of these sermons and the clergy's influence in early America:

> The clergy were generally consulted by the civil authorities; and not infrequently the suggestions from the pulpit, on election days and other special occasions, were enacted into laws. The statutebook, the reflex of the age, shows this influence. The State was developed out of the Church.
>
> The sermon is styled the Election Sermon, and is printed. Every representative has a copy for himself, and generally one or more for the minister or ministers of his town. As the patriots have prevailed, the preachers of each sermon have been the zealous friends of liberty; and the passages most adapted to promote the spread and love of it have been selected and circulated far and wide by means of newspapers, and read with avidity and a degree of veneration on account of the preacher and his election to the service of the day.[149]

These election sermons were preached in America for about 250 years (into the 1870s).

3. The Artillery Sermon — These were periodic addresses given to the military on such topics as "a defensive war in a just cause is sinless" and the sin of cowardice.

4, Special Fast, Thanksgiving, and Anniversary Sermons — These sermons were preached in observance of victories, calamities, and special events.

A study published in the American Political Science Review (1984) showed that 10% of all political writings in the Founding Era were sermons and asserted therefore that colonial clergymen must be considered part of our "Founding Fathers" in America.[150]

During his lifetime, the average adult in colonial America listened to about 15,000 hours of biblical exposition by the clergy. Ministers' influence on public opinion was equivalent to that of the modern media today. For us to ever see a restoration of the American Christian Republic, political educational efforts such as those in early America must once again become a regular part of the clergy's weekly responsibilities in their churches.

The Pulpits Produced the American Revolution

An artillery sermon preached to General Washington and his troops on the eve of the Battle of Brandywine reveals the force that motivated the colonists. Rev. Jacob Troute's sermon was entitled "They that Take the Sword Shall Perish by the Sword."

> Soldiers, and Countrymen: — We have met this evening perhaps for the last time. We have shared the toils of the march, the peril of the fight, and the dismay of the retreat, alike. We have endured the cold and hunger, the contumely of the internal foe, and the scourge of the foreign oppressor. We have sat night after night by the campfire. We have together heard the roll of the reveille which calls us to duty, or the beat of the tattoo which gave the signal for the hardy sleep of the soldier, with the earth for his bed and the knapsack for his pillow.
>
> And now, soldiers and brethren, we have met in this peaceful valley, on the eve of battle, in the sunlight that tomorrow morn will glimmer on the scenes of blood. We have met amid the whitening tents of our encampments; in the time of terror and gloom we have gathered together. God grant that it may not be for the last time.
>
> It is a solemn moment! Brethren, does not the solemn voice of nature seem to echo the sympathies of the hour? The flag of our country droops heavily from yonder staff. The breeze has died away along the green plaid of Chadd's Ford; the plain that spreads before us glitters in the sunlight; the heights of Brandywine arise gloomy and grand beyond the waters of yonder stream; all nature holds a pause of solemn silence on the eve of the uproar and bloody strife of tomorrow.
>
> "They that take the sword shall perish by the sword."
>
> And have they not taken the sword?
>
> Let the desolate plain, the blood-sodden valley, the burned farmhouses, blackening in the sun, the sacked village and the ravaged town, answer. Let the withered bones of the butchered farmer, strewed along the fields of his homestead, answer. Let the starving mother, with

her babe clinging to the withered breast that can afford no sustenance, let her answer—with the death-rattle mingling with the murmuring tones that marked the last moment of her life; let the mother and the babe answer.

It was but a day past, and our land slept in the quiet of peace. War was not here. Fraud and woe and want dwelt not among us. From the eternal solitude of the green woods arose the blue smoke of the settler's cabin, and golden fields of corn looked from amid the waste of the wilderness, and the glad music of human voices awoke the silence of the forest.

Chaplain James Caldwell distributing Watts Hymnals to Revolutionary soldiers during the heat of battle. J.T. Headley explains how Caldwell ran to a nearby church and filled his arms with hymn books. "Hastening back with them into the battle, he scattered them about in every direction, saying as he pitched one here and another there, 'Now put Watts into them, boys.' With a laugh and a cheer they pulled out the leaves, and ramming home the charge did give the British Watts with a will."

Now, God of mercy, behold the change. Under the shadow of a pretext, under the sanctity of the name of God, invoking the Redeemer to their aid, do these foreign hirelings slay our people. They throng our towns, they darken our plains, and now they encompass our posts on the lonely plain of Chadd's Ford.

"They that take the sword shall perish by the sword."

Brethren, think me not unworthy of belief when I tell you the doom of the British is sealed. Think me not vain when I tell you that, beyond the cloud that now enshrouds us, I see gathering thick and fast the darker cloud and thicker storm of Divine retribution.

They may conquer tomorrow. Might and wrong may prevail, and we may be driven from the field, but the hour of God's vengeance will come!

Ay, if in the vast solitudes of eternal space there throbs the being of an awful God, quick to avenge and sure to punish guilt, then the man George Brunswick, called king, will feel in his brain and heart the vengeance of the eternal Jehovah. A blight will light upon his life—a withered and an accursed intellect; a blight will be upon his children and on his people. Great God, how dread the punishment! A crowded populace, peopling the dense towns where the men of money thrive, where the laborer starves; want striding among the people in all forms of terror; an ignorant and God-defying priesthood chuckling over the miseries of millions; a proud and merciless nobility adding wrong to wrong, and heaping insult upon robbery and fraud; royalty corrupt to the very heart, and aristocracy rotten to the core; crime and want linked hand in hand, and tempting the men to deeds of woe and death:—these are a part of the doom and retribution that shall come upon the English throne and English people.

Soldiers, I look around upon your familiar faces with strange interest! Tomorrow morning we go forth to the battle—for need I tell you that your unworthy minister will march with you, invoking the blessing of God's aid in the fight? We will march forth to the battle. Need I exhort you to fight the good fight—to fight for your homesteads, for your wives and your children?

My friends, I urge you to fight, by the galling memories of British wrong. Walton, I might tell you of your father, butchered in the silence of the night in the plains of Trenton. I might picture his gray hairs dabbled in blood. I might ring his death-shrieks in your ears. Shaefmyer, I might tell you of a butchered mother and sister outraged, the lonely farmhouse, the night assault, the roof in flames, the shouts of the troops as they dispatched their victims, the cries for mercy, and the pleadings of innocence for pity. I might paint this all again, in the vivid colors of the terrible reality, if I thought courage needed such wild excitement.

But I know you are strong in the might of the Lord. You will march forth to battle tomorrow with light hearts and determined spirits, though the solemn duty—the duty of avenging the dead—may rest heavy on your souls.

And in the hour of battle, when all around is darkness, lit by the lurid cannon-glare and the piercing musket-flash, when the wounded strew the ground and the dead litter your path, then remember, soldiers, that God is with you. The eternal God fights for you; He rides on the battle-cloud. He sweeps onward with the march of a hurricane charge. God, the awful and infinite, fights for you, and you will triumph.

"They that take the sword shall perish by the sword."

You have taken the sword, but not in the spirit of wrong or revenge. You have taken the sword for your homes, for your wives and your little ones. You have taken the sword for truth, justice and right, and to you the promise is, be of good cheer, for your foes have taken the sword in defiance of all that men hold dear, in blasphemy of God; they shall perish by the sword.

And now, brethren and soldiers, I bid you all farewell. Many of us will fall in the battle of tomorrow, and in the memory of all will ever rest and linger the quiet sense of this autumnal eve.

Solemn twilight advances over the valley. The woods on the opposite height fling their long shadows over the green of the meadow. Around us are the tents of the Continental host, the suppressed bustle of the camp, the hurried tramp of the soldiers to and fro, and among the tents the stillness and awe that mark the eve of battle.

When we meet again, may the shadows of twilight be flung over the peaceful land. God in heaven grant it! Let us pray.[151]

Without a doubt, the moral force and unified biblical worldview exhibited in the American Christian Revolution was a product of the pastoral cultivation of liberty for 150 years. Historian Alice Baldwin said, "The Constitutional Convention and the written Constitution were the children of the pulpit."[152]

Thomas Jefferson's Seal
"Rebellion to Tyrants is Obedience to God"

Chapter 10

The American Christian Revolution

The Origins of the American Christian Revolution

Without the Great Awakening (1740-1760) there would have been no American Revolution (1760-1790). The ideas, the motivation, the biblical worldview, and the great virtuous statesmanship seen in the Founder's era were all birthed in this great revival led by Jonathan Edwards and George Whitefield.

George Washington, Samuel Adams, Thomas Jefferson and others who guided us throughout independence and beginnings as a nation were young men during this time period. The godly environment of the Awakening deeply affected and helped prepare them for their destiny.

During this Great Awakening the Spirit of God swept mightily throughout the colonies. The number of people in the churches more than doubled. Whole towns were converted to Christ. Benjamin Franklin wrote in his *Autobiography* that "it seem'd as if all the world were growing religious, so one could not walk thro' the town in an

George Whitefield

evening without hearing psalms sung in different families of every street."[153]

Many new revivalist universities were established to cultivate and propagate seeds of liberty and raise up a learned clergy. The clergy trained at these universities helped to spread biblical principles to all the colonies. They continued to cultivate the Christian ideas of liberty up to the Revolution.

The Harvest of Christian Ideas of Liberty – 1772

Although Rev. Jonathan Mayhew was the first to propose the idea of using circular letters to unite the colonies, he died shortly thereafter. It was brought to pass by the man who became known as the "Father of the Revolution"— Samuel Adams. George Bancroft wrote that Adams

> was a member of the church; and the austere purity of his life witnessed the sincerity of his profession. Evening and morning his house was a house of prayer; and no one more revered the Christian Sabbath. … The walls of his modest mansion never witnessed anything inconsistent with the discipline of the man whose desire for his birthplace was that "Boston might became a Christian Sparta."[154]

Samuel Adams, the Father of
the American Revolution

The title, the "Father of the American Revolution," was applied to Samuel Adams due to his unequaled efforts promoting the Revolution. He understood the conflict between the colonies and England was more than an economic or political struggle. He recognized, as only a Christian truly could, that the British government had violated the colonists' rights as men, Christians, and subjects.

Not only did Samuel Adams understand the principles upon which the American Revolution was based, but he also saw that in order for independence to be realized these ideas would have to be dispersed throughout the colonies. He worked for twenty years promoting the cause of liberty.

In 1772 Samuel Adams proposed "Committees of Correspondence" to be established throughout the colonies because he desired all people to be educated in order that they could reason out their rights and political convictions based upon biblical principles. His desire was for the colonies to be united "not by external bonds, but by the vital force of distinctive ideas and principles."[155] This unity of ideas and principles helped to promote union among the colonists. The common ideas sown within the colonists by Samuel Adams and many other Christian thinking men of that and earlier generations resulted in the external union of the colonies into the United States of America.

The response of other colonies to Adams' Committees of Correspondence was not immediate because to educate in principles, as Adams desired, is much more difficult and requires more time than just teaching issues. Nevertheless, Samuel Adams did not lose heart for he had faith in the cause of independence. One incident revealing his faith was seen when Adams received a letter from a Plymouth patriot concerning establishing a committee in that area of Massachusetts. In the letter, the patriot expressed fear that most people would not join in the effort for "they are dead," he wrote, "and the dead can't be raised

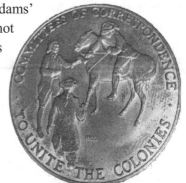

In 1772 Samuel Adams proposed Committees of Correspondence to educate and unite the colonies.

without a miracle." Adams replied that there was no place for despair within their lives and that "all are not dead; and where there is a spark of patriotic fire, we will rekindle it."[156]

The first letter circulated among the colonists in 1772 was called the *Rights of the Colonists* and was written by Sam Adams. It was the "most systematic presentation of the American cause and the first public denial of the right of the British Parliament to tax the Colonists." He wrote: "The supreme power cannot justly take from any man any part of his property, without his consent in the person or by his representative." He said that "the natural rights of the Colonists are these: First, a right to life; Secondly, to liberty; Thirdly, to property; together with the right to support and defend them in the best manner they can. ... The rights of the Colonists as Christians," he said, "may be best understood by reading and carefully studying the institutes of the great Law Giver and Head of the Christian Church, which are to be found clearly written and promulgated in the New Testament." Samuel Adams, understood that the principles necessary for changing a society are discovered through "the study and practice of the exalted virtues of the Christian system."[157]

American Christian Ideas Lead to American Christian Unity

For many decades England had embraced a philosophy of government that gave the Colonies representation in matters relating to themselves. This begin to change with the Stamp Act in 1765. To raise revenue for the war debt, accrued through defending the Colonies from the French and Indians, England's Parliament imposed a tax upon the colonists without their having any say in the matter. The colonists recognized that it was their responsibility to pay for the cost of their defense, but they opposed the principle of the Parliament being able to tax them without their consent, or the consent of their representatives. Due to their protest, the Stamp Act was repealed, but England's change in governmental policy continued with the Townsend Act in 1767 and then the Tea Act in 1773. The colonists would no longer tolerate this arbitrary power of the King or Parliament to take their property without their consent. They claimed it violated the English Constitution guaranteeing the fundamental right of property. It was not that they were poor and would not pay, but rather they were free and would not submit to tyranny.

The Boston Tea Party – December 1773

After Parliament imposed a tax upon all British tea sold in the colonies, the colonists gathered together and determined that they would boycott the tea and not purchase it. As ships full of tea were on their way to America, patriots in Philadelphia, Boston, New York, and Charleston, the major destination ports for the ships, held town meetings. When the ships arrived in Boston, the patriots put a guard at the docks to prevent the tea from being unloaded. Almost 7,000 people gathered at the Old South Meeting House to hear from Mr. Rotch, the owner of the ships. He explained that if he attempted to sail from Boston without unloading the tea, his life and business would be in danger. The colonists decided, therefore, that in order to protect Mr. Rotch, they must accept the tea, but they wouldn't have to drink it! By accepting the shipment, they were agreeing to pay

Old South Meeting House

for it, but they would make a radical sacrifice in order to protest this injustice before the eyes of the world. Thus ensued the "Boston Tea Party." To make it even more newsworthy, as well as to protect individuals involved, the men disguised themselves as Indians.

Historian Richard Frothingham records the incident:

> The party in disguise…whooping like Indians, went on board the vessels, and, warning their officers and those of the customhouse to keep out of the way, unlaid the hatches, hoisted the chests of tea on deck, cut them open, and hove the tea overboard. They proved quiet and systematic workers. No one interfered with them. No other property was injured; no person was harmed; no tea was allowed to be carried away; and the silence of the crowd on shore was such that the breaking of the chests was distinctly heard by them. "The whole," [Governor] Hutchinson wrote, "was done with very little tumult."[158]

Soon after this, ships arrived at Philadelphia, New York and Charleston and were convinced to return to England. This confrontation brought about much unity throughout the colonies and brought the first proposal for a Continental Congress.

The Boston Tea Party: a protest of taxation without representation.

Boston Port Bill – June 1774

England, however, embarrassed and infuriated, decided to retaliate. They passed the Boston Port Bill which was intended to shut down all commerce on June 1st and starve the townspeople into submission. Committees of Correspondence spread the news by letter through all the colonies. The colonies began to respond. Massachusetts, Connecticut and Virginia called for days of fasting and prayer. Thomas Jefferson penned the resolve in Virginia "to invoke the divine interposition to give to the American people one heart and one mind to oppose by all just means every injury to American rights."[159] Frothingham writes:

On the day [June 1] the Port Act went into effect, a cordon of British men-of-war was moored around the town of Boston. Not keel nor a raft was permitted to approach the wharves. The wheels of commerce were stopped. The poor were deprived of employment. The rich were cut off from their usual resources. The town entered upon its period of suffering.

Virginia Capitol, the meeting place of the House of Burgesses, the elected legislature.

The day was widely observed as a day of fasting and prayer. The manifestations of sympathy were general. Business was suspended. Bells were muffled, and tolled from morning to night; flags were kept at half-mast; streets were dressed in mourning; public buildings and shops were draped in black; large congregations filled the churches.

In Virginia the members of the House of Burgesses assembled at their place of meeting; went in procession, with the speaker at their head, to the church and listened to a discourse. "Never," a lady wrote, "since my residence in Virginia have I seen so large a congregation as was this day assembled to hear divine service." The preacher selected for his text the words: "be strong and of good courage, fear not, nor be afraid of them; for the Lord thy God, He it is that doth go with thee. He will not fail thee nor forsake thee." "The people," Jefferson says, "met generally, with anxiety and alarm in their countenances; and the effect of the day, through the whole colony, was like a shock of electricity, arousing every man and placing him erect and solidly on his centre." These words describe the effect of the Port Act throughout the thirteen colonies.[160]

The colonies responded with material support as well, not by governmental decree but, more significantly, by individual action. A grassroots movement of zealous workers went door to door to gather patriotic offerings. These gifts were sent to Boston accompanied with letters containing phrases such as: "Stand firm, and let your intrepid courage show to the world that you are Christians."[161] Out of the diversity of the colonies, a deep Christian unity was being revealed on a national level for the first time. In the *Boston Gazette* on July 11, 1774, the following words appeared in a published letter:

> My persecuted brethren of this metropolis, you may rest assured that the guardian God of New England, who holds the hearts of his people in his hands, has influenced your distant brethren to the benevolence.[162]

This was the greatest miracle of the Revolution: unity out of diversity. This is why *E. Pluribus Unum* ("one from the many") was such a significant motto. John Adams said,

> The colonies had grown up under the constitutions of government so different, there was so great a variety of religions, they were composed of so many different nations, their customs, manners and habits had so little resemblance, and their intercourse had been so rare, and their knowledge of each other so imperfect, that to unite them in the same principles in theory, and the same system of action, was certainly a very difficult enterprise. The complete accomplishment of it, in so short a time and by such simple means, was, perhaps, a singular example in the history of mankind—thirteen clocks were made to strike together; a perfection of mechanism which no artist had ever before effected.[163]

According to Rosalie Slater, "Within the space of two months, for the first time in Christian history, three million people achieved Biblical Christian Unity."[164]

The First Continental Congress – September 1774

Further evidence of national unity and union is found in the call for a Continental Congress that convened for the first time on September 5, 1774. B.F. Morris writes:

No doubt the assembly of the first Continental Congress may be regarded as the era at which the Union of these States commenced. This event took place in Philadelphia, the city distinguished by the great civil events of our early history, on the 5th of September, 1774, on which day the first Continental Congress assembled...

The proceedings of the Assembly were introduced by religious observances and devout supplications to the throne of grace, for the inspiration of wisdom and the spirit of good counsels. The first act of the first session of the Continental Congress was to pass the following resolution:

Tuesday, September 6, 1774 — Resolved, that the Rev. Mr. Duché be desired to open Congress tomorrow morning with prayer, at Carpenter's Hall, at nine o'clock.[165]

The Journal of the Proceeding of Congress records for September 7, 1774:

Agreeable to the resolve of yesterday, the meeting was opened with prayers by the reverend Mr. Duché. Voted, That the thanks of the Congress be given to Mr. Duché, by Mr. Cushing and Mr. Ward, for performing divine service, and for the excellent prayer, which he composed and delivered on the occasion.[166]

A beautiful reminiscence of this event was recorded by John Adams in a letter to his wife:

When the Congress met, Mr. Cushing made a motion that it should be opened with prayer. It was opposed by Mr. Jay of New York and Mr. Rutledge of South Carolina because we were so divided in religious sentiments—some Episcopalians, some Quakers, some Anabaptists, some Presbyterians, and some Congregationalists—that we could not join in the same act of worship. Mr. Samuel Adams arose and said "that he was no bigot, and could hear a prayer from any gentleman of piety and virtue who was at the same time a friend to his country. He was a stranger in Philadelphia, but had heard that Mr. Duché deserved that character, and therefore he moved that Mr. Duché, an Episcopal clergyman, might be desired to read prayers to Congress tomorrow morning." The motion was seconded, and passed in the affirmative. Mr. Randolph, our president, waited on Mr. Duché, and received for [an] answer that if his health would permit, he certainly would. Accordingly next morning he appeared with his clerk, and his pontificals, and read the Psalter for the seventh day of September, which was the Thirty fifth Psalm. You must remember this was the next morning after we had heard the rumor of the horrible cannonade of Boston. I never saw a greater effect produced upon an audience. It seemed as if Heaven had ordained that Psalm to be read on that morning.

After this, Mr. Duché, unexpectedly to everybody, struck out into extemporary prayer which filled the bosom of every man present.[167]

When the First Continental Congress met in September, 1774, they prayed fervently for America, for Congress, for Massachusetts, and for Boston.

Mr. Duché concluded his prayer:

Be Thou present O God of Wisdom, and direct the councils of this honorable assembly: enable them to settle all things on the best and surest foundation, that the scene of blood may be speedily closed, that order, harmony, and peace may be effectually restored, and truth and justice, religion and piety, prevail and flourish among the people. Preserve the health of their bodies and the vigor of their minds; shower down on them and the millions they here represent, such temporal blessings as thou seest expedient for them in this world, and crown them with everlasting glory in the world to come. All this we ask in the name and through the merits of Jesus Christ, Thy Son, our Savior, Amen![168]

Responding to this prayer, John Adams wrote:

> I must confess I never heard a better Prayer or one, so well pronounced. Episcopalian as he is, Dr. Cooper himself never prayed with such fervour, such Ardor, such Earnestness and Pathos, and in Language so elegant and sublime—for America, for the Congress, for The Province of Massachusetts Bay, and especially the Town of Boston, It has had an excellent Effect upon every Body here."[169]

Connecticut Delegate Silas Deane wrote, "The Congress met and opened with a prayer made by the Revd. Mr. Duché which it was worth riding one hundred mile to hear. He read the lessons of the day...and then prayed without book about ten minutes so pertinently, with such fervency, purity, and sublimity of style and sentiment...that even Quakers shed tears."[170]

Leadership of the Clergy in the Revolution

The primary force or catalyst for this miracle of unity and mutual support among the colonies were the preachers of the era. Jedidiah Morse writes in his *Annals of the American Revolution:*

> The prayers and public discourses of the clergy,...who were friends to their country, (and there were few who were not) breathed the spirit of patriotism; and as their piety and integrity had generally secured to them the confidence of the people, they had great influence and success in encouraging them to engage in its defence. In this way, that class of citizens aided the cause of their country; and to their pious exertions, under the Great Arbiter of human affairs, has been justly ascribed no inconsiderable share of the success and victory that crowned the American arms.[171]

Proclamation Recognizing Ministers – December 1774

A significant proclamation from the period affirms this crucial role of the clergy in shaping public opinion (see page 140 for a copy). On December 6, 1774, the Provincial Congress of Massachusetts under the leadership of John Hancock, issued this statement:

> When we contemplate the friendship and assistance our ancestors — the first settlers of this Province — received from the pious Pastors of the Churches of Christ,...we cannot but acknowledge the goodness of Heaven in constantly supplying us with preachers of the Gospel whose

concern has been the temporal and spiritual happiness of this people; In a day like this,…we cannot but place great hopes in an Order of Men, who have ever distinguished themselves in their country's cause, and do therefore recommend to the Ministers of the Gospel…that they assist us in avoiding that dreadful slavery with which we are now threatened by advising the people of their several congregations.[172]

The voluntary aid that came to Boston during the Port Bill and other similar instances throughout the war were primarily due to the leadership of the clergy. Alice Baldwin writes:

Beginning in 1767 and continuing throughout the War, the ministers did all in their power to encourage the non-importation agreements and home manufactures. There are many instances in each of the New England colonies of all-day spinning bees

A minuteman leaving for action, as a minister bestows his blessing.

held in the rooms and on the lawns of the minister's homes. … One good clergyman [Rev. Judah Champion of Litchfield, Conn.] during the war felt so keenly the need of clothes for the soldiers [in the cold northern winter] at Quebec that he excused the women of the town from afternoon service and set them all to spinning on the Sabbath Day. … Frequently before the end of the day the minister would address the women and girls on the issues of the time. … In this manner the ministers showed knowledge of human nature by arousing competition between town and town, and between churches in the same town, and even between married and unmarried women, as well as by making the whole affair a great social occasion through having the men come to supper and join in an evening of fun with music and singing of songs written by the "Sons of liberty."[173]

The clergy were also a motivating force behind the organization of militia for military defense. The churches would form *minutemen* from out of their male membership and the deacon of the church would often be responsible for drilling them. Richard Frothingham writes that, "On the days of drill the citizen soldiers sometimes went from the parade ground to the church where they listened to exhortation and prayer." He records part of an admonition given to these minutemen by the Provincial Congress: "You are placed by Providence in the post of honor, because it is the post of danger;...The eyes not only of North America and the whole British Empire, but of all Europe, are upon you. Let us be, therefore, altogether solicitous that no disorderly behavior, nothing unbecoming our characters as Americans, as citizens and Christians, be justly chargeable to us.[174]

On April 15, 1775, the Provincial Congress, led by John Hancock, called for a Day of Fasting and Prayer with these words:

> In circumstances dark as these, it becomes us, as Men and Christians, to reflect that, while every prudent measure should be taken to ward off the impending judgements;...at the same time, all confidence must be withheld from the means we use; and reposed only on that God who rules in the armies of Heaven, and without whose blessing the best human counsels are but foolishness—and all created power, vanity. It is the happiness of his Church that, when the powers of earth and hell combine against it, and those who should be nursing fathers become its persecutors—then the Throne of Grace is of easiest access—and its appeal thither is graciously invited by the Father of Mercies, who has assured it, that when his children ask bread he will not give them a stone.[175]

Jonas Clark and the Battle of Lexington – April 1775

The most historic band of minutemen was led by Deacon Parker under the auspices of Rev. Jonas Clark. Clark was pastor of a church in Lexington, Massachusetts. Since the struggle over the Stamp Act in 1765, this clergyman had become the town's principal leader in its town meetings and issues of liberty and government. Almost every crucial state paper written to represent Lexington was authored by Jonas Clark. His home was a frequent meeting place for men like Samuel Adams and John Hancock when safe locations could not be assured inside Boston. Such was the case on the night of April 18th, 1775. Adams and Hancock were visiting for the night, unaware that the British had decided to send troops to Lexington to destroy the town's military supplies and capture these two men. One of Clark's house guests asked him on that night if the Lexington people would fight if necessary. Clark, who had taught them for years the duty of self-defense and preservation of inalienable rights, responded confidently: "I have trained them for this very hour!"[176] Clark had prepared this people so well in the Scriptures as they related to the issues of the day, that the first shots of the entire war were providentially selected to be fired on his church lawn.

William Wells describes well this first battle in his book *The Life and Public Service of Samuel Adams.* He explains how Paul Revere had agreed to give the signal to the colonists across the Charles River.

> If the British went out by water, he would display two lanterns in the North Church Steeple, and if by land, one, as a signal that the news might be conveyed to Lexington, should the communication with the peninsula be cut off. Having instructed a friend to that effect, he was rowed across the Charles River. It was the young flood, the ship was winding, and the moon rising. Landing in Charlestown, Revere found that his signal had been understood. He then took a horse, and rode toward Lexington.
>
> After several adventures on the way, in which he narrowly escaped capture, he reached the house of Mr. Clark about midnight, and gave the alarm. He was just in time to elude the vigilance of the British in Boston; for Earl Percy, having accidentally ascertained that the secret was out, gave orders to allow no person to leave the town. Revere found the family at rest, and a guard of eight men stationed at the house, for the protection of Adams and Hancock. He rode up, and requested admittance, but the Sergeant replied that the family before retiring had desired that they not be disturbed by any noise about the house. "Noise!"

Old North Church

replied Revere, "you'll have noise enough before long. The Regulars are coming out." He was then admitted.

About one o'clock on the morning of the 19th, the militia were mustered on the green near the meeting-house, and messengers sent for additional information. By two o'clock the countrymen numbered one hundred and thirty. The guns were loaded with powder and ball in the presence of Adams, Hancock, and Clark. One of the messengers returning with the report that no troops could be seen, and the weather being chilly, the men were dismissed with orders to appear again at the beat of the drum. Most of them retired to Buckman's Tavern, near by.

Paul Revere warns of the approaching British troops.

Colonel Smith had marched his column but a few miles, when the ringing of bells and firing of guns satisfied him that the country was alarmed. He immediately detached six companies of light infantry, under command of Major Pitcairn, with orders to press forward, and secure the two bridges at Concord, while he sent back for reinforcements. By capturing those whom he met upon the road, Pitcairn prevented the news of his approach from going before him, until he came within a mile and a half of Lexington meeting-house, when a horseman, who had succeeded in eluding the troops, galloped into the village. Then, about seventy townspeople assembled as the drums beat, and at the sound the British halted to load. The advance guard and grenadiers then hurried forward at double quick, and when within five or six rods of the Provincials, Pitcairn shouted, "Disperse, ye villains! Ye rebels, disperse! Lay down your arms! Why don't you lay down your arms and disperse?"

Most of the minutemen, undecided whether to fire or retreat, stood motionless, having been ordered by their commander not to fire first. Some were joining the ranks, others leaving them, when Pitcairn in a loud voice gave the word to fire, at the same time discharging his pistol. The order was obeyed at first by a few guns, which did no execution, and immediately after by a deadly discharge from the whole British force. A few of the militia, no longer hesitating, returned the fire, but without serious effect. Parker, seeing the utter disparity of forces, ordered his men to disperse. The Regulars continued their fire while any of the militia remained in sight, killing eight and wounding ten. The village green, where this event took place, has been aptly termed by the historian, "a field of murder, not of battle."

A few farmers had assembled, willing to defend their homes, but determined not to commence hostilities, and unsuspicious of the sudden onslaught. The firing was soon over, and the royal troops remained masters of the field; but the sacrifice of that little band revolutionized the world. It was the first scene in the drama which was to carry with it the destinies of mankind.

Adams and Hancock, as the soldiers made their appearance, were persuaded to retire to the adjacent village of Woburn, their safety being regarded as of utmost importance. Passing through the fields, while the sunlight glistened in the dew of the fresh spring morning, Adams felt his soul swell with uncontrollable joy as he contemplated the mighty future, and with prophetic utterance of his country's dawning independence, he exclaimed, "O! what a glorious morning is this!"[177]

It *was* a glorious morning. Why? Because as Rev. Jonas Clark preached: "From this day will be dated the liberty of the world!"[178]

The providential Hand of God is evident in this event. About one month earlier the Governor of Connecticut had called upon the colony to observe a "Day of public Fasting and Prayer…that God would graciously pour out his Holy Spirit on us, to bring us to a thorough repentance and effectual reformation;…That He would restore, preserve and secure the liberties of this, and all the other American Colonies, and make this land a mountain of Holiness and habitation of Righteousness forever. — (and) That God would preserve and confirm the Union of the Colonies in the pursuit and practice of that Religion and virtue which will honour Him."[179] (A copy of the proclamation is on p. 202)

What day had Governor Jonathan Trumbull selected for them to be praying? "Wednesday, the nineteenth Day of April!" — the very day fighting had begun in the war for American independence.

The Battle of Lexington: "From this day will he dated the liberty of the World!"

The Mecklenburg Declaration — May 1775

As soon as word of the battle of Lexington reached a convention of delegates in North Carolina, they declared independence from England. George Bancroft writes:

> The first public voice in America for dissolving all connections with Great Britain, came not from the Puritans of New England, the Dutch of New York, nor from the planters of Virginia, but from the Scotch-Irish Presbyterians "who were meeting in convention as delegates of Mecklenburg County, North Carolina."[180]

Over a year before the Declaration of Independence, these Presbyterians—many of them preachers—wrote the following declaration:

> Resolved, That we do hereby declare ourselves a free and independent people, are, and of a right ought to be, a sovereign and self-governing Association, under the control of no power, other than that of our God

and the General Government of the Congress; to the maintenance of which independence, we solemnly pledge to each other, our mutual cooperation, our lives, our fortunes, and our most sacred honor.[181]

Continental Congress Calls for a Day of Fasting and Prayer — July 1775

On June 12, 1775, England declared that the Colonies would now be put under martial law. The Christian Continental Congress, in response, employed their most trusted weapon: Prayer. They appealed to "The Great Governor of the World" who "frequently influences the minds of men to serve the wise and gracious purposes of His providential government." It was "recommended to Christians of all denominations to assemble for public...Humiliation, Fasting and Prayer" on the 20th of July.[182]

When the special day came, the entire Congress went as a group to the church of Jacob Duché and heard his sermon from Psalm 80:14. They were joined that day for the first time by delegates from Georgia, who were led by Rev. John Zubly. Now all thirteen Colonies were united in Congress.

Elsewhere, on that day, Rev. David Jones preached one of the day's most eloquent sermons entitled *Defensive War in a Just Cause Sinless.* In this sermon he appealed to the history of Israel and noted that "when vice and immorality became prevalent; when they forsook and rebelled against their God, [then] they lost their martial spirit." Then the nation experienced revival under the leadership of Nehemiah who stirred the people to arm themselves with these words: "Be not ye afraid of them: Remember the Lord, which is great and terrible, and fight for the brethren, your sons and your daughters, your wives and your houses!" Rev. Jones proved from many Scriptural examples how a defensive war is sinless before God, and when it is proper to use force against a tyrant. Then he says:

> The reason why a defensive war seems so awful to good people, is, they esteem it to be some kind of murder: but this is a very great mistake; for it is no more murder than a legal process against a criminal. The end is the same, the mode is different. In some cases it is the only mode left to obtain justice. And surely that religion is not from Heaven, which is against justice on earth. Remember all men are not converted; if they were, there could be no necessity of war in any sense. For, says the Scripture, "they shall not hurt nor destroy." But, remember, this is when the earth shall be filled with the knowledge of the Lord. Alas! this is not the case now; for darkness, gloomy darkness, prevails throughout the

kingdoms of this world. Oh! that the kingdom of Jesus was come, when we should have occasion to learn war no more."[183]

Just a few months prior to this sermon, Patrick Henry, the orator of the Revolution, urged the Virginia Convention of the delegates to take up arms since they had exhausted every means of protest and flight. He said:

Sir, we have done everything that could be done to avert the storm which is now coming on. We have petitioned—we have remonstrated— we have supplicated—we have prostrated ourselves before the throne, and have implored its interposition to arrest the tyrannical hands of the ministry and parliament. Our petitions have been slighted; our remonstrances have produced additional violence and insult; our supplications have been disregarded; and we have been spurned, with contempt, from the foot of the throne. In vain, after these things, may we indulge the fond hope of peace and reconciliation. There is no longer any room for hope. If we wish to be free...we must fight! — I repeat it, sir, we must fight! An appeal to arms and to the God of Hosts is all that is left us! ... Three millions of people, armed in the holy cause of liberty...are invincible by any force which our enemy can send against us. Besides, sir, we shall not fight our battles alone. There is a just God who presides over the destinies of nations; and He will raise up friends to fight our battles for us. The battle, sir, is not to the strong alone; it is to the vigilant, the active, the brave. ... There is no retreat but in submission and slavery!...

Patrick Henry making "an appeal to arms and to the God of Hosts."

Gentlemen may cry, "Peace! peace!" — but there is no peace. ... Is life so dear, and peace so sweet, as to be purchased at the price of chains and slavery? Forbid it, Almighty God! I know not what course others may take; but as for me, give me liberty or give me death![184]

"The Black Regiment"

The war effort was blessed with the inspirational leadership of the colonial clergy, who the British called "the Black Regiment," in reference to the color of their pulpit gowns that they wore even on the battlefront.

Saint John's Episcopal Church, Richmond. Here Patrick Henry in 1775 proclaimed, "Give me liberty or give me death!"

One month after the Battle of Lexington, Rev. Samuel Langdon, President of Harvard, preached an Election Sermon to the leaders of Massachusetts entitled *Government Corrupted by Vice and Recovered by Righteousness*. He said that:

> Vice will increase with the riches and glory of an empire; and this generally tends to corrupt the Constitution and in time bring on its dissolution. This may be considered not only as the natural effect of vice, but a religious judgement from Heaven, especially upon a nation which has been favored with the blessings of religion and liberty and is guilty of undervaluing them.[185]

He went on to call for repentance, as well as action, in faith that God had heard them, to set up their banners and fight in the name of the Lord. Langdon then personally led them to the heights of Bunker Hill to begin their entrenchments for that historic battle. Shortly after that battle, Rev. Langdon felt called of God to devote himself full-time to ministering to the troops as their chaplain. He recorded in his journal the following:

> June 20, 1775 — This has been one of the most important and trying days of my life. I have taken leave of my people for the present, and shall at once proceed to the American camp at Boston and offer my services as chaplain in the army. Ever since the battle of Bunker Hill my mind has

been turned to this subject. God's servants are needed in the army to pray with it and for it. This is God's work; and his ministers should set an example that will convince the people that they believe it to be such. But the scene in the house of God today has tried me sorely. How silent, how solemn, was the congregation and when they sang the sixty-first Psalm, commencing — "When overwhelm'd with grief, My heart within me dies. ..." Sobs were heard in every part of the building. At the close, I was astonished to see Deacon S., now nearly sixty years of age, arise and address the congregation. "Brethren," said he, "our minister has acted right. This is God's cause; and as in days of old the priests bore the ark into the midst of the battle, so must they do it now. We should be unworthy of the fathers and mothers who landed on Plymouth Rock, if we do not cheerfully bear what Providence shall put upon us in the great conflict now before us. I had two sons at Bunker Hill, and one of them, you know, was slain. The other did his duty, and for the future God must do with him what seemeth him best. I offer him to liberty. I had thought that I would stay here with the church. But my minister is going, and I will shoulder my musket and go, too." In this strain he continued for some time, till the whole congregation was bathed in tears. Oh God must be with this people in the unequal struggle, or else how could they enter upon it with such solemnity and prayer, with such strong reliance on his assistance, and such a profound sense of their need of it? Just before separating, the whole congregation joined in singing — "O God our help in ages past, Our hope for years to come."[186]

Peter Muhlenberg — December 1775

In the U.S. Capitol building today, there stands a statue honoring another one of the *Black Regiment* (see picture on page 201). Benson J. Lossing writes:

In those days politics were preached in the pulpits and men were led to action on the side of freedom by faithful pastors. The eminent General Muhlenberg was one of this stamp. When the war for independence was kindling, he was a clergyman in Virginia, and at the close of 1775, he concluded a sermon with the words of Scripture: "There is a time for all things — a time to preach and a time to pray;" but those times, he said, had passed away; and then, in a voice that sounded like a trumpet-blast through the church, he exclaimed: "There is a time to fight, and that time has now come." Then laying aside his sacerdotal gown, he stood before his flock in the full uniform of a Virginia colonel. He ordered the drums to be beaten at the church door for recruits; and almost the entire male audience, capable of bearing arms, joined his standard. Nearly three hundred men enlisted under his banner on that day.[187]

Rev. Peter Muhlenberg became one of Washington's primary Brigadier Generals in the Continental Army. Other clergymen followed Muhlenberg's example and led in battle, including Rev. Robert Smith of South Carolina and Rev. John Craighead of North Carolina.

Peter Muhlenberg

J. Wingate Thornton declared in his book *The Pulpit of the American Revolution:*

> Thus it is manifest, in the spirit of our history, in our annals, and by the general voice of the fathers of the republic, that, in a very great degree, — to the pulpit, the Puritan pulpit, we owe the moral force which won our independence.[188]

Massachusetts affirmed this truth as they looked for the most effective way to promote the Declaration of Independence in that state. Large numbers of the Declaration were printed with the following addendum (see page 176):

> Ordered, that the Declaration of Independence be printed; and a copy sent to the Ministers of each parish, of every denomination, within this state; and that they severally be required to read the same to their respective congregations, as soon as divine Service is ended;…And after such publication thereof, to deliver the said Declaration to the Clerks of their several towns or districts; who are hereby required to record the same in their respective town or district books.[189]

John Quincy Adams said in a July 4th oration, as summarized by Thornton: "The highest glory of the American Revolution…was this: it connected, in one indissoluble bond, the principles of civil government with the principles of Christianity."[190]

IN

CONGRESS,

JULY 4, 1776.

A DECLARATION

BY THE

REPRESENTATIVES

OF THE

UNITED STATES OF AMERICA,

IN GENERAL CONGRESS ASSEMBLED.

WHEN in the Course of human Events, it becomes necessary for one People to dissolve the political Bands which have connected them with another, and to assume among the Powers of the Earth, the separate and equal Station to which the Laws of Nature and of Nature's God entitle them, a decent Respect to the Opinions of Mankind requires that they should declare the Causes which impel them to the Separation.

We hold these Truths to be self-evident, that all Men are created equal, that they are endowed by their Creator with certain unalienable Rights, that among these are Life, Liberty, and the Pursuit of Happiness:—That to secure these Rights, Governments are instituted among Men, deriving their just Powers from the Consent of the Governed, that whenever any Form of Government becomes destructive of these Ends, it is the Right of the People to alter or to abolish it, and to institute new Government, laying its Foundation on such Principles, and organizing its Powers in such Form, as to them shall seem most likely to effect their Safety and Happiness. Prudence, indeed, will dictate that Governments long established should not be changed for light and transient Causes; and accordingly all Experience hath shewn, that Mankind are more disposed to suffer, while Evils are sufferable, than to right themselves by abolishing the Forms to which they are accustomed. But when a long Train of Abuses and Usurpations, pursuing invariably the same Object, evinces a Design to reduce them under absolute Despotism, it is their Right, it is their Duty, to throw off such Government, and to provide new Guards for their future Security. Such has been the patient Sufferance of these Colonies; and such is now the Necessity which constrains them to alter their former Systems of Government. The History of the present King of Great-Britain is a History of repeated Injuries and Usurpations, all having in direct Object the Establishment of an absolute Tyranny over these States. To prove this, let Facts be submitted to a candid World.

He has refused his Assent to Laws, the most wholesome and necessary for the public Good.

He has forbidden his Governors to pass Laws of immediate and pressing Importance, unless suspended in their Operation until his Assent should be obtained; and when so suspended, he has utterly neglected to attend to them.

He has refused to pass other Laws for the Accommodation of large Districts of People, unless those People would relinquish the Right of Representation in the Legislature, a Right inestimable to them, and formidable to Tyrants only.

He has called together Legislative Bodies at Places unusual, uncomfortable, and distant from the Depository of their public Records, for the sole Purpose of fatiguing them into Compliance with his Measures.

He has dissolved Representative Houses repeatedly, for opposing with manly Firmness his Invasions on the Rights of the People.

He has refused for a long Time, after such Dissolutions, to cause others to be elected; whereby the Legislative Powers, incapable of Annihilation, have returned to the People at large for their Exercise; the State remaining in the mean Time exposed to all the Dangers of Invasion from without, and Convulsions within.

He has endeavoured to prevent the Population of these States; for that Purpose obstructing the Laws for Naturalization of Foreigners; refusing to pass others to encourage their Migrations hither, and raising the Conditions of new Appropriations of Lands.

He has obstructed the Administration of Justice, by refusing his Assent to Laws for establishing Judiciary Powers.

He has made Judges dependent on his Will alone, for the Tenure of their Offices, and the Amount and Payment of their Salaries.

He has erected a Multitude of new Offices, and sent hither Swarms of Officers to harass our People, and eat out their Substance.

He has kept among us, in Times of Peace, Standing Armies, without the Consent of our Legislatures.

He has affected to render the Military independent of, and superior to the Civil Power.

He has combined with others to subject us to a Jurisdiction foreign to our Constitution, and unacknowledged by our Laws; giving his Assent to their Acts of pretended Legislation:

For quartering large Bodies of armed Troops among us:

For protecting them, by a mock Trial, from Punishment for any Murders which they should commit on the Inhabitants of these States:

For cutting off our Trade with all Parts of the World:

For imposing Taxes on us without our Consent:

For depriving us, in many Cases, of the Benefits of Trial by Jury:

For transporting us beyond Seas to be tried for pretended Offences:

For abolishing the free System of English Laws in a neighbouring Province, establishing therein an arbitrary Government, and enlarging its Boundaries, so as to render it at once an Example and fit Instrument for introducing the same absolute Rule into these Colonies:

For taking away our Charters, abolishing our most valuable Laws, and altering fundamentally the Forms of our Governments:

For suspending our own Legislatures, and declaring themselves invested with Power to legislate for us in all Cases whatsoever.

He has abdicated Government here, by declaring us out of his Protection and waging War against us.

He has plundered our Seas, ravaged our Coasts, burnt our Towns, and destroyed the Lives of our People.

He is, at this Time, transporting large Armies of foreign Mercenaries to compleat the Works of Death, Desolation, and Tyranny, already begun with Circumstances of Cruelty and Perfidy scarcely paralleled in the most barbarous Ages, and totally unworthy the Head of a civilized Nation.

He has constrained our Fellow Citizens, taken Captive on the high Seas, to bear Arms against their Country, to become the Executioners of their Friends and Brethren, or to fall themselves by their Hands.

He has excited domestic Insurrections amongst us, and has endeavoured to bring on the Inhabitants of our Frontiers, the merciless Indian Savages, whose known Rule of Warfare, is an undistinguished Destruction of all Ages, Sexes, and Conditions.

In every Stage of these Oppressions we have petitioned for Redress, in the most humble Terms: Our repeated Petitions have been answered only by repeated Injury. A Prince, whose Character is thus marked by every Act which may define a Tyrant, is unfit to be the Ruler of a FREE PEOPLE!

Nor have we been wanting in Attention to our British Brethren. We have warned them from Time to Time of Attempts by their Legislature to extend an unwarrantable Jurisdiction over us. We have reminded them of the Circumstances of our Emigration and Settlement here. We have appealed to their native Justice and Magnanimity, and we have conjured them by the Ties of our common Kindred to disavow these Usurpations, which would inevitably interrupt our Connexions and Correspondence. They too have been deaf to the Voice of Justice and of Consanguinity. We must, therefore, acquiesce in the Necessity which denounces our Separation, and hold them, as we hold the rest of Mankind, Enemies in War; in Peace, Friends.

We, therefore, the Representatives of the UNITED STATES OF AMERICA, in General Congress assembled, appealing to the SUPREME JUDGE of the World for the Rectitude of our Intentions, do, in the Name and by the Authority of the good People of these Colonies, solemnly Publish and Declare, That these United Colonies are, and of Right ought to be, Free and Independent States; that they are absolved from all Allegiance to the British Crown; and that all political Connexion between them and the State of Great-Britain, is, and ought to be totally dissolved; and that as Free and Independent States, they have full Power to levy War, conclude Peace, contract Alliances, establish Commerce, and to do all other Acts and Things which Independent States may of Right do. And for the Support of this Declaration, with a firm Reliance on the Protection of Divine Providence, we mutually pledge to each other our LIVES, our FORTUNES, and our SACRED HONOR.

Signed by Order and in Behalf of the Congress,

JOHN HANCOCK, PRESIDENT.

Attest, CHARLES THOMPSON, Secretary.

IN COUNCIL, JULY 17th, 1776.

ORDERED, That the Declaration of Independence be printed; and a Copy sent to the Ministers of each Parish, of every Denomination, within this State; and that they severally be required to read the same to their respective Congregations, as soon as divine Service is ended, in the Afternoon, on the first Lord's-Day after they shall have received it:—And after such Publication thereof, to deliver the said Declaration to the Clerks of their several Towns, or Districts; who are hereby required to record the same in their respective Town, or District Books; there to remain as a perpetual Memorial thereof.

In the Name, and by Order of the Council, R. DERBY, Jun. President.

A true Copy Attest, JOHN AVERY, Dep. Sec'y.

SALEM, Massachusetts-Bay: Printed by E. Russell, by Order of Authority.

A printed version of the Declaration distributed by the government of Massachusetts to the churches requiring them to read it to their congregations.

Chapter 11

How God Defends Christian Liberty

Christian character and principles were the foundation of the actions of the colonists which led to the American Revolution. The people, soldiers, and leaders exemplified the same Christian character during the war with Great Britain. In this chapter we will see the Christian character of the Continental Congress and the Continental Army as well as witness how God providentially protected the Continental Army on numerous occasions. God was more than just supporting Christian individuals in the war; He was supporting the entire cause of liberty.

The Christian Continental Congress — 1775

The colonists did not initially want to separate from England. They endured mistreatment for many years, always hoping British leaders would respond to their petitions to stop their tyrannical behavior. Even after fighting had begun, they still sought legal redress to be reconciled with England for 14 months before declaring independence.

In December of 1775, when King George III rejected their petitions and declared them all rebels and enemies, they realized their lives, liberty, and property were no longer protected by the English government. This meant they were now in a "state of nature," and therefore they needed to establish their own government to protect their lives and liberty. The Declaration of Independence states that, "He [the King] has abdicated Government here, by declaring us out of his Protection and waging War against us."

Why the King and Parliament would treat the petitions of their own colonies in such a stupid way is incomprehensible. It can only be compared in history to the hardening of Pharaoh's heart so that God's purposes might be fulfilled (and many sermons were preached during this time making this comparison).

July 1776

During the first days of July in 1776 the Continental Congress was considering one of the most important events of all time — the declaration by thirteen colonies to become the new nation of the United States of America.

On the issue of independence all the colonies were agreed, but a few of the most cautious delegates still were not sure about the timing. Rev. John Witherspoon, a delegate from New Jersey, answered their concerns as he said:

> There is a tide in the affairs of men. We perceive it now before us. To hesitate is to consent to our own slavery. That noble instrument should be subscribed to this very morning by every pen in this house. Though these gray hairs must soon descend to the sepulchre, I would infinitely rather that they descend thither by the hand of the executioner than desert at the crisis the sacred cause of my country![191]

The delegates went on to approve the Declaration of Independence. After the announcement of the vote, silence moved over the Congress as the men contemplated the magnitude of what they had just done. Some wept openly,

John Hancock

while others bowed in prayer. After signing the Declaration with unusually large writing, the President of the Continental Congress, John Hancock, broke the silence as he declared, "His majesty can now read my name without glasses. And he can also double the price on my head."[192] Then he went on to say at the tense moment, "We must be unanimous; there must be no pulling different ways; we must all hang together."

Benjamin Franklin responded in his characteristic wit, "Yes, we must indeed all hang together, or most assuredly we shall all hang separately!"[193]

A brief chuckle followed and then Samuel Adams, whom men of that day ascribed "the greatest part in the greatest revolution of the world,"[194] rose and stated:

> We have this day restored the Sovereign to Whom alone men ought to be obedient. He reigns in heaven and…from the rising to the setting sun may His kingdom come.[195]

The men who helped give birth to America understood what was taking place. They saw in the establishment of America the first truly Christian nation in history.

As Franklin suggested, they did "hang together," but even so, many of these signers as well as tens of thousands of colonists lost their lives, property, families, and reputations in order to purchase liberty for themselves and their posterity.

What was it that motivated these people to risk everything in order that they might have freedom? What was it that brought about the events leading to the colonists declaring their independence? John Adams, our second President and a leader in the cause of independence, revealed what he and many others thought as he wrote on the day that the colonies declared their independence:

> It is the will of Heaven that the two countries should be sundered forever. It may be the will of Heaven that America shall suffer calamities still more wasting and distresses yet more dreadful. If this is to be the case,…the furnace of affliction produces refinement in states as well as individuals;…but I…submit all my hopes and fears to an overruling Providence, in which, unfashionable as the faith may be, I firmly believe.[196]

John Adams

John Hancock had earlier expressed his reliance upon God and the belief that the destiny of nations is in the hand of God as he said:

> Let us humbly commit our righteous cause to the great Lord of the Universe… Let us joyfully leave our concerns in the hands of Him who raises up and puts down the empires and kingdoms of the earth as He pleases.[197]

This firm reliance upon God was so universally adhered to among those in America that the Continental Congress insisted it be included in the Declaration of Independence. While reviewing Thomas Jefferson's original draft of the Declaration, the committee assigned to the task added the words, "they are endowed by their Creator with certain unalienable rights." Then, when the Declaration was debated before Congress, they added the phrase, "appealing to the Supreme Judge of the World, for the rectitude of our intentions," as well as the words "with a firm reliance on the protection of divine Providence."[198]

Most of the revisions of Jefferson's original work had to do with the Lord. Thus, we see the Continental Congress declaring to all the world their Christian convictions.

Not only does the Declaration of Independence reflect our Founders' faith in God, but as we have seen previously, this document only came into being as a result of biblical ideas that had been sown in the hearts of the colonists for one hundred and fifty years.

The American Revolution was a revolution of ideas long before it was a revolution of war. As the clergy and other leaders taught the colonists their God-given rights as men, Christians, and subjects, the inevitable result was a nation birthed in liberty.

The Signing of the Declaration of Independence. After President Hancock signed his name, Samuel Adams stated: "We have this day restored the Sovereign to Whom alone men ought to be obedient. He reigns in heaven and from the rising to the setting sun, may His kingdom come."

The Seal of the United States

The Seal of the United States (also known as "the Great Seal") is a symbol of our nation's sovereignty. It is affixed to various official national documents that are signed by the President.

Shortly after the adoption of the Declaration of Independence in 1776, a committee (composed of Thomas Jefferson, John Adams, and Benjamin Franklin) was appointed to formulate an official seal for the new nation. The seal was to reflect the heart of the new nation and the principles upon which she was built. Franklin's description of his proposal for the seal was as follows:

> Moses standing on the shore, and extending his hand over the sea, thereby causing the same to overwhelm Pharaoh who is sitting in an open chariot, a crown on his head and a sword in his hand. Rays from a pillar of fire in the clouds reaching to Moses, to express that he acts by command of the Deity. Motto: Rebellion to tyrants is obedience to God.[199]

Jefferson proposed that one side of the seal be

> Pharaoh sitting in an open chariot, a crown on his head & a sword in his hand, passing through the divided waters of the Red Sea in pursuit of the Israelites: rays from a pillar of fire in the cloud, expressive of the divine presence & command, reaching to Moses who stands on the shore &, extending his hand over the sea, causes it to overwhelm Pharaoh.[200]

Jefferson's proposal for the Seal of the United States

Both of these men saw that the birth of America was accomplished sovereignly and miraculously by the hand of God, as He similarly had done with ancient Israel. While almost every member of Congress agreed with this, they also felt God was doing something more with America. Consequently, Congress did not immediately adopt any official seal. It was not until 1782 that a seal was approved. Both sides of the Seal are found on the back of our one-dollar bill today.

Following is a description of the reverse side given in a Department of State bulletin which was taken from the *Journals of Congress:*

> Reverse. A pyramid unfinished—of 13 layers of stone. In the zenith, an eye of Divine Providence, surrounded with a glory proper. Over the

eye these words, "Annuit Coeptis" [Latin words that mean "He (God) has blessed our undertakings."] On the base of the pyramid the numerical letters MDCCLXXVI. And underneath, the following motto, "Novus Ordo Seclorum." [Latin for "A New Order of the Ages"][201]

Charles Thomson, the Secretary of the Congress that approved the Seal, wrote that "the Pyramid signifies Strength and Duration. The Eye over it and the Motto allude to the many signal interpositions of Providence in favour of the American cause."[202]

James Wilson, a Justice on the first Supreme Court said that, "A free government has often been compared to a pyramid;…it is laid on the broad basis of the people."

The Great Seal

Chaplains Appointed

One of the first acts of the American Congress after declaring independence was to appoint chaplains to open the daily meetings of Congress in prayer. On July 9, Rev. Jacob Duché, Rev. Patrick Allison (a Baptist), and Rev. William White (an Episcopal) were among the first chaplains appointed. Congress also ordered that chaplains be provided for the Continental Army and for the various hospitals and that they be paid at the rank of colonel.

Days of Fasting and Prayer

Throughout the war with Britain, the American Congress frequently declared Days of Fasting and Prayer to beseech God for His aid and assistance in their struggle for freedom. They also declared Days of Thanksgiving to acknowledge the Hand of God after victories in battle and other significant events. We saw in the last chapter that this was their response to the Boston Port Bill of June 1, 1774, and to declaration of martial law on July 20, 1775. Later in this chapter, we will see a few more of the many times our Congress declared such days of acknowledgement of God. To date, our Congress has declared over 200 National

Days of Prayer, and state governments have declared hundreds more. During the colonial era, governments declared more than 1000 Days of Prayer and Fasting or Prayer and Thanksgiving.[203]

Importation of Bibles — September 1777

In the book, *The Bible of the Revolution,* Robert Dearden and Douglas Watson wrote:

> Revolutionary America without Bibles presented an impossible situation. In no country in the world was the Good Book then so relied upon. Faith in Divine Providence and the consolation and guidance of Holy Writ were necessary to all patriots in the struggle for Liberty...
>
> Before the rupture with the mother country, the Colonies had depended largely for their literature upon England, and entirely so for their Bibles in their native tongue. The Revolutionary War stopped importation, and at length the situation reached such an acute stage that the Chaplain of Congress, the Rev. Patrick Allison, D.D., placed before that body a petition praying for immediate relief. The memorial was assigned to a special committee which weighed the matter with great care, and on September 11, 1777, it reported:
>
> "...that the use of the Bible is so universal and its importance so great that your committee refer the above to the consideration of Congress, and if Congress shall not think it expedient to order the importation of types and paper, the Committee recommend that Congress will order the Committee of Congress to import 20,000 Bibles from Holland, Scotland, or elsewhere, into the different parts of the States of the Union."
>
> Whereupon it was resolved accordingly to direct said Committee to import 20,000 copies of the Bible.[204]

A flag of the Revolutionary War

This is another action of our early Congress that reveals their Christian values. The importance they gave to this legislation of importing Bibles is magnified when one considers the day upon which it occurred. The committee's report to import 20,000 Bibles took place on September 11, 1777, the same day that the Battle of Brandywine was claiming the lives of 1200 Americans and which resulted in a defeat for the Colonial Army. Congress was meeting within earshot of the cannon fire of this battle.

The Christian Character of the Continental Army

The winter of 1777-1778 was one of the most important in our nation's history, for that winter was the turning point of the American Revolution. During that winter the American Army faced as great an ordeal as any army in history. Prior to its movement to Valley Forge in December 1777, Washington's army was an undisciplined mob with few victories to show for their efforts; however, the next spring those same men marched out of camp as a well-disciplined band committed to their general and the cause of liberty and prepared for victory.

What was the ordeal this army faced? How did such a change occur during the months at Valley Forge? What was the cause behind this change?

George Washington

When the army entered Valley Forge, the troops lacked clothes, tents, and blankets. Washington wrote that being "without shoes" their "marching through frost and snow…might be traced by the blood from their feet, and almost as often without provisions as with."[205] And their situation only worsened after December 19th. Washington pleaded for supplies for his men from Congress. In a December 23, 1777, letter to Congress, Washington wrote that a number of men were confined to hospitals and in farmers' houses "for want of shoes. … [W]e have, by a field return this day made no less than 2898 Men in Camp unfit for duty because they are barefoot and otherwise naked."[206]

About one third of all his troops were unfit for service, and this number increased as winter progressed. "The unfortunate soldiers were in want of everything. They had neither coats, hats, shirts, nor shoes," wrote Lafayette. "The men," said Baron Von Steuben, "were literally naked, some of them in the fullest extent of the word."[207]

Hunger was an even greater danger. "The army frequently remained whole days without provisions," said Lafayette. "One soldier's meal on a Thanksgiving Day declared by Congress was a 'half a gill of rice and a tablespoonful of vinegar!' In mid-February there was more than a week when the men received no provisions at all."[208] Dr. Albigence Waldo gave this description:

There comes a soldier, his bare feet are seen through his worn out shoes, his legs nearly naked from the tattered remains of an only pair of stockings; his breeches are not sufficient to cover his nakedness, his shirt hanging in strings, his hair dishevelled, his face meagre. His whole appearance pictures a person forsaken and discouraged. He comes and cries with an air of wretchedness and despair, "I am sick, my feet lame, my legs are sore, my body covered with this tormenting itch."[209]

The troops suffered greatly at Valley Forge.

Due to this lack of food and clothing, hundreds of Washington's troops fell sick. Many men's "feet and legs froze till they became black, and it was often necessary to amputate them."[210] During most of January and February there were "constantly more than 4,000 soldiers who were incapacitated as a result of exposure, disease, and undernourishment."[211]

And in the midst of all of this they persevered! Beyond this, the patient attitude with which they endured this misery was no less than supernatural. On April 21, 1778, Washington wrote to a congressional delegate:

For without arrogance, or the smallest deviation from the truth it may be said, that no history, now extant, can furnish an instance of an Army's suffering such uncommon hardships as ours has done, and bearing them with the same patience and Fortitude. ... [Their] submitting without a murmur, is a mark of patience and obedience which in my opinion can scarce be parallel'd.[212]

What could possibly have kept the army together through this ordeal? Friedrich Von Steuben observed that no European army could have held together under such circumstances. How, then, could an inexperienced army stick together? Was it due to good discipline? "With regard to military discipline," Von Steuben stated, "no such thing existed."[213]

Could it have been the financial reward they would receive? Their paltry pay was already four to five months past due, and complete payment would never come for many of them. Most historians agree that the army persevered at Valley Forge because of the troops' love of liberty and their devotion to Washington. George Bancroft commented that "love of country and attachment to their General sustained them under their unparalleled hardships; with any other leader, the army would have dissolved and vanished."[214]

Washington's character and encouragement inspired the army to follow his example, and his heart was devoted to his men as well as to his country. From the beginning, he tirelessly traveled throughout the camp, his presence bringing strength to the men. After observing his naked and distressed soldiers, he said: "I feel superabundantly for them, and from my Soul pity those miseries, wch. it is neither in my power to relieve or prevent."[215]

Washington knew that the cause for which they fought was worth any price — even the suffering at Valley Forge — for they purchased liberty not only for themselves but for the generations to come. But at Valley Forge, blood was not shed in battle, and still the army shed much blood. "The blood that stained this ground," wrote Henry Brown, "did not rush forth in the joyous frenzy of the fight; it fell drop by drop from the heart of a suffering people. They who once encamped here in the snow fought not for conquest, not for power, not for glory, not for their country only, not for themselves alone. They served here for Posterity; they suffered here for the Human Race; they bore here the cross of all the peoples; they died here that freedom might be the heritage of all."[216]

If Washington's character helped to sustain the army, one must ask, "What sustained Washington?" This question could easily be answered by Washington's soldiers, because they knew his trust was in God. The army had frequently received orders from its general to attend church and to observe days of prayer and fasting and days of thanksgiving. Plus, he had secured chaplains for the army. Rev. Henry Muhlenberg recalled how Washington "rode around among his army…and admonished each and every one to fear God, to put away the wickedness that has set in and become so general, and to practice the Christian virtues."[217]

General Washington "rode around among his army…and admonished each and every one…to practice the Christian virtues."

Almost every man in the army personally knew that his general "regularly attends divine service in his tent every morning and evening, and seems very fervent in his prayers."[218] Henry Knox was one who recounted that Washington frequently visiting secluded groves to lay the cause of his bleeding country at the throne of grace.[219]

A number of people recounted the story of Isaac Potts, a Tory Quaker, who came upon Washington while he was on his knees in prayer in the woods. G.W.P. Custis related that Potts later remarked to his wife:

If there is anyone on this earth whom the Lord will listen to, it is George Washington; and I feel a presentiment that under such a commander there can be no doubt of our eventually establishing our independence, and that God in his providence has willed it so.[220]

On May 6, 1982, President Reagan remarked on this event in his National Day of Prayer Proclamation:

> The most sublime picture in American history is of George Washington on his knees in the snow at Valley Forge. That image personifies a people who know that it is not enough to depend on our own courage and goodness; we must also seek help from God, our Father and Preserver.

In this most difficult of times, Washington constantly relied upon God and trusted in Him for success. God was faithful to answer his prayers, and through Washington, He eventually established America's independence and secured the beginning of the most free and prosperous nation the world has ever seen.

How did God answer Washington's prayer? One miracle occurred that winter that helped to eliminate the army's situation of near-starving. Bruce Lancaster described the event:

> One foggy morning the soldiers noticed the Schuylkill River seemed to be boiling. The disturbance was caused by thousands and thousands of shad which were making their way upstream in an unusually early migration. With pitchforks and shovels, the men plunged into the water, throwing the fish onto the banks. Lee's dragoons rode their horses into the stream to keep the shad from swimming on out of reach. Suddenly and wonderfully, there was plenty of food for the army.[221]

Using pitchforks and shovels to gather a miraculous supply of fish.

Baron Von Steuben

God's providence could also be seen in the arrival of Baron Von Steuben at Valley Forge on February 23. No one could have been more valuable at the time, for he trained and drilled the men into a well-disciplined army. His rigorous instruction gave the troops confidence in themselves as soldiers even as Washington had given them confidence as men. Not only had godly character and strength been forged and tempered within the army, but military skill had also been imparted to them at last.

Another providential event occurred that winter when France became an ally to America. This meant much needed money and additional troops would pour into the new nation. The Continental Congress acknowledged this as the hand of God when the representatives declared a National Day of Thanksgiving on May 7, 1778. At Valley Forge on May 5, Washington proclaimed:

It having pleased the Almighty ruler of the Universe propitiously to defend the Cause of the United American States and finally by raising up a powerful Friend among the Princes of the Earth to establish our liberty and Independence upon lasting foundations, it becomes us to set apart a day for gratefully acknowledging the divine Goodness and celebrating the important Event which we owe to his benign Interposition.[222]

The troops' survival, the molding of a disciplined army, Washington's amazing leadership, and all the miraculous occurrences during the winter at Valley Forge can only be attributed to Almighty God. Washington certainly acknowledged Him in the events of the war, writing in 1778: "The hand of Providence has been so conspicuous in all this, that he must be worse than an infidel that lacks faith, and more than wicked, that has not gratitude enough to acknowledge his obligation."[223] And later he wrote:

The man must be bad indeed who can look upon the events of the American Revolution without feeling the warmest gratitude towards the great Author of the Universe whose divine interposition was so frequently manifested in our behalf.[224]

The Hand of God Protects the Continental Army

During the Revolutionary War, God performed many miracles on behalf of the American Army because God desired to see America win its struggle for freedom, become a nation, and fulfil its divine purposes. We will look at a number of these miracles.

The Evacuation of Long Island — August 1776

One incident revealing God's supernatural care occurred shortly after the signing of the Declaration of Independence in August of 1776. During fighting on Long Island, British General Howe and his army of 32,000 men had inflicted heavy losses on the Continental army but had not succeeded in capturing or destroying it. Howe then prepared to attack the 8000 American troops on Brooklyn Heights.

The British army had surrounded Washington's troops in a great semicircle, with their backs to the nearly mile-wide East River. Here an amazing thing occurred, for General Howe held this position for two days and did not attack. Had he struck, victory would have been certain for the superior British force.

Washington, greatly outnumbered, realized that to fight would mean defeat and the likely end of the war. Surrender was unthinkable. As difficult as it would be, he decided to retreat across the East River since all land routes were blocked by the British. The Continental army could have easily been surrounded by the British, but providentially, adverse weather conditions kept British ships from sailing up the East River. As a result, the Continentals were able to escape.

To make sure the British did not discover their retreat, Washington evacuated his army in great secrecy, even from his own troops. He sent orders for every rowboat, sailboat, and seagoing vessel in the area to be collected. At eight o'clock on the night of August 29, 1776, the evacuation of the troops began.

Washington prayed often throughout the Revolutionary War.

The day before about one thousand men had come over to reinforce Washington's army. Part of these reinforcements included Glover's regiment of Massachusetts fishermen. These men, some of the best mariners in the world, manned the boats that were evacuating not only the troops, but all their supplies, guns, carts, cattle, and horses.

Many providential occurrences took place during the retreat from Long Island.

A heavy rain was falling as the evacuation began and the adverse winds, which hindered the British ships, continued. In this weather the sailboats were of little use, and only the few rowboats were employed in the retreat. But at the rate at which the oarsmen could work, a successful evacuation seemed impossible. At eleven o'clock that evening, however, the northeast wind that had been raging for three days amazingly stopped, and the water became so calm that the boats could be loaded with extra weight. A gentle breeze also blew in from the south and southwest, which favored the Continental's progress across the river to New York.

Yet as the adverse weather changed, a new problem was created. Under the light of a full moon, the British were sure to see the movement of the American troops. Miraculously, though, the Americans retreated all night without being heard or seen. God's hand was surely upon the army and, as was stated in their newly ratified Declaration of Independence, their "firm reliance on the protection of Divine Providence" was proving invaluable.

During the pre-dawn hours of Friday, August 30, through mistaken orders, General Mifflin prematurely withdrew his men, who were the covering party for the retreat. They were to be the last to be evacuated. However, he ran into General Washington, who knew that they should not be removed, and he ordered them to return. Though they were gone 45 minutes from their post the British had not even noticed.

The retreat continued through the darkness of the pre-dawn, but as the sun began to rise, many troops were yet to be evacuated. Death seemed imminent, but again an astonishing thing occurred. Major Benjamin Tallmadge, who was still on the island, recorded what happened in his memoirs:

> As the dawn of the next day approached, those of us who remained in the trenches became very anxious for our own safety, and when the dawn appeared there were several regiments still on duty. At this time a very dense fog began to rise (out of the ground and off the river) and it seemed to settle in a peculiar manner over both encampments.
>
> I recall this peculiar providential occurrence perfectly well, and so very dense was the atmosphere that I could scarcely discern a man at six yards distance. ... We tarried until the sun had risen, but the fog remained as dense as ever.[225]

The fog remained until the last boats left Long Island.

Another miraculous event occurred during this retreat, and Washington Irving described it in his *Life of Washington*. Near the ferry where the troops were being evacuated, a family lived who favored the British cause. Upon seeing the army's embarkation, the lady of the house sent a servant to alert the British of what was happening. The servant managed to slip past the American guards, but upon reaching the British lines, he halted at an outpost of German-speaking mercenaries and was unable to communicate with them.

The servant was put under guard as a suspicious person until the next morning, when a British officer questioned him. Upon hearing the news of the American evacuation, some Redcoats were sent to confirm the report. They cautiously approached the Continental camp only to find it completely empty!

British troops hurried to the river. As they arrived, the fog lifted enough for them to see four boats on the East River. The only boat near enough to be captured contained three vagabonds who had lingered in the camp to plunder it.

Otherwise, 8000 men, with nearly all their supplies, had miraculously retreated to New York.

American General Nathanael Greene called the withdrawal from Long Island "the best effected retreat I ever read or heard of."[226] This extraordinary retreat was one of the most improbable and important events of the war, and many attributed the fortunate series of events to "a peculiar Providence."[227] Surely God was defending American liberty.

Trenton and the Crossing of the Delaware — December 1776

A few months after the retreat from Long Island, Washington found himself in as desperate a situation as on Long Island. He was not engaged in battle or surrounded by the enemy, but his army was dwindling as the men's enlistment times were up. It was now December and at the first of the year most of the men's duty was over and few had re-enlisted. Defeat after defeat had brought the army's and the nation's morale to its lowest point. Washington knew he had to make a bold stroke and go on the offensive.

In a desperate move, Washington decided to cross the Delaware River in pre-dawn hours in order to surprise the enemy. He chose the early morning of December 26 to attack the Hessian garrison quartered at Trenton, for he knew their accustomed drinking on Christmas would help assure their deep slumber on that early morning.

As the troops prepared to cross the Delaware River, a violent snow and hailstorm suddenly came up. This hardship, however, worked in their favor by inducing the enemy's sentries to seek cover and reducing the visibility to near zero.

The Americans entered Trenton so unexpectedly and with such surprise to the

Washington crossing the Delaware River

Hessians that about 1000 prisoners were taken captive after only 45 minutes of battle. Only three Americans were wounded in the fighting. Two had died, but not in fighting; they froze to death on the march. Henry Knox described the event as follows: "The hurry, fright and confusion of the enemy was not unlike that which will be when the last trump will sound."[228]

This much needed victory helped raise the spirit of the army and the nation, strengthening them to continue their struggle for liberty. As Knox wrote of the victory at Trenton, "Providence seemed to have smiled upon every part of this enterprise."[229] Here was another instance of God defending American liberty.

Defeat of Burgoyne at Saratoga — October 1777

On October 17, 1777, British General John Burgoyne was defeated by Colonial forces at Saratoga. This was a much needed victory and an answer to prayer. General Washington had experienced many defeats at the hands of the British, such as the Battle of Brandywine the month before where 1200 Americans lost their lives. In great need, Washington prayed fervently, and when God answered with this victory, he called it a "signal stroke of Providence."[230]

Others recognized the precarious position of the American cause. One Sunday in Sharon, Connecticut, Rev. Smith proclaimed that though a long night of disaster had been occurring, God would soon bring a signal victory for the American army. Before the service ended, a messenger arrived with news that British General Burgoyne had surrendered at Saratoga!

The providence of God was evident in this victory. Earlier, General Howe was supposed to have marched north to join Burgoyne's 11,000 men at Saratoga. However, in his haste to leave London for a holiday, Lord North forgot to sign the dispatch to General Howe. The dispatch was pigeonholed and not found until years later in the archives of the British army. This inadvertence, plus the fact that contrary winds kept British reinforcements delayed at sea for three months, totally altered the outcome at Saratoga in favor of America.

This battle has been called one of the seven most significant battles in history, because once France learned of this triumph, they saw that their longtime enemy might be defeated, and thus Louis XVI decided to ally with the colonies in the war. French support in terms of troops, munitions, ships, and money was invaluable to the American cause.

The Continental Congress proclaimed a Day of Thanksgiving and Praise to God after the surrender of General Burgoyne.

In response to the victory, the Continental Congress proclaimed a Day of Thanksgiving and Praise to God. In part they stated:

> Forasmuch as it is the indispensable duty of all men to adore the superintending providence of Almighty God,...and it having pleased Him in His abundant mercy...to crown our arms with most signal success...it is therefore recommended...to set apart Thursday, the 18th day of December, for solemn thanksgiving and praise.

They recommended for everyone to confess their sins and humbly ask God, "through the merits of Jesus Christ, mercifully to forgive and blot them out of remembrance" and thus He then would be able to pour out His blessings upon every aspect of the nation.[231]

Providential Discovery of Benedict Arnold's Treason — September 1780

Miss Hall and Miss Slater write of another miraculous event during the Revolutionary War:

> An example of God's Providential protection against such "imminent, though unseen dangers" was in the amazing capture of the British spy

Major Andre which revealed the treachery of Benedict Arnold. Of this event, Washington himself wrote to John Laurens:

> "In no instance since the commencement of the War has the interposition of Providence appeared more conspicuous than in the rescue of the Post and Garrison of West Point from Arnold's villainous perfidy. ... A combination of extraordinary circumstances."

Benedict Arnold

Washington's letter of September 26, 1780 to Major General William Heath gives more details on what happened.

> "Major General Arnold has gone to the enemy. He had an interview with Major Andre, Adjutant General of the British Army, and had put into his possession a state of our Army; of the Garrison at this post; of the number of Men considered as necessary for the defence of it, a Return of Ordinance and the disposition of the Artillery Corps in case of Alarm. By a most Providential interposition, Major Andre was taken in returning to New York with all these papers in General Arnold's hand writing, who hearing the matter kept it secret, left his Quarters immediately under pretence of going over to West point on Monday forenoon, about an hour before my arrival, then pushed down the river in the barge, which was not discovered till I had returned from West point in the Afternoon."

Major Andre was finally brought to General Washington on the 26th, and then the full story of his capture came to light. On September 23, three young militiamen had posted themselves on the Old Post Road close to Tarrytown, waiting to waylay "cowboys" who were stealing cattle and driving them into the British lines. Suddenly, about 9:30 in the morning, they saw a solitary rider coming toward them. They stopped him and learned that he was on his way to New York. It was Major Andre who believed that they were loyalists who had established a look-out for the British. He didn't show them his pass and talked so freely that the young militiamen began to be suspicious. They made him strip off his clothes and discovered the incriminating papers stuffed in the feet of his stockings. Realizing the game was up, Andre then tried to bribe the boys, but they contemptuously dismissed his efforts and took him to the nearest outpost which was North Castle.[232]

The following is General Washington's message (delivered by General Greene) to his troops concerning Arnold's treason and its discovery:

GENERAL ORDERS—Head Quarters, Orangetown, Tuesday, September 26, 1780

Treason of the blackest dye was yesterday discovered! General Arnold who commanded at Westpoint, lost to every sentiment of honor, of public and private obligation, was about to deliver up that important Post into the hands of the enemy. Such an event must have given the American cause

Major Andre's capture was, according to Washington, due to a providential train of circumstances.

a deadly wound if not a fatal stab. Happily the treason has been timely discovered to prevent the fatal misfortune. The Providential train of circumstances which led to it affords the most convincing proof that the liberties of America are the object of Divine Protection.[233]

Following is the official response of Congress to this event:

Journals of Congress Wednesday, October 18, 1780

Congress took into consideration the resolution reported for setting apart a day of thanksgiving and prayer, and agreed to the following draught:

Whereas it hath pleased Almighty God, the Father of all mercies, amidst the vicissitudes and calamities of war, to bestow blessings on the people of these states, which call for their devout and thankful acknowledgments, more especially in the late remarkable interposition of his watchful providence, in rescuing the person of our Commander in Chief and the army from imminent dangers, at the moment when treason was ripened for execution; in prospering the labours of the husbandmen, and causing the earth to yield its increase in plentiful harvests; and above all, in continuing to us the enjoyment of the gospel of peace;

It is, therefore, recommended to the several States to set apart Thursday, the seventh day of December next, to be observed as a day of public thanksgiving and prayer; that all the people may assemble on that day to celebrate the praises of our Divine Benefactor; to confess our unworthiness of the least of his favours, and to offer our fervent supplications to the God of all grace; that it may please him to pardon our heinous transgressions and incline our hearts for the future to keep all his laws; to comfort and relieve our brethren who are any wise afflicted or distressed; to smile upon our husbandry and trade; to direct our publick councils, and lead our forces, by land and sea, to victory; to take our illustrious ally under his special protection, and favor our joint councils and exertions for the establishment of speedy and permanent peace; to cherish all schools and seminaries of education, and to cause the knowledge of Christianity to spread over all the earth.

Done in Congress, the 18th day of October, 1780, and in the fifth year of the independence of the United States of America.[234]

Miraculous Retreat from Cowpens — February 1781

In *The American Covenant* Foster and Swanson relate another event revealing the providence of God:

Led by George Morgan, the Americans defeated Colonel Tarleton's entire detachment at the Battle of the Cowpens, January 17, 1781. Lord Cornwallis, leading the large British army in the south, was infuriated by this defeat. Destroying his heavy baggage, he headed for the Catawba River to cut off the retreat of the small American army.

Cornwallis reached the Catawba River just two hours after General Morgan had crossed. Confident of victory, the British general decided to wait until morning to cross. But during the night a storm filled the river detaining his troops. Twice more in the next ten days Cornwallis nearly overtook the American Army. On February 3, he reached the Yadkin River in North Carolina, just as the Americans were landing on the eastern slopes. But, before he could cross, a sudden flood cut off the British troops again! On February 13, the Americans reached the Dan River that would lead them into friendly Virginia territory. They crossed and a few hours

later, when Cornwallis arrived, rising waters once again stopped him from defeating the American Army. Even Clinton, the commander-in-chief of Lord Cornwallis, acknowledged that Divine Providence had intervened. He wrote: "here the royal army was again stopped by a sudden rise of the waters, which had only just fallen (almost miraculously) to let the enemy over, who could not else have eluded Lord Cornwallis' grasp, so close was he upon their rear."

The significance of the Battle of Cowpens and the safe retreat of the patriots that followed is that our small

General Cornwallis

army in the south was saved by God's providence so that it could harass General Cornwallis and drive him to the sea, which set the stage for the final defeat of the British at Yorktown in October 1781.[235]

The Battle of Yorktown — October 1781

In October of 1781, British General Cornwallis had his troops stationed at Yorktown, Virginia. While Cornwallis waited for reinforcements, Washington marched his troops from New York to Yorktown. Unknown to Washington or Cornwallis, a French fleet under Admiral De Grasse arrived just in time to defeat the British fleet sent to relieve General Cornwallis at Yorktown.

Without reinforcements, Cornwallis was barely holding out against the siege of the American and French forces. As a last resort he decided to attempt a retreat across the York River. At 10 o'clock on the night of October 17th, sixteen large boats were loaded with troops and embarked for Gloucester. After the first few boats had landed a great turn of events occurred. In the official dispatch to his superior, Cornwallis wrote: "But at this critical moment, the weather, from being moderate and calm,

A miraculous weather change stopped the escape of the British troops.

changed to a violent storm of wind and rain, and drove all the boats, some of which had troops on board, down the river."[236] Due to this miraculous weather change, Cornwallis was unable to complete his intended retreat and found his force divided when Washington's batteries opened at daybreak. When the boats finally returned he ordered them to bring back the troops that had passed during the night. Later that day he surrendered his forces to General Washington. This essentially marked the end of the war.

General Washington and our Congress recognized the Providence of God in the battle of Yorktown. The Journals of the Continental Congress record this entry:

> Resolved, that Congress will, at two o'clock this day, go in procession to the Dutch Lutheran Church, and return thanks to Almighty God, for crowning the allied arms of the United States and France, with success, by the surrender of the Earl of Cornwallis.[237]

And in his congratulatory order to the allied army on the day after the surrender, General Washington concluded:

> The General congratulates the army upon the glorious event of yesterday. ... Divine service is to be performed tomorrow in the several brigades and divisions. The commander-in-chief recommends that the troops not on duty should universally attend with that seriousness of

deportment and gratitude of heart which the recognition of such reiterated and astonishing interpositions of Providence demand of us.[238]

The Surrender at Yorktown. In response, Congress went in procession to church "to return thanks to Almighty God, for crowning the allied arms...with success."

Rev. Peter Muhlenberg's statue in the U.S. Capitol Building showing him removing his pulpit gown exposing his officer's uniform. In 1775 Muhlenberg left his church in Virginia and enlisted in the Continental Army. He served throughout the war, eventually becoming a Brigadier General. He was at Yorktown when the British surrendered (pictured above among the mounted officers behind General Washington, who is the central figure on the white horse).

By the HONORABLE

JONATHAN TRUMBULL, Esquire,

Governor of the Englifh Colony of *Connecticut*, in *New-England*, in
AMERICA;

A PROCLAMATION.

*ALTHOUGH we have great Reafon to adore the Divine Goodnefs, for the Plenty, and general
Health, we have enjoyed in the paft Year ; yet we ought, with humble Reverence, to take Notice
of the Frowns of GOD, in vifiting divers Towns and Places, with Sicknefs and Mortality,
efpecially amongft the Children :—And alfo, in ftill holding his Rod of Correction over us,
threatning the Lofs of our Privileges and Liberty ; and confidering that we fee not a fpirit
of Repentance and general Reformation, under his awful Threatnings,—and that all our
Salvation, and the fupply of all our Wants, depend on his Pleafure ;—to whom we are to
feek for all Good.*

HAVE therefore thought fit, by and with the Advice of the Council, to appoint,
and do hereby appoint, *Wednefday*, the *nineteenth* Day of *April* next, to be obferved
as a Day of publick Fafting and Prayer, throughout this Colony, by all Chriftian
Churches and Societies in it ;—hereby exhorting both Minifters and People to humble
themfelves fincerely before GOD,—and mourn for all our Sins, which are the pro-
curing Caufe of all the Tokens of Divine Difpleafure that we are under ;—and deprecate the awful
Judgments we are threatened with, in the lofs of our ineftimable Privileges. Particularly, to
lament that careleffnefs and unteachablenefs of Spirit which appears amongft us ;—that we are no
more awakened, humbled and reformed, when the awful Judgments of GOD are threatened to punifh
us ;—Earneftly to beg the pardon of our Sins,—and that GOD would gracioufly pour out his
HOLY SPIRIT on us, to bring us to a thorough Repentance and effectual Reformation, that our
Iniquities may not be our Ruin :—That He would reftore, preferve and fecure the Liberties of
this, and all the other *Britifh American* Colonies, and make this Land a mountain of Holinefs, and
habitation of Righteoufnefs forever.—That GOD would preferve and confirm the Union of the
Colonies in the purfuit and practice of that Religion and Virtue which will honour Him,—and be
our greateft Honour and Security.

And to offer our fervent Prayers to Almighty GOD for his Bleffing on our rightful Sovereign, King
GEORGE the Third, that He may have the Divine Direction in all his Adminiftrations ; and his
Government be juft, benign, gracious and happy to the Nation, and thefe Colonies :—That He
would blefs our gracious Queen CHARLOTTE, the Prince of WALES, and the reft of the Royal
Family :—That He would blefs, guide and affift the Rulers of this Colony ; give them Wifdom and
Firmnefs, in this dark and difficult Day ; lead them into right Meafures, in all the adminiftrations
of Government, and fucceed them :—Unite the Hearts of the People to live in all Godlinefs and
Honefty ; and preferve all our juft Rights and Liberties :—That He would blefs and fucceed the
Gofpel Miniftry, and make it the Power of GOD to the Salvation of many Souls ; and build up
the Churches in Faith and Holinefs :—Blefs and fmile on the College and means of Education, that
our Children may be trained up in the love of GOD and their Country, and in all ufeful Knowledge ;—and fucceed the Endeavours ufed to civilize and chriftianize the Heathen :—That it would
pleafe GOD to bring forward the fpringing of the Year, and give fuitable Seafons ;—caufe the Earth
to yield its Fruits and Increafe ;—fmile upon the Labours of his People ;—difpofe them to Induftry
and Frugality ;—give them Opportunity quietly to attend their Bufinefs ;—and crown the Year
with his Bleffing ;—caufe Glory to dwell in our Land, and give Peace to Ifrael.

And all fervile Labour is forbidden on faid Day.

*GIVEN under my Hand in Lebanon, the twenty-fecond Day of March, in the fifteenth Year
of the Reign of Our Sovereign Lord GEORGE the Third, by the Grace of GOD of Great-
Britain, France and Ireland, KING, Defender of the Faith, &c. Annoque Domini,* 1775.

Jonath. Trumbull.

GOD fave the KING.

NEW-LONDON : Printed by Timothy Green, *Printer to the* GOVERNOR *and* COMPANY.

Connecticut Governor Jonathan Trumbull's Proclamation for a Day of
Prayer and Fasting, observed April 19, 1775 — the very day fighting began
in the war for American independence.

Chapter 12

The Power Behind the American Republic

While the Battle of Yorktown was the last major battle of the war, a peace treaty between the United States and England was not signed until September 3, 1783. Fighting had stopped, yet the new nation of America still faced many difficulties. A number of the problems that existed were due to weaknesses in the *Articles of Confederation,* which was our national governing document from 1777-1789.

Some of the major weaknesses of the *Articles of Confederation* included:

1. Congress had no power to raise money.
2. Congress had no power to enforce any of its decisions.
3. There was a lack of supreme authority to lead—no executive.

As a consequence of these things, many times during the war, the army lacked supplies and received no pay. This was one reason why the troops suffered so at Valley Forge, and also contributed to members of the military threatening a coup in 1783.

As time went on, it became evident that something must be done to correct the flaws of the *Articles of Confederation.* While many were proposing amending the Articles, some men, such as James Madison, George Washington, and Noah Webster, felt we must draw up a whole new Constitution. When delegates from the various states met in the State House in Philadelphia in the spring of 1787, most of them were expecting to amend the *Articles of Confederation.* However, the Virginia delegates were prepared to propose a new form of government.

The Constitutional Convention — 1787

Thirteen years earlier, on July 4th, men sat in the very same room and put their "lives, fortunes and sacred honor" on the line. The Pennsylvania State House would be renamed "Independence Hall" for that heroic act. Now, however, a different spirit prevailed among those delegates who had arrived in May. When they heard of the thorough reform proposed by Madison and Washington, hesitancy, fear, and doubt surfaced. Many of them believed that half-measures would be far more acceptable in the eyes of the people—any change this complete was sure to fail.

George Washington rose and addressed the Convention in a brief but immortal speech. He agreed that it was "too probable that no plan we propose will be adopted." If so, then he believed that it was entirely possible that they would have to endure another dreadful war. But, he continued, "If, to please the people, we offer what we ourselves disapprove, how can we afterward defend our work?"[239]

The Constitutional Convention. Washington declared "the event is in the hands of God!"

Washington then concluded by urging them to "raise a standard" of the best government they could devise and then trust in this fact: "THE EVENT IS IN THE HANDS OF GOD!"[240] This lofty statement by Washington was crucial during the first ten days of the Convention.

The Framers of the Constitution unabashedly declared that the forming of that document was a miracle of God. Franklin was the least orthodox of them all and yet he wrote:

> Our General Convention...when it formed the new Federal Constitution, [was]...influenced, guided, and governed by that omnipotent and beneficent Ruler in whom all...live, and move, and have their being.[241]

James Madison, the Father of the Constitution, writing to Thomas Jefferson in France just a few weeks after the Convention, said: "It is impossible to conceive the degree of concord which ultimately prevailed, as less than a miracle."[242] And later Madison wrote:

> It is impossible for the man of pious reflection not to perceive in it [the Constitutional Convention] a finger of that Almighty hand.[243]

Perhaps the greatest affirmation of this came from the most influential of all the framers of the Constitution — George Washington. In a letter to his good friend Governor Jonathan Trumbull of Connecticut, he wrote that the "adoption of the proposed General Government"

James Madison

disposed him to be of the opinion "that miracles have not ceased." For, he said, one could "trace the finger of Providence through those dark and mysterious events, which first induced the States to appoint a general Convention and then led them one after another...into an adoption of the system recommended by that general Convention.[244]

On June 28, 1787, the Constitutional Convention was on the verge of complete rupture. For over a month the delegates wrestled with the issue of representation with no breakthroughs, and now patience was wearing thin, emotions were on edge.

A somber George Washington, presiding over this assembly, began to despair of seeing success in the Convention. But the oldest delegate in attendance, Dr. Benjamin Franklin, asked for permission to speak. This was unusual since up to this point, the 81-year-old Pennsylvanian wrote out his remarks and had someone else read them due to his infirmity. But this time he was stirred to rise and address the delegates himself:

The small progress we have made after four or five weeks...with each other...is a melancholy proof of the imperfection of the human understanding. ... In this situation of this Assembly, groping as it were in the dark to find political truth, and scarce able to distinguish it when presented to us, how has it happened, Sir, that we have not hitherto once thought of humbly applying to the Father of lights to illuminate our understandings?

On the brink of rupture, Franklin called the Constitutional Convention to prayer.

In the beginning of the contest with Britain, when we were sensible of danger, we had daily prayers in this room for Divine protection. Our prayers, Sir, were heard and they were graciously answered. All of us who were engaged in the struggle must have observed frequent instances of a superintending Providence in our favor. ... Have we now forgotten this powerful Friend? Or do we imagine we no longer need His assistance?

I have lived, Sir, a long time, and the longer I live, the more convincing proofs I see of this truth: that God governs in the affairs of man. And if a sparrow cannot fall to the ground without his notice, is it probable that an empire can rise without His aid? We have been assured, Sir, in the Sacred Writings that "except the Lord build the house, they labor in vain that build it" [Psalm 127:1]. I firmly believe this, and I also believe that without His concurring aid we shall succeed in this political building no better than the builders of Babel. We shall be divided by our little partial local interests; our projects will be confounded and we ourselves shall become a reproach and bye word down to future ages.

I therefore beg leave to move that, henceforth, prayers imploring the assistance of Heaven and its blessing on our deliberation be held in this assembly every morning...and that one or more of the clergy of this city be requested to officiate in that service.[245]

A delegate from New Jersey, Mr. Dayton, wrote:

The doctor sat down; and never did I behold a countenance at once so dignified and delighted as was that of Washington at the close of the address; nor were the members of the convention generally less affected. The words of the venerable Franklin fell upon our ears with a weight and authority even greater than we may suppose an oracle to have had in the Roman Senate.[246]

Mr. Sherman seconded the motion for prayer, and it was carried with only one negative, but then Mr. Williamson of North Carolina pointed out that they had no funds to pay for a chaplain. This part of Franklin's motion, therefore, failed, but Mr. Randolph then proposed that they obtain clergy who would volunteer their time as much as possible to lead in prayer, and especially "that a sermon be preached, at the request of the convention, on the Fourth of July, the anniversary of Independence."[247]

They apparently were successful in obtaining clergymen to volunteer on some of the mornings, for Mr. Dayton refers to one opening the session on the first day after the three-day recess. Dayton also notes that "every unfriendly feeling had been expelled, and a spirit of conciliation had been cultivated which promised at least a calm and dispassionate reconsideration" of the representation issue.[248]

This speech marked the turning point of the Convention. Breakthroughs followed shortly and within a year the Constitution was ratified by eleven states to establish the first Christian form of government in history.

The nation as a whole distrusted any national centralization of power. The Anti-Federalists emphasized the fallen, carnal nature of man and fought against a national union under the Constitution. The Federalists on the other hand, acknowledging the sinful nature of man, emphasized the importance of Christian character, virtue, and morality in the rulers of a nation that delegated certain limited powers under the Constitution. More wisdom, trust, and love are required when power is granted beyond the state level. In the Constitution's delicate balance between unity and diversity, the nation and the state can only be preserved by virtuous and knowledgeable representatives elected by virtuous and knowledgeable citizens.

The struggle between the Federalists and the Anti-Federalists was intense. Although the Federalist perspective prevailed in the ratification of the Constitution, many of the Anti-Federalist positions were established in the passage of the Bill of Rights. This brought a balance of both Christian perspectives. George Washington wrote:

George Washington

I doubt whether the opposition to the Constitution will not ultimately be productive of more good than evil. … They have given the rights of man a full and fair discussion, and explained them in so clear and forcible a manner, as cannot fail to make a lasting impression.[249]

Within one month of Washington's statement five states ratified the Constitution, and six more followed within six more months. Over fifty clergy from various denominations were prominent in the state ratifying conventions, but they were especially numerous in Massachusetts, North Carolina, and New Hampshire. In Massachusetts, twenty clergy served as delegates in their state convention and one of them urged ratification on the grounds that this "union" was the rock of their national "salvation." The support of these clergymen was crucial, since the Massachusetts convention ratified the Constitution by only nineteen votes (187 to 168). In Connecticut, Rev. William Samuel Johnson preached to his state's convention that the one harmonious system of government that came out of Philadelphia was a sign of God's hand. In South Carolina celebration broke out when the ratification vote was announced to the state delegates. When order was restored the elderly statesman Christopher Gadsden said that he would probably not live long enough to see the happy results, but declared: "I shall say with good old Simeon [when he saw the Christ child brought into the Temple], 'Lord, now lettest Thou Thy servant depart in peace, for mine eyes have seen the salvation of my country.'"[250]

Just prior to the official ratification of the Constitution by the ninth state, New Hampshire, George Washington summed up the whole era by again referring to the hand of God:

Should everything proceed as we anticipate, it will be so much beyond anything we had a right to imagine or expect 18 months ago that it will demonstrate the finger of Providence in human affairs greater than any event in history.[251]

The First Inauguration — 1789

George Washington was unanimously elected (via electors from each of the states as prescribed by the Constitution) as the first President of the new Republic under the newly ratified Constitution. He and the new Congress gathered in New York City in the spring of 1789. On April 30, Washington took the oath of office with his hand on a Bible opened to Deuteronomy 28, which promises blessings or curses on a nation according to its faithfulness to keep God's Word. At the end of the oath he added the words "So help me God"[252] and leaned over and kissed the Bible. Every president since Washington has repeated this same appeal to God. Washington then gave his inaugural address to Congress, and then obeyed

After being sworn in as the first President. Washington leaned over and kissed the Bible.

their own official resolution on April 29th: "After the oath shall be administered to the President…the Speaker and the members of the House of Representatives, will accompany him to St. Paul's Chapel, to hear divine service performed by the chaplains [Rev. Provost]."[253]

Washington acknowledged the providence of God in his Inaugural Address:

> It would be peculiarly improper to omit, in this first official act, my fervent supplications to that Almighty Being who rules over the universe, [and] who presides in the councils of nations. … No people can be bound to acknowledge and adore the Invisible Hand which conducts the affairs of men more than the people of the United States. Every step by which they have advanced to the character of an independent nation seems to have been distinguished by some token of providential agency. … We ought to be no less persuaded that the propitious smiles of Heaven can never be expected on a nation that disregards the eternal rules of order and right which Heaven itself has ordained.[254]

Public acknowledgement and adoration of God was universally affirmed and practiced by every aspect of our government in its early years. Our Founders considered this an indispensable element to the success of our form of government. It was "the Spirit of the Constitution." All three branches of the government, both at the national and state level, emphasized its importance.

Christianity and the Congress

The first Congress under the Constitution proposed a Bill of Rights on September 25, 1789. Foremost of these rights was the freedom of religion in the First Amendment. On that very same day, Congress also passed the Northwest Ordinance which said that, "religious liberty... [is] the basis whereon these republics, their laws and constitutions are erected" and that, being necessary to good government, "religion, morality and knowledge...shall forever be encouraged" through the schools.[255] Also, on that same day, Congress passed a resolution for a National Day of Prayer. The *Journals of Congress* record that:

St. Paul's Chapel, New York, where Congress and Washington worshiped after the first inauguration.

> Mr. Sherman justified the practice of thanksgiving on any signal event, not only as a laudable one in itself, but as warranted by precedents in Holy Writ: for instance, the solemn thanksgiving and rejoicing which took place in the time of Solomon after the building of the temple was a case in point. This example he thought worthy of imitation on the present occasion.[256]

This resolution was unanimously adopted, and President Washington issued a proclamation for the people of the United States to thank "the great Lord and Ruler of Nations" for enabling us "to establish constitutions of government for our safety and happiness, and particularly the national one now lately instituted." He said it is "the duty of all nations to acknowledge the providence of Almighty God, to obey his will, to be grateful for his benefits, and humbly to implore his protection and favor."[257]

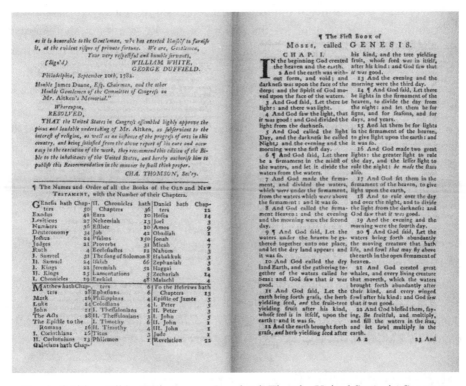

Front of Aitken Bible: "Whereupon, Resolved, That the United States in Congress assembled…recommend this edition of the Bible to the inhabitants of the United States."

Our Congress and Presidents have fulfilled this duty over 200 times in our nation's history under the Constitution. We have seen that the Continental Congress had already established official Days of Fasting and Prayer on the national level beginning in 1775. These proclamations were not bland, "deistic" documents; they were Christian. For example, on November 1, 1777, Congress called for a National Day of Thanksgiving and Prayer for the victory at Saratoga. In this, the people of the United States were urged to ask "Jesus Christ mercifully to forgive and blot out [our sins]" and "to prosper the means of religion for the promotion and enlargement of that Kingdom which consisteth in righteousness, peace, and joy in the Holy Ghost."[258] Three years later on October 18, 1780, Congress called for a Day of Thanksgiving and Prayer for the discovery of Benedict Arnold's plot to commit treason. Again the people were urged to ask God "to cause the knowledge of Christianity to spread over all the earth."[259]

In 1782, Congress acted the role of a Bible society by officially approving the printing and distribution of the "Bible of the Revolution," an American translation prepared by Robert Aitken. The endorsement of Congress in the front of the Aitken Bible read: "Whereupon, Resolved, That the United States in Congress assembled…recommend this edition of the Bible to the inhabitants of the United States."[260]

In the same year that the Constitution was framed, 1787, Congress urged the people to thank God for providing us "the light of Gospel truth" and to ask Him to "raise up from among our youth men eminent for virtue, learning and piety, to His service in the Church and State; to cause virtue and true religion to flourish;…and to fill the world with His glory."[261]

Congress renegotiated and ratified the Treaty with Tripoli in 1805 after deleting the phrase: "The United States of America is not, in any sense, founded on the Christian religion."[262]

In 1854, the House of Representatives passed a Resolution proclaiming that "the great vital element in our system is the belief of our people in the pure doctrines and divine truths of the gospel of Jesus Christ."[263] Even recently, Congress and President Reagan proclaimed 1983 as the "Year of the Bible."

Christianity and the Supreme Court

Both the Congress and the Supreme Court begin with prayer even to this day. A crier proclaims these words each day when the Supreme Court officially opens: "Oyez, Oyez, Oyez,…God save the United States and this honorable court!" Over the head of the Chief Justices is a carved marble relief containing a tablet on which are the Ten Commandments.

The Supreme Court of the state of Maryland recognized Christianity as the established religion in America and the basis of our form of government as early as 1799. In *Runkel v. Winemiller* the court stated that, "By our form of government, the Christian religion is the established religion."[264]

In 1892, in *Church of the Holy Trinity* v. *The United States,* the U.S. Supreme Court declared that:

> These, and many other matters which might be noticed, add a volume of unofficial declarations to the mass of organic utterances that this is a Christian nation.[265]

The Illinois Supreme Court ruled in Richmond v. Moore 1883:

Our laws and our institutions must necessarily be based upon and embody the teachings of the Redeemer of mankind. It is impossible that it should be otherwise. In this sense and to this extent, our civilizations and our institutions are emphatically Christian.

In 1952, the U.S. Supreme Court said, "We are a religious people whose institutions presuppose a Supreme Being" (Zorach v. Clauson). The Court upheld our national motto as constitutional in 1979, and also upheld paid chaplains in the Legislative branch of government in 1983.

"The Bible is the Rock on which our Republic Rests."
President Andrew Jackson, June 8, 1845

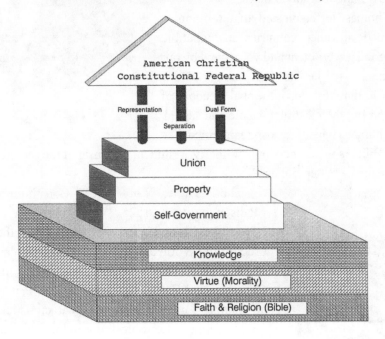

"Religion and morality are the essential pillars of society." - George Washington 1797
"If Virtue and Knowledge are diffused among the People, they will never be enslaved." - Samuel Adams 1779
"...in your faith supply moral excellence, and in your moral excellence, knowledge; and in your knowledge, self-control." - 2 Peter 1:5-6

Our Founding Fathers Emphasized Christian Faith and Morality

"Virtue...Learning...Piety." These words are found throughout our official documents and statements of our Founders. Sometimes they are called "Morality," "Knowledge," and "Religion," such as are found in the Northwest Ordinance. "Religion" meant Christianity. "Morality" meant Christian character. "Knowledge" meant a biblical worldview. These were consistently emphasized by our Founders as the indispensable foundations or supports of our system of government. If they are lost, then our nation will eventually collapse.

John Adams said it best in 1798: "Our Constitution was made only for a moral and religious people. It is wholly inadequate for the government of any other."[266]

Thomas Jefferson said that religion is "deemed in other countries incompatible with good government and yet proved by our experience to be its best support." He believed that "the constitutional freedom of religion [is] the most inalienable and sacred of all human rights." He also maintained that

John Adams

"The Bible is the cornerstone of liberty;...student's perusal of the sacred volume will make us better citizens."[267]

The Father of the Constitution, James Madison, wrote in 1825, "the belief in a God All Powerful wise and good, is...essential to the moral order of the World and to the happiness of man."[268]

George Washington, President of the Constitutional Convention, said in 1783 that "without an humble imitation" of the "characteristics of the Divine Author of our blessed religion...we can never hope to be a happy nation."[269] Later, in his Farewell Address in 1796, he said: "Of all the dispositions and habits which lead to a political prosperity, religion and morality are indispensable supports."[270] He said they

James Madison

"are the essential pillars of society" in 1797.[271]

The Father of the American Revolution, Samuel Adams, said that to change any society the people must "study and practice the exalted virtues of the Christian system. … While the people are virtuous they cannot be subdued; but when once they lose their virtue they will be ready to surrender their liberties to the first external or internal invader. … If virtue and knowledge are diffused among the people, they will never be enslaved. This will be their great Security."[272]

Signer of the Declaration Benjamin Rush wrote in 1806: "Christianity is the only true and perfect religion, and that in proportion as mankind adopt its principles and obeys its precepts, they will be wise and happy."[273]

In 1838 the Legislature of New York stated: "Our Government depends for its being on the virtue of the people, — on that virtue that has its foundation in the morality of the Christian religion; and that religion is the common and prevailing faith of the people."[274]

Benjamin Rush

In a book entitled *American Political Writings During the Founding Era,* Dr. Donald Lutz and Charles Hyneman collected 76 of the most representative pamphlets and essays written by our Founders. In these 76 essays, "virtue" is emphasized as vital over 300 times.

One Nation Under God

Many sincere people have the mistaken belief that our Constitution requires complete neutrality toward religion. Nothing could be further from the truth. Our Constitution establishes us as a nation "under God" in a variety of ways, but especially in Article 6.

Article 6 deals with supremacy. In paragraph one it declares that the national government had supreme responsibility for debts. In paragraph two it declares the Constitution to "be the supreme law of the land," but then in paragraph three it declares God to be supreme over both our laws and our leaders: "all…officers, both of the United States and of the several States, shall be bound by oath" taken, of course, with their hand on a Bible.

The Framers of the Constitution wrote that the "definition of an oath is a solemn appeal to the Supreme Being, for the truth of what is said. In administering an oath, it is only necessary to inquire if the person who is to take it 'believes in a Supreme Being and in the future state of rewards and punishment'…otherwise there would be nothing to bind his conscience on."[275]

Sol Bloom was appointed by Congress in the mid-1930s as the Chairman of the Sesquicentennial Commission of the Constitution. In his authorized book, *The Story of the Constitution,* Bloom asks the question: "Can an atheist become President of the United States?" Then he answers: "I maintain that the spirit of the Constitution forbids it. The Constitution prescribes an oath or affirmation which the President must take in order to qualify for his office. This oath or affirmation in its essence is a covenant with the people which the President pledges himself to keep with the help of Almighty God."[276] Since 1862, the words "so help me God" have also been legally required at the end of the oath.

The Constitution goes even further in its recognition of Christianity and biblical law in Article 1, Section 7, Paragraph 2, where the President has "Sundays excepted" for deciding on legislation. A Senate Committee on the Judiciary commented on this provision in 1853:

French Revolutionary pocket watch. After their revolution, the French leaders started a new calendar with year one from the time of the revolution. They also instituted a ten-day week. This watch has the ten days around the outer edge. These changes were part of removing Christianity from public life. This new calendar lasted only about 12 years, as it was contrary to God's created order.

> In the law, Sunday is a *"dies non;"* it cannot be used for the services of legal process, the return of writs, or other judicial purposes. The executive department, the public establishments, are all closed on Sundays; on that day neither House of Congress sits; … Here is a recognition by law, and by universal usage, not only of a Sabbath, but of the Christian Sabbath, in exclusion of the Jewish or Mahammedan Sabbath; … The recognition of the Christian Sabbath [by the Constitution] is complete and perfect.[277]

The final recognition of Christianity in the Constitution itself is found in the two-fold date employed by our Founders in Article 7: "in the year of our Lord 1787, and of the independence of the United States of America the 12th." Our Founders dated this document in this way to deliberately recognize the two most significant sources of authority to our Constitution: the birth of Christ and the birth of independence. Indeed, Scripture has said that "Where the Spirit of the Lord is, there is liberty" (2 Corinthians 3:17).

Christianity and the States

After declaring independence in 1776, most states began to write new constitutions. By 1780 all but two had done so. Many of these documents not only required an oath of public officials, but also mandated religious tests, which differed in each state according to the denomination that was officially established there. Of the thirteen states, eight had favored one denomination above others, and four had required general affirmations of faith in Protestant Christianity. Only Rhode Island had no religious test whatsoever. A few examples follow.

Delaware's Constitution was non-denominational, yet emphatically Christian:

> Everyone appointed to public office must say, "I do profess faith in God the Father, and in the Lord Jesus Christ his only Son, and in the Holy Ghost, one God and blessed forevermore; and I do acknowledge the Holy Scriptures of the Old and New Testaments to be given by divine inspiration."[278]

New Hampshire's Constitution was typical of the New England establishment of Congregationalism where the legislature was empowered to adopt measures "for the support and maintenance of public Protestant teachers of piety, religion and morality."[279]

South Carolina's Constitution was typical of the establishment of Episcopal churches in the southern states: "The Christian Protestant religion shall be deemed, and is hereby constituted and declared to be, the established religion of the State. ... No person should be eligible to a seat in the Senate unless he be of the Protestant religion."[280]

Most states had Sabbath laws and blasphemy laws. Maryland required of its public officials belief in Christianity until 1864. New Hampshire specifically required that only Protestants hold office until 1902, after which it was switched to any "Christian." These religious tests and established churches were not unconstitutional on the state level. However, a Christian movement toward disestablishment of favored denominations was growing in the states. This led the Framers of the Constitution to write Article 6, which first required an oath, but also prohibited any "religious test" on the national level.

In 1838, the Legislature of New York rejected by a nearly unanimous vote a petition calling for "a repeal of the laws for the observance of the Sabbath." Their report declared that:

> In all countries, some kind of religion or other has existed in all ages. No people on the face of the globe are without a prevailing national religion. Magistrates have sought in many countries to strengthen civil government by an alliance with some particular religion and an intolerant exclusion of all others. But those who have wielded this formidable power have rendered it a rival instead of an auxiliary to the public welfare, — a fetter instead of a protection to the rights of conscience. With us it is wisely ordered that no one religion shall be established by law, but that all persons shall be left free in their choice and in their mode of worship. Still, *this is a Christian nation.* Ninety-nine hundredths, if not a larger proportion, of our whole population, believe in the general doctrines of the Christian religion. Our Government depends for its being on the virtue of the people, — on that virtue that has its foundation in the morality of the Christian religion; and that religion is the common and prevailing faith of the people. There are, it is true, exceptions to this belief; but general laws are not made for excepted cases. There are to be found, here and there, the world over, individuals who entertain opinions hostile to the common sense of mankind on subjects of honesty, humanity, and decency; but it would be a kind of republicanism with which we are not acquainted in this country, which would require the great mass of mankind to yield to and be governed by this few.[281]

The First Amendment

Justice Joseph Story, in his *Commentaries on the Constitution,* wrote that:

> The clause requiring no religious test for office is…designed to cut off every pretence of an alliance between the Church and State in the administration of the National Government. The American people were too well read in the history of other countries, and had suffered too much in their colonial state, not to dread the abuses of authority resulting from

religious bigotry, intolerance, and persecution. … The same policy which introduced into the Constitution the prohibition of any religious test, led to the more extended prohibition of the interference of Congress in religious concerns [i.e. the First Amendment]. We are not to attribute this prohibition of a national religious establishment to an indifference to religion in general, and especially to Christianity which none could hold in more reverence than the framers of the Constitution. … Probably at the time of the adoption of the Constitution and of the Amendments to it, the general, if not universal, sentiment in America was that Christianity ought to receive encouragement from the State, so far as such encouragement was not

incompatible with the private rights of conscience and the freedom of religious worship. An attempt to level all religions, and to make it a matter of state policy to hold all in utter indifference, would have created universal disapprobation, if not universal indignation. … In some of the states, Episcopalians constituted the predominant sect; in others, Presbyterians; in others, Congregationalists; in others, Quakers; … It was impossible that there should not arise perpetual strife and jealousy…if the national government were left free to create a religious establishment. … Thus the whole power over the subject of religion is left exclusive to the state governments.[282]

The First Amendment to the Constitution is misunderstood today, even by the Supreme Court. It begins by stating: "Congress shall make no law respecting an establishment of religion." The only government forbidden of favoring a particular denomination is the U.S. Congress, not the state legislatures.

Thomas Jefferson, who was never a strict separationist, wrote in *the Kentucky Resolutions of 1798* that, "no power over the freedom of religion [is]…delegated to the United States by the Constitution, … all lawful powers respecting the same did of right remain, and were restored, to the States, or to the people."[283] In his 1805 Inaugural Address he said, "In matters of religion I …have left them, as the Constitution found them, under the direction and discipline of the church or state authorities acknowledged by the several religious societies." Again, in a letter in 1808, Jefferson said, "I consider the government of the United States as interdicted by the Constitution from intermeddling with religious institutions, their doctrines, discipline, or exercises. ... It must then rest with the states as far as it can be in any human authority."[284]

Jefferson never promoted the concept of a secular state. While serving in the Virginia House of Burgesses, he personally introduced a resolution for a Day of Fasting and Prayer in 1774. Then while President, he chaired the school board for the District of Columbia and authored its plan of education using the Bible and Watt's Hymnal as reading texts. He also proposed a treaty with the Kaskaskian Indians which included using Federal money to build a church and support a clergyman. When he established the University of Virginia, he encouraged the teaching of religion and set apart space in the Rotunda for chapel services. He also praised the use of the local courthouse in his home town for religious services.[285]

Thomas Jefferson

So our Founders' view of "separation of church and state" was far different from the way it is interpreted by the courts and secularists today. Modern courts have used the Fourteenth Amendment as grounds to declare prayer, Bible-reading, and other such traditions in the states as unconstitutional by saying this amendment caused the First Amendment (and others) to have application to the states. However, the same Congress that passed the Fourteenth Amendment defeated the proposed Blaine Amendment and numerous other attempts to apply the First Amendment to the states. The Blaine Amendment (1876) read: "No **state** shall make any law respecting the establishment of religion."

What the people of the United States have never done by due constitutional means, an activist liberal Supreme Court has done unconstitutionally. No matter how much the secularists may want to remove the influence of Christianity from public life, no matter how heterogeneous or diverse we become, they have no real constitutional grounds for demanding the banishment of Christianity until an amendment is passed to that effect. The First Amendment does not guarantee freedom from religion and a secular state, but freedom of religion and a truly non-denominational Christian state. It guaranteed that the "Spirit of the Constitution" would be forever free to flourish as the foundation of our republic.

Harvey Cox, of Harvard University, has pointed out that secularism is a religion and a very intolerant one at that. It does not concede that any other religious perspective can be promoted in public, and it calls upon the government to enforce its beliefs. "Pluralism" today, although a Christian idea originally, now claims to protect the freedom of all religions, but this is a farce. There is one religion which does not have free exercise—Christianity.

In 1952 Justice William O. Douglas wrote for the Supreme Court that "we find no constitutional requirement...for government to be hostile to religion and to throw its weight against efforts to widen the effective scope of religious influence."[286]

In 1984 the Supreme Court made a surprising statement in *Lynch* v. *Donnelly:*

> The Constitution [does not] require complete separation of church and state; it affirmatively mandates accommodation, not mere tolerance, of all religions, and forbids hostility toward any. ... Anything less would require the 'callous indifference' we have said was never intended by the Establishment Clause. ... Indeed, we have observed such hostility would bring us into 'war with our national tradition as embodied in the First Amendment's guarantee of the free exercise of religion.'"[287]

Chief Justice John Marshall (Justice from 1801-35) stated:

> The American population is entirely Christian, & with us, Christianity & Religion are identified. It would be strange, indeed, if with such a people, our institutions did not presuppose Christianity, & did not often refer to it, & exhibit relations with it.[288]

The Christian religion, Christian virtue, and a biblical worldview are the "Spirit of the Constitution" — the power behind our form of government.

John Marshall

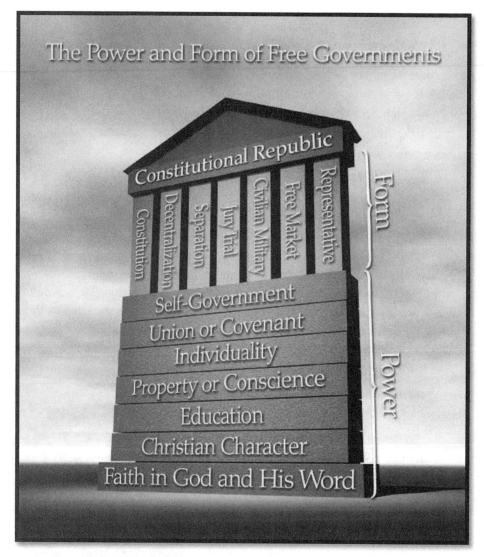

The Power and Form of the American Christian Constitutional Federal Republic.

Chapter 13

The Christian Form of Our Government

What makes America a Christian nation? Many Christians erroneously believe it depends on whether or not our Founders were Christians. Others believe it depends on if a vast majority of Americans are Christians. The problem with these criteria is when one or more of our Founders are found not to be Christians, does that negate the rest? Who determines the arbitrary percentage of a population that must be Christian to qualify? 100%? 51%? What about when our Christian Founding Fathers came short of God's glory and sinned against the Native Americans or in other ways? Does the fallibility of Christians in a Christian nation negate the claim? Of course not. Even as an individual Christian fails morally now and then, he still can claim the name of Christ without reservation. Modern "Christian" books such as *In Search of Christian America* have made these fundamental mistakes in how one determines a Christian nation.

A Christian nation is determined by its **form** of government, not **who** formed it. If the form of a nation's government is shaped by biblical ideas of man and government, in contrast to pagan or man centered ideas, then the nation is a Christian nation. (Remember, a Christian form of government flows from Christian ideas. Hence, a Christian nation is one founded upon biblical ideas, which will be reflected in its form of government.)

In 1867 *The North American Review* declared that "the American government and Constitution is the...political expression of Christian ideas."[289] Our Founders were universally convinced of this truth. Even unbelievers such as Benjamin Franklin often publicly cited Scripture. In the Constitutional Convention Franklin said:

We have been assured, Sir, in the Sacred Writings that "except the Lord build the house, they labor in vain that build it" [Psalm 127:1]. I firmly believe this, and I also believe that without His concurring aid we shall succeed in this political building no better than the builders of Babel [Gen. 11].[290]

At the convention Franklin declared, "God governs in the affairs of men."

The ideas embodied in our Constitution stem primarily from the Bible. Our Founders reasoned from the Bible far more than any other source. Almost all Americans understood this until modern revisionist historians began to promote the view that rationalistic enlightenment thinkers were the major influence behind the Constitution. How can we know for sure?

Dr. Donald Lutz, a professor of political science from the University of Houston, conducted an exhaustive ten-year research of about 15,000 political documents of the Founders' Era (1760-1805) and recorded every quote or reference to another written source. This list of the 3,154 citations of the Founders was analyzed and published in Volume #78 of the *American Political Science Review* in 1984. The results give an accurate measure of the influence of various sources of thought on the Constitution and are surprisingly contradictory to "modern scholarship." By far, the most often quoted source of their political ideas was the Bible. This accounts for over one-third (34%) of all their citations. The next most quoted source is not even cited one-fourth as frequently (Montesquieu—8.3%, Blackstone—7.9%; and both of these men have a Christian view of law). Another 50% of all references can be attributed to authors who themselves derived their ideas from the Bible. Therefore, it can be said that 84% of the ideas in our Constitution are based either directly or indirectly on the Bible.[291]

The Bible and civil liberty are inseparable. Even *Newsweek,* on December 26, 1982, acknowledged after a major analysis of the Bible's influence in America that, "Now historians are discovering that the Bible, perhaps even more than the Constitution is our Founding document."[292] Honest historians are beginning to recognize that Franklin's references to "the Sacred Writings" and to "the builders of Babel" in the Convention's search for "political truth" were not an aberration.

The Christian Constitution

The Preamble to the Constitution provides evidence that the U.S. Constitution is the product of Christianity and its ideas of man and government. In the Preamble is found a summary of the purpose of civil government. These five basic functions are revealed in Scripture as legitimate.

The **first** purpose of civil government presented in the Preamble is **"to establish justice."** The Bible says in 1 Peter 2:14 that civil rulers exist "for the punishment of evildoers and the praise of those who do right." In Genesis 9:6, God told Noah that "Whoever sheds man's blood, by man his blood shall be shed." This is justice.

The **second** purpose of civil government is **"to insure domestic tranquility."** This is found in Scripture in 1 Timothy 2:1-2 where Paul urges Christians to pray for civil rulers "in order that we may lead a tranquil and quiet life in all godliness and dignity."

A Scripture verse is engraved on the Liberty Bell: "Proclaim Liberty throughout all the land, unto all the inhabitants thereof. Lev. XXV X"

Third, government is **"to provide for the common defense."** The protection of innocent human life is at the base of not only capital punishment and a domestic police force, but also in this third provision of an army for protection from external threats. Romans 13:4 affirms that civil government "does not bear the sword for nothing." The "sword" in Scripture is equivalent to any military weapon used today, even nuclear weapons. The only thing that would make any weapons "immoral" is if there is not a sufficient amount to bring "wrath upon one who practices evil." If external threats have a huge arsenal of nuclear weapons, there must be at least equal amounts to deter aggression upon innocent human beings. Even Jesus Christ taught His disciples the legitimacy of being armed militarily, saying in Luke 22:36, "Now...let him who has no sword sell his robe and buy one."

Fourth, government should **"promote the general welfare."** Romans 13:4 says civil rulers are servants "to you for good." The common good of all classes of citizens must be promoted by governmental laws guaranteeing equal opportunity. Notice, our Framers' choice of words here: promote, not provide. Scripture makes it clear that God is the provider, not the state, and that needy individuals are to be cared for by private acts of charity done voluntarily. A biblical free-enterprise system will promote compassionate use of wealth, but socialism (and other forms of statism) is contrary to biblical definitions of civil government, as it seeks to provide for the people material things by using force to take from the productive and give to others.

Lastly, civil government exists to **"secure the blessings of liberty."** *Blessings* are a gift of one's Creator, not a privilege granted by government. The most basic of these Creator-endowed blessings are listed in the Fifth Amendment of the Constitution and include "life, liberty, [and]…private property." Scripture declares God as the source of life in Genesis 1:27: "And God created man in His own image." He is the author of liberty as well: 2 Corinthians 3:17 says, "Where the Spirit of the Lord is, there is liberty;" and Leviticus 25:10 says, "Proclaim liberty throughout the land to all its inhabitants." Scripture also presents God as the source of private property and "the pursuit of happiness" (as expressed in the Declaration of Independence): Ecclesiastes 5:19 states, "For every man to whom God has given riches and wealth, He has also empowered him to eat from them…and rejoice in his labor; this is the gift of God;" and in 1 Chronicles 29:12, "Both riches and honor come from Thee."

Contrary to the belief of a majority of Americans today, public education is **not** guaranteed in the Constitution. Our Founders knew that the Bible does not teach this is a function of civil government.

Structures Based on Christian Presuppositions in the Constitution

Our Founders, while not all born-again Christians, firmly believed in the biblical ideas of man and government. They believed that man's sinful nature meant that he should not be entrusted with too much power, even if he was regenerated through the blood of Jesus Christ.

A nation's form of government depends greatly upon a people's view of the nature of man. James Madison wrote in the *Federalist* No. 51, "What is government itself, but the greatest of all reflections on human nature?"[293] One's view of human nature profoundly affects one's view of government.

Pagan governments, which are not based on the belief that men are sinners, establish too much centralized power in the hands of men. This has always resulted in oppression and tyranny at the expense of individual liberty. There are really only two types of national union—pagan and Christian. Pagan union is held together by external force and intimidation. Christian union, in contrast, is held together by internal unity of purpose and principles. Christian union always protects diversity and individuality.

When our Founders declared independence from England, they were well aware that great oppression was possible not only when power is concentrated in a monarchy but also in the hands of an elite. Parliament was a national legislature with supreme authority. When our Founders drafted the *Articles of Confederation* in 1777, a National Congress was established but with very little power. The Confederation placed supreme authority in the thirteen state legislatures. The Continental Congress was merely a committee of the thirteen sovereign states and its "president" was simply a chairman elected annually. Our Founders wanted to keep power decentralized.

Federalism

The problem with a confederation or confederacy, however, is that it is too weak or inefficient to maintain a strong nation. It required voluntary, unanimous consent of all 13 states in order to make every decision. By 1787 the delegates in the Philadelphia convention realized that there needed to be a change. They achieved this in the establishment of a form of national union that is unique in the world today—Federalism.

Federalism is the principle that most powers should be decentralized among state and local governments, but that a few defined powers are delegated to a national government. James Madison described a federation when he said: "The powers delegated by the...Constitution to the federal government are few and defined. Those which are to remain in the State governments are numerous and indefinite."[294]

James Madison, the chief architect of the Constitution, received much of his training from Rev. John Witherspoon.

Jefferson said that "the way to have good and safe government is not to trust it all to one, but to divide it among the many."[295]

The Constitution does not make the states merely administrative arms of the national government. It establishes, in effect, a dual form of government—both the national government and the state governments having supreme authority over their defined areas of jurisdiction. This means that every American citizen has two law-making bodies to which he must submit. He must obey federal laws as well as state laws equally. But what if one conflicts with the other? The answer is they do not and never will (if they both act according to the Constitution), because they make laws dealing with completely different areas of life. The national government can only make laws dealing with such items as the regulation of interstate and foreign commerce, coining money, the postal services, copyrights, citizenship laws, and the armed forces. The state governments can only make laws dealing with such things as public education, voting procedures, marriage and divorce, corporations and traffic. Neither can interfere in the area of the other without being unconstitutional and thus subject to indictment. Each sovereign government is held in check from encroaching on the other by the higher law of the Constitution, declared supreme in Article 6, paragraph 2.

The Constitution establishes only 18 powers for the national government in Article 1, Section 8. Then it declares these powers off-limits to the states in Section 10. But then it reserves every other undefined power to the states in the 10th Amendment:

> The powers not delegated to the United States by the Constitution, nor prohibited by it to the states, are reserved to the states respectively, or to the people.

These 18 powers delegated to the national government were permanently surrendered. They could not be altered except by amendment to the Constitution. This makes the federation a permanent union, unlike the uncertainty of a confederation. The Civil War was precipitated by the secession of the "Confederate" states from the Union. Our Founders established a permanent union of states by a national covenant—the Constitution. The Latin word for covenant is *foedus* (from which we get our word *federal*). The bottom line of any covenant, whether in marriage or in church or in civil government, is that there should be no divorce. All problems and conflicts must therefore be patiently discussed and debated until they are resolved. This requires Christian character and virtue in order to work.

The idea of an unbreakable union was rooted in the federal theology of the colonial churches. A sermon by Ezra Stiles in 1760 entitled *Christian Union* was one of the most widely published and distributed pamphlets of the Founders' Era.

The idea of an unbreakable covenant was not the only idea the Founding Fathers borrowed from the churches. They also borrowed the idea of dual sovereignty. Federalism means dual government. The only model in history to which our founders could refer was in the primitive churches of the first century. No civil government in history had ever attempted such a scheme, but in the New Testament church our founders saw evidence of dual government to which every Christian was submitted. Each local church was governed by its local presbytery of elders (1 Timothy 3:1-5, 4:14, 5:17). Yet there was a measure of authority exercised by apostles and prophets in the mother church at Jerusalem that was also binding on the church at large (Acts 15:2, 6; 16:4). These dual governments were also operating in the denominational arrangements of the Colonial churches. A Presbyterian in Virginia was loyal to his local church leadership, but also to the Presbyterian denominational leadership at large. Separatist leader Rev. John Robinson, pastor of the Pilgrims, emphasized loyalty to the local congregation (or the principle of self-government). Puritan clergyman William Ames emphasized loyalty to the Church of England at large (or the principle of union). They debated their points equally well and many of the colonial churches achieved a balance of both.

One of the delegates in the Constitutional Convention was James Wilson of Pennsylvania, who later was named as a justice of the first Supreme Court. He said that a free republic is best symbolized by a pyramid with a majority of powers decentralized among the people and only a few granted to the national government.[296] (This is why our founders put a pyramid on our national seal, which can be found on the dollar bill.) This is federalism, based on the Christian doctrine of the sin nature of man.

The pyramid on the national seal represents a republic.

Separation of Powers

Fearing centralization, our Founders, after they had apportioned most of the powers of government to the states, went even further, due to their mistrust of sinful men, and separated the few and limited powers of the national government into three branches that would check each other. James Madison wrote that, "The

Montesquieu

accumulation of all powers, legislative, executive, and judiciary, in the same hands whether of one, a few, or many … may justly be pronounced the very definition of tyranny."[297] Furthermore, he wrote in the *Federalist* No. 47 that "the three great departments of power should be separate and distinct. The oracle who is always consulted and cited on this subject is the celebrated Montesquieu."[298]

Montesquieu and our Founders separated the powers of government into these three divisions because that is how the Bible defined God's government of the universe in Isaiah 33:22 — "For the Lord is our judge [Chief Justice], the Lord is our lawgiver [Legislature], the Lord is our King [Chief Executive]; He will save us." Since God is perfect and infallible, He can possess all three powers and still be just and fair, but sinful men cannot.

Just as federalism was an idea rooted in church government, so also is the concept of the three branches of government. The Protestant Reformation produced three distinct movements of Christians who emphasized three different forms of church government. The Episcopalians emphasized the rule of one from the top down. The Presbyterians emphasized the rule of a few elders. Congregationalists emphasized the rule of many. By the design of Providence, each of these groups colonized America and formed their colonial civil governments in patterns similar to their churches. The northern colonies, settled predominantly by Congregationalists, established a form of democracy. The southern colonies, being mostly Episcopalian, established "Royal Provinces" which were a form of monarchy. The middle colonies were proprietary, and being influenced greatly by Reformed Presbyterianism established more aristocratic governments.

God allowed these isolated geographical groupings to experience the strengths and weaknesses of their particular form of government for more than one century before bringing them all together through the American Revolution. When delegates arrived in Philadelphia in 1787, they were experienced experts on all three forms and blended them together beautifully. They decided, in the words of James Madison, that "the essential qualities of a monarchy—unity of council, vigor, secrecy...—will enable the President to execute the laws with energy and dispatch."[299] They established an unelected Supreme Court and U.S. Senate in order to give "to this part of the system all the advantages of an aristocracy—wisdom, experience, and a consistency of measures."[300] Finally, elements of democracy were established in the House of Representatives which would be elected directly by the people every two years (these three elements are also seen on the state level in governors, judges and state legislators).

Our federal government — specifically the first three Articles of the Constitution — is therefore a reflection of church government. The Episcopalian form of church government is not the biblical model found in the New Testament, neither is the Presbyterian or Congregational. A blending of all three is what makes a balanced biblical Christian church government. Such is the case in civil government as well. If our founders had all been Congregationalists, our Constitution would probably have established more of a pure democracy in America. But that alone would not be the biblical model of civil government. God providentially shaped the colonization of America in such a way that democracy, aristocracy, and monarchy would be blended together into a balanced Christian Republic — the first in history.

Representative government is also an aspect of our Constitution that is biblical. It will be dealt with in Chapter 18.

The Declaration of Independence and the Constitution were clearly founded upon Christian ideas of man and government. Our Founders were the first men to "hold these truths" and establish a nation upon them. Without Christianity, there never would have been a Constitution. As Noah Webster, the father of the dictionary and a key Federalist in the passage of the Constitution, said:

> The religion which has introduced civil liberty, is the religion of Christ and his apostles, which enjoins humility, piety, and benevolence; which acknowledges in every person a brother, or a sister, and a citizen with equal rights. This is genuine Christianity, and to this we owe our free constitutions of government.[301]

Noah Webster

Ministers in early America taught a comprehensive worldview using regular Sunday sermons as well as special sermons, including Election Sermons (top left), Execution Sermons (top center), and Artillery Sermons (top right). Sermons not only addressed personal matters, but all spheres of life as seen in the sermons above: Left: "Moral View of Railroads," Middle: "A Discourse Occasioned by the Earthquake," Right: "A Sermon Containing Reflections on the Solar Eclipse."

Chapter 14

Principles of Christian Economics

Much of the material in this chapter was adapted from an article on "The Principle Approach to American Christian Economics" by Charles Hull Wolfe in the book *A Guide to American Christian Education for the Home and School, the Principle Approach* by James B. Rose. After much study on Christian economics, we found Mr. Wolfe's approach to be the most clear, complete, and easily understood. We are deeply indebted to him to allow us to borrow so freely of his ideas.

Defining Christian Economics

Since economics is the science that deals with production, distribution, and consumption of goods and services, Christian Economics is the "discipline that studies the application of Biblical principles or laws to the production, distribution, and consumption of goods and services." It entails "how men use God-given natural resources, ideas, and energy to meet their human needs and glorify Him."[302]

A Christian Economy will Flow from the Heart of Man Outward

Christianity produces internal liberty in man, which is the foundation for a Christian economy. The internal change of heart that Christ brings produces Christian character and self-government which is necessary for an economy to be prosperous. Christian character and self-government produce:

- People who will not steal. Billions of dollars are lost each year by American businesses to theft by their employees. This theft is much greater than that by non-employees.
- People with a strong work ethic who will labor hard and be productive. This will cause an economy to grow.
- People who will save and invest to acquire greater return later.
- People who have concern for their posterity and will seek to pass on a greater estate than they received.

The truth of the gospel also imparts new ideas and creativity to man which assists him in increasing his material welfare. This occurs as man creates new and better tools. In addition, man gains the understanding that God has given him an abundance to rule the earth, and if he seeks His supply he will find it.

Besides bringing internal liberty to man, the introduction of Christianity in a nation will also manifest itself externally in political freedom. A government acting on biblical principles is needed for a Christian economy. As Verna Hall stated, "government is the house in which the economy lives." Its policies must promote and protect economic freedom.

Economic freedom will then flow from personal and governmental freedom. Charles Wolfe states that this freedom includes "a people's freedom to own their own property...to choose their own occupation...to keep the fruits of their labors...to buy and sell in a free market, where wages and prices are determined not by government mandate but by voluntary exchanges of free men and women."[303]

Factors of Production in a Society

Stated in a simple manner, man's material welfare is a product of natural resources mixed with human energy and coupled with the use of tools. Mr. Wolfe represents this by the following formula:

$$\text{N.R.} \quad + \quad \text{H.E.} \quad x \quad \text{T.} \quad = \quad \text{M.M.W.}$$

Natural Resources + Human Energy x Tools = Man's Material Welfare

If natural resources increase, so does man's material welfare. If human energy is exerted, man's material welfare increases. If better tools are created, man's material welfare will also increase.

This equation for man's material welfare is applicable for every nation in the world, yet there is a great difference in how men in a Christian society view the world and apply their physical and mental energies as compared to those men in a secular society. We will examine the factors of production in both a Christian and secular society.

In a Christian Society with Great Economic Freedom

Natural Resources

God created man and knew that he would have certain basic needs, such as food, clothing, and shelter. God created everything that was needed to meet those needs. One, God created natural resources. Those men with a Christian worldview believe that God has provided all that they need and, consequently, they have faith to seek, find, and process abundant natural resources. As the natural resources available to man increase, his material welfare increases as well.

Human Energy

God not only created natural resources, but He also created man with human energy. God told him to "have dominion" or rule over the earth (Genesis 1:26). Man was placed in the garden to cultivate and keep it (Genesis 2:15), which required labor. After the fall, cultivating the ground required an additional "sweat of [man's] face" (Gen. 3:19).

In a Christian society, men will be inspired by God to work. In addition, in a nation of economic freedom, men will be able to partake of the fruit of their labors which will encourage them to exert more energy. As man works harder and exerts more human energy, his material welfare (and that of the nation) will increase.

Tools

From the beginning, man was unable to cultivate the ground and rule over the earth, or even meet his basic needs well, with his bare hands alone. Mr. Wolfe writes that "to take the natural resources God [had] created and turn them into…food, clothing, and shelter" to meet man's needs, tools were needed to help him "till the soil, to cut down trees and saw timber, to mine and refine minerals, and to tend sheep and weave wool."[304] Knowing this, God gave man "ideas for inventing and making tools." Man was given "intelligence and physical strength," that is "mental and muscular energy," to take the natural resources and create tools to meet his needs.[305]

Man has used tools from the beginning. Adam and Cain were farmers and likely used simple tools (possibly a digging stick or simple plow) and some kind of sickle or cutting tool to harvest grain. Abel was a shepherd and likely had a rod and staff.

The Bible has many references to tools. Wolfe states these include "hammers, axes,...plows drawn by oxen, millstones for grinding meal,...furnaces for refining silver and gold, ovens, and baking and frying pans."[306]

Wolfe writes: "The usefulness of each tool is measured by the amount of time and energy it saves; by the increase in the quantity and (or) quality of the goods and services that can be produced through its use."[307] The following chart reveals how advancements in agricultural tools have produced economic progress:[308]

Time Period	Tool	Production by One Man
Adam	Simple tools	Probably enough food for Eve and himself
Abraham	Wooden plow drawn by oxen	Food for large family
18th Century	Horse drawn iron plow	Food for 3 families
1940's	Tractor	Food for 14 families
Today	Advanced tractors & tools	Food for 60 families

Development of better tools has primarily occurred in nations where people have had access to the truth of the Bible (and hence the mind of Christ) which has enabled them to receive many ideas for inventing new and better tools. As we have seen, these advancements in tools have caused man's material welfare to improve.

We should remember that man's productivity is a result, not only of better, but also of better use of those tools. That is why we must be diligent in our work.

God has given man all he needs for his human welfare—natural resources, human energy, and ideas for creating tools—but man must labor to take what God has given and transform it into the food, clothing, shelter, and other things that meet his human needs. Labor is the title deed to property.

In a Secular Society with Limited Economic Freedom

The factors of production in the equation, N.R. + H.E. x T. = M.M.W., are viewed differently in a secular society by those with a non-Christian worldview than those in a Christian society.

Natural Resources

A secular society will lack faith in God's providence and, consequently, men will find fewer natural resources. The secularist or socialist has a limited resource mentality and views the world as a pie (there is only so much) that needs to be cut up so that everyone can get a piece. In contrast, the Christian knows that the potential in God is unlimited and that there is no shortage of resources in God's earth. The resources are waiting to be tapped.

We do not live in a resource short world. God created renewable resources, through photosynthesis and reproduction.

We do not live in a resource-short world. Known reserves of minerals and energy resources are greater today than in 1950 despite increasing consumption. Ideas allowing us to tap into unused natural resources are limitless. For example, 150 years ago the American Indians wiped oil on their faces. Today, new uses of that natural resource have transformed our economy and brought a higher standard of living for everyone. In recent years, the computer world has been revolutionized by the silicon chip, which is made from the same material as sand.

While many secularists view the world as over-populated, Christians know that God has made the earth sufficiently large, with plenty of resources to accommodate all the people He knew would come into existence. There is plenty of room and food for the entire world population today. All the nearly eight billion people on the earth could live in the states of Texas and New Mexico in single family homes with front and back yards and be fed by production in the rest of the United States. Present world agricultural areas, if developed by present technology, could feed 31 billion people. Our earth has plenty of room and plenty of natural resources.

Human Energy

Those with a secular worldview will lack a God-inspired strength and work ethic. Such strength and character would cause them to be more productive through hard labor, honesty, investment in the future, etc. In addition, the lack of incentives of freedom found in secular nations with limited economic freedom cause men to exert less energy since they cannot eat of the fruit of their labor. The net result is that man's material welfare suffers.

Tools

Secularists are cut off from the Bible and the mind of Christ (the chief source of creativity), and so they get fewer ideas for inventing new and better tools. Lack of new and better tools keeps production and man's material welfare from increasing.

Comparing the factors of production in Christian and secular societies reveals why some countries prosper and some do not. Mr. Wolfe writes: "While men and women in every country try to multiply their human energies with the help of tools in order to transform natural resources into useful goods and services, Christian free societies generally do it more efficiently than others."[309]

A study by Dr. Browning of incomes of different nations and people groups confirms this observation. He found that "between protestant and catholic groups it was noted consistently that the protestant countries had higher per capita income than the catholic countries. But those that were not Christian had no income or low incomes or were starving to death."[310]

There are a few exceptions to this finding. The most notable is the nation of Japan. However, the reason that Japan has prospered is that "they have simply imitated the principles and techniques on which America's original prosperity was built"[311] — principles that grew out of our Christian society (and which have in part been abandoned today).

As Mr. Wolfe reveals, the Japanese have imitated our Puritan work ethic, Yankee ingenuity, the idea that "a penny saved is a penny earned," individual responsibility for quality of work, giving workers a voice in the decision making process of businesses, and encouraging workers and managers to come together in a kind of voluntary union.

While application of these principles have caused the material welfare of the Japanese to increase greatly, this increase has come at the expense of greater life and liberty in other areas. Material welfare is not the only aspect of a Christian economy. The pressure to succeed is so great upon many Japanese youth today that many are not holding up under the stress. Many are also "sold out" to their jobs and work so much they have no time for anything else.

In a Christian economy people will earn more with less work which means:

- People will have more free time for worship of God, instruction, recreation, and service to others.
- People will have more money to give to churches, charities, and foreign missionary efforts.
- People can acquire more luxuries.

The Real Wealth of a Nation

While America has in recent years abandoned some of the principles that produced our prosperity, we are still the most prosperous nation in the world. Wolfe writes that "the best way to compare the real wealth of the people of one country with the wealth of the people of another is how many hours of work it takes a factory worker to earn the money needed to buy the same basic commodities in retail stores in that country."[312]

To purchase a kilogram of bread, a factory worker must work 18 minutes in Moscow, 12 minutes in London, and 8 minutes in Washington. To purchase a car (Volga, Ford), that work time is 35 months in Moscow, 8.5 months in London, and 4.1 months in Washington.[313]

If you visit the Philippines, you will find that clothes are on-third to one-quarter the price of those in the United States. While this may be of benefit to the American traveler, this price reflects a much greater percentage of the average Filipino income than Americans spend on clothes. An American worker's average income is about 10 times that of the average worker in Manila. So the average Filipino spends more of his income on clothes and food than the average American, even though these items are less expensive in Manila than the United States. Filipinos spend much more on other items because appliances, cars, and other things not made in the Philippines, cost more than they do in the States.

Why Are Some Nations in Poverty?

As we have seen, the equation, N.R. + H.E. x T. = M.M.W., applies to every country in the world. Those societies built on Christian principles will have a proper view of natural resources, the character to exert human energy, and access to the creativity of God leading to better tools, all of which cause man's material welfare to increase. While any nation adhering to this truth will see the material welfare of its citizens increase, most people and nations are quite poor. In fact, 46% of the world lives in poverty today. Why? Some claim that it is because many nations lack natural resources. Yet, some nations, such as Japan, with few natural resources are quite prosperous. There are also many nations with abundant natural resources that are much less prosperous than other nations with fewer natural resources.

The primary reason that nations are in poverty is lack of spiritual resources and truth. A secularist worldview keeps each element of the factors of production from increasing, which stifles man's material welfare. India is a good example of how a people's religion directly affects its economic prosperity. Today, India has widespread hunger problems, yet these are not due to a lack of food, but are a result of the people's religious beliefs. The majority of Indians are Hindus. The Hindu religion teaches that people who die are reincarnated as animals; therefore, their laws and religion prohibit the people from killing rats, mice, cows, or other animals.

There are 200 million "sacred cows" in India. Each cow eats enough food to feed seven people. So the grain consumed by these cows would feed 1.4 billion people, which is about one-fifth the world's population. The mice and rats, which they will not kill, eat much of their grain as well. This grain, not to mention the meat from the cows, would supply plenty of food for all the starving people of India.[314]The economic state of a nation depends upon its religion.

Profit Motive

We have seen that man's material welfare increases in a Christian society because Christian faith and character help "enlarge, vitalize, and improve" the three factors of production. Moreover, as Charles Wolfe writes:

> The economic incentives of freedom are also important. To find and process natural resources such as oil and minerals is extremely costly. So is the protracted process of researching, developing and producing new and more efficient power tools. The profit motive provides individuals

with the needed incentive in a Christian free economy based on individual enterprise.

History shows that in a Christian free economy…men tend to invent more and better tools, invest more in producing those tools, and use those tools more efficiently than in a secular society with limited economic freedom.[315]

In the latter part of the 20th century, prominent communist nations found the only way they could survive economically was to allow some individual enterprise, which was contrary to their communistic economic principles. They discovered the profit motive caused people to be much more productive. Two such nations were Russia and China.

Russia began to allow "each farming family 2-3 acres of ground to operate privately and sell its produce in the local market. These tiny private farm plots produce[d] more meat, vegetables and fruit than all of the huge government farms combined."[316]

Communal farming with no individual incentive does not even work with Christians who have common vision, goals, and purposes. The Pilgrims gave us

In 1623, when the Pilgrims instituted an individual farming system, much more corn was planted than in the previous two years. However, a drought threatened all their crops. In response, Governor Bradford wrote, "they set apart a solemn day of humiliation, to seek the Lord by humble and fervent prayer… And He was pleased to give them a gracious and speedy answer."

this example in their first two years in America. Compelled by the contract with their financial backers, the Pilgrims farmed the land communally. The lack of incentive to work resulted in such a poor crop that the Pilgrims almost starved during the first two winters. To alleviate this problem, the leaders shifted to an individual enterprise system where every family farmed their own parcel of land, and ate the fruit of their own labor. Governor Bradford wrote that "this had very good success; for it made all hands very industrious. ... The women now went willingly into the field, and took their little ones with them to set corn, which before would allege weakness, and inability; whom to have compelled would have been thought great tyranny and oppression."[317] They produced an abundant crop and never lacked for food again. Their example shows that "the taking away of property, and bringing in community into a common wealth,"[318] does not make people happy or cause them to flourish, as many ancients, such as Plato, or modern men, such as Marx, have espoused.

The Wheel of Progress in a Christian Economy

The diagram of the "Wheel of Progress in a Christian Economy," as given by Charles Wolfe, is an excellent depiction of the necessary elements of a growing and prospering economy. We will look at the individual parts of the wheel.

Lawful Enterprise (A Christian Constitutional Form of Government)

The Hub of God-Given Liberty

We saw earlier how a Christian economy revolves around or flows out of the heart of man — from the internal liberty that Christ brings. This God-given liberty, which begins internally but is manifested externally, is the hub of the wheel of progress in a Christian economy.

It is important to recognize that this liberty or freedom is granted by God and not by man or the state. Mr. Wolfe writes that "if the hub of the wheel is seen as freedom granted by man or the state, rather than by God Himself, then that freedom can readily be taken away, in whole or in part, and there is no reliable basis for a continuing, consistent free economy."[319]

The hub, seen as God-given liberty, has a reliable core "to which the various spokes — the Biblical principles of economics — can be securely attached." In fact, only a hub of God-given liberty can give rise to the various spokes, for it is only in an economy of liberty that men are allowed to practice individual enterprise, economic self-government, and manifest each aspect of the spokes.[320]

Rim of Stewardship and Law

The spokes in the wheel of progress in a Christian economy will be held together, and the wheel will run smoothly, by the discipline of God's law and the practice of Christian stewardship. These make up a rim of responsibility which keep economic freedom under God's control.

In an economy, as in all society, the great challenge is not merely to maintain freedom, but to maintain freedom with order. To do this, people must be disciplined from within so they do not infringe upon the rights of others. Therefore, men must understand and obey God's law in order to have a Christian economy, for as they do, the following will result:

- Men will respect each other's property.

  In many nations today, people must have a half dozen locks on their cars, and walls, fences, and guards protecting their houses and businesses to keep other citizens from stealing their property. Growth of the economy will be hindered greatly in this environment.

- They will not steal or cheat one another.

  A recent visitor to the United States from Latin America was amazed at many things he witnessed in this country. One thing that he especially took note of were newspaper stands. He marveled that people would put in a quarter and take only one newspaper. He said that this would never happen in his country, because the first person to get there in the morning would put in his quarter, take all the newspapers, and go and sell them on the street. This is a small example of how dishonesty hinders economic freedom. We mentioned before how businesses lose more money by theft from their employees than outside forces. For a nation's economy to grow, the people must be honest.

- They will abide by contracts.
- When citizens are elected or appointed to positions in government, they will not use their power to secretly erode the value of the people's money through inflation, nor will they gradually restrict the people's economic freedom through excessive regulation.

A Christian businessman in a developing country needed to get some raw materials through customs so that he could fill large orders for various customers. Before these materials could be released he needed to get 46 different signatures of government officials. Most of these officials wanted a bribe before they gave their signature, and when the businessman refused, there was such a delay in getting his materials released that he was unable to fill his orders in time, and he lost hundreds of thousands of dollars. Excessive regulation and dishonesty stifle economic growth.

To maintain economic freedom, individuals must also practice Christian stewardship. Wolfe says that they must:

- Be industrious in earning money
- Be disciplined in saving money
- Be wise in investing money
- Be obedient to God's law in how they share it with their church and with those in need
- Practice "the self-denial necessary to restrain themselves from buying many things that would bring immediate gratification, in order to save and invest enough to provide for emergencies and their later years, without having to turn to government for assistance."[321]

In other words, people must work all they can, earn all they can, save all they can, and give all they can.

The Title Deed to Property Is Labor

John Locke writes:

> Though the Earth, and all inferior Creatures be common to all Men, yet every Man has a Property in his own Person: This no Body has any right to but himself. The Labour of his Body, and the Work of his Hands, we may say, are properly his. Whatsoever then he removes out of the State that Nature hath provided, and left in it, he hath mixed his Labour with, and joyned to it something that is his own, and thereby makes it his Property. It being by him removed from the Common State Nature hath placed it in, it hath by this Labour something annexed to it, that excludes the common Right of other Men.[322]

John Locke

All property you possess was acquired by labor, either your labor or someone else's. You take possession or title to property in proportion to your labor or individual enterprise. This is not only true of external property but also internal property. Rosalie Slater writes:

> We might use the example of learning of a subject in school as an illustration of this principle which Locke is setting forth. God has given the knowledge contained in this subject to all of us—you might say it's our common possession. Yet no one actually has title to it—can prove that he owns it. If any student makes the effort to learn the subject—he acquires title to what he learns. This effort on his part hasn't in the least diminished the amount of the subject which we all still have in common. It's still there. But the student who made the effort to learn the subject does have a title to something which no one can take from him and which he would not have had if he had not added or invested his own effort. He has property rights in the subject.[323]

The Measure of Property

If through labor people acquire more property, what is to be the measure of how much one accumulates? John Locke tells us that the measure of property is not how much one wants, but how much one needs — that is what is sufficient for an individual to fulfill God's will in his life.

The Title to Internal Property Is Obtained by Consent.

Miss Slater explains this idea well:

> Just as the Christian values the talents which God has placed in trust with him, and just as he works for their productive fruition in our Lord's service, so he carefully guards the use and disposal of his property. Today much concern is expressed about "property rights" and the infringement upon individual or private enterprise. But the first invasion of property rights occurs internally when the individual consents to the disposal or use or misuse of his opinions, his religious convictions, and his faculties. Often this consent is tacit consent. John Locke differentiated between express consent and tacit consent. The word tacit means:
>
> Tacit: "Silent; implied, but not expressed. Tacit consent is consent by silence, or by making no objection.
>
> "So we say, a tacit agreement or covenant of men to live under a particular government, when no objection or opposition is made; a tacit surrender of a part of our natural rights."
>
> Thus the surrender of an individual or a nation can occur by *silence,* or by making *no objection.* Christianity, unlike any other religion, requires an *active confession* of faith, an *active acceptance* of Jesus Christ as Lord and Saviour. So a Christian also must refuse, through whatever duly constituted means are at his disposal, to permit his rights of conscience, his convictions, or, indeed, his very faculties, and talents, to be used contrary to what he knows to be good and true, and in accord with the laws of God. *Consent* is one's title to the property of conscience. And as John Locke reminds us only *express consent* makes one a "member of any Commonwealth." So only *express refusal* to have one's property used for purposes which do not support righteous government can make one truly faithful to the stewardship of conscience.[324]

The Spokes

1. Individual Enterprise

The idea of individual enterprise follows from God's Principle of Individuality. Every person on earth is distinct, unique, and important in an economic sense. It follows that:

- Each person has "special God-given talents as a producer." This leads to specialization and division of labor (which leads to greater wealth in a nation).

- Each person has "individual desires as a customer."
- Each person has "individual rights, such as the right to enter an occupation of one's choice" (which promotes greater productivity), "the right to start one's own business, and the right to buy the goods one prefers."
- Each person has "individual economic responsibilities." Each citizen should provide for themselves and their family rather than rely upon the civil government to meet their needs. They should also voluntarily help the poor and those with genuine need. According to the Bible, providing for the poor is the responsibility of individuals and the church. The state has assumed this responsibility in the United States as the church and individuals gave it up.[325]

Caring for the Poor

Welfare states are not biblical and do not work. America in recent decades has shown this to be true. While government money spent on welfare has increased dramatically, the nation's poverty has not declined. Today, only 30 cents of each welfare dollar actually goes to meet the need of the poor. The other 70 cents is consumed by the governmental bureaucracy. Since President Johnson announced his war on poverty in the 1960's, America has spent trillions of dollars on the fight, yet poverty is at about the same level as at the beginning of the huge expenditures. Government money is not the solution to poverty. Compare the following figures:

- In 1950, 1 in 12 Americans lived below the poverty line.
- In 1951, government spent about $4 billion on social welfare programs.
- In 1979, 1 in 9 Americans lived below the poverty line.
- In 1981, government spent $316.6 billion on social welfare programs.[326]

The Bible says that the family and church are the primary institutions of health, education, and welfare. As we reassume our responsibilities, we can eliminate the need for the civil government to spend trillions of dollars on welfare.

Individual enterprise opposes economic collectivism and its emphasis upon the group and forced common production. Individual enterprise applies the Bible principle, "as you sow, so shall you also reap," which encourages productivity.

2. Economic Self-Government (Free Enterprise)

An individual who governs himself will direct and control his own economic affairs in a responsible manner. He will be:

- "A self-governed producer"—"not needing constant supervision...to assure the quality and quantity of his work."
- "A self-governed customer"—"buying only what he needs and never spending in excess of his income."
- "A self-governed saver"—"regularly saving some of his earnings to assure a strong economic future."
- "A self-governed manufacturer or retailer"—"producing and selling quality goods and services, with due concern for the rights and needs of employees and customers."[327]

A nation of self-governed people will cause the economy to grow and remain free.

3. Christian Character (Honest Enterprise)

We have already seen how Christian character is the foundation for a free and prosperous society. A few specific character qualities that effect the economy of a nation include:

- Diligence and industry—hard work increases productivity which brings about increased prosperity.
- Faith in God's Providence—hard work alone does not guarantee prosperity; we must also trust and obey the Lord to experience His blessings (Matthew 6:33; Deuteronomy 28). Individuals and the nation must put their faith in God to experience His blessings.
- Love for our neighbor—as we express Christian love, we will care for the needy in the land.
- Honesty—honest employees will not steal from their employers; an honest civil government will not steal from its citizens by use of fiat money.

Honest Money

A biblical economy will have an honest money system. Leviticus 19:35-37 states:

> You shall do no wrong in judgment, in measurement of weight, or capacity. You shall have just balances, just weights, a just ephah, and a

just hin: I am the Lord your God, who brought you out from the land of Egypt. You shall thus observe all My statutes, and all My ordinances, and do them: I am the Lord.

Money is a commodity. It is something of genuine value in the marketplace, whether cattle, coconuts, shells, silver or gold—all of which have been used as money. Historically, exchange began with barter. Money makes exchange much easier, because people can trade their goods for money and use the money to buy other things they want. In the Bible money was silver or gold, a precious metal. This is money based on principle.

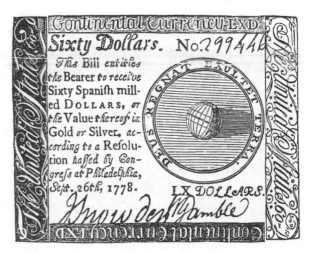

"Paper money initially is not money. It is a substitute for money, and is useful because it is difficult to fold coins into a wallet. But if paper money is honest, it will always be backed by a specific amount of real, 'hard' money and redeemable at any time."[328]

The worthlessness of "Continental Money" motivated our founders to establish a currency consisting of the precious metals.

America was on a gold standard throughout most of her history. In 1933 we shifted to a silver standard. In 1968 our silver certificates were replaced with Federal Reserve Notes, thus eliminating honest money from our nation. When we had honest money there was never any prolonged inflation in this nation. Today's paper money is not backed by anything except the government's promise that it is good. Compared to a 1932 dollar, the dollar today is worth less than 5 cents. It is interesting to note that an ounce of gold today will purchase about the same amount of goods that an ounce of gold bought 90 years ago.

Money with no precious metal backing, *fiat* money (money by *decree* of the government), allows the central government to spend more than it collects in taxes, because the FED (Federal Reserve Board) can print new "money" (increase the money supply) anytime there is a need. This is inflationary.

Inflation

Greg Anthony writes that "one of the Biblical signs of a nation backsliding is the condition of its currency and the degree of honesty in its weights and measures. When nations began backsliding in history, dross (common-based metal) began to appear in their coinage."[329] In rebuking Israel from turning from God, Isaiah points out how "your silver has become dross" (Isa. 1:22).

To many people today, inflation means an increase in prices. This, however, is simply the symptom of the national government increasing the money supply to pay for their budget deficits. When the money supply is increased, either through printing more money or credit-expansion, the purchasing power of each dollar falls, and businesses must increase the prices they charge to keep up with their own higher costs.

Anthony says, "the only one to benefit from inflation is the first one to spend money (i.e. the government). It is a hidden form of tyrannical taxation because as the government spends more and more money created from thin air, the purchasing power of the citizen's bank account goes down and down. Inflation is theft! Remember the Bible declares, 'thou shalt not steal' (Ex. 20:15). If a private citizen decides to set up a printing press and make some money, he is called a criminal (counterfeiting); if the government does the same thing it is called 'monetizing the debt' or 'stimulating the economy.' What is the difference?"[330]

Inflation discourages savings by promoting a "spend now" attitude. It encourages debt, deceives people about pay increases and future wealth accumulations, and decreases capital available for investment. It is a hidden theft tax.

To get rid of inflation we should abolish the central bank (Federal Reserve), repeal all tender laws, and return to a gold warehouse receipt standard. In addition, we must also end fractional reserve banking.

Basics of Banking

Banks were places for the safe keeping of money. People who used this service paid a fee for it. Gradually, banks began to act not only as warehouses to store money, but as intermediaries between savers who were willing to lend, and others who wanted to borrow. Banks could only loan out what they had in reserve. If a bank was lending your money for you, you could not get it back until the borrower repaid it. You earned interest for your investment.

Today, American banks, international banks, and most banks in other nations have a fractional reserve banking system. Banks only need to keep a small percentage of "cash" in their vaults (around 10%), and can loan the rest. This is inflationary because "money" is created through the loaning process.[331]

4. Private Property (Private Enterprise)

A person's property is whatever he has exclusive right to possess and control. Property is first internal. A person's conscience is his most precious aspect of property because it tells him what is right and wrong in his actions. Each person in a free government must be a good steward of his conscience and keep it clear. By doing so, he will know what is right and wrong from within and, therefore, he will be able to live his life in a right manner.

How one takes care of his internal property will determine how he takes care of his external property. The following chart reveals various aspects of internal and external property:

Internal Property	External Property
Thoughts	Land / Estate
Opinions	Money
Talents	Freedom of Speech
Conscience	Freedom of Assembly
Ideas	Bodily Health
Mind	Possessions
Affections	Freedom of Worship

Governments exist to protect property of every sort, most importantly, liberty of conscience. Tyrannical governments will usually invade rights of conscience before invading external property rights. The power that can invade liberty of conscience can also usurp civil liberty. Internal property rights must, therefore, be guarded at all costs, for as they are diminished, every inalienable right of man is jeopardized.

Private property rights are a basic necessity for any society that desires to be free and prosperous. Noah Webster wrote:

The liberty of the press, trial by jury, the Habeas Corpus writ, even Magna Charta itself, though justly deemed the palladia of freedom, are all inferior considerations, when compared with a general distribution of real property among every class of people. ... Let the people have property and they will have power—a power that will forever be exerted to prevent a restriction of the press, and abolition of trial by jury, or the abridgement of any other privilege. The liberties of America, therefore, and her forms of government, stand on the broadest basis.[332]

Noah Webster

A Christian nation will "let the people have property" and hence power.

The famous British political scientist, John Locke, wrote in his treatise *Of Civil Government:*

> For Men being all the Workmanship of one Omnipotent, and infinitely wise Maker: All the Servants of one Sovereign Master, sent into the World by His Order, and about His Business, they are His Property, whose Workmanship they are, made to last during His, not one anothers Pleasure.[333]

Locke goes on to state that while we are God's property, God has given us the responsibility to be good stewards over our persons. He wrote that "every Man has a Property in his own Person."[334] It follows we have a God-given right to everything necessary to preserve our persons, to internal and external property.

Before any property can be taken from us, we must give our consent. If our property can be taken without our consent, then we really have no property. This is why any taxes imposed by a government on its citizens must be done by elected representatives. We give our consent to taxes or laws affecting our property rights through our representatives. If they do not represent our views, we should work to replace them in a lawful manner.

A people standing on the principle of property will take action to prohibit government or other citizens from taking anyone's personal property without their consent, or from violating anyone's conscience and rights. Lack of this principle in the lives of citizens will lead to unjust taxation, a government controlled economy, and usurpation of both internal and external property rights.

5. Local Business (Local Enterprise)

Economic growth occurs as small businesses (that may grow into large businesses) are started locally by responsible individuals who have prepared themselves — people who do not depend on someone else to employ them, but who save their money, get an idea for serving others, become self-employed, win customers, and then employ others. This is how new jobs are created. This is how our economy grows.

Christian education will produce such knowledgeable and motivated individuals in our nation. These people will not look to the government to create jobs but will be entrepreneurs and assume that responsibility themselves.

6. Voluntary Union (Free Market)

A voluntary working together of all peoples and regions of a nation will encourage economic growth. This would prohibit any tariff barriers within a nation and create a nationwide "common market." This would allow each person in each region or district of a nation to do what he could do best (and working with the natural resources in his locality), and exchange it for the production of others, using honest money as the medium of exchange. Each person is free to sell or not to sell at whatever price they want to offer, but they cannot force anyone to buy. Exchange of goods and services is voluntary and will occur as all involved believe they benefit from the exchange.

The prices of goods and services will be determined by "supply and demand." In a free market the supply of goods and services will balance out the demand for those goods and services at a price buyers are willing to buy and sellers are willing to sell. The greater the supply of any particular kind of good or service, the more the price will tend to go down. The greater the demand for any kind of good or service, the more the price will tend to go up.

The free market is based upon the idea that men are to be free under God to pursue their calling and provide for themselves and their families.

The Road Bed: A Christian Constitutional Form of Government (Constitutional/Lawful Enterprise)

A civil government built on biblical principles provides the road on which the wheel of economic progress can turn with great efficiency. Such a government, rooted in the Law and the Gospel and based on the Christian idea of man and government, will assist economic progress by providing an environment of freedom with order in which production and exchange can flourish, protecting private property, punishing theft and fraud, and not providing for the people's economic needs.

Such a government will be "limited in its functions and cost — to have just enough power to guard the citizen's rights, but not the power to interfere with honest economic activities."[335]

The Constitution and Money

Most of the powers of Congress, according to the Constitution, deal either with money or the military. Our Constitution declared in Article 1, Section 8, Paragraph 1 that all taxation would "be uniform throughout the United States," yet today we have a graduated income tax system, not uniform at all. Those who labor more diligently so as to earn more money are penalized by a higher tax bracket. Congress was given power to borrow money, but our Founders believed it should be as sparingly as possible. Jefferson said: "We shall all consider ourselves unauthorized to saddle posterity with our debts, and morally bound to pay them ourselves."[336] Deficit spending and graduated taxation were virtually unheard of until the passage of the 16th Amendment establishing a federal income tax in 1913. Income taxes began to be automatically withheld from wages by employers in 1943. Over the years our taxes have grown dramatically, where the total tax rate today averages over 40% of each individual's income.

Congress refuses to balance its budget as a routine practice — it has only balanced the budget a few times in the last 60 years. How do they get away with what state governments must do according to their law, what private businesses must do to exist, and what individuals must do to stay out of jail? The answer is that they just print or create more money!

The Constitution says in Article 1, Section 8, paragraph 5 that only Congress has power "to coin money." This means that they are not allowed to print paper money. James Madison records in his notes of the Constitutional Convention that originally the delegates considered allowing the Congress to "emit bills of credit" (or paper money), but the phrase was struck out in order, according to Delegate Elseworth, "to shut and bar the door against paper money."[337] Section 10, Paragraph 1 of the Constitution states that only "gold and silver coin" would be legal "tender in payment of debts." Andrew Jackson said: "It is apparent from the whole context of the Constitution as well as the history of the time which gave birth to it, that it was the purpose of the Convention to establish a currency consisting of the precious metals."[338]

Andrew Jackson

For about 80 years we had just that. But during the emergency of the Civil War, we began using paper money and never stopped. At least it was redeemable in gold or silver upon demand until 1933 when Franklin Delano Roosevelt used economic "emergency" powers to abolish the gold standard. Then in 1968 the silver standard was suspended, and our currency became completely unredeemable — merely *fiat* money. Now every time Congress wishes to pay off some of its excessive spending, instead of facing the public with higher taxes, it simply orders more money to be printed (or created as blips on computer screens) and then borrows it. When this happens everyone's money is automatically devalued in its purchasing power. It is a hidden tax, a form of theft.

Taxation

Jesus' admonition to "Render unto Caesar the things that are Caesar's and unto God the things that are God's" underscores our duty to pay taxes. Civil governments need money to accomplish their responsibilities of providing defense, punishing evildoers, and keeping the peace. Gary DeMar writes:

In the United States the Constitution is our "Caesar." We are bound to pay what it stipulates is our due. But, neither citizens nor civil representatives must assume that Jesus gave rulers a blank check in the area of taxation. ... Paul informs citizens to pay taxes due to civil authorities (Romans 13:7). Notice that Paul does not say "What they want." The state must limit taxing authority to those areas specified by God's word. For the most part, our original Federal Constitution (prior to the 1913 passage of the 16th Amendment) has been faithful to the biblical mandate of limited taxation for a specific limited function. ... The tax limiting effects of the Constitution (Article I, Section 8), seemingly were nullified with the passage of the 16th Amendment in 1913. This amendment effectively gave the Federal Government unlimited taxing power.[339]

This amendment also gave us the progressive income tax, which is a nonbiblical means of taxation that destroys personal property rights. These oppressive forms of taxation have come upon our nation as we have refused to govern and provide for ourselves as God intended. When Israel stopped wanting to be self-governed and asked for a king to rule over them, they got a king with greater centralization of power. One consequence of this was the confiscation of their property through taxes (see 1 Samuel 8).

Types of Taxes

1. **Income tax**—"Another word for taxes is tribute. If God requires only 10% (tithe), to give civil government more would indicate the giving of greater allegiance. This is idolatry."[340]

2. **Property tax**—"Civil government in the United States, in direct violation of biblical law, owns all the land in the country, and rents some of it to its citizens. If you do not pay the property tax (rent), you will be evicted. This is theft. The government has no right whatsoever to tax property, and the principle of eminent domain is a claim to deity. It is specifically forbidden in Scripture (I Sam. 8:14; I Kings 21; Ezek. 46:18)."[341]

3. **Inheritance taxes**—"Nowhere does the Bible allow the fruit of a man's labor to be taken from him after he dies and before his children receive it. This is one way that the kingdom is continued and built. Godly children should not have to start at the bottom when they begin. This increases the wealth in the kingdom of God."[342]

In a Christian economy the children will be wealthier than their parents because the estate will continue to grow and be built up with each generation.

Biblical Taxes

The Bible mentions two kinds of taxes:

1. **Head Tax or Poll Tax (Ex. 30:11-16)**—This tax supported the state in its duties. It was a uniform tax that each male aged 20 and over paid. It was of necessity small so the poor would not be oppressed in paying it.

2. **Tithe**—A tenth of each person's increase was given to the priests and Levites for them to meet the necessary ecclesiastical and social functions of society. It supports the church and aspects of welfare, education, and other godly social needs. We could say the tithe is a "tax" on people's income. If citizens would tithe, the amount of money the civil government would need to collect would be drastically less.[343]

Hugo Grotius (1583-1645) was a Dutch lawyer, theologian, statesman, and poet who wrote *The Rights of War and Peace* in 1625. James Madison called him "the father of the modern code of nations." He, along with the German thinkers Pufendorf and Vattel, developed the concept of a God-given "Law of Nations" that is mentioned in Article 1, Section 8 of the Constitution.

Chapter 15

Christian Principles of Foreign Affairs

Freedom and Peace through Strength

The history of Israel, and myriads of other countries, reveals that a nation can only have liberty and peace through strength. America's founders agreed. They recognized that a free and prosperous society will face continual threats from outside forces who are no friends of liberty. Consequently, to secure their liberty and peace, the United States Constitution empowered the Congress to "provide for the common Defense [and] promote the general Welfare...[of] the United States."

Consider the following quotes of some of the founders of America:

George Washington

"There is a rank due to the United States among nations, which will be withheld, if not absolutely lost, by the reputation of weakness. If we desire to avoid insult, we must be able to repel it; if we desire peace...it must be known that we are at all times ready for war."

"To be prepared for war is one of the most effectual means of preserving peace."[344]

General Washington

Benjamin Franklin

"Let us...beware of being lulled into a dangerous security...of neglect in military exercises and discipline, and in providing stores of arms and munitions of war to be ready on occasion; for all these are circumstances that give confidence to enemies, and diffidence to friends; and the expenses required to prevent a war are much lighter than those that will, if not prevented, be absolutely necessary to maintain it."

"There is much truth in the Italian saying, 'make yourselves sheep and the wolves will eat you.'"[345]

Benjamin Franklin

Thomas Jefferson

"Whatever enables us to go to war, secures our peace."[346]

A Christian Foreign Policy

A Christian nation should relate to foreign nations in much the same way a Christian should relate to an unbeliever. We are to be peacemakers, mercy-givers, teachers, and defenders of the helpless and the oppressed. We should not try to impose our will upon other nations, but we should sow the truth within the heart of the people in a nation, knowing that this internal change will affect the public affairs of a nation.

Washington's Farewell Address

George Washington set forth some basic principles of a proper foreign policy in his 1796 *Farewell Address*. Three general principles follow.

1. Cultivate peace with all nations and maintain impartiality

Washington wrote:

> Observe good faith and justice towards all nations; cultivate peace and harmony with all. Religion and morality enjoin this conduct. ... It will be worthy of a free, enlightened, and...great nation to give to mankind the...novel example of a people always guided by an exalted justice and benevolence...

Harmony, liberal intercourse with all nations, are recommended by policy, humanity, and interest...

In the execution of such a plan nothing is more essential than that permanent, inveterate antipathies against particular nations, and passionate attachments for others, should be excluded; and that, in place of them, just and amicable feelings towards all should be cultivated. The nation, which indulges towards another an habitual hatred or an habitual fondness, is in some degree a slave. It is a slave to its animosity or to its affection, either of which is sufficient to lead it astray from its duty and its interest. Antipathy in one nation against another disposes each more readily to offer insult and injury, to lay hold of slight causes of umbrage, and to be haughty and intractable, when accidental or trifling occasions of dispute occur. Hence, frequent collisions, obstinate, envenomed and bloody contests. The nation prompted by ill will and resentment sometimes impels to war the government, contrary to the best calculations of policy. The government sometimes participates in the national propensity, and adopts through passion what reason would reject; at other times,

Washington stressed impartiality in relating to other nations.

it makes the animosity of the nation subservient to projects of hostility instigated by pride, ambition, and other sinister and pernicious motives. The peace often, sometimes perhaps the liberty, of nations has been the victim.

So, likewise, a passionate attachment of one nation for another produces a variety of evils. Sympathy for the favorite nation, facilitating the illusion of an imaginary common interest, in cases where no real common interest exists, and infusing into one the enmities of the other, betrays the former into a participation in the quarrels and wars of the latter without adequate inducement or justification. It leads, also, to concessions to the favorite nation of privileges denied to others, which is apt doubly to injure the nation making the concessions; by unnecessarily parting with what ought to have been retained; and by exciting jealousy, ill will, and a disposition to retaliate in the parties from whom equal privileges are withheld.[347]

2. With trading, keep political connections to a minimum

The great rule of conduct for us, in regard to foreign nations, is, in extending our commercial relations, to have with them as little political connections as possible. … But, even our commercial policy should hold an equal and impartial hand; neither seeking nor granting exclusive favors or preferences; consulting the natural course of things… constantly keeping in view, that it is folly in one nation to look for disinterested favors from another; that it must pay with a portion of its independence for whatever it may accept under that character.[348]

It should be left entirely to the private sector to decide who to trade with, not the government. However, if our national security is threatened, trade can and should be limited. In addition, it is the role of government to assure that the market is both free and fair, and hence government has a role in this regards.

3. No long-term entangling alliances

It is our true policy to steer clear of permanent alliances with any portion of the foreign world…taking care always to keep ourselves by suitable establishments, on a respectable defensive posture, we may safely trust to temporary alliances for extraordinary emergencies.[349]

Gary North defines these "permanent alliances" that Washington warned against as "the creation of international treaties that would bind together the United States and other nations to perform certain military actions under specified future circumstances."[350] The U.S. did not enter into such a treaty until well into the twentieth century.

The main points were summarized by Jefferson in his First Inaugural Address: "Peace, commerce, and honest friendship with all nations, entangling alliances with none."[351]

America's impartiality toward all nations and her non-engagement in long-term entangling alliances would allow her to be an example to other nations and in this way positively affect them. If we treat nations equally, and not act as the policemen of the world, then they will more readily seek our advice and judgment, allowing us to sow Christian truth within them.

Thomas Jefferson

The Monroe Doctrine

America's foreign policy was further defined by James Monroe in 1823. In a message delivered to Congress on December 2, Monroe stated:

James Monroe

The American continents, by the free and independent condition which they have assumed and maintain, are henceforth not to be considered as subjects for future colonization by any European powers.... The political system of the allied powers is essentially different...from that of America. ... We owe it, therefore, to candor and to the amicable relations existing between the United States and those powers to declare that we should consider any attempt...to extend their system to any portion of this hemisphere as dangerous to our peace and safety. With the existing colonies or dependencies of any European power we have not interfered and shall not interfere. But with the governments who have declared their independence...we could not view any interposition for the purpose of oppressing them...by any European power in any other light than as the manifestation of an unfriendly disposition toward the United States.[352]

Intervention Should Be Based on Just Principles

The cause of those nations which seek intervention by us should be based on just principles (on the Christian idea of man and government). We must realize that no nation perfectly adheres to these principles, but that should be the desire.

Therefore, the basis for one nation becoming involved in the affairs of another nation includes: 1) Legitimate officials ask for help. 2) A nation's own security is threatened by action in another. 3) Their cause is based on just principles. If it is determined that it is legitimate to give assistance, then the type of aid must be decided, whether money, goods, weapons, troops, etc.

Perversion of Our Foreign Policy in the Twentieth Century

In the first part of America's history, we largely maintained a foreign policy based on the above principles. However, during the second half of the 20th century we began to act on other ideas. Formerly, we were generally respected in the eyes of the whole world. More recently, since we have compromised these principles, we are found supporting oppressive regimes and have lost much respect.

Congress wisely rejected Woodrow Wilson's treaty setting up a League of Nations in 1919, but capitulated to the U.N. Charter after World War II. We thus entered into a long-term entangling alliance that George Washington warned against.

The President of the United States is not only our Commander-in-Chief, but also our Chief Diplomat. He establishes foreign policy and proposes treaties, but they must be approved by the Senate. However, in 1945 Franklin D. Roosevelt negotiated a secret treaty at Yalta with Churchill and Stalin that was never submitted to Congress. In it we consented to allow the Soviet Union to take control of Eastern Europe and enslave millions of people under the yoke of communism.

The Law of Nations

Nations cannot do whatever they want to, even if their law permits it. Everyone is subject to the higher law of God, and as a Christian nation we must not allow other nations to violate our God-given rights.

The United States Constitution gives Congress the right "to declare war" and "to define and punish Piracies and Felonies committed on the high Seas, and Offences against the Law of Nations." John Eidsmoe writes:

> The United States established war tribunals to bring foreign officials to trial for atrocities committed in violation of the Law of Nations or international law, based on this clause of the Constitution. The fact that such officials could be held to a higher standard of conduct and that simple "obedience to orders" was not considered an absolute defense to charges of violating international law, indicates further recognition that the laws of man are subject to the law of God.[353]

A Christian nation will be an exporter of Christian ideas.

Marshall Foster writes of how the United States as a Christian nation should relate to other nations:

> As we repair our nation and put it in order, we shall then be in a position to do what we were meant to do originally—to "colonize ideas,"

specifically, the Christian idea of man and government so that it does not stop on these shores, but goes on to cover the globe. Our historians used to believe that it was part of our mission to colonize America's unique political ideas, but as we have forgotten what our Founding Fathers achieved—forgotten the source of our freedom and affluence—we have failed to do this.

This does not mean that we can export our structure and system of government to other countries and expect it to make sense to them without an understanding of the Christian principles of self-government that underlie the structure. We have learned that self-government begins first with the individual aligning himself with the will of God, then caring for himself and others and applying biblical principles to all areas of his life until he produces a civil government that reflects his godly self-government. All merely external forms of democratic structure which we may attempt to promote in other lands are doomed to failure and will inevitably bring cries of "American imperialism" or cries of an attempt to exercise external control over other nations.

Attempts to throw money at the acute problems in Africa and Latin America, when there is little understanding of Christian self-government in these lands, is a tragic waste of resources. If a fraction of the resources now spent on military hardware was spent on colonizing the ideas of our Founders, a proper foundation would be laid for the development of liberty and self-government in these lands.

The communists know the values of ideas and have for years been colonizing theirs which lead only to chaos and bondage. On the other hand, our political ideas, under the Providence of God, have achieved more civil and religious liberty and more self-government and genuine prosperity than the world has ever known before.[354]

Missionaries and Christian businessmen should be the ambassadors of Christian nations.

In his article on "Can We Make a Deal for Peace?" Lee Grady writes:

To the humanist, peace is really pacifism. My dictionary accurately defines pacifism as "opposition to war or to the use of military force for any purpose; an attitude of mind opposing all war and advocating settlement of international disputes entirely by arbitration." I agree with Dean London of New York University: people majoring in the current "Peace studies" programs in U.S. colleges should be called pacifism majors. No professor in any of these universities is offering any way to achieve peace according to the true definition.

Gary North, in *Healer of the Nations,* powerfully refutes this notion by reminding us of the history of U.S. foreign policy. When the Department of State was created in 1789 by President Washington, the staff consisted of six persons. In 1870, slightly less than 100 years later, the entire personnel consisted of only 53 persons—in spite of the great expansion of our borders and growth in population. By 1909 it grew to 202 persons, and rapid expansion ensued after the World Wars. By 1980, the figure had climbed to 23,497. This included over 3,500 Foreign Service Officers, the elite corps of specialists who staff our embassies and consulates.

How, you may ask, could the U.S. function as a world power with such a tiny State Department for so many years of its history? Who was conducting the summits? Who was drawing up the treaties and doing all the research? Who was hammering out the peace plans?

Answer: No one. The United States had made one treaty with France in 1778, which it abrogated in 1800. We made absolutely no entangling alliances with any nations during the 19th century. Dexter Perkins, a specialist in U.S. foreign policy, writes in his *History of the Monroe Doctrine* that "nothing is more characteristic of American diplomacy than its general aversion to contractual agreements." On the contrary, nothing could be more characteristic of our present foreign policy than our infatuation over contractual agreements, as well as summits, treaties, alliances, pacts, and deals between world powers. We also have a recent fixation over meddling in disagreements between other nations.

Gary North writes: "This centralization came at the expense of private activities and responsibilities. In the field of international relations, no one before this era had perceived a need for the United States government to send official representatives to every nation or to seek alliances, agreements, and arrangements with every nation. People assumed that private interests would be the basis of the vast bulk of international relations."

This is the heart of the problem in foreign policy, according to Dr. North. "Voters in the West have passively turned over the conduct of foreign policy to professional diplomats." Now, you may ask: If professional diplomats aren't supposed to be conducting foreign policy, then who is? That brings us to Dr. North's most important theme in his book.

Practically, foreign policy in this Christian world order will be conducted by missionaries and members of the Christian business and trade community who know how to represent the cause of Christ abroad. Their business as ambassadors of Christ is not to work out terms of compromise; it is to persuade men and governments to surrender to the government of Christ.[355]

Take the example of American businesses in South Africa: they were one of the greatest influences in ending apartheid in that country through their business policies and employment practices. When many began leaving that country for various reasons, change slowed to a minimum. They no longer exerted their positive influence. (Their leaving also financially hurt those they wished to help.)

Lee Grady continues:

The prophet Isaiah spoke of a progressive, worldwide surrender to the gospel when he wrote: "The law will go forth from Zion...and He [God] will judge between the nations, and will render decisions for many peoples; and they will hammer their swords into plowshares, and their spears into pruning hooks. Nation will not lift up sword against nation, and never again will they learn war" (Isaiah 2:4).

It is important to note that the act of transforming swords into plowshares takes place after the peoples of the earth voluntarily confess, "Come and let us go unto the mountain of the Lord, that He may teach us His ways" (v. 3). God is waiting for knees to bow in submission before He resolves international conflict. That is His condition for peace.

North summarizes this idea: "There can never be peace in history outside of Christ. There can be temporary cease-fire agreements, but never a lasting peace. What Christians must understand is that peace is attained through the preaching of the gospel and the discipling of the nations. There is no other way. God will not permit peace on any other terms."[356]

Chapter 16

Advance of Liberty in Early America: Fruit of the Seed of the American Republic

The Declaration of Independence and U.S. Constitution

For over 150 years people who were primarily the product of the Protestant Reformation came to America and planted seeds that were to become a new nation, an exceptional nation, though not without faults. As we have seen, Christianity was the unifying factor of the Christian union that resulted from the American Revolution. The American Revolution was a Christian revolution. It was based upon biblical ideas,[357] and God's hand was evident throughout the events leading up to the war, during the eight years of fighting, and through the establishment of the United States Constitution in 1789 (see Chapters 9-13).

The Americans certainly saw God's hand in these events. George Washington summarized the colonists' view of God's involvement in the war when he wrote in 1778, referring to the first three years of the conflict: "The hand of Providence has been so conspicuous in all of this, that he must be worse than an infidel that lacks faith, and more than wicked, that has not gratitude enough to acknowledge his obligations."[358]

John Quincy Adams linked the founding of America to Christ's incarnation and God's plan to liberate mankind. He wrote in an 1837 oration:

Is it not that, in the chain of human events, the birthday of the nation is indissolubly linked with the birthday of the Saviour? That it forms a leading event in the progress of the gospel dispensation? Is it not that the Declaration of Independence first organized the social compact on the foundation of the Redeemer's mission upon earth? That it laid the cornerstone of human government upon the first precepts of Christianity and gave to the world the first irrevocable pledge of the fulfillment of the prophecies announced directly from Heaven at the birth of the Saviour and predicted by the greatest of the Hebrew prophets 600 years before?[359]

Adams believed the principles of civil government and the principles of Christianity were linked together in the birth of America. The Declaration of Independence was our founding covenant, and its power and form were Christian. The same was true for the United States Constitution. It was formed with the view that men are sinful and cannot be entrusted with too much power. A constitution is needed to "chain down" rulers, by specifying the limited role of government, separating powers, and setting up checks and balances among the branches of government. In addition, frequent and fair elections were needed to hold officials accountable.[360]

Signing of the Constitution

As previously stated, the Framers of the Constitution declared that the forming of that document was a miracle of God. James Madison, wrote that the outcome of the Convention, was "a miracle,"[361] and that "a finger of that Almighty hand"[362] was clearly evident. George Washington concurred and added that he thought the Constitution would most likely lay "a lasting foundation for tranquility and happiness," but knowing the source of blessing, his "earnest prayer" was "that the same good Providence may still continue to protect us and prevent us from dashing the cup of national felicity just as it has been lifted to our lips."[363]

The Declaration and Constitution, arguably the most valuable civil documents for the advancement of liberty in history, were the fruit of the Christian seeds planted in the prior generations. These seeds produced much more good fruit. Great advancement and blessings came from the biblical foundation of America. After all, God promises that great blessing comes to those who obey His Word.

Advancement in Inventions, Technology, Scientific Discovery, Transportation, and Communication

The new nation of the United States, with its great liberty, provided the perfect environment for growth and advancement in every sphere of life. Beginning with the birth of America, there was an outburst of human energy, an exponential increase of inventions, and a great growth of wealth never seen before in history. Why? Was it because of great natural resources? Not primarily, for many nations have as many or more. Was it due to the special qualities of the European settlers? No, for some of these same people were starving in Europe. Was it because Americans worked harder than others in the world? Not really (though diligent labor was important in America's prosperity — the Puritan work ethic is foundational for America's success). What then? The primary reason was due to people living in Christian liberty. This liberty was a result of people having a biblical idea of man, family, education, government, law, and economics. A biblical worldview released character and ideas in men that propelled them forward in taking dominion over God's creation.

A nation is cultivated in direct relation to the amount of liberty it embodies — more liberty, greater productivity. Liberty is more important than type of soil, climate, natural resources, or other factors (though these, of course, have an effect). Free Americans turned the desolate plains into a garden; they turned the desert of Arizona into a fruit field; inhospitable Idaho into a potato mine, and so on.

Christianity produced personal liberty in the hearts and minds of men, which in turn produced religious, political, civil, and economic liberty. The ability to live free, direct their future, and benefit from their physical and mental labor brought many new ideas and inventions to Americans, which produced great transformation in society.

Patent and copyright laws helped propel the many new inventions. These laws were based on the principle of property because the product of man's brain is property as well as the product of his hands. (Property is both external and internal.) Some of those inventions, discoveries, and advances include: Cotton gin, 1793; Bowditch publishes *The ... Navigator* in 1802; Steamboat, 1807; Erie Canal, 1825; Railroad, 1826; Steam locomotive, 1830; McCormick reaper, 1831; Telegraph, 1832 (first line in 1844); Deere plow, 1833; Goodyear vulcanized rubber, 1839; Matthew Maury charts ocean currents, 1842; Safety pin, 1849; Sewing machine, 1846; Transatlantic cable, 1858; Transcontinental telegraph line, 1861; Transcontinental railroad line, 1869. Other inventions include the: electric light, telephone, phonograph, radio, mass produced automobile, airplane, television, and computer. Advances occurred in many other fields as well, including medicine, business, and the social arena (e.g., the end of slavery, women's rights). Freedom and the ability to benefit from one's labor caused the United States of America to be the most inventive, progressive, and prosperous nation in history.

The McCormick Reaper

Cyrus Hall McCormick, the inventor of the reaper (a machine which cut grain), was a great example of a Christian inventor and businessman. He was a "reaper" in the Kingdom of God who instituted many new principles of business which reflected his biblical view of life. He advanced civilization and destroyed famine by using his God-given talents to fulfill his calling.

His invention of the reaper, and the ensuing business of making and selling reapers, lay the foundation for the advancement and prosperity of

Cyrus McCormick

America, for it enabled one man to do the work of many, increasing his productivity many-fold. One biographer wrote:

> He instructed the wheat-eating races how to increase the "seven small loaves" so that the multitudes should be fed. He picked up the task of feeding the hungry masses – the Christly task that had lain unfulfilled for eighteen centuries, and led the way in organizing it into a system of international reciprocity.[364]

Cyrus, born in 1809, grew up on a farm in the Shenandoah Valley of Virginia. His father had worked to invent a reaper from the time Cyrus was a child, but was unsuccessful. Seeing his father's attempts was part of his inspiration to invent. Another motive came from experiencing the back-breaking work of harvesting grain by hand. For thousands of years mankind had harvested grain by hand using simple tools, sickles or scythes. When the crops ripened, men labored day and night to gather the grain before it rotted in the field. The size of their planted fields depended upon the amount of manual labor available for the harvest. McCormick's reaper multiplied the potential productivity of men and transformed farming.

Workshop where McCormick invented his reaper.

Cyrus' first successful reaper was tested in July 1831 on a small patch of wheat on his father's farm. Cyrus gave a public exhibition a few days later at the nearby town of Steele's Tavern. With his reaper drawn by two horses he cut six acres of oats in an afternoon. This was an amazing feat equal to the work of six laborers with scythes or 24 peasants with sickles.

In 1832, he gave a large-scale public exhibition to one hundred people in the town of Lexington. This brought a wider recognition of his invention and praise from many sources. A noted professor declared that "this machine is worth a hundred thousand dollars." No praise was more encouraging than the words of his father who said, "It makes me feel proud to have a son do what I could not do."[365]

Many other people had attempted to invent a reaper—Cyrus was the 47th person to secure a patent for a reaper — but none of them worked properly or could have developed into a successful machine for they lacked the proper operational design. His invention combined for the first time the seven mechanical elements necessary for a working reaper. Those who built their own reapers after this time copied McCormick's basic design.

Cyrus Hall McCormick is remembered as the inventor of the reaper, but he did much more than that. He also invented the business of making and selling reapers, and he did it in a biblical manner, with Kingdom fruit. His work impacted the world. "He did more than any other member of the human race to abolish the famine of the cities and the drudgery of the farm — to feed the hungry and straighten the bent backs of the world."[366]

McCormick had built a successful reaper, but no one knew about it. Promoting the value and importance of the reaper was just as important as building it. He built the machine, so now he had to build the business. Cyrus worked harder and longer to build his business than he did to build his reaper. "His whole soul was wrapped up in his Reaper," said one of his neighbors.[367]

In the summer of 1832 while looking out over rolling fields of wheat the thought came to him, "'Perhaps I may make a million dollars from this Reaper.'

McCormick Reaper

This thought was so enormous that it seemed like a dream—like dwelling in the clouds—so remote, so unattainable, so exalted, so visionary."[368] For years it appeared only that, a vision. In fact, it took **nine years** before McCormick found anyone with enough money and courage to buy a reaper from him. He had invented a machine that would transform every farmer that obtained one (and, in time, agriculture the world over) yet no one bought one for nine years. During that time he struggled greatly and instead of making any money toward his vision of a million dollars, he actually lost money. He even had to give up his farm to creditors, but he held on to his reaper. His indomitable spirit would not give up on his vision.

In 1839 he opened the first of the world's reaper factories in the little log workshop near his father's house and began to make reapers. But even so it was not until over a year later that he sold his first reaper to Abraham Smith. During those first years of failure "Cyrus McCormick hung to his Reaper as John Knox had to his Bible."[369] In the next decade as he traveled around the country and promoted his reaper, he became so identified with his invention that he was often called "the Reaper Man."

During the 1840s, he gradually began to sell more and more reapers, but as he looked to expand his business he recognized Virginia was not the place to do it, so he traveled to the Midwest and opened up a factory in a little mud-town called Chicago. As he looked for ways to sell his reapers throughout the states he created "a new species of commercial organization which is by many thought to be fully as remarkable as his invention of the Reaper."[370]

Cyrus McCormick probably did more than any man in history to elevate men out of poverty, and he did so in a biblical way. He did not seek to use governmental force to take from the productive and give to the nonproductive (as modern socialist states do), but he gave the common farmer a tool that made him twenty or thirty times more productive, hence increasing greatly his wealth creation potential.

The Morse Telegraph

Samuel F. B. Morse invented the telegraph in 1832 and worked during the next decade to improve it. The first inter-city line was tested in 1844, when a message was sent from the Capitol Building in Washington to Baltimore.

The invention of the telegraph was one of the most significant technological discoveries in history. It ranks with the printing press in its impact in the area of communication. The message from Washington to Baltimore took a few minutes, which before would have taken about a day. When cables were laid across the Atlantic and across the continent, messages that would have taken days and weeks, now took just a moment.

Samuel F.B. Morse said of his telegraph, "Not what hath man, but 'What hath God wrought!'"

The *New York Herald* declared Morse's telegraph "is not only an era in the transmission of intelligence, but it has

Plaque of Morse in US Capitol

originated in the mind...a new species of consciousness." Another paper concluded that the telegraph is "unquestionably the greatest invention of the age."[371]

Morse was a Christian who believed he had been chosen by God to invent the telegraph and, for the first time, harness the use of electricity. This discovery would contribute greatly to the advancement of man and the fulfilling of God's purpose for mankind. Annie Ellsworth, a friend of Morse's, composed the first message sent over the Washington-Baltimore line on May 24, 1844. She "selected a sentence from a prophecy of the ancient soothsayer Balaam" — "What hath God wrought!"[372] Of this message Morse wrote:

Nothing could have been more appropriate than this devout exclamation, at such an event, when an invention which creates such wonder, and about which there has been so much scepticism, is taken from the land of visions, and becomes a reality.[373]

Morse considered it remarkable that he, an artist, "should have been chosen to be one of those to reveal the meaning of electricity to man! How wonderful that he should have been selected to become a teacher in the art of controlling the intriguing 'fluid' which had been known from the days when the Greeks magnetized amber, but which had never before been turned to the ends of common man! 'What hath God wrought!' As Jehovah had wrought through Israel, God now wrought through him."[374] Morse wrote to his brother:

That sentence of Annie Ellsworth's was divinely indited, for it is in my thoughts day and night. "What hath God wrought!" It is His work, and He alone could have carried me thus far

Morse Telegraph 1837

through all my trials and enabled me to triumph over the obstacles, physical and moral, which opposed me.

"Not unto us, not unto us, but to Thy name, O Lord, be all the praise."

I begin to fear now the effects of public favor, lest it should kindle that pride of heart and self-sufficiency which dwells in my own as well as in others' breasts, and which, alas! is so ready to be inflamed by the slightest spark of praise. I do indeed feel gratified, and it is right I should rejoice with fear, and I desire that a sense of dependence upon and increased obligation to the Giver of every good and perfect gift may keep me humble and circumspect.[375]

Morse would remark in a speech many years later:

If not a sparrow falls to the ground without a definite purpose in the plans of infinite wisdom, can the creation of an instrumentality, so vitally affecting the interests of the whole human race, have an origin less humble than the Father of every good and perfect gift? I am sure I have the sympathy of such an assembly as is here gathered, if in all humility and in the sincerity of a grateful heart, I use the words of inspiration in ascribing honor and praise to him to whom first of all and most of all it is pre-eminently due. "Not unto us, not unto us, but to God be all the glory." Not what hath man, but "What hath God wrought!"[376]

Matthew Maury Charts Ocean Currents

Inspired in his life work by Scripture, Matthew Fontaine Maury was sustained by industry derived from his Christian faith. As an enlightened seer in new fields of science and guided by his biblical worldview, he played a significant role in advancing civilization. He was one of the greatest men America has ever produced.

Maury's accomplishments include: 1) He was the father of oceanography, 2) He charted the ocean and wind currents, 3) He mapped out and proposed sea routes, including laying down lanes for steamers in the North Atlantic, 4) He developed the National

Matthew Maury

Observatory, 5) He was instrumental in founding of U.S. Naval Academy, 6) He proposed the idea for a U.S. Meteorological Society or National Weather Bureau, 7) He was a key consultant for the laying of the transatlantic telegraph cable, 8) He invented the first floating mines and the first electric torpedoes, 9) He wrote many influential science books. Matthew Maury literally fulfilled the ancient mandate of God to take dominion over the earth (Gen. 1:26-28).

Scriptural Inspiration

Matthew Maury's faith was evident in his work and in his writings, where he often quoted the Bible. He said the same God who was the author of the Bible was also the author of nature. In both, God gave a divine revelation of Himself to mankind, and that the message of the two were never contradictory. He also said "to remember that the earth was made for man."[377]

Maury was originally inspired to find the ocean currents as Scripture was read to him. A monument honoring Maury was dedicated in Richmond, Virginia, in 1929. A writer for the Richmond Times, Virginia Lee Cox, spoke of this biblical inspiration in describing the monument in a newspaper article of the day. Cox wrote:

> On the plinth of the monument in the flattest relief are figures of fish, representing Maury's interest in the paths of the sea. The story goes that once when Maury was ill he had his son[378] read the Bible to him each night. One night he read the eighth Psalm, and when he came to the passage—"The fishes of the sea and whatsoever walketh through the paths of the sea" — Maury had him read it over several times. Finally he said, "If God says there are paths in the sea I am going to find them if I get out of this bed." Thus the Psalm was the direct inspiration for his discoveries...

> In his right hand are the pencil and the compass, and in his left hand a chart. Against his chair is the Bible, from which he drew inspiration for his explorations. The sculptor has caught amazingly the spirit of the man.[379]

Maury Monument in Richmond. "Against his chair is the **Bible**, from which he drew inspiration for his explorations."

Another Maury Monument—in the Goshen Pass on the bank of the North Anna River, erected by the state of Virginia in 1923—also reveals his biblical inspiration. The bronze tablet on the monument contains these words:[380]

MATTHEW FONTAINE MAURY, Pathfinder of the Seas, The Genius who first snatched from ocean & atmosphere the secret of their laws. Born January 14th, 1806. Died at Lexington, Va., February 1st, 1873... Every mariner for countless ages as he takes his chart to shape his course across the seas, will think of thee. His Inspiration Holy Writ: Psalms 8 & 107, Verses 8, 23, & 24; Ecclesiastes Chap. 1, Verse 8; A Tribute of his Native State Virginia, 1923

The Scriptures that inspired Maury were: Psalm 8:8 — "The fowl of the air, and the fish of the sea, and whatsoever passeth through the paths of the seas." Psalm 107: 23-24 — "They that go down to the sea in ships, that do business in great waters; these see the works of the Lord, and his wonders in the deep." Eccl. 1:8—"All things are full of labor; man cannot utter it: the eye is not satisfied with seeing, nor the ear filled with hearing."

Maury looked to the Bible when it gave insight into scientific knowledge. For example, he writes in *The Physical Geography of the Sea*:

And as for the general system of atmospherical circulation...the Bible tells it all in a single sentence: "The wind goeth toward the south, and turneth about unto the north; it whirleth about continually, and the wind returneth again according to his circuits." – Eccl., i., 6.[381]

Maury frequently mentioned the work of God in his scientific writings. "The ocean of air like the ocean of water, is never at rest. It has its waves and its currents." After giving three offices of winds that make life on earth possible, Maury wrote: "Discharging these various offices, they verify the Psalmist's words, 'God maketh the winds his messengers.'"[382]

Maury believed giving yourself to a useful and God-ordained occupation was the secret of happiness. He "found that occupation, for some useful end or other, was the true secret of happiness."[383] Once a man found this occupation, Maury believed industry was essential for success. He wrote: "It's the talent of industry that makes a man. I don't think that so much depends upon intellect as is generally supposed; but industry and steadiness of purpose, they are the things."[384]

A Biblical Seer

Maury was able to accomplish so many significant things because he attempted to look at creation from a lofty position, from the view of the Creator. One of his biographers wrote:

The thing above all others that made Maury a great man was his ability to see the invisible. He was a seer. He saw the cable before it was laid. He saw a railroad across the continent before it was built. He saw a ship canal from the Mississippi to the Great Lakes before it was dug. ... He was a seer and a pathfinder not only on the seas, but under the seas, across the lands, and among the stars.[385]

He saw so much because he knew the Bible, believed it, and saw the harmony between what it taught and the natural sciences. He wrote that, "Physical geography confesses the existence, and is based on the biblical doctrine that the earth was made for man. Upon no other theory can it be studied; upon no other theory can its phenomena be reconciled."[386] In the same speech, he also declared:

Matthew Maury said concerning Psalm 8:8, "If God says there are paths in the sea I am going to find them."

I have been blamed by men of science, both in this country and in England, for quoting the Bible in confirmation of the doctrines of physical geography. The Bible, they say, was not written for scientific purposes, and is therefore of no authority in matters of science. I beg pardon! The Bible is authority for everything it touches. ... The Bible is true and science is true. The agents concerned in the physical economy of our planet are ministers of His who made both it and the Bible. The records which He has chosen to make through the agency of these ministers of His upon the crust of the earth are as true as the records which, by the hands of His prophets and servants, He has been pleased to make in the Book of Life. They are both true; and when your men of science, with vain and hasty conceit, announce the discovery of disagreement between them, rely upon it the fault is not with the Witness or His records, but with the "worm" who essays to interpret evidence which he does not understand.[387]

Maury, as has been true of most of the significant scientists in history, accomplished his great work because he had a biblical view of life and science. He realized the Creator of the Universe is orderly and caused His creation to operate according to set laws. Maury believed God wants man to discover and apply those laws as part of his mission to take dominion over the earth. Maury wrote:

As a student of physical geography I regard the earth, sea, air and water as parts of a machine, pieces of mechanism not made by hands, but to which, nevertheless, certain offices have been assigned in the terrestrial economy. It is good and profitable to seek to find out these offices, and point them out to our fellows; and when, after patient research, I am led to the discovery of any one of them, I feel with the astronomer of old as though I had 'thought one of God's thoughts!' — and tremble.[388]

There are many other technological and scientific advances that were part of the good fruit of the American republic.[389] Christians were ubiquitous in this and all spheres of advancement. An engraving on the base of a statue in the United States Capitol of Dr. Crawford W. Long says:

Statue of Dr. Crawford W. Long in the U.S. Capitol

Discoverer of the use of sulphuric ether as an anaesthetic in surgery on March 30, 1842 at Jefferson, Jackson County, Georgia U.S.A. "My profession is to me a ministry from God."

Growth of Education

Education for all people is a Christian idea. It motivated the early colonists to start schools and colleges, and is why the Bible was their central textbook. Americans' biblical faith continued to be manifested through education in the nineteenth century.

Noah Webster

We previously mentioned Noah Webster (see Chapter 8), the most important educator of the nineteenth century. He was a devout Christian whose biblical philosophy of education is clearly reflected in his enormous work. He produced a series of self-teaching textbooks out of his desire to teach truth to the American people and make the nation intellectually independent of England and Europe. This series

Noah Webster

> IM-MOR′AL, *a.* [*in* and *moral.*] Inconsistent with
> . moral rectitude ; contrary to the moral or divine law ;
> wicked ; unjust ; dishonest ; vicious. Every action
> is *immoral* which contravenes any divine precept, or
> which is contrary to the duties which men owe to
> each other.

Webster's definition of immoral reflects the Biblical worldview of early America—
"divine precept" was the standard for immoral behavior. Modern definitions reflect
the relativistic ideology of most Americans—"accepted norm" is now the standard.

included his well-known best-seller, the *Blue Backed Speller,* which did more for
American education than any other single book except for the Bible. As
Americans settled the west, they carried their Bible and Webster's speller.

William McGuffey

Another important educator of the 19th century that
was mentioned in Chapter 8 was William Holmes
McGuffey (1800-1873), a Presbyterian minister,
university professor, and an author. He taught at a
number of different colleges, ending his career as the
professor of moral philosophy at the University of
Virginia (the last 28 years of his life). He greatly
impacted the nation through his biblical textbooks, the
McGuffey Readers (the first two volumes published in
1836, with six volumes by 1857), which sold 122 million
copies in 75 years.

William McGuffey

Colleges

Previously we mentioned the Christian foundation of most of the early
colleges and universities, from the first college, Harvard, to those that sprang up
during the First Great Awakening. This continued into the 1800s. In 1860 there
were 246 colleges in the United States. Over 90 percent of these were Christian
or were started for a Christian purpose.[390] Ministers remained as presidents of
most colleges up to the end of the nineteenth century.

Even though the Christian faith was central at most schools, seeds of
secularism began to be planted. In the early 1800s Unitarians took control of

Harvard University. Though originally rooted in the Bible, Unitarianism gradually drifted farther and farther away from biblical ideology, with a corresponding shift occurring in Unitarian churches and in colleges controlled by that belief system.

The rise of modern state education began in Massachusetts due to the efforts of Horace Mann. In 1838 he became the first secretary of education of Massachusetts public schools. Many today see this as a great step forward, but his action paved the way for a state financed, state directed, and ultimately state controlled education system that has usurped not only the authority of localities, but more importantly that of parents to direct the education of children. The Bible remained in the schools for generations (though it was no longer THE text, but one of many texts), but over time it has not only ceased to be used as a text, but the liberating philosophy of a biblical worldview has been replaced by a secular, immoral, man-centered view of life.

The first compulsory school laws were enacted in Massachusetts in 1852 and over time every state has followed suit. As a consequence, the government now compels youth to learn certain ideas, including moral and religious ideas since all education is ultimately religious.

Political and Geographical Advancement

After independence, western exploration and settlement occurred rapidly, adding many new states to the original thirteen. In 1775 Daniel Boone blazed the Wilderness Road through the Cumberland Gap to explore and settle Kentucky. He would later explore and move farther west. John Chapman was a missionary explorer who sowed the Word of God to any pioneers he encountered. As he traveled west he also planted many apple trees to provide food for future settlers. Chapman, who became known as Johnny Appleseed, sought to provide spiritual and physical sustenance.

The purchase from France of the Louisiana Territory under President Thomas Jefferson in 1803 nearly doubled the size of the United States. Lewis and Clark first explored this territory, but many

Gail Borden was the first person baptized in the Gulf of Mexico west of the Mississippi River.

other explorers followed them, including Jedidiah Smith who always packed his Bible.

One of the leaders in Texas' independence from Mexico in 1836 was Gail Borden. He ran the only newspaper in the area and printed important government papers and news of the war. Though professing the Christian faith years before, it was not until 1840 that Borden was baptized. That year was the first time an ordained Baptist minister came to Galveston, where Borden lived, to organize a church. Gail and his wife Penelope were the first to ask for this ordinance. "It was reputedly the first baptismal service in the Gulf west of the Mississippi River."[391] Borden later invented condensed milk, the reason most people know his name today.

Missionaries Marcus and Narcissa Whitman blazed the Oregon Trail, in 1836. The first great emigration was led by Marcus in 1843. He was also instrumental in the United States acquiring the Oregon Territory in 1846.[392]

Barbary Powers War (1801-05, 1815), America's First War against Muslim Terrorists

America's war with Muslim terrorists did not begin after the bombing of the Twin Towers in New York City on September 11, 2001. Nor did it begin with the bombing of the Beirut Barracks in Lebanon in 1983. In fact, the first war we fought as a new nation was against Islamic terrorists.

Muslims have long been at war with Christendom, on and off for fourteen centuries. By the late eighteenth century a "peaceful warfare" had developed. To carry on commerce within the Mediterranean Sea without fear of molestation from the Muslims, it was the custom for European powers to pay tribute to the pirates of the Barbary States (Algiers, Morocco, Tripoli, and Tunis). These states

President Jefferson directed our first war against Muslim terrorists.

were located in North Africa, which the Muslims had controlled for centuries. European nations found it easier to pay the bribes than fight. Thus the unholy alliance of the Muslim states with nations like England, France, and Spain only served to build up the terrorists. The economic system of tribute, ransom, and bribery was well established when America entered onto the scene.

After American independence, American crews and ships came under the direct threat of the pirates as they began to sail under a new flag. The pirates saw the opportunity for fresh booty in ships and slaves. The U.S. Ambassadors to France, Thomas Jefferson, and Britain, John Adams, were ordered to do what they could to make peace. Jefferson argued the best long-term solution was to establish a navy, writing, "I very early thought it would be best to effect a peace through the medium of war."[393] He pointed out that the cost of establishing and maintaining a navy "would amount to little more than we must pay, if we buy peace,"[394] that is, pay the tribute demanded by the pirates.

In May 1786, Jefferson and Adams met in London with the resident Tripolitan ambassador, Sidi Haji Abdul Rahman Adja, to try and negotiate a treaty to end the threat from the Barbary pirates. They asked the ambassador why the Muslim states were so hostile to the new American republic that had done nothing to provoke such animosity. Ambassador Adja answered, "that it was founded on the Laws of their Prophet, that it was written in their Koran, that all nations who should not have acknowledged their authority were sinners, that it was their right and duty to make war upon them wherever they could be found, and to make slaves of all they could take as Prisoners, and that every Musselman who should be slain in Battle was sure to go to Paradise."[395] (Jefferson would later read the Koran to learn for himself if it really taught this strange doctrine.)

With no means of resistance, the United States concluded a treaty in 1786 with the ruler of Morocco where the U.S. would pay money and give presents in exchange for captive Americans and future immunity.

Stephen Decatur boarding a Muslim pirate gunboat during the bombardment of Tripoli, August 3, 1804.

This treaty still applied in 1789 when the new U.S. Constitution went into effect. Paying tribute had been going on for centuries. Great Britain made a treaty with the Barbary States in 1662 to purchase immunity for its merchant shipping.[396] Having no other option, since the newly founded United States had no navy, President Washington continued the custom of paying tribute. This irked him greatly, but this was the only way to protect American commerce and American citizens from capture and imprisonment. Without the tribute payment, and at times with it, the pirates would capture ships and hold the captains and crew for ransom. They were held in horrid conditions, and many died from hardships of captivity.

Under Washington, funds had been appropriated to build a navy. Adams had access to these ships but did not think the American people were prepared for a protracted war in far off northern Africa, so he continued paying tribute. When Jefferson became President, he had had enough. He decided to use our treasury, not, in the words of the U.S. Consul to Tunis William Eaton, "to buy oil of roses to perfume that pirate's beard," but rather to send "gun batteries to chastise his temerity."[397] When Jefferson refused to pay tribute to the Barbary pirates, they declared war of sorts upon the United States and began to attack American ships in the area, stealing property and imprisoning citizens. Jefferson sent troops to protect American interests. War continued until 1805 when a treaty of peace was signed on June 10 where the Barbary pirates agreed to end hostilities.

In 1815, while America was fighting the War of 1812, the leader of the Muslim terrorists in Algiers (having the title, the Dey) renewed his plunder of American commerce thinking the war would keep the U.S. from being able to respond. After pirates seized American vessels and citizens, Congress approved action against the Barbary powers. Capt. Stephen Decatur sailed from New York with 10 ships and captured enemy ships and sailed into the harbor of Algiers. He forced the Dey to release all prisoners without ransom and to agree to a peace treaty where no tribute would be paid again, nor American commerce molested. Decatur obtained similar guarantees from Tunis (July 26) and Tripoli (August 5).

America set an example for Europe of chastising and humbling a lawless band of pirates and ended the practice of paying tribute to Muslim terrorists. Expressions of submission were obtained from these powers by the United States such as had not been obtained by any other nation. Pope Pius VII said: "The Americans have done more for Christendom against the pirates of Africa than all the powers of Europe united."[398]

Political Figures

Just as during the founding era, the majority of the governmental leaders of the nineteenth century were Christians, including such men as Chief Justices John Jay and John Marshall, Presidents John Quincy Adams and James Garfield, and Senator Daniel Webster. President Andrew Jackson was converted later in life, and President Abraham Lincoln likely embraced the Christian faith as well.[399]

Daniel Webster

Daniel Webster

Daniel Webster was a great Christian statesman and orator, and served almost a decade in the U.S. House, nearly two decades in the U.S. Senate, and as the Secretary of State for three different Presidents. He believed that to become a great orator one must study the Word of God. He practiced his own oratory by reciting the Bible aloud.

Webster's old Senate desk is still in the Capitol, in the current Senate Chamber. It is used by the senior Senator from New Hampshire, the state of Webster's birth. As a Senator he used a penknife to inscribe his name in the bottom of his desk. (Others have followed his example.) He developed a love for penknives at an early age. One of Daniel's first school teachers, Master James Tappan, told the story of how he got his first penknife (at around age 6-8):

> Daniel was always the brightest boy in the school. ... He would learn more in five minutes than any boy in five hours. ... One Saturday, I remember, I held up a handsome new jack-knife to the scholars and said the boy who would commit to memory the greatest number of verses in the Bible by Monday morning should have it. Many of the boys did well; but when it came to Daniel's turn to recite, I found that he had committed so much [to memory] that after hearing him repeat some sixty or seventy verses, I was obliged to give up, he telling me that there were several chapters yet that he had learned. Daniel got that jack-knife.[400]

Webster's love for the Bible remained throughout his life. He understood obedience to God's truth produces great blessings for a nation. He said,

"Whatever makes men good Christians, makes them good citizens."[401] He gave this warning that is very pertinent for today:

> If we and our posterity shall be true to the Christian religion, if we and they shall live always in the fear of God and shall respect His Commandments...we may have the highest hopes of the future fortunes of our country; ... But if we and our posterity neglect religious instruction and authority, violate the rules of eternal justice, trifle with the injunctions of morality, and recklessly destroy the political constitution which holds us together, no man can tell how sudden a catastrophe may overwhelm us that shall bury all our glory in profound obscurity.[402]

Senator Webster was known for his great oratorical skills – skills which he said were acquired through much labor. One day as the Senate was discussing the extent of the British Empire, Webster displayed his great eloquence when he remarked:

> She has dotted the surface of the whole globe with her possessions and military posts, whose morning drum-beat, following the sun and keeping company with the hours, circles the earth daily with one continuous and unbroken strain of the martial airs of England.

When they left the Senate one member complimented Mr. Webster on his brilliant language, and said that his remarks struck him greatly, especially considering they were impromptu. To this Webster replied:

> You are mistaken, the idea occurred to me when I was on the ramparts of Quebec some months ago. I wrote it down and rewrote it, and after several trials got it to suit me, and laid it up for use. The time came today, and so I put it in.[403]

Daniel Webster is representative of the many Christians who served in civil government in early America.

Arts and Literature

Like all other areas of life, arts and literature advanced after independence. Quaker Benjamin West was the first prominent American painter, beginning his career before the American Revolution and conducting most of his work in England. Many others followed him including Washington Allston, Charles Wilson Peale, Thomas Sully, Samuel F.B. Morse, John Trumbull, and Emanuel Leutze.

American Landscape Painters

American painting has suffered the same fate as American history – its Christian and moral foundations have been covered up, distorted, and lost. It is especially evident with the landscape painters of the nineteenth century. The prominent painters of the Hudson River School, covering the years 1825-1860, included Frederic Edwin Church, Thomas Cole, Jasper Francis Cropsey, and Asher Brown Durand.

"For these painters there was a moral purpose in being an artist; art was a sacred obligation. … The paintings of the Hudson River School…are filled with light, the most obvious manifestation of God's presence, expressing man's harmony with nature, seen as a second chance for mankind in the new Eden of the American wilderness."[404]

These were not "religious" paintings of obvious religious themes, like many from the Middle Ages, but Christian paintings, reflecting God's nature and light in His creation, through the excellence of the scenes, styles, and techniques.

In the modern relativistic world, "Beauty [has] suffered the same fate as morality."[405] Just as there is no standard for moral behavior, there is no standard for beauty when looking at art — beauty is only in the eye of the beholder. The random strokes of a monkey on a canvas can be just as beautiful as the masterful brush of Da Vinci on the Last Supper. It all depends on who is evaluating them. The recent tax-payer funded work that demeaned Christ can be art to

Jasper Francis Cropsey, Wyoming Valley

some modern subjective viewers, for there is no objective standard by which to judge beauty or art.

But a secular humanistic worldview is not founded upon truth and cannot sustain itself. Thus, beauty and goodness continue to be acknowledged.

"Beauty...has survived its harshest critics." "Goodness, beauty, and truth have thus outlasted the critique of those that constituted modernism."[406]

The Hudson River Painters are the fruit of the American Christian Republic. Art, like every other field, reflects the Christian foundation of America; but art also helps to preserve and propagate the Christian seed. The Hudson River School reflected the biblical morality and worldview of the founding generation of Americans. They "saw the American landscape as blessed by God." These artists believed that "the arts play a critical role in a civilization, not only in defining and disseminating core values, but also as a barometer of moral character." Jasper Cropsey wrote in 1846: "No moral and refined work of art could be produced by an immoral man." For Cropsey, "the artist was a knight who wields not a sword but a brush in his pursuit of spiritual and moral perfection." He saw himself on "a holy quest," involved in "spiritual warfare."[407]

Filmmakers today are like these artists of earlier centuries. In the 1800s people paid money to see paintings, which would at times be displayed in traveling exhibits. Before the invention of the camera there were few pictures, so they had a great effect on the viewers. "There was a moral purpose in being an artist." "One was called to art much as one was called to the ministry. It became a sacred obligation. And nowhere was the obligation more important than in the new republic."[408]

"Genesis instructed these nineteenth-century artists that, when God created the Earth, Seas, Heaven, Sun, Moon, Man, Woman, and all living and growing things, he saw that it was good: 'And God saw the light, that it was good: and God divided the light from the darkness.' This process of creating and seeing was repeated each time, until at the end of the sixth day, 'God saw everything that he had made, and behold, it was very good...and he rested on the seventh day.' The human ability to see, to judge, to comprehend the universe, was understood to be part of the divine spirit. Seeing implies an aesthetic function, but it was far more than that for these artists. Ruskin wrote that 'the greatest thing a human soul ever does in this world is to see something...to see clearly is poetry, prophesy, and religion, — all in one.' We are drawn to the artists of the Hudson River School because they enable us to see what they saw with fresh eyes: the beauty of nature, the glory of God, and the virtue of America."[409]

The Hudson River Painters had a vision to transmit God's paradise and preserve it through biblical renewal in all spheres of life. They were aware of the gradually encroaching secularism in Western Civilization, especially seen in European art and culture. They hoped to keep this destructive force from overtaking America, not by using all their energy to attack that which was pagan, but by presenting godly beauty and truth in their art. They understood that "cultural renewal is not about destroying a golden calf — an image of a bankrupt ideology — but about creating works of the highest standards that celebrate the beauty of holiness."[410]

Authors

While some of the early American authors were not Christians, like Edgar Allen Poe, Herman Melville, and Henry David Thoreau, they often reflected a Christian view of man and life in their writings. For example, Poe clearly reveals the negative consequences of man's sinfulness, though he fails to give a biblical solution to this problem. Others uphold higher biblical themes, like Henry Wadsworth Longfellow, James Fenimore Cooper, and Washington Irving.[411]

Lew Wallace, Statue in U.S. Capitol

One of the bestselling novels of all time was written by a Christian, General Lew Wallace. He is honored by a statue in the U.S. Capitol Building. Wallace wrote *Ben Hur: A Tale of the Christ* after he was challenged by "the great agnostic," Robert Ingersoll, to try to prove that Jesus was the Son of God. Through his extensive research and travels to the Holy Land, he became a Christian and went on to write the great Christian classic and bestselling novel of the nineteenth century. *Ben Hur* undermined Ingersoll's message and advanced Christianity mightily. It influenced many, including President Ulysses S. Grant, who read it through in a day-and-a-half. President Garfield wrote a nationally published letter recommending *Ben Hur*.

Challenges to Liberty and the Need of Continual Energetic Faith

With increasing liberty comes the need for increasing godly character among the citizens to support the liberty. Without this internal support, a free society will quickly become depraved. The decay begins in man's heart, but will quickly express itself in society. A declining society, with increasing crime and corruption, leads to the need for greater external constraints to control the uncivil, which leads to loss of liberty. Biblical revival and renewal, therefore, are needed for liberty to grow.

The Second Great Awakening

As a new nation, America had more liberty and prosperity than any people in history. Yet in spite of this, their internal divine fire began to go out. God in His mercy moved on the nation again in what is called the Second Great Awakening.

The Second Great Awakening occurred in different phases over many years. It began in the late 1700s in the wilderness of Kentucky in the days of Daniel Boone. Over time, it spread throughout the nation. Many prominent individuals were impacted. When this revival swept through Connecticut in 1808, the well-known educator Noah Webster was dramatically converted, although he had attended church all his life and generally had a biblical worldview. He was just beginning his twenty-year labor on his *American Dictionary of the English Language*. His definitions and biblical references reflect the transformation he experienced. The awakening continued on and off in different parts of America up until and during the Civil War. Other nations saw revival as well.

Salvation came to many, in camp meetings in the western wilderness, in homes and businesses, and in churches in the North and South. Because of this revival and the biblical foundation of the nation, Christianity continued to be the predominate force in the first half of the 1800s. The Founding Fathers started and served as officers in numerous Bible societies. The American Bible Society formed in 1816 when 35 Bible Societies joined together, and 85 other local societies joined with it the first year. Elias Boudinot, President of the Continental Congress in 1782, became its first president. Its officers included the first Chief Justice of the U.S. Supreme Court, John Jay, President John Quincy Adams, and Supreme Court Chief Justice John Marshall.

In addition to Bible Societies, Christianity gave impetus for the founding of abolition societies, philanthropic societies, the American Tract Society, the American Sunday School Union (1824), and America's first branches of the YMCA (in Boston, 1851) and YWCA (in Boston, 1866).

Missions Movements and Missionaries

Modern missions were birthed in the eighteenth century in Great Britain and the United States. We have seen that a central motive for the colonization of the original thirteen colonies was the propagation of the Gospel. This motive continued to influence the establishment of other states after we became a nation. Ministers led the settlement of the Oregon Territory, Rev. Jason Lee in the state of Oregon and Marcus and Narcissa Whitman in Washington.

Marcus Whitman, a medical missionary and Christian patriot, was the man who saved the Oregon Territory and assured it would be a part of the United States. Called to the Northwest by a desire to see the Indians taught the liberating principles of the Bible, the daring action of this "man of destiny" paved the way for the establishment of the states of Washington, Oregon, and Idaho. Biographer William Mowry writes:

> Braving the cold and the snows of the Rocky Mountains, he crossed the continent on horseback to warn our government at Washington and to encourage the hardy pioneers of the frontier to emigrate to Oregon, assuring them that they could carry their wagons and their families through to the Columbia, for he had gone there himself with his wife and his wagon.[412]

Statue of Marcus Whitman in the U.S. Capitol with his Bible in one hand and his medical bag in the other.

The tragic and sad end of the story of Marcus and Narcissa Whitman reminds us that "the blood of the martyrs is the seed of the church." Their story clearly reveals the providence of God in the march of history—that nations do not, in the words of historian George Bancroft, "float darkling down the stream of the ages without hope or consolation, swaying with every wind and ignorant whither they are drifting" but that "there is a superior intelligence and love, which is moved by justice and shapes their courses." The Whitmans' story will also inspire us to practice "heroic, patriotic, and Christian virtues."[413]

When Marcus & Narcissa reached the Continental Divide, July 4, 1836, on their initial trip to the northwest, they claimed the Oregon Territory for God and the United States. Rev. Spalding wrote: "They alighted from their horses and kneeling on the other half of the continent, with the Bible in one hand and the American flag in the other, took possession of it as the home of American mothers and of the Church of Christ."[414]

In the winter of 1842-43, Whitman made a daring trip over the Rocky Mountains and traveled to Washington, DC, to meet with President John Tyler and Secretary of State Daniel Webster (above) and urge them to not give away the Oregon Territory.

Christian Philosophy of Government in the United States

Americans had a biblical philosophy of government. What governments did in Europe the private sector did in the United States, and that much more effectively. Alexis De Tocqueville wrote how America assisted the poor and established voluntary associations for every imaginable purpose, meeting needs much better than in Europe. In Europe the state controlled the development of the telegraph, in America the private sector did so. Comparing the growth of the telegraph in the USA and Europe shows the superiority of the free market system. A New York newspaper wrote in 1846, two years after Samuel F. B. Morse's line from Washington to Baltimore was complete:

> While England by her government has got with great labor 175 miles of telegraph into operation...the United Sates, with her individual enterprise, has now in successful operation 1269 miles. This is American enterprise.[415]

This comparison reflects different governmental philosophies in the new Christian republic and the old European statist governments. This "American enterprise" is still reflected today in many ways. You can find a huge variety of almost any kind of product and service. The growth of homeschool materials is one example. Americans are still a creative and productive people because they have the freedom to pursue their ideas and to benefit from the fruit of those ideas.

Samuel F.B. Morse exhibiting the telegraph. Alexander Hamilton wrote that the free enterprise system encourages industry and invention.

However, more government control, regulation, and taxes are stifling creativity and productivity. Businesses are growing in states with less taxes and regulations (many states in the South) and leaving others with high taxes and more controls (like California and various New England states). Some businesses are going to other nations to escape big government.[416]

The Diminishing Influence of Christianity

During the nineteenth century a number of factors contributed to a gradual diminishing influence of Christianity in America. One of those was the rise of Unitarianism. Today Unitarianism is often non- and sometimes anti-Christian, but in its beginning in America in the late 1700s into the early 1800s it held the Bible and the Words of Jesus as its standard for theological belief. This is why some of our Christian Founders, like John Quincy Adams and Joseph Story, could associate with early Unitarianism. However, over time it was slowly reshaped into an ethical theism which embraced humanism, pragmatism, evolutionism, and other anti-Christian beliefs. Many churches and colleges were influenced by Unitarianism.[417]

A second factor that caused biblical Christianity's influence to decline in America was the influx of immigrants from Europe who did not adhere to *sola scriptura*, that belief in the centrality of the Bible held by the first colonists.

Cotton Mather: "Religion begot prosperity, but the daughter hath consumed the mother."

Liberty in America attracted many immigrants, most coming from Europe during the nineteenth century. Some were Protestants, and many were Catholics, who often held to a form of religion but were usually deficient in biblical knowledge and worldview. Some were non-Christians. To maintain liberty and prosperity, a Christian nation must impart to new citizens the biblical character and worldview that initially formed the foundation of the nation. If this is not done, the nation will gradually decline. While many of the new immigrants were infused with a vibrant Christian faith, large numbers were not, and their non-biblical ideology negatively affected the nation.

A third factor contributing to the diminishing influence of Christianity in the nineteenth century was the rise of materialism. Prosperity is the natural by-product of biblical faith. However, we must be careful not to let the love of money creep into our lives. A prominent puritan minister of the late seventeenth century Cotton Mather said: "Religion begot prosperity, but the daughter hath consumed the mother." Christianity laid the foundation for the great prosperity that arose in the United States, but for many people, seeking wealth became more important than seeking the source of wealth, God Himself. God told the children of Israel that when they entered the Promised Land they would prosper if they obeyed Him, but He warned them not to forget Him and worship other Gods, for if they did they would perish (Deuteronomy 30:5, 8-10, 17-18; 8:11-14, 17-18). Many Americans have failed to heed this warning, beginning in the nineteenth century but even more so today.

The Church Must Continually Disciple the Nation.

Eternal vigilance is the price of liberty. Each generation must maintain and propagate the principles of liberty. The American Revolution was a product of the pulpit. The church imbued the citizens with the character and ideas necessary for freedom. Parents in turn transmitted these to their children. However, as the nation moved toward the mid-1800s the church failed to carry on the example of the Revolutionary era. Consequently, the negative factors mentioned above began to grow. In addition, the failure of the new American nation to deal with the institution of slavery was devastating.

Chapter 17

The War for the Union

Every American ought to master three basic documents: The Declaration of Independence, the Constitution, and George Washington's Farewell Address. When our eminent first President was leaving office in 1796, he presented one of the most insightful political documents in history. He already perceived some trends in the national life that were dangerous to our union. His deep concern was evident when he wrote:

> You should properly estimate the immense value of your national Union to your collective and individual happiness;...indignantly frowning upon the first dawning of every attempt to alienate any portion of our country from the rest. ... Your Union ought to be considered as a main prop of your liberty, and the love of one ought to endear to you the preservation of the other.[418]

Washington then begins to identity some things which may "disturb our Union:"

1. The Spirit of Party

> Men may endeavor to excite a belief, that there is a real difference of local interests and views. One of the expedients of party [in order] to acquire influence within particular districts is to misrepresent the opinions and aims of other districts;...The alternate dominion of one faction over another, sharpened by the spirit of revenge...will gradually incline the minds of men to seek security and repose in the absolute power of an individual;...[also] it opens the door to foreign influence and corruption, which find a facilitated access to the government itself through the channels of party passions.[419]

2. The Spirit of Encroachment

Washington urged each branch or individual official to "confine themselves within their respective constitutional spheres, avoiding in the exercise of the powers of one department to encroach upon another. The spirit of encroachment tends to consolidate the powers of all the departments in one, and this to create, whatever the form of government, a real despotism;…Let there be no change by usurpation; for, though this, in one instance, may be the instrument of good, it is the customary weapon by which free governments are destroyed."[420]

Washington then goes on to emphasize the real protection against these dangers: religion, morality and knowledge. In other words, the "letter" of the Constitution will never work perfectly if the "spirit" of the Constitution departs. It does not work for a people without Christian character. In this light we can begin to understand the events leading to the War Between the States.

The Issue of Slavery

England outlawed slavery in 1833 due to the influence of Christians, especially William Wilberforce. America's road to end slavery was much more difficult.

The majority of the Founding Fathers believed slavery was fundamentally wrong; it was an evil institution that needed to be abolished. Charles Carroll, signer of the Declaration from Maryland, expressed the majority view when he said, "slavery…is admitted by all to be a great evil."[421] Washington wrote, "that there is not a man living who wishes more sincerely than I do to see a plan adopted for the abolition of it [slavery]."[422]

However, slavery had been around since time began, present in almost every

Confederate troops

nation in history; thus they believed such an entrenched social problem must be overcome gradually. Some of them owned slaves and yet were leaders in anti-slavery organizations which were working to change the laws as well as educate and prepare slaves for independence.

During the drafting of the Declaration of Independence in 1776 Jefferson wanted to condemn slavery outright, but some thought it potentially too divisive to deal with while they were trying to present a united front. They also avoided it in their Articles of Confederation in 1777 since most considered it under the jurisdiction of the states.

Many states and individuals had already been acting upon their anti-slavery beliefs. Some of the first anti-slavery laws in history were enacted in colonial New England. There had always been free blacks in America who owned property, voted, and had the same rights as other citizens. Black slaves who fought during the Revolutionary War won their freedom in every state except South Carolina and Georgia. Many of the Founders started and served in anti-slavery societies. With independence came the freedom for the states to enact new laws—by 1804 eight northern states had abolished slavery. In the South, many individuals, including George Washington, who owned slaves set them free.

The issue of slavery was considered at the Constitutional Convention. Though most delegates were opposed to slavery, they compromised on the issue when the representatives from Georgia and South Carolina threatened to walk out. The delegates realized slavery would continue in these states with or without the union. They saw a strong union of all the colonies was the best means of securing their liberty (which was by no means guaranteed to survive). They did not agree to abolish slavery as some wanted to do, but they did take the forward step of giving the congress the power to end the slave trade after 20 years. No nation in Europe or elsewhere had agreed to such political action.

Even so, many warned of the dangers of allowing this evil to continue. George Mason of Virginia told the delegates:

> Every master of slaves is born a petty tyrant. They bring the judgement of heaven upon a country. As nations cannot be rewarded or punished in the next world, they must be in this. By an inevitable chain of causes and effects, Providence punishes national sins by national calamities.[423]

George Mason

The constitutional provision of counting the slaves as three-fifths for purposes of representation was not pro-slavery or black dehumanization; it was a political compromise between the North and the South. The three-fifths provision applied only to slaves and not free blacks, who voted and had the same rights as whites (and in some Southern states this meant being able to own slaves). While the Southern states wanted to count the slaves in their population to determine the number of congressmen from their states, slavery opponents pushed to keep the Southern states from having more representatives, and hence more power in Congress.

The former slave and famous abolitionist Frederick Douglass, who first thought the Constitution was pro-slavery, saw the liberating nature of the Constitution after he escaped slavery and studied the document, writing:

> [T]he Constitution is a glorious liberty document. Read its preamble; consider its purposes. Is slavery among them? Is it at the gateway? Or is it in the temple? It is neither. … [I]f the Constitution were intended to be, by its framers and adopters, a slaveholding instrument, why neither slavery, slaveholding, nor slave can anywhere be found in it? … Now, take the Constitution according to its plain reading and I defy the presentation of a single pro-slavery clause in it. On the other hand, it will be found to contain principles and purposes entirely hostile to the existence of slavery.[424]

Frederick Douglass

National Sins

Congress passed and President Washington signed the Northwest Ordinance in 1789, which prohibited slavery in the new states. They also banned the exportation of slaves from any state in 1794. All intentions of that generation were united in their goal to abolish slavery. God wanted to show the world how a Christian nation would deal with such a major social problem. However, America failed to deal with slavery as God had intended. It had begun to take steps to end slavery but failed to follow through to completion. One reason for this failure was greed.

In 1783, Eli Whitney invented the cotton gin. This made slavery much more profitable. Thus, as a new generation of Americans arose with less convictions on the matter than their fathers, we began to compromise. The trend towards emancipation came to a halt in the South, and some churches even began to justify slavery for the first time around 1810. By then all slave trading had been made illegal, yet slave owning became more entrenched. In the 1830s, the three major Protestant church denominations split over the issue of slavery. Once the churches divided, it was almost certain that the nation would divide.

Around this same time, Southern statesmen arose who began to argue that each state was free to decide if it wanted to allow slavery or not. They appealed to the fact that our Founders left it this way in the Constitution; yet by so doing, they were holding to the "letter" of the law, but rejecting the "spirit" or intentions behind it. This principle of self-government (or states' rights or popular sovereignty) was championed eloquently by John C. Calhoun in the U.S. Senate in the 1840s. His arguments by the "letter" were right and often unanswerable, yet were being used to defend something wrong.

A number of years later in 1858, a popular candidate, Stephen O. Douglas was speaking for "popular sovereignty" in his debates with Abraham Lincoln. Lincoln agreed that his opponent's doctrine was "absolutely and eternally right. But it has no just application as here attempted ... whether a negro is not or is a man." He said when

"Slavery is wrong and ought to be dealt with as wrong." — Abraham Lincoln

self-government is used to oppress another man then it is "despotism." "Slavery is wrong," Lincoln stated, "and ought to be dealt with as wrong."[425]

The anti-slavery movement became well-organized in 1834 with one-third of its leaders being clergyman. Daniel Dorchester writes:

The prime impulse [of the anti-slavery movement] was Christian and...many eminent divines acted...the leading part in the abolition movement. The first anti-slavery convention stated:

"We also maintain that there are at the present time the highest obligations resting upon the people of the free states to remove slavery by moral and political action, as prescribed in the Constitution of the U.S.

"These are our views and principles—these our designs and measures. With entire confidence in the overruling justice of God, we plant ourselves upon the Declaration of Independence and the truths of divine revelation as upon the everlasting rock.

"We shall organize anti-slavery societies, if possible, in every city, town and village in our land.

"We shall send forth agents to lift up the voice of remonstrance, of warning, of entreaty and rebuke.

"We shall circulate unsparingly and extensively anti-slavery tracts and periodicals.

"We shall enlist the pulpit and the press in the cause of the suffering and the dumb.

"We shall aim at a purification of the churches from all participation in the guilt of slavery.

"We shall encourage the labor of freemen over that of the slaves by giving a preference to their productions...

"We shall spare no exertions nor means to bring the whole nation to speedy repentance."[426]

These evangelical abolition societies (as opposed to some which were anti-religious and anti-constitutional) eventually helped birth the Republican party in 1854.

As new states were entering the Union, there was a great struggle over which ones would allow slavery or forbid it. Senator Henry Clay of Kentucky was one statesman who worked to preserve the Union by compromise. The Congress determined that all states south of a certain line could have slavery, but those north of it could not. This measure was overturned, however, in 1857, when the Supreme Court declared that blacks were not persons, but mere "property." The Court said the constitutional right to property made it illegal for any state to forbid slavery. Abraham Lincoln criticized this decision as fundamentally wrong.

John Brown had been working for years against slavery by political means, but after the Court's Dred Scott decision he felt that the issue could never be resolved by mere legal action. He, therefore, devised a plan of flight for the slaves, which, if it succeeded, would "destroy the money-value of slave property" by rendering it insecure in the eyes of slaveholders. His plan was to use the Appalachian mountain range (running through most of the slave states) as his base of operations from which five-man squads would go down to the fields and induce the slaves to flee with them to the mountains.

He never planned an insurrection and slaughter of slave masters, but he did plan to supply the runaway slaves with arms and ammunition in case they needed to defend themselves in the mountains from attack.

His plans, however, without sanction of any legitimate civil authorities were illegitimate, and quickly turned lawless. He was captured at Harper's Ferry and eventually hung for treason and murder. He was trying to do a good thing, but in an unbiblical way. Before his death he stated:

John Brown after his capture.

I have no regret for the transaction for which I am condemned. I went against the laws of men, it is true, but "whether it be right to obey God or men, judge ye." Christ told me to remember them that were in bonds as bound with them, to do toward them as I would wish them to do towards me in similar circumstances. My conscience bade me do that. I tried to do it, but failed.

I, John Brown, am now quite certain that the crimes of this guilty land will never be purged away but with blood. I had, as I now think vainly, flattered myself that without very much bloodshed it might be done.[427]

The Principle of Union

As the principle of self-government was being championed by Calhoun, the principle of union was articulated best by Christian statesman Daniel Webster. The speeches of Webster, Clay, and Calhoun took place in the "golden-era" of the Congress.

We pointed out earlier that the principles of self-government and union must be kept in balance or tension, as was established by our Founders; if not, the end result is either centralism or disintegration. Though the Civil War focused on the issue of slavery, the principle at stake was union. Our Founders had rejected the loose-knit confederation for a permanent federation when they drafted the Constitution.

Daniel Webster

This is likened to a marriage covenant—if there are problems, you must patiently work through them; divorce is not an option.[428]

In President Lincoln's perspective, we should not break our Federal union (as long as there are constitutional avenues for redress), thus secession of the Southern states over slavery became legitimate grounds for Lincoln to go to war. It would be inaccurate to think that the North was more godly or Christian than the South. In reality, the South had become the center of true revival and the bastion of Calvinism, while part of the North had drifted into Unitarianism and dead formalism.

Henry Clay

John C. Calhoun

The Almighty Has His Own Purpose

The Civil War is unique in history. America was a Christian nation, in both North and South, but America had compromised in dealing with slavery. God could not allow slavery to continue and hinder his long-term destiny for America in the eyes of the world. He used the war to judge us and yet deliver us at the same time.

A history of the individuals involved is intriguing, for some of the greatest Christian generals and statesmen existed on both sides. Abraham Lincoln described it best in his Second Inaugural Address:

> Both read the same Bible and pray to the same God, and each invokes His aid against the other. It may seem strange that any men should dare to ask a just God's assistance in wringing their bread from the sweat of other men's faces, but let us judge not that we be not judged. The prayer of both could not be answered. That of neither has been answered fully. The almighty has His own purposes. Woe unto the world because of offences, for it must needs be that offences come, but woe to that man by whom the offence cometh.
>
> If we shall suppose that American slavery is one of those offences which, in the providence of God, must needs come, but which having continued through His appointed time, He now wills to remove, and that He gives to both North and South this terrible war as the woe due to those by whom the offence came, shall we discern there any departure from those divine attributes which the believers in a living God always ascribe to Him? Fondly do we hope, fervently do we pray, that this mighty scourge of war may speedily pass away. Yet if God wills that it continue until all the wealth piled by the bondsman's two hundred and fifty years of unrequited toil shall be sunk, and until every drop of blood drawn with the lash shall be paid by another drawn with the sword, as was said three thousand years ago, so still it must be said, that the judgements of the Lord are true and righteous altogether.[429]

God accomplished two things in this time period: He eradicated slavery and preserved the union. How He did it is fascinating.

When Lincoln was elected President, he never intended to emancipate the slaves. In fact, he could not legally, but he did eventually under the authority of emergency war powers. But he did not do so until 1863, motivated by the North losing almost every major battle. Lincoln wrote shortly before his assassination:

> On many a defeated field there was a voice louder than the thundering of a cannon. It was the voice of God, crying, "Let My people go." We were all very slow in realizing it was God's voice, but after many

humiliating defeats the nation came to believe it as a great and solemn command. Great multitudes begged and prayed that I might answer God's voice by signing the Emancipation Proclamation, and I did it, believing we never should be successful in the great struggle unless the God of Battles has been on our side.[430]

Between 1861 and 1863, associations of clergymen representing Methodists, Baptists, Episcopalians, Lutherans, Quakers, Congregationalists, United Brethren, missions boards and YMCA groups, all over the North sent 79 official condemnations of slavery to President Lincoln, thanking him for his stand, and urging him to further action.

General Stonewall Jackson and his men at prayer.

Within a few months' time, 125 remonstrances signed by New England clergymen alone poured into Congress. One memorable protest concerning the extension of slavery in the territories, signed by 3050 New England clergymen, was 200 feet long.[431]

Senator Charles Sumner thanked ministers, saying, "In the days of the Revolution, John Adams, yearning for Independence, said, 'Let the pulpits thunder against oppression, and the pulpits thundered. The time has come for them to thunder again.'"[432]

A religious periodical of the day reports:

It became the general [consensus] that we were passing through an ordeal of purification rather than destruction. A profound moral feeling began to pervade the sorrow-stricken mind of the country. Good men betook themselves to importunate prayer. Public fasts were observed; religious assemblies were held in behalf of the country. Almost every pulpit discussed public affairs from a religious standpoint;…and millions of devout men and women mourned in their closets of devotion over the national sins and perils…

The religious spirit of the nation, instead of decaying, is daily making men's hearts more reverent, more humble, more courageous, and more worthy of our first national heritage of liberty, which God is now a second time purifying by fire![433]

But it wasn't without cost. An awesome example of God's explicit judgment for all of those who compromise is revealed by the aftermath of the war. One state had its cities and land devastated more than any other: Georgia. For every wound laid on the back of a slave, God used General Sherman to lay a stripe down the middle of the state. Another result of the war was major division in religious bodies. The three denominations that suffered the worst splits were those that held the most slaves: the Presbyterians, the Methodists, and the Baptists. Such is the curse of compromise.

Why was the North losing all the battles? Because God induced the greatest generals to fight for the South.

The Christian Character of the Generals

Colonel Robert E. Lee of Virginia was offered command of the troops that President Lincoln ordered to South Carolina in response to her seceding from the Union. After much prayer, he declined saying: "I look upon secession as anarchy. If I owned the four millions of slaves in the South, I would sacrifice them all to the Union—but how can I draw my sword upon Virginia, my native state?"[434]

Lee later accepted the command of the Army of Virginia. This may have not been the best decision, yet it seems that Providence had willed it, so that the two greatest generals would lead the Confederate army to victory until the slaves were emancipated.

In a conversation with a minister shortly after the start of the war, Lee was asked: "Is it your expectation that the issue of this war will be to perpetuate the institution of slavery?" Lee replied: "The future is in the hands of Providence, but if the slaves of the South were mine, I would surrender them all without a struggle to avert the war." The minister then tells us:

Robert Edward Lee

> I asked him next upon what his calculations were based in so unequal a contest, and how he expected to win success; was he looking to divided counsels in the North, or to foreign interposition? His answer showed how little he was affected by the hopes and fears which agitated ordinary minds.
>
> "My reliance is in the help of God."
>
> "Are you sanguine of the result?" I ventured to inquire.
>
> "At present I am not concerned with results. God's will ought to be our aim, and I am contented that His designs should be accomplished and not mine."[435]

Lee did much to promote revival in his army and saw every soldier as a soul to be saved. So concerned was Lee for the spiritual welfare of his soldiers that one of his biographers says, "One almost feels as if he cared more for winning souls than battles, and for supplying his army with Bibles than with bullets and powder."[436]

The same was true of another Christian General, Thomas Jonathan "Stonewall" Jackson. Jackson was one of the best (if not best) military leaders in our nation's history. The confederate troops under his command (for the first few years of the war) obtained victory after victory over the Union Army. In a majority of these battles, the Union forces greatly outnumbered Jackson's men. Jackson's fearlessness in battle earned him the name "Stonewall." Mark Grimsley writes:

> He displayed extraordinary calm under fire, a calm too deep and masterful to be mere pretence. His apparent obliviousness to danger attracted notice, and after First Manassas someone asked him how he managed it.
>
> "Captain, my religious belief teaches me to feel as safe in battle as in bed," Jackson explained. "God has fixed the time for my death. I do not concern myself about that, but to be always ready, no matter when it may overtake me." He added pointedly, "Captain that is the way all men should live, and then all would be equally brave."

As a field commander, Jackson's religion came into play in various ways. During military operations he prayed frequently, lived simply, and in his reports habitually gave God all credit for the slightest success. "Without God's blessing," Jackson declared, "I look to no success, and for every success my prayer is, that all the glory may be given to Him to whom it is properly due." Whenever possible he also avoided marching or fighting on the Sabbath.

Jackson considered his army to be, among other things, an enormous opportunity to further the gospel. In prayer he pleaded with God to "baptize the whole army with His Holy Spirit." In practice he worked

ceaselessly to sharpen the spiritual devotion of his men. Orders that religious services be conducted frequently found their way into his military correspondence, and although he stopped short of declaring them mandatory, Jackson had a way of seeing to it the services were well-attended. Riding through the camps one Sunday to make sure his men were at worship, Jackson came upon a captain, indolently smoking a pipe. The captain greeted him uneasily. Without returning the "good morning," Jackson went straight

Jackson pleaded with God to "baptize the whole army with His Holy Spirit."

to the point: "Captain, is divine service going on in your camp?" "I don't know, sir." "Where is your Colonel's headquarters" The captain pointed them out and inquired, "Shall I take you to them, sir." "Yes," Jackson clipped, and as they neared the headquarters tent, added, "I see service is going on…Captain, the next time I order divine service, won't you promise me to attend?" The captain made the only safe response — "Yes, sir" — and joined the assemblage.

During the winter of 1862 and 1863, while the Confederate army bivouacked along the Rappahannock, a religious revival swept the entire command. Jackson, of course, enthusiastic, bent his energies toward facilitating the tide of Christian sentiment that bathed the army. He also strove to better organize the chaplains of the army, arguing they should meet together and "through God's blessing devise successful plans for spiritual conquests."[437]

While the Confederate Army was enjoying revival (up to 150,000 Southern troops were saved during the war), it also enjoyed phenomenal success in almost every major battle. This induced Abraham Lincoln to seek God for the reasons why. He concluded that the nation's chief sins were slavery and pride.

On September 22, 1862, he issued the Emancipation Proclamation which declared all slaves free in states that were still in rebellion as of January 1, 1863. Then he called for a national Day of Humiliation, Fasting and Prayer throughout the North on April 30th of 1863. He stated in part:

The Emancipation Proclamation

It is the duty of nations as well as of men to own their dependence upon the overruling power of God; to confess their sins and transgressions in humble sorrow, yet with assured hope that genuine repentance will lead to mercy and pardon; and to recognize the sublime truth, announced in the Holy Scriptures and proven by all history, that those nations only are blessed whose God is the Lord;

And insomuch as we know that by His divine law nations, like individuals, are subject to punishments and chastisements in this world, may we not justly fear that the awful calamity of civil war which now desolates the land may be but a punishment inflicted upon us for our presumptuous sins, to the needful end of our national reformation as a whole people? We have been the recipients of the choicest bounties of Heaven. We have been preserved these many years in peace and prosperity. We have grown in numbers, wealth, and power as no other nation has ever grown; but we have forgotten God. We have forgotten the gracious hand which preserved us in peace, and multiplied and enriched and strengthened us; and we have vainly imagined, in the deceitfulness of our hearts, that all these blessings were produced by some superior wisdom and virtue of our own. Intoxicated with unbroken success, we have become too self-sufficient to feel the necessity of redeeming and preserving grace, too proud to pray to the God who made us;

It behooves us, then, to humble ourselves before the offended Power, and confess our national sins, and to pray for clemency and forgiveness.[438]

Interestingly, within two days, one of the most crucial providential occurrences of the entire war occurred. God had removed the stigma of slavery from this nation and gave Lincoln and others in the North a measure of repentance. Providence now turned to a new objective: preserve the Union of the United States as one whole people. Within just two days of this Day of Prayer, General Stonewall Jackson, who had never lost a battle, was providentially removed from the scene.

Stonewall Jackson

In an accident of war, Stonewall Jackson was shot by his own men. Anguished staff officers brought him to a battlefield operating table; a surgeon chloroformed him and amputated his left arm.

Upon learning of Jackson's fate the next morning, General Robert E. Lee lamented, "He lost his left arm, but I have lost my right."[439]

Shortly after this on May 10, 1863, Jackson died. However, even in his odd death (previously, Jackson had many times lead his men into battle and exposed himself to enemy fire, yet he remained unharmed, protected, as he believed, by God), he believed God was fulfilling His purposes and causing "all things to work together for good to those that love God." Had God not removed him the outcome of the war may have been different.

Just around the corner was the battle that marked the turning point of the war—Gettysburg. This was a major offensive for the South but without Jackson and Providential assistance, they would never succeed. Immediately following the battle, William Johnson records how Union General Sickles asked President Lincoln whether or not he had been anxious about the battle at Gettysburg.

Lincoln gravely said, "No, I was not; some of my Cabinet and many others in Washington were, but I had no fears." General Sickles inquired how this was, and seemed curious about it. Mr. Lincoln hesitated, but finally replied: "Well, I will tell you how it was. In the pinch of your campaign up there, when everybody seemed panic-stricken, and nobody

could tell what was going to happen, oppressed by the gravity of our affairs, I went to my room one day, and I locked the door, and got down on my knees before Almighty God, and prayed to Him mightily for victory at Gettysburg. I told Him that this was His war, and our cause His cause, but we couldn't stand another Fredericksburg or Chancellorsville. And I then and there made a solemn vow to Almighty God, that if He would stand by you boys at Gettysburg, I would stand by Him. And after that (I don't know how it was, and I can't explain it), soon a sweet comfort crept into my soul that God almighty had taken the whole business into his own hands and that things would go alright at Gettysburg. And that is why I had no fears about you."[440]

As General Lee was retreating from this major defeat, that he probably knew sealed the doom of the Confederacy, an encounter with a wounded Union soldier revealed his great Christian character. The Northern soldier wrote afterwards:

I had been a most bitter anti-South man, and fought and cursed the Confederates desperately. I could see nothing good in any of them. The last day of the fight I was badly wounded. A ball shattered my left leg. I lay on the ground not far from Cemetery Ridge, and as General Lee ordered his retreat, he and his officers rode near me.

As they came along I recognized him, and, though faint from exposure and loss of blood, I raised my hands, and looked Lee in the face, and shouted as loud as I could—"Hurrah for the Union!"

The General heard me, looked, stopped his horse, dismounted, and came toward me. I confessed I at first thought he meant to kill me. But, as he came up, he looked down at me with such a sad expression upon his face that all fear left me, and I wondered what he was about. He extended his hand to me, grasping mine firmly, and looking right into my eyes, said, "My son, I hope you will soon be well."

If I live a thousand years, I shall never forget the expression on General Lee's face. There he was, defeated, retiring from a field that had

Pickett's charge at Gettysburg.

cost him and his cause almost their last hope, and yet he stopped to say words like these to a wounded soldier of the opposition who had taunted him as he passed by! As soon as the General had left me, I cried myself to sleep there on the bloody ground.[441]

After such a defeat, Lee saw the opportunity to continue to promote revival. General Lee often issued orders for his troops to observe days of fasting and prayer, and attend services. In one such order on Thursday, August 13, 1863, Lee told his army to cry out to God for forgiveness of their sins and humble themselves before Him. He asked God to save their enemies as well as their own troops, and declared that "God is our only refuge and our strength."[442] Chaplain William Jones related the effect this order had:

General Robert E. Lee

I can never forget the effect produced by the reading of this order at the solemn services of that memorable fast-day. A revival was already in progress in many of the commands—the day was almost universally observed—the attendance upon preaching and other services was very large. The solemn attention and starting tear attested the deep interest felt, and the work of grace among the troops widened and deepened and went gloriously on until over fifteen thousand of the soldiers of Lee's army professed repentance toward God and faith in Jesus as a personal Saviour. How far these results were due to this fast-day, or to the quiet influence and fervent prayers of the commanding general, eternity alone shall reveal."[443]

Lee would personally pray with his men. Jones recorded:

While the Army of Northern Virginia confronted General Meade at Mine Run, near the end of November, 1863, and a battle was momentarily expected, General Lee, with a number of general and staff officers, was riding down his line of battle, when…[they] came upon a party of soldiers held on the eve of battle. An attack from the enemy seemed imminent—already the sharpshooting along the skirmish line had begun—the artillery was belching forth its hoarse thunder, and the mind and heart of the great chieftain was full of the expected combat. Yet, as he saw those ragged veterans bowed in prayer, he instantly dismounted, uncovered his head and devoutly joined in the simple worship. The rest of the party at once followed his example, and those humble privates found themselves leading the devotions of their loved and honored chieftain.[444]

Lee at the soldiers' prayer meeting.

On almost the same date in November, Lincoln returned to the field where Gettysburg was fought to dedicate it as a national cemetery. In about three minutes, perhaps the greatest speech in history was delivered:

Fourscore and seven years ago our fathers brought forth upon this continent a new nation, conceived in liberty, and dedicated to the proposition that all men are created equal. Now we are engaged in a great civil war, testing whether that nation, or any nation so conceived and so dedicated, can long endure. We are met on a great battlefield of that war. We have come to dedicate a portion of that field as a final resting-place for those who here gave their lives that that nation might live. It is altogether fitting and proper that we should do this. But in a larger sense we cannot dedicate, we cannot consecrate, we cannot hallow this ground. The brave men, living and dead, who struggled here, have consecrated it far above our power to add or detract. The world will little note, nor long remember, what we say here, but it can never forget what they did here. It is for us, the living, rather to be dedicated here to the unfinished work which they who fought here have thus far so nobly advanced. It is rather for us to be here dedicated to the great task remaining before us, that from these honored dead we take increased devotion to that cause for which they gave the last full measure of devotion; that we here highly resolve that these dead shall not have died in vain; that this nation, under God, shall have a new birth of freedom, and that the government of the people, by the people, and for the people, shall not perish from the earth.[445]

Shortly before his death an Illinois clergyman asked Lincoln, "Do you love Jesus?" Mr. Lincoln solemnly replied: "When I left Springfield I asked the people to pray for me. I was not a Christian. When I buried my son, the severest trial of my life, I was not a Christian. But when I went to Gettysburg and saw the graves of thousands of our soldiers, I then and there consecrated myself to Christ. Yes, I do love Jesus."[446]

A year and a half later, General Robert E. Lee surrendered to Ulysses S. Grant at Appomattox.

On the day of the receipt of the news of the capitulation of Lee, the Cabinet meeting was held an hour earlier than usual. Neither the President nor any member was able, for a time, to give utterance to his feelings. At the suggestion of Mr. Lincoln all dropped on their knees, and offered, in

Lincoln delivering his Gettysburg address. While at Gettysburg Lincoln said, "I then and there consecrated myself to Christ."

silence and in tears, their humble and heartfelt acknowledgments to the Almighty for the triumph He had granted to the national cause.[447]

Later that year, slavery was abolished by Constitutional amendment. Lincoln was assassinated, and Lee became president of what is now Washington and Lee University, where men were being trained for the ministry. There he is buried, while thousands of other American soldiers have been buried around his former home which still stands at Arlington National Cemetery.

Effects of the War Between the States

Since America did not deal with the evil institution of slavery, God did. And He used a devastating war to do so — a war that brought judgment upon both the North and South, with the loss of over half a million lives. The South, the place where slavery was entrenched, was especially hard hit, as one out of seven adult males of child-bearing age was killed during the war.

The Civil War had both positive and negative results. The positive: slavery was abolished and the union was preserved. The negative: power began to be centralized in the national government, and the idea of federalism incorporated into the nation by the Founders (with a balance of power between the state and national governments) began to be lost.

Through it all, the principles of the Declaration prevailed; in particular, the idea that all men are created free and have equal rights before the Creator, including a right to life, liberty, and property. This Christian idea continued to advance in history. The elimination of slavery in America was the catalyst that led to the overthrow of slavery throughout much of the world.

Francis Scott Key, author of "The Star-spangled Banner" (1814). He writes
in the final verse:

> Then conquer we must,
> For our cause it is just,
> And this be our motto:
> "In God is our Trust!"

Chapter 18

Christian Liberty Impacts All Citizens

Advancements of Liberty after the Civil War

After the Civil War, the foundational Christian ideas of the American Republic brought advancements in all spheres of life and new opportunities for all citizens, especially minorities and women. African Americans had new liberties that were not common prior to the ending of slavery. Free blacks had lived in America from the early years of colonization, and in some states had the same rights as other settlers. This included the right to vote, own property, run for office, start businesses, and more. But such privileges were not available to most blacks until slavery ended and legal barriers began to be removed.

Blacks, including many who were born into slavery, made significant contributions to American life in our antebellum history. These included such people as Richard Allen, the founder of the African Methodist Episcopal (AME) denomination; Phyllis Wheatley, author and poet; Benjamin Banneker, scientist, inventor, philosopher and author; James Armistead and Peter Salem, heroes of the American Revolutionary War; Absalom Jones, the first black bishop of the Episcopal Church in America; William Nell, historian and civil servant; Frederick Douglas, orator, author, and political activist; Sojourner Truth and Harriet Tubman, leaders in the anti-slavery movement; and Henry Garnet, minister and first African American to speak in the halls of Congress, delivering a sermon to that body in commemoration of the passage of the 13th Amendment.

These opportunities, however, were limited due to unjust laws. But this changed with the ending of slavery after the Civil War and the triumph of biblical principles of liberty. The Chain of Liberty was continuing to grow and Christian liberty was continuing to advance. Not only was America effected but so were many other nations, as advancing liberty ended serfdom in much of Europe. Technological advancements in the U.S. and Europe produced the radio, automobile, airplane, television, computer, and space flight. Economic and agricultural advances occurred due to the influence of such Christian men as George Washington Carver and John Wanamaker.

George Washington Carver Applied the Truth and Transformed the Economy of the South

George W. Carver was born into slavery just before the close of the Civil War. His mom was a slave, but after emancipation she stayed in Missouri with the family who had owned her. George and his mother were carried off from the Carver family by raiders when he was just a baby. Mose Carver offered 40 acres and a horse (since he had no cash) to a man to find the mother and child. He brought back George, but was unable to find the mother. George, therefore, grew up on the Carver farm, but in relative poverty.

As a child he loved the woods and plants and things related to botany. He was very observant of nature and always asked questions. He also enjoyed using his hands. At about age ten he left the farm and worked his way through high school. As a young man he worked hard and saved money to go to a certain college, but was not allowed to attend. A couple helped him to go to an artist school, but he found there were no jobs for an artist. He eventually was able to study his first love, agriculture.

After obtaining his university degree, Carver was invited by Booker T. Washington to teach at his newly formed Tuskegee Institute in Alabama. His work while there transformed the economy of the South and affected many nations as well.

Carver would rise every morning at 4:00 AM, read the Bible, and seek God concerning what He wanted him

George Washington Carver

to do. Toward the end of his life Carver remarked: "The secret of my success? It is simple. It is found in the Bible, 'In all thy ways acknowledge Him and He shall direct thy paths.'"[448]

One thing Carver sought God concerning was how to improve the economy of the southeastern part of the United States. Continual planting of cotton had depleted the soil and the invasion of the boll weevil was destroying much of the cotton crop.

Biographer Rackham Holt wrote that, "He devoutly believed that a personal relationship with the Creator of all things was the only foundation for the abundant life. He had a little story in which he related his experience:

> I asked the Great Creator what the universe was made for.
> "Ask for something more in keeping with that little mind of yours," He replied.
> "What was man made for?"
> "Little man, you still want to know too much. Cut down the extent of your request and improve the intent."
> Then I told the Creator I wanted to know all about the peanut. He replied that my mind was too small to know all about the peanut, but He said He would give me a handful of peanuts. And God said, "Behold, I have given you every herb bearing seed, which is upon the face of the earth…to you it shall be for meat. … I have given every green herb for meat: and it was so."
> I carried the peanuts into my laboratory and the Creator told me to take them apart and resolve them into their elements. With such knowledge as I had of chemistry and physics I set to work to take them apart. I separated the water, the fats, the oils, the gums, the resins, sugars, starches, pectoses, pentosans, amino acids. There! I had the parts of the peanuts all spread out before me.[449]

Carver's story teaches us the importance of preparation in fulfilling God's plan for our lives. Carver had labored hard to develop his skills of chemistry. Consequently, God could answer the question Carver posed to Him. God could not reveal the answer to this question to me today; I would need much preparation before I would be in a position to understand and act upon the answer. Diligent preparation is vital to understand and fulfill our calling. God may not answer many of our inquiries or lead us deeper into our providential purpose because we have not learned enough or been properly prepared to hear and understand what

He may say. It is important to learn this lesson. To continue with Carver's story, he relates:

> I looked at Him and He looked at me. "Now, you know what the peanut is."
>
> "Why did you make the peanut?"
>
> The Creator said, "I have given you three laws; namely, compatibility, temperature, and pressure. All you have to do is take these constituents and put them together, observing these laws, and I will show you why I made the peanut."
>
> I therefore went on to try different combinations of the parts under different conditions of temperature and pressure, and the result was what you see.[450]

The results: Carver discovered over 300 uses for the peanut. Food items included nuts, soup, a dozen beverages, mixed pickles, sauces, meal, instant and dry coffee. Other items included: salve, bleach, tan remover, wood filler, washing powder, metal polish, paper, ink, plastics, shaving cream, rubbing oil, linoleum, shampoo, axle grease, synthetic rubber.

He produced milk which would not curdle in cooking or when acids were added. Long-lasting cream and cheese could be made from this milk. "This milk proved to be truly a lifesaver in the Belgian Congo. Cows could not be kept there because of leopards and flies, so if a mother died her baby was buried with her; there was nothing to nourish it. Missionaries fed the infants

George Washington Carver said: "My purpose alone must be God's purpose — to increase the welfare and happiness of His people."

peanut milk, and they flourished."[451]

George worked with many other plants and items — making 107 products from sweet potatoes; making synthetic marble from sawdust; and making wallboard from many different Southern plants.

For his work, Carver received many awards and became the advisor to many world leaders, including President Franklin Roosevelt, Mahatma Gandhi, and Thomas Edison. In all his work he never failed to acknowledge God. In 1921 when he testified before a committee of Congress, he was asked by the Chairman:

> "Dr. Carver, how did you learn all of these things?"
> Carver answered: "From an old book."
> "What book?" asked the Senator.
> Carver replied, "The Bible."
> The Senator inquired, "Does the Bible tell about peanuts?"
> "No Sir" Dr. Carver replied, "But it tells about the God who made the peanut. I asked Him to show me what to do with the peanut, and he did."[452]

Carver looked for divine direction and saw God as the revealer of truth. He said:

> I discover nothing in my laboratory. If I come here of myself I am lost. But I can do all things through Christ. I am God's servant, His agent, for here God and I are alone. I am just the instrument through which He speaks, and I would be able to do more if I were to stay in closer touch with Him. With my prayers I mix my labors, and sometimes God is pleased to bless the results.[453]

He knew his purpose in life: "My purpose alone must be God's purpose — to increase the welfare and happiness of His people."[454] Godly service, not money or fame, was his primary motivation. In fact, Edison offered him a job with a six-figure income, a fortune in those times, but he turned it down so he could continue his agricultural work in his laboratory that he called "God's little workshop." "George Washington Carver worked for the riches of God rather than the wealth of this world."[455]

Carver helped transform the economy of the South, and affected agriculture all over the world. Carver had to overcome all kinds of obstacles to fulfill his destiny (only a few have been mentioned here). In all of these he persevered, labored hard, and pursued the desires in his heart. He had a great impact upon many people, upon agriculture, and the economy at large.

John Wanamaker

John Wanamaker was the founder of the modern department store and a business pioneer. In 1911 he opened a new store in Philadelphia that was so noteworthy that President Taft dedicated it. He said that the department store that Wanamaker pioneered was "one of the most important instrumentalities in modern life for the promotion of comfort among the people,"[456] and that it would be "a model for all other stores of the same kind throughout the country and throughout the world."[457] Thirty thousand people attended this event. Words on the dedication tablet reveal the success of the

John Wanamaker

Wanamaker store was due to "freedom of competition and the blessing of God."[458]

When John Wanamaker was a boy, he went to a jewelry store in Philadelphia on a Christmas Eve to buy his mom a gift. He said,

> "I had only a few dollars saved up for the purpose. I wanted to buy the best thing these dollars would buy. I guess I took a long time to look at the things in the jewelry cases. The jeweler was growing impatient. Finally I said 'I'll take that,' indicating a piece — just what it was I do not recall.
>
> "The jeweler began wrapping it up. Suddenly I saw another piece that I thought would better please my mother. 'Excuse me, sir,' I said, 'but I have changed my mind, I'll take this piece instead of the one you are wrapping.'
>
> "You can imagine my surprise and chagrin when the jeweler answered; 'It's too late now. You've bought the first piece and you must keep it.' I was too abashed to protest. I took what I had first bought, but as I went out of the store I said to myself:
>
> "'When I have a store of my own the people shall have what they want...and what they ought to have.'"[459]

This incident helped create the foundation of his business.

John Wanamaker was much more than a successful merchant. He founded a new system and philosophy of business, based upon the biblical view of man. He was a merchant pioneer who believed that "the Golden Rule of the New Testament has become the Golden Rule of business."[460] Though at times he was cynically called "Pious John" by those who thought religion had no place in business, he showed that Christianity was essential for good business.

Christianity provided the character necessary to keep the many temptations of business from blowing the merchant "over the precipice and be ruined"[461] and also the principles necessary to build a successful business. He understood stores were much more than buildings with stocks and fixtures, saying the soul of the workmen must give life to the structure, not only providing needed goods for people but "meeting the greater future of the nation" and leading "the world in its nobler civilization by its advancing education and commerce."[462]

He revolutionized business by establishing the one-price system, the money-back guarantee, the marking of the quality of goods, and the service oriented store. He was the "father of modern advertising," in that the volume of advertising became so great as other merchants followed his lead of having daily ads in newspapers, that this gave birth to the modern newspaper and magazine, making them affordable to all.

Money did not motivate John Wanamaker to build a successful business. His desire was to serve the people. Money came as a by-product of service.

He exemplified the historical truth that capitalism is a product of Calvinism. Calvinism taught that work is an important part of Godliness; that God requires

Wanamaker's Philadelphia store

uprightness in all one's dealing in business; that keeping account of one's dealings in business is like God keeping account of man's actions before God. Calvinism imparts a zealousness to succeed and an understanding of the importance of savings and frugality.

He had poor health (he was rejected for service in the Civil War because of this), but labored six days a week in the business and community, as well as every Sabbath (in teaching in the church and Sunday school) for 70 years.

He had only about two years of formal schooling, yet became one of the world's leaders in business, served in the cabinet of President Benjamin Harrison as Postmaster-General, and assisted in many voluntary associations. President Taft called him "the greatest merchant in America."[463]

He applied the Golden Rule to employees and customers. He promoted better working conditions, including fewer work hours per week, retirement plans, medical plans, better work environment (with lockers, cafeterias, recreation clubs). He operated with the view that all his employees were part of the Wanamaker family. With both customers and employees in view, he pioneered store comforts: heat and ventilation, elevators, electric lights, and ease of access.

His Philadelphia store became the largest in the world. It was much more than just its physical size. It had a spirit, a personality. The employee sought to serve the customer and had his well-being in mind. The store entertained, educated, and performed special services. People enjoyed visiting, whether they bought items or not, and were refreshed from the visit. Universities studied his stores to learn successful economic principles. They could see them at work. His success came from his character.

Wanamaker said, "Commerce...is the very life blood that pulsates through every fibre of a healthy body politic."[464] What Wall Street or investment banks did was of no matter unless commerce was full of life and advancing.

He believed strongly in the free market and individual enterprise, with government involved only in keeping the market free and fair. The best means of advancing the economy and producing the growth of business in a nation was to keep taxes low, cut government regulations, and encourage competition. "Business thrives on competition," he wrote, "and that the people's interests in getting better merchandise and lower prices are always improved when competition is unstifled!"[465]

For men in commerce to succeed, biblical civil leaders are needed because the government is the house in which the economy lives. America had many good leaders after the war, including for the first time many African Americans. James Garfield and William McKinley were two of those Christian presidents who lived out their faith in public service.

James Garfield

In 1881 James A. Garfield was inaugurated the twentieth President of the United States. About six months after taking office he was assassinated. Were it not for God's Providence, he would have died many years earlier in his youth.

As a boy, Garfield worked on a canal. He was unable to swim which almost proved fatal one day when he fell into the water. While gasping for breath and trying to keep above water, he grabbed hold of a tow rope that had accidentally fallen into the water. As he was sinking he somehow managed to throw the rope, which wrapped around a fixture on the barge, and he then pulled himself to safety. After recovering, Garfield attempted for three hours to throw the same rope around the same fixture and have it attach, but he was unable to duplicate the feat.

James Garfield

Garfield concluded that God had providentially saved his life. He went on to attend seminary and became a minister for the Disciples of Christ denomination. He led hundreds to Christ, publically debated evolutionists, and influenced the public sector in many different ways. He was elected to Congress and eventually became President.

In 1876, at the Centennial of our Declaration of Independence, Garfield wrote these words, which must be understood by Americans today:

> Now, more than ever before, the people are responsible for the character of their Congress. If that body be ignorant, reckless, and corrupt, it is because the people tolerate ignorance, recklessness, and corruption. If it be intelligent, brave, and pure, it is because the people demand these high qualities to represent them in national legislature. ... Congress must always be the exponent of the political character and culture of the people; and if the next centennial does not find us a great nation, with a great and worthy Congress, it will be because those who represent the enterprise, the culture, and the morality of the nation do not aid in controlling the political forces which are employed to select the men who shall occupy the great places of trust and power.[466]

William McKinley

William McKinley was one of many political leaders of the 19th century who was a Christian. McKinley, the 25th President of the United States, was assassinated in 1901 during the first year of his second term of office. His lifelong Christian faith was evident in that he forgave his murderer immediately after he fired the shot (on September 6) – "Don't let them hurt him,"[467] was his first cry – and his last conscious words before he died (on September 14) from the wounds were, "It is His will, not ours, that will be done."[468]

McKinley was born in Ohio in 1843 and raised in a Methodist home. Many people were being converted to the fast-growing revivalist Methodist movement in the mid-nineteenth century. He was saved at a camp meeting at around age ten, and in 1859, after attending another series of camp meetings, Will was baptized and became a full member of the Methodist Church. He may have pursued the ministry, but the civil war intervened. He did not leave his faith behind when he joined the Twenty-third Ohio Volunteer Infantry, which was so devout it was called "the psalm-singers of the Western Reserve."[469] McKinley

McKinley taking oath of office.

described to his sister their Christian regimen: "religious exercises in the company twice a day, prayer meetings twice a week, and preaching in the regiment once on a Sabbath."[470] He even called himself a soldier of Jesus.

His strong faith remained with him throughout his life and was expressed in his speeches and testified to by his friends. In his First Inaugural Address (1897) he said: "Our faith teaches that there is no safer reliance than upon the God of our fathers, who has so singularly favored the American people in every national trial, and who will not forsake us so long as we obey His commandments and walk humbly in His footsteps."[471]

As President, he regularly read the Bible and often hosted hymn sings in the White House. One biographer stated, "His evenings were spent with Mrs. McKinley and friends, often reading the Bible aloud, until ten."[472] McKinley wrote in 1899: "My belief embraces the Divinity of Christ and a recognition of Christianity as the mightiest factor in the world's civilization."[473]

Numerous friends testified of his strong Christian faith. McKinley's pastor and friend, Methodist Bishop Andrews, said of him: "He believed in God and in Jesus Christ, through whom God was revealed. He accepted the divine law of the Scripture; he based his hope on Jesus Christ, the appointed and only Redeemer of men."[474]

On the evening of his death, McKinley softly chanted the words of his favorite hymn, "Nearer, My God to Thee," and then uttered his last words, "His will be done."[475]

African American Leaders

Modern minority history often focuses on the first individuals to do something, but of more importance in God's eyes are those who carry on their vocation with Christian character and a biblical worldview. Such people are who we should emulate and who God can especially use to accomplish His purposes for mankind.

Frederick Douglass was one of the most significant black leaders of the 19th century. Born into slavery, he escaped to the North, and in 1839 was licensed as a preacher by the AME Zion Church in New Bedford, Massachusetts, and there began his anti-slavery work. By 1851 Douglass changed his negative view of America's founding (as expressed in his earlier 1845 *Narrative*) and began supporting the Constitution as an anti-slavery document (see his quote on page 300). His faith was central to his public life, writing in 1852 that there is

one great political idea. … The best expression of it I found in the Bible:…righteousness exalts a nation, and sin is a reproach to any people— Proverbs 14:34. Now this constitutes my politics—the negative and positive of my politics and the whole of my politics.[476]

With the passage of the 13th, 14th, and 15th Amendments, blacks had opportunities to not only vote but also to hold elected and appointed office. Beginning in 1867, Douglass received Presidential appointments from Republican Presidents Ulysses S. Grant,

Frederick Douglas

Rutherford B. Hayes, and James A. Garfield. Democratic President Grover Cleveland removed Douglass from office but Republican Benjamin Harrison reappointed him.

Douglass, like all black public officials in the 19th century, identified with the Republican Party, and virtually all blacks voted for that party for about 70 years after the Civil War. In 1867 Rev. Hiram Revels of Mississippi became the first black elected to the U.S. Senate. In the years just after the war, there were two black senators and 14 black congressmen elected to national office. Many others were elected to state and local offices, including Pinckney Pinchback of Louisiana, the first black elected as governor of a state (in 1872).

Unfortunately, it wasn't long before these new-found freedoms began to be restricted when the Democratic Party returned to power in the South in the later part of the 19th century. The rise of the Ku Klux Klan, lynchings,[477] black codes, and Jim Crow laws all contributed to suppressing the voice and political power of African Americans.

The First Blacks in Congress. From left: Senator Hiram Rhodes Revels, Mississippi; Congressmen: Benjamin Turner, Alabama, Robert De Large, South Carolina, Josiah Walls, Florida, Jefferson Long, Georgia, Joseph Hayne Rainey, South Carolina, and Robert Brown Elliott, South Carolina.

After the implementation of segregation laws, Booker T. Washington advanced his vision to educate blacks for service in all spheres of life by starting Tuskegee Institute in 1881. (George W. Carver began teaching at Tuskegee in 1896.) Washington would later tell his story of rising from slavery to founding a college in his popular book *Up From Slavery* (1891). This educator, Republican Party leader, and advisor to President Theodore Roosevelt put his faith first. Booker T. Washington understood the liberating nature of Christianity, writing:

> If no other consideration had convinced me of the value of the Christian life, the Christ-like work which the Church of all denominations in America has done during the last thirty-five years for the elevation of the black man would have made me a Christian.[478]

Even though many of their rights began to be restricted, African Americans provided leadership in many different arenas.

Booker T. Washington

Religious leaders around the turn of the 19th century included Amanda Smith, a popular black female evangelist and missionary, and Rev. William Seymour. In 1906, Seymour led an interracial revival in California at the Azuza Street Mission that launched Pentecostalism, a religious movement that over the next century became the largest Christian movement in the world with the most racially diverse churches in history.

W.E.B. DuBois was a prominent social leader who issued a declaration in 1905 calling for an end of voting restrictions and segregation. He and several others helped start the National Association for the Advancement for Colored People on February 12, 1909. Unfortunately, DuBois rejected Christianity and supported socialism and Marxism. While he was an effective voice against racism, his appeal to non-Christian ideas of government affected many members of the African-American community. His endorsement of the Democratic Party presidential candidate Woodrow Wilson in 1912 was a shocking action for any black in the country at that time.

During the Great Depression some blacks for the first time became advisors to the Democratic Party, like Mary M. Bethune, who was a Republican but advised the Democratic President Franklin Roosevelt. Her most important advice:

Faith is the first factor in a life devoted to service. Without faith, nothing is possible. With it, nothing is impossible. Faith in God is the greatest power, but great, too, is faith in oneself. ... Our greatest Negro figures have been imbued with faith.[479]

While most early black leaders were Christians, this was changing as secularism began to rise in the nation. Two prominent labor leaders and civil rights pioneers, A. Philip Randolph and James Farmer were secular humanists. In addition, many of those who professed Christianity began to embrace many non-biblical views of government and social change, mirroring many white Christians.

Promises for assistance from President Franklin Roosevelt caused some black support to shift to the Democrats. However, it was not until Harry Truman ordered the integration of the military after World War II that a significant majority of blacks for the first time started identifying more with the Democratic Party.

In 1954 the Supreme Court struck down segregation of schools and public institutions in *Brown v. Board of Education* saying that separate is inherently unequal. This started the trend for integration of other public services, often forced by peaceful demonstrations. The best known protest was initiated by Rosa

Parks, a Republican Christian who refused to give up her seat on a bus in Montgomery, Alabama in 1955. She said that in her church, "I learned people should stand up for their rights, just as the

Rosa Parks said God gave her the strength to protest unjust policies and that God's peace flooded her soul.

Children of Israel stood up to the Pharaoh." Regarding her decision not to move from her seat, she remarked:

I instantly felt God give me the strength to endure whatever would happen next. ... God's peace flooded my soul, and my fear melted away. All people were equal in the eyes of God, and I was going to live like a free person.[480]

Parks' action started a bus boycott organized by Republican and Baptist minister Rev. Martin Luther King, Jr. King's political work was rooted in his faith. He wrote:

We need to recapture the gospel glow of the early Christians who were nonconformists in the truest sense of the word. ... Their powerful gospel put an end to such barbaric evils as infanticide and bloody gladiatorial contests. Finally, they captured the Roman Empire for Jesus Christ.[481]

Martin Luther King Jr.'s Christian faith motivated and guided his social activism.

He challenged his hearers:

If any earthly institution or custom conflicts with God's will, it is your Christian duty to oppose it. You must never allow the transitory, evanescent demands of man-made institutions to take precedence over the eternal demands of the Almighty God.[482]

Rev. King was clear where it starts:

By opening our lives to God in Christ, we become new creatures. This experience, which Jesus spoke of as the new birth, is essential if we are to be transformed nonconformists. ... Only through an inner spiritual transformation do we gain the strength to fight vigorously the evils of the world in a humble and loving spirit.[483]

In the famous march on Washington, D.C. in 1963 (which was organized by Republican A. Philip Randolph), Rev. King gave his historic speech on the American dream. His call for civil rights for all Americans, in which he appealed to the ideals of the Declaration of Independence and of the Christian faith, helped shift more national Democratic leaders to join with the almost unanimous Republican politicians to finally pass civil rights legislation between 1963-1965.

In 1966 the first black in a century was elected to the U.S. Senate — Edward Brooke, Republican of Massachusetts. And that same year the first black justice was appointed by Democratic President Johnson to the Supreme Court – Thurgood Marshall.

In 1968 Dr. King was assassinated (President Ronald Reagan made a national holiday in his honor in 1983). Around this time many in the Democratic Party sought to atone for its racist policies of the past; consequently, many black clergy and other black leaders became aligned with that party, and the general voting trend of African Americans became solidly Democratic. Unfortunately, many of the clergy (like Jesse Jackson and Al Sharpton) moved away from embracing a biblical worldview.

The first black Democrats elected to the Senate (in 1993) and to the Presidency (Barack Obama in 2008) reflect the changing political alliance of African Americans, as well as the general political philosophy of the Democratic Party, where Christianity has negligible influence in people's personal lives, worldview, and policies. (The current platform of the Democratic Party is extremely anti-Christian.)

The kingdom of God transcends all political parties, and no one party is without faults. Racism has been found in both the Democratic and Republican parties and in both white and black racial groups because racism is primarily due to sin, not skin. Blacks were extremely loyal to the Republican Party for about 80 years and then shifted to the Democratic Party for the last 60 or so years.

Political party or race should not be the primary basis for why Christians support certain candidates. A Christian's loyalty should always be to principle, and he should always be willing to shift support when adherence to biblical truth mandates it. It is certainly best to have Christians at the highest levels of leadership in all major parties and to have their actions align with biblical values. A party that ignores God's moral and political principles must be abandoned. As of the writing of this book, most African Americans and Hispanic and Asian Americans do not support homosexuality, same-sex marriage, removal of religious expression in public life, abortion, denial of private school choice, promotion of immorality and violence in popular media, and other such unbiblical positions; yet, most of them still support the Democratic party, which does embrace these policies. Why would they do this? Partly due to their history of supporting that party in the last 60 or so years, and partly to not being educated in school or church in a biblical worldview.

Clearly, the Democratic Party needs to be changed. The Republican Party has shortcomings as well and it, likewise, needs to be changed. Among other things, it needs more black Christians involved in it so both parties can be used by God to provide leadership that is good for the nation.

Elevation of Women

The biblical ideas upon which America was founded have not only brought advancements in race relations, but they also have elevated the role of women in society. As with all Christian societal change, this has been gradual.

In colonial and early American history, there were numerous Christian women who contributed to the nation's progress and growth, including Anne Hutchinson, Deborah Moody, Mary Starbuck, Hannah Penn, Barbara Heck, Mercy Otis Warren, Henrietta Zinzendorf von Watteville, Dolley Madison, Elizabeth Seton, Narcissa Whitman, and Eliza Spalding.

During this time women could not hold public office or vote,[484] and property ownership was restricted (this was true in America and most nations), but people began to speak out and take action for change. For example, in the 17th century Margaret Brent became the first woman to own land in the Maryland colony. She also petitioned for the right to vote, although without success. In the following century, Abigail Adams spoke strongly for women's rights, telling her husband John that women should not be bound by laws where they have no representation.

In the early 19th century Emma Willard championed the cause of education for women. She wrote *An Address to the Public...for Improving Female Education* in 1819, which, along with other Christians' efforts, contributed to the opening of more schools and colleges for women. Oberlin College in Ohio even became coed in 1833. Quaker Sarah Grimke wrote *Letters On the Equality of the Sexes* in 1838, and was widely held to be the mother of the women's suffrage movement.

Narcissa Whitman helped to blaze the Oregon Trail along with her husband Marcus, a medical missionary.

Non-Christian leaders joined with these Christians and held the first Women's Rights Convention at Seneca Falls in 1848. Led by Quaker Lucretia Mott and Elizabeth Cady Stanton, the attendees (both women and men) issued a Declaration of Sentiments calling for various rights for women, including the right to vote. In 1854 Susan B. Anthony collected 6000 signatures demanding similar rights.

After the war, the women's movement began to see more success. In 1866 numerous women — including Stanton, Anthony, Martha Wright and Ernestine Rose — founded the American Equal Rights Association. In 1869 the federal territory of Wyoming gave women the right to vote and Congress guaranteed equal pay for equal work in federal jobs. Four years later the Supreme Court ruled that women could select any occupation (the state of Illinois had prohibited women from the practice of law), and in 1875 they ruled that women were included in the 14th Amendment's use of the term "persons" (*Miner v. Hoppersatt*).

In spite of these advances, the popular opinion supporting universal women's rights lagged behind. A new wave of Christian leadership helped change this. Educator Frances Willard was an important part of promoting biblical equality of the sexes. She was converted to Christianity in 1859 and later did much to promote revival, participating in many outreach crusades with evangelist Dwight L. Moody. She even preached in one of Moody's crusades in Boston in 1877. In 1874 she and others launched the National Women's Christian Temperance Union (WCTU). Her faith motivated her religious and social work. Willard wrote:

> How glorious a thing it is to be at peace with Him by whom I was created, by whom I am preserved. Let me truly repent, and help me to please Thee, and to be useful in the world, I ask it very humbly and sincerely, *only* for Christ's sake.[485]

A Methodist and a Republican, she became the president of the national WCTU in 1879. The movement primarily focused on abuse of alcoholic beverages, but it also mobilized women and added legitimacy to their work for suffrage and equality.

Frances Willard

The people of Wyoming, which became a state in 1890, elected the first woman to office, Republican Estelle Reel in 1894. In that same year polygamy was outlawed. Elizabeth Cady Stanton published her autobiography in 1898—a history that ignored the religious influence on the women's movement, reflecting her own bias. Yet, the Christian support of women's rights was vital.

In 1904 Rev. Anna Shaw, ordained by the Methodist Church in 1880, became president of the National American Woman Suffrage Association (NAWSA) and led it for over a decade. NAWSA's membership grew to about two million, making it the largest voluntary organization in America. It played a key role in passing the 19th Amendment to the Constitution, which granted all women the right to vote. After its passage in 1920, many of the Christian women in the movement withdrew, leaving the control of NAWSA, and the movement in general, in the hands of non-Christians. Ever since, the women's movement has been largely controlled by those embracing non-biblical, immoral ideas. It gradually morphed into the feminist movement, which has pushed for the removal of laws barring sexual immorality, divorce, and abortion. Margaret Sanger, the racist founder of Planned Parenthood, promoted abortion and birth control as a means of reducing the number of "inferior" minority races in the American population.

As women (and men) were working to secure their voting rights, many women began to expand their work in ministry. Toward the end of the 19th century, Maria Woodworth-Etter began an itinerant multi-racial evangelistic and healing ministry that made her the most prominent female preacher at the time. She helped found the Assemblies of God denomination in 1914. Anna Carpenter Spencer became minister of Bell Street Chapel in Providence, Rhode Island, in 1891. Alma White organized the independent Methodist Pentecostal Church in 1901 (later its first bishop in 1917). While some churches and denominations do not agree theologically with women taking such a leadership role, it is undeniable that many women have been used by God in very effective service. This is true in other spheres of life as well.

Clara Barton organized and led the American Red Cross. Jane Stanford, with her husband, founded Stanford University. Maud Booth of the Salvation Army started the Volunteers of America, and Evangeline Booth became leader of the U. S. Salvation Army. In 1903 African-American Maggie Walker became the first woman bank president in Baltimore. Most of these were strong Christian women. Many women today serve as CEOs of major corporations, earning on average as much as men.

Maggie Walker was the first African American woman to charter a bank in the United States.

Women from both major parties have been elected and appointed to the highest places of government (except the Presidency as of 2020). The first woman elected to the House of Representatives was Republican Jeannette Rankin in 1917; first elected to U. S. Senate was Democrat Hattie Caraway in 1931. Female firsts include: Supreme Court Justice Sandra Day O'Connor, appointed by President Reagan in 1981; Attorney General Janet Reno (1993) and Secretary of State, Madeleine Albright (1997), both appointed by President Clinton; and Speaker of the House, Nancy Pelosi (2007).

On the state level, the first women elected to the legislature occurred in 1894, when five were elected. The first elected female governor was Nellie Ross (1925). Today there is virtually no job where women are not leaders.

Hispanic and Asian Americans

America has been called a melting pot, referring to the multi-national, multi-racial make-up of the nation. Most of the settlers of the 17th century were white Christian Europeans, especially from the Protestant nations of England, Germany, Scotland, and the Netherlands. A few blacks from Africa, the majority of whom were slaves, came in the latter part of the 1600s and increased greatly in the 18th century, making up about 19% of the population in 1790 (with about 4% of the 19% free blacks).

As in the 17th century, immigrants of the 18th century came predominantly from Protestant Europe, but some came from Catholic nations, like the French Protestant Huguenots who immigrated to America when persecution arose in their nation. Others came from Hispanic Catholic nations like Spain and various Latin American regions, but the number was small.

In 1790 about 1.5% of the American population were free non-whites, where about half of these were free blacks, with Hispanics the next largest group. Since the number of Hispanics who were citizens in early America was very small (only in the thousands), their greatest contribution to the rise of the Republic would be felt in territories that would later become a part of the United States.[486]

Spanish Christians of the Roman Catholic faith were used by God to discover, explore and settle many areas in the southeastern and southwestern parts of the present-day United States, and to contribute in other ways as well. Some of these men included: Cabeza daVaca, Bernardo de Galvez, Francisco de Miranda, Joseph Marion Hernández, Juan Nepomucene Seguin, and Rafael Gonzales.

Junipero Serra (1713-1784) was a Roman Catholic Spanish priest who founded the first nine Spanish missions in California from San Diego to San Francisco. He is honored for his work by a statue in the U.S. Capitol. Successful rancher Andres Pico (1810-1876) helped negotiate protections for Californios[487] after the Mexican-American War (1846-1848). After California became a state in 1850, Pico was elected to the state Assembly and Senate. The state's new constitution was drafted with help from Mexican Americans, Pablo de la Guerra, Mariano Vallejo, and Jose Antonio Carrillo.

The Gadsden Purchase of 1853 added more land to the territories of Arizona and New Mexico, which had not long before been obtained by the U.S. after the Mexican-American War. Importantly, the treaty under which the purchase occurred, guaranteed the civil rights and land titles of Mexican Americans, which although not consistently enforced, affirmed in principle what would eventually become the norm. One of the early delegates from the New Mexico Territory to the U.S. Congress was Trinidad Romero.

Statue of Junipero Serra in the United States Capitol

Nearly 10,000 Mexican Americans fought during that Civil War, including Philip Bazaar, a Chilean member of the U.S. Navy who was awarded the Congressional Medal of Honor in 1865. The most famous Hispanic patriot during this period was Admiral David G. Farragut. Congress awarded him the rank of Admiral, the first in the history of the U.S. Navy, after his famous victory for the North at the Battle of Mobile Bay.

After the war and throughout the 20th century, more and more Hispanics have been elected and appointed to public office, on the state and national levels. They have started businesses, organized workers, founded churches, become involved in education and the arts, and contributed in many other ways to the American republic.

Puerto Ricans, like activists Ramon Emeterio Betances and Luis Munoz Riveram, began to become a part of the American story during the first of the 20th century. Rivera served in the U.S. Congress, started the paper *La Democracia,* and worked successfully for Puerto Ricans to get full citizenship in 1917. Prominent Mexican Americans included Romualdo Pacheco, who served as both a member of the U.S. House of Representatives and as governor from the state of California, and Octaviano Ambroso Larrazolo of New Mexico. Larrazolo had intended to become a priest, but found his calling in the civil arena after joining the Republican Party. In 1928 he was elected as the first Mexican American U.S. Senator from his state. Cesar Chavez's Catholic faith motivated him to form the Farm Workers Association in 1962. A few other Hispanics who came to serve in government included Cuban Americans Bob Martinez, governor of Florida, and John Sununu, governor of New Hampshire and White House Chief of Staff. Both were Republicans. Sonia Maria Sotomayor was appointed an Associate Justice of the Supreme Court of the United States in 2009 by Democratic President Barack Obama. While a majority of Hispanics currently vote Democratic, most evangelical Hispanics vote Republican because of their opposition to abortion and homosexuality, and their support for the family and biblical morality.

Asians have only lately emerged in the American story, beginning to assume political leadership after World War II. On the national level, Hiram Fong, a Chinese American, was elected in 1959 as Republican U.S. Senator from the new state of Hawaii. Japanese American, S. I. Hayakawa, became a U.S. Senator from California in 1977. More recently, Indian Americans Bobby Jindal and Nikki Haley were elected governors of Louisiana and South Carolina, respectively. Haley was appointed as Ambassador to the United Nations by President Donald Trump. In 2008, Anh Cao of Louisiana became the first Vietnamese American elected to Congress. David S. Chang was the first Korean American to chair a state political party.

As was the case with blacks and women, the rights and liberties guaranteed in our Declaration and Constitution have been extended to Hispanics, Asians, and all the other people groups who have flocked to the nation. And over the past two centuries, unlike anything seen in history, tens of millions of people from nations all over the world have immigrated to America, attracted by the great freedom and its corresponding blessings.[488] This great interest in coming to America will continue as long as we live according to the Christian principles upon which this nation was built.

The fruit of these Christian principles has brought advancements in all spheres of life and to all races. Due to the spread of biblical ideas, women have come to obtain the same respect and standing in society as men. Women have shown they can compete with men and succeed, in almost every arena.

While the influence of women has been growing in many ways during the past century and a half, it has been diminished in other ways, especially regarding preparing posterity to maintain the American Christian Republic. Up until the 1860s, the vast majority of American children were taught at home by their parents, especially their mothers. They understood that the home was the primary place where principles of liberty were transferred from one generation to the next. Without such a transfer of this way of life, liberty cannot advance or even be maintained.

With the death of hundreds of thousands of men, and many more disabled, during the Civil War, many women had to work outside the home to help provide for their families. Coinciding with this was the rise of state controlled education and the secular idea that government is the primary educator. Consequently, parents began to give up responsibility to educate their children to the government. To make matters worse, America's public schools have, over time, adopted an unbiblical, immoral, man-centered system of education.

Whoever educates the children in a nation, controls the future. Christian families used to do this, but today this has largely shifted to the state. The bad fruit of secular education gradually began to affect every aspect of American life, as we will explore in the next chapter.

On the base of the Pilgrim Mother Statue in Plymouth is the inscription: "They brought up their families in sturdy virtue and a living faith in God, without which nations perish."

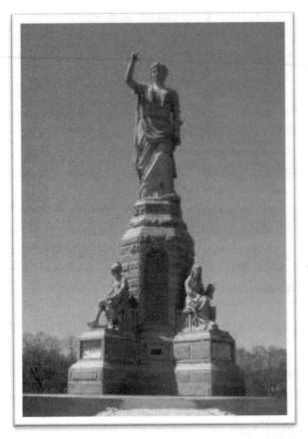

The National Monument to the Forefathers

The National Monument to the Forefathers, located in Plymouth, Massachusetts, commemorates the Pilgrims, their planting the colony of Plymouth, and their contribution to the American nation at large. This marvelous eighty-one-foot-tall granite structure also provides a matrix for how to build a free society based upon the biblical ideals and worldview of these early settlers.

The monument is composed of numerous statues; the most prominent is the heroic figure of *Faith*, standing with her right hand pointed to the heavens and the other holding a Bible. At the base of the pedestal where *Faith* stands are four seated statues representing *Morality, Law, Education*, and *Liberty*—emblems of the principles upon which the Pilgrims built their Commonwealth, each also having a symbol referring to the Bible that *Faith* possesses. Flanking these allegorical figures are smaller engravings representing more components of the template of liberty.

The monument provides us a matrix of liberty based upon the worldview of our forefathers. Their ideas gave birth to the most free, prosperous, virtuous, and just nation the world has ever seen. If we apply those same principles today and build according to the successful pattern, we can expect the same results.

(For more on the monument see Stephen McDowell, *The Forefathers Monument, A Matrix of Liberty*, Providence Foundation, 2019.)

Chapter 19

The American Apostasy and Decline

Biblical truth is powerful, so much so that its seed continues to bear fruit for many generations. For the past century and more, we have sown ungodly, humanistic ideas in all areas of life; yet even so, we still remain the most free and prosperous nation in the world (though in recent times we have been losing ground). We owe our freedom to the Christian foundations of the nation, coupled with the efforts of many people to continue to transmit biblical Christianity and truth.

Towards the end of the nineteenth and into the twentieth century, advancements continued from the Christian seeds while at the same time thorns began to grow from non-Christian ideas. The biblical seeds of liberty also affected other nations, especially the Protestant nations of Western Europe. Advancements occurred in all areas of life – science, technology, commerce, business, agriculture, government, medicine, communications, etc. Unfortunately, as the 20th century progressed, the rise of statism and secularism in the nation began to stifle the free market and limit liberty in many ways.

Rise of Secularism/Statism

Secularism, or secular humanism, is the belief that there is no god—no ultimate authority—outside of man, and that man is the center of the universe. As such he is the source of law; he is the sovereign one. He determines what is truth, or even if truth exists. Secular man sits upon the throne of the universe. Atheism, materialism, and evolution are at the heart of this worldview (religion).

Secularism is the mother of many worldviews, including all forms of statism, and (in practical working) all man-made religions.

Statism — which includes socialism, communism, Marxism, fascism, democratic socialism, and most modern democracies — goes hand-in-hand with secularism. Statism is the belief that the civil government (or man via civil government) is the ultimate authority in the earth and as such is the source of law, morality, and righteousness (that which is right and wrong). Statism is a religious belief. How has this false religion gained such prominence in America today?

Finding the Cause of America's Problems

Only if we correctly identify and diagnose the true cause of America's problems, can we begin to really solve them. Many Christians today place the blame on various conspiracies of men: the humanists, the ACLU, the big bankers, the Trilateral Commission, the New Age Movement, the World Council of Churches, the homosexuals, the feminists, the communists, the Democrats, the Pope, etc. Information regarding such groups and their activities can be useful, yet they must never be regarded as the primary source of our problems. God forbid it in Isaiah 8, verse 12 and 13:

> You are not to say, "It is a conspiracy!" in regard to all that this people call a conspiracy. And you are not to fear what they fear or be in dread of it. It is the Lord of hosts whom you should regard as holy. And He shall be your fear, and He shall be your dread.

Many Christians today seem to fear these groups more than they do God. This is wrong, for it diminishes the true biblical understanding that God is sovereign over the earth. God sees human conspiracies and laughs at them for He knows what He has planned will prevail. This should be our perspective toward conspiracies. Psalm two says:

> Why are the nations in an uproar, and the people devising a vain thing? The kings of the earth take their stand, and the rulers take counsel together against the Lord and against His Anointed: "Let us tear their fetters apart, and cast away their cords from us!" He who sits in the heavens laughs; the Lord scoffs at them. Then He will speak to them in His anger and terrify them in His furry: "But as for Me, I have installed My King upon Zion, My holy mountain." I will surely tell of the decree of the Lord: He said to me, "Thou art My Son, today I have begotten Thee. Ask of Me,

and I will surely give the nations as Thine inheritance..." Now therefore, O kings, show discernment; take warning, O judges of the earth. ... Do homage to the Son, lest He become angry, and you perish in the way.

This prophecy was, of course, describing the first coming of Christ, when He died, rose again, and was given absolute authority to reign. Just prior to His ascension, Jesus delegated this responsibility and authority to His church. Matthew 28:18-19 says:

And Jesus came up and spoke to them, saying, "All authority has been given to Me in heaven and on earth. Go therefore and make disciples of all nations."

Christians Are Responsible

The church has been given authority to shape history. If our nation is in an awful condition, God holds us responsible. In 2 Chronicles 7:14 He says:

If...My people who are called by My name humble themselves and pray, and seek My face and turn from their wicked ways, then I will hear from heaven, will forgive their sin, and will heal their land.

The power for healing our land rests with God's people.

America's decline has not occurred because the ideas and leadership of various ungodly organizations have overcome biblical ideas. Rather, it is because we abdicated our responsibility to lead and left a void or vacuum in the public realm that has been surrendered by default. Rosalie Slater says it well:

For one hundred and fifty years and more, up to the time of our Revolution, the seven years of that long struggle, and through the ratification of our Constitution—even through the perilous years of the French Revolution—we maintained our Christian character as a nation. Then began our period of "falling away" when we worshipped the "effect" of our great success—and forgot the "cause." This vacuum was readily filled with man-centered philosophies which replaced the internal battles of conscience with the social, economic and political struggles of society.

Thus we veered from a period when, even our governmental proclamations were filled with the language of salvation and the recognition that Christ alone could change the hearts of men, to a pre-occupation with educational, social, economic, and eventually political arrangements, which claimed to insure progress and improvement for society and hence for man.[489]

"If…My people…humble themselves and pray. I will heal their land." (2 Chron. 7:14)

America has repeated the folly of Israel. God warned Israel of the danger of apostasy once they entered the Promised Land and began to enjoy prosperity and peace. Within a short time a generation arose in Israel that was unfaithful to the God and traditions of their fathers. They began to neglect the things that produced their freedom in the first place. Likewise, this happened in America. We lost our virtue and our self-government and became prey to what Samuel Adams called "internal invaders:"

A general Dissolution of Principles and Manners will more surely overthrow the Liberties of America than the whole Force of the Common Enemy. While the People are virtuous they cannot be subdued; but when once they lose their Virtue they will be ready to surrender their Liberties to the first external or internal Invader. … If Virtue and Knowledge are diffused among the People, they will never be enslaved. This will be their great Security.[490]

Samuel Adams

The only way that "tares" can be sown is when the church is "asleep," that is, neglecting her role in society (Matthew 13:24, Proverbs 24:30-34). This neglect by God's people is the primary reason for the rise of secularism in America.

Rise of Secularism in Education

In the early 1800's the clergy and church began to gradually cease providing leadership in our public universities and schools. Thus Harvard was taken over by the Unitarians, and as the quality of public education declined, Horace Mann convinced Massachusetts that the answer was to let civil government take charge of it instead of the private sector (families and churches). Rosalie Slater writes:

Horace Mann

> In the years 1837-1848 Horace Mann, whom John Dewey designated as "the father of progressive education," made a series of Annual Reports to the Massachusetts Board of Education of which he was Secretary. These reports paved the way for a state financed, state directed, and ultimately a state controlled education program superseding local control through the demand for "standardization: of school structures, textbooks, curriculum, and teacher training and certification." But even this might not have proved so effective in the "secularization" of education had we not deliberately removed the Bible as the basis of our Christian character and substituted for salvation and regeneration of heart a psychological atheism which found man innately "good" and society "bad."

There were many alert clergymen of the time of Horace Mann who were aware of this "condition" for the drive to achieve "universal public education." This "condition" was that Christianity be neutralized for the larger goal of building, not Christian character and conscience, but humanitarians with benevolent inclinations toward mankind. And for those individuals who wished the schools to teach a patriotism which indicated how great was "the faith of our fathers" there was substituted a bland form of non-controversial democracy and "citizenship in the state."

Thus the public school was able to accomplish that which the hired European mercenaries of England never could—namely to separate our patriotism from our Christian conviction.[491]

In the late 1800s and early 1900s, secularists Charles and Mary Beard began to popularize Marxist, socialist ideas in the many revisionist history books they wrote and introduced to schools. These were so radical that even modern academics reject much of what they taught, but their ideas were, nonetheless, sown throughout the nation. In the first half of the twentieth century the godfather of modern progressive education, John Dewey, had much success in introducing socialistic ideas in colleges, especially through training teachers. They in turn carried this philosophy to local secondary schools.

John Dewey

Colleges, which were originally started by churches or for Christian reasons, gradually became more and more secular. Ministers ceased to be hired as their presidents. Today 80-90% of the staff of most major universities is liberal. Christian professors are becoming a rare item, and many must keep their belief quiet if they want to keep their job.

Today, public schools, in essence, serve as the pulpits for the modern religion of secular humanism, spreading its tenets of relativism, positivism, and humanism.[492] All citizens are compelled via their tax dollars to support this religion, whose ideology is undermining liberty and destroying the unique nation our Founders gave us. All teachers and administers are certainly not ungodly, as there are many godly people involved in public education and many still communicate truth and biblical ideals, but the philosophy, content, and structure of the public educational system has long ago abandoned its biblical roots and is becoming more and more hostile to the Christian faith.

Rise of Secularism in Law

In his *Spirit of the Common Law*, Roscoe Pound, who was president of Harvard Law School in the 1920s, revealed the nature of the rise of secularism in law in America. (The secularization of law had begun decades before at Harvard Law School under the direction of Christopher Columbus Langdell.[493]) Pound recognized the Christian foundation of law in the United States but did not directly attack it. In fact, he said that the old Christian legal foundation was good and produced many good results; but, he went on to say that this foundation was not good enough to bring us into the modern era. According to him, we needed a new law system, one founded on a different premise. Pound and others claimed that law was rooted in the best that society had to offer—in the consensus of the society and what they deemed best for mankind—and as society grew and became better, the law would change with it. Evolving law and the sovereignty of the state replaced the absolutes of God's law. Pound said "the state takes the place of Jehovah."[494]

Roscoe Pound

Many people in the judicial system began to embrace this evolving view of law and rejected the Christian understanding of absolute law rooted in a Higher Power. For example Supreme Court Justice Benjamin Cardozo (appointed in 1932) said:

> If there is any law which is back of the sovereignty of the state, and superior thereto, it is not law in such a sense as to concern the judge or lawyer, however much it concerns the statesmen or the moralist.[495]

Relativism began to affect judicial philosophy and constitutional interpretation, as reflected in the words of Charles Evans Hughes, Supreme Court Chief Justice from 1930 to 1941: "We are under a Constitution, but the Constitution is what the judges say it is."[496]

A humanistic view of law, with its moral relativism, has spread to the point where today a majority of Americans embrace this idea. Its dissemination and influence is such that, according to one recent poll even a majority of those who claim to be Christian reject moral absolutes.[497]

Charles Evans Hughs

As evolving law and the sovereignty of the state has replaced the absolutes of God's law, judges have also moved from making decisions based upon established law to becoming activists, legislating through their decisions. Activist judges are a great problem today.

Rise of Secularism in Government and the Economy

Statism is the general term we could use to describe a secular view of government and the economy. Statism began when Adam and Eve disobeyed God, desiring to determine for themselves what was good and evil (Genesis 3:5). The Tower of Babel was perhaps the first public expression of statism or socialism, with corporate man seeking to be his own god. So when Karl Marx's book, *The Communist Manifesto*, was published in 1848, it was not presenting new ideas. Marxist socialism had been around from the very beginning.

Socialism Is a Religion.

Socialism has been one of the great enemies of liberty and of Christianity in the past. It will be one of the greatest threats to Christianity in the twenty-first century. Socialism can be defined as government control or ownership of property and/or the production of goods and services. Socialistic governments claim authority over all property. This is bad enough, but such states' claim of ownership goes much further — they also claim authority over the children in a nation. Thus, the state seeks to educate, provide for, direct and regulate their activities. The state seeks to be the parent.

God created individuals and three divine institutions: family, church, and state. He has given certain authority and responsibilities to each of these. No one institution has absolute authority over any other institution. Today, the state has come to be seen as the all-encompassing authority over men and other institutions. This is socialism. When government bureaucrats (elected or not) act under this belief they are like blind men, who will lead the blind into the ditch (Luke 6:39). To limit the all-powerful state, men must be self-governed under God and His law.

Only God is supreme and can exercise supreme power. No man or institution should ever exercise supreme power, especially regarding matters of the economy. Therefore, no central planning agency should rule over the entire economy (as in communist countries). The flow of authority should be from the bottom up, not the top down. In building the communist party in Russia, Lenin rejected the bottom upwards attempts of the less revolutionary socialists for a top down approach. He said, "My idea…is 'bureaucratic' in the sense that the Party is built from the top downwards."[498]

Socialism is a religion that assumes:[499]

1. All property belongs to society, that is, the state.

2. There should be no private property.

3. Men will work as hard for society in general as they would for themselves and their family.

These ideas have been shown not to work every time they have been attempted throughout history, even among Christians. But socialist adherents still press on to impose this philosophy on nations, even though it will bring stagnation and loss of liberty. Why? Because it is a religion to them.

Socialists have certain views about God, man, and law which are rooted in their faith, or fundamental presuppositions of life. They think the socialistic means of ownership and production will change the nature of man, will bring a utopia to earth, which is what people in communist U.S.S.R. were taught. They had not experienced a utopia yet, but they just needed more time to get rid of the left-over influence of free and private enterprise, and then it would come. These people were blinded by this false religion.

Karl Marx

Productivity declines in a socialist state. Why? One reason is no individual incentive to produce, since individuals do not benefit directly from the fruit of their labor. Another reason is this: when men see that their property is easily confiscated by the state, which will then use it as it thinks best, then men are going to attempt to gain political power so they can control property. Gaining control of government then becomes more important than being productive. People will exert energy to gain control of government, using whatever means possible to do so, rather than using their energy to give to society needed goods and services. Economic productivity will decline.

Socialism hates a flat tax or small head tax. Graduated taxation is the means of redistribution of wealth. Karl Marx's second plank of his program to destroy capitalism was a highly graduated income tax. Socialist governments seek to control by many means, most especially via taxation. As socialist governments assume more and more authority, they need more and more money to fulfill their ever expanding role in life.

Socialism and communism are forms of humanism, in that they all adhere to the idea of man as the supreme ruler. In socialism this supremacy is placed in political man — man exercising authority through the government.

4. Socialism says the world is naturally productive, but that human laws and institutions stifle man and nature from this natural productivity.

Socialists believe that if these laws and institutions could be removed or restructured, then this natural productivity could be released. Socialists think the central state planners must remove the obstacles. They must either own the means of production (which is communism or socialism) or direct the means of production (fascism or corporate state). In both cases a central elite body of planners claim to know what is best for everyone. They plan for everyone's life. These monopolistic central planners are acting like God, knowing what must be done in all areas of business, what unique skills each person has, and what the wants and desires of each consumer are. They are the agents to transform society; they are the agents of salvation. But they believe in salvation by force and by man-made laws.

Socialism claims authority over all property, including children. Thus, the socialist state seeks to educate children, provide for them, and direct and regulate their business and activities. The state seeks to be the parent. In order to provide all that God says the family is to provide (including education, retirement, and so on), the state must seek higher and higher taxes. Thus, socialist leaders implement graduated income taxes, inheritance taxes, all kinds of licenses and fees, and more. The state becomes the substitute parent, but also the substitute child, by providing for people when they get old.

A society that rejects God's order for family responsibility will find the state becoming the educator and provider, and thus requiring a "double portion" of the inheritance (like the first born[500]), an ever-increasing tax burden, and an ever-increasing control, in order to fulfill its duties.

Socialism is ultimately demonic since it is Satan's attempt to control God's earth. At the Fall, Satan seized Adam's inheritance of the earth. Since Jesus has restored this to man, Satan continues to try to rob man of his inheritance in God. He uses the tool of the state to try to seize the capital of modern man, thus keeping man in bondage. Those who embrace the idea of the state as welfare agent are collaborating with the devil and delaying the advance of God's Kingdom in the earth. They are keeping man from the great blessing of his inheritance in God.

Growing Socialism in America

America is becoming more and more socialist. Seeds of socialism were planted in various colleges and schools in the early twentieth century and through various organizations like the Intercollegiate Socialist Society. These ideas began to influence public policy, including these past and recent actions:

- Graduated income taxes (beginning in 1913 with the 16th Amendment to the Constitution)
- Establishment of the Federal Reserve Bank (Fed), a central bank in hands of private bankers, in 1913[501]
- Rise of progressivism under President Woodrow Wilson
- Rise of the socialist state under President Franklin D. Roosevelt[502]
- Social security system
- Social programs under President Johnson. Since Johnson launched his war on poverty, America has spent trillions of dollars to help the poor, yet there are more people in poverty today than then. Most of the money (70-80%) for these social programs has not gone to the poor but to government workers to run the programs. Sadly, this well-intentioned but statist run war has destroyed many poor families in America, especially African-American families.
- Soaring government expenditures, especially in areas outside its jurisdiction. (Non-defense spending was 57% in 1965; it was 80% in 2005. Social security and Medicare/Medicaid spending was 40% of federal budget in 2005 and 53% in 2009.)
- Increased taxes and deficit spending. The tax burden has gradually increased on the American people during the twentieth century (with some reprieves here and there, as under President Reagan). But the American people can only be taxed so much, so our statist national government gets more money by borrowing it or creating money out of nothing (as blips on computer screens). This diminishes the wealth of people who have labored hard and saved over their lifetime, plus it lays a burden upon future generations. Our current national debt is over $22 trillion.[503]
- Excessive regulation of land use and private property.
- Bailouts of AIG, Fannie Mae and Freddie Mac, and loans to American automobile corporations (with borrowed or newly created fiat money).
- $750 billion bailout agreed to in the fall of 2008, much of which was used to prop up faltering financial institutions.

- In early 2009, the nearly one trillion dollar "stimulus plan" which was really primarily a socialist spending plan.

The massive stimulus did not produce the desired results of restoring the economy to a firm foundation. It only increased our debt (increasing the burden on our children and grandchildren), and worse, it contributed to the increase of the power and size of government, which will result in loss of liberty and prosperity.[504]

In 1986, Ronald Reagan summarized the modern socialist government: "Government's view of the economy could be summed up in a few short phrases: If it moves, tax it. If it keeps moving, regulate it. And if it stops moving, subsidize it."

Ronald Reagan said: "Government's view of the economy could be summed up in a few short phrases: If it moves, tax it. If it keeps moving, regulate it. And if it stops moving, subsidize it."

Rise of Global Government

The tendency of fallen man is to look to himself, in particular to corporate man via the state, as savior and provider. When problems arise in society, man usually seeks to centralize power to attempt a solution, which rarely, if ever, succeeds since all sinful actions begin in sinful hearts. Human governments cannot change the heart. In fact, man's "solutions" are usually worse than the problems. History reveals that more centralization of power leads to loss of liberty. The rise of secularism in America has led to greater centralization of power. A pagan view of government has also led the nations of the world to seek to centralize power globally, especially in the past century with the League of

Nations, the United Nations, the European Union, and world courts. While working in union with those having a common worldview can be of benefit, the underlying secularism of the move to global government will only result in a continued loss of liberty.

The United Nations, like the Tower of Babel, is an attempt by corporate man to save himself.

Rise of Secularism in Science

Charles Darwin wrote his book *Origin of the Species* in 1859, but its evolutionary ideas did not become predominant in public education until after the Scopes trial of 1925. Evolutionary forces lost this trial but eventually won the battle of ideas. Evolutionists first argued for free expression of ideas, desiring evolution to be taught alongside of creationism. Today, evolutionists have a grip on public education and take great measures to suppress any mention of creationism or intelligent design, or of allowing any professors to consider such beliefs. Their behavior shows the great intolerance of the "tolerant" liberals.

Charles Darwin

Forest and Flame in the Bible

See pictures on the page following: While secularism was on the rise during the twentieth century, the fruit of Christianity was still evident in private and public life. Consider the government pamphlet produced by the U.S. Department of Agriculture, Forest Service, in 1961. The Foreword states:

> There are many passages in the Bible that tell how our forests serve us and how we should protect them. ... The Bible urges us to the protection and wise use of our forests, range, and woodlands. ... As the Bible foretells, destruction of our natural resources will bring us punishment in the form of loss and misery. ... In this booklet we selected Biblical passages of great wisdom and beauty.

Even 60 years ago we still held to at least a form of godliness, yet as we have lost the power of the Christian faith, there has grown an increasing hostility to God in public (and private) life.

Pictures, top: Pamphlet front cover, showing the Bible, and back cover, showing Smokey the Bear praying; bottom: two insides pages, listing Scriptures regarding natural resources and creation.

... and please make
people careful, amen

Remember - Only you can
PREVENT FOREST FIRES!

YES . . . *Most* forest fires can be prevented if you will follow these rules:

1. **CRUSH OUT YOUR SMOKES—BREAK YOUR MATCH IN TWO—DROWN YOUR CAMP AND WARMING FIRE.** Be sure that every spark is dead out.

2. **USE CARE IN BURNING BRUSH OR TRASH—NEVER BURN LAND OF OTHERS.** Respect your neighbor's property rights.

Yes, care will prevent many fires from starting. Fires which are deliberately set on lands of others should be brought to the attention of law-enforcement officers.

AND THOSE WHO SET FIRES WILL BE CALLED UPON TO MAKE AMENDS TO THOSE WHO HAVE SUFFERED

Exodus 22:6

"If a fire break out, and catch in thorns, so that the stacks of corn, or the standing corn, or the field, be consumed *therewith*; he that kindled the fire shall surely make restitution."

FOR THE RESOURCES OF NATURE ARE MAN'S LIFE

Deuteronomy 20:19

". . . (for the tree of the field *is* man's life) . . ."

SO SPARE THE EARTH AND THE TREES

1 Chronicles 16:33

"Then shall the trees of the wood sing out at the presence of the Lord, . . ."

Deuteronomy 20:19

"When thou shalt besiege a city a long time, in making war against it to take it, thou shalt not destroy the trees thereof by forcing an axe against them: for thou mayest eat of them, and thou shalt not cut them down . . . to employ *them* in the siege:"

14

AND IF A TREE BE CUT OR BURNED, GROW OTHERS IN ITS STEAD

Isaiah 44:14

"He heweth him down cedars, and taketh the cypress and the oak, which he strengtheneth for himself among the trees of the forest: he planteth an ash, and the rain doth nourish *it*."

Job 14:7

"For there is hope of a tree, if it be cut down, that it will sprout again, and that the tender branch thereof will not cease."

AND FROM THE EARTH WILL SPRING THE TREE ONCE MORE!

Genesis 1:11

"And God said, Let the earth bring forth grass, . . . *and* the fruit tree yielding fruit after his kind, whose seed is in itself, upon the earth: and it was so."

Revelation 22:1

"And he shewed me a pure river of water of life, clear as crystal, proceeding out of the throne of God and of the Lamb."

Revelation 22:2

"In the midst of the street of it, and on either side of the river, *was there* the tree of life, which bare twelve *manner of fruits, and* yielded her fruit every month: and the leaves of the tree *were* for the healing of the nations."

Genesis 1:12

". . . and God saw that it *was* good."

15

Rise of Secularism in Arts, Music, and Media

Music, arts, and the media are a means of communicating a worldview. While primarily Christian in our earlier years, today these are mostly humanistic. With the rise of secularism, the biblical Hudson River Painters, and others like them, who believed in truth and objective beauty, have been supplanted by relativistic artists who embrace a completely subjective view of beauty, and seek to shock viewers with more and more bizarre and perverted images.

Hollywood once produced many excellent biblical movies such as Sergeant York, Mr. Smith Goes to Washington, and Ben Hur, and never made immoral movies. They usually promoted a love of family, love of Christian character, love of God, and similar themes. Today, the opposite is true. While some good movies and television shows are produced today, the majority of them reflect non-Christian values and a secular worldview, and many are evil.

In early America, the church was the primary source of news. Ministers were the newsmen presenting events from a providential perspective. The first newspapers generally sought to communicate truth. Today, the secular bias of the major media helps to keep most Americans ignorant and in bondage.

America's Problem Today

Jesus taught that we are to render to Caesar the things that are Caesar's and to God the things that are God's (Matthew 22:15-21), but today Christians throughout the world have been rendering to Caesar the things that are God's. It is not surprising that secularists will do this because, since they have no god (but themselves), the state readily becomes their default god. However, it is surprising that Christians are worshiping this golden calf.

Does this mean they are worshiping the civil government? Do people have images of the Capitol in their house that they bow down to each day? Do they have bobble-heads of some elected official on their coffee tables that they pray to each day? No, their idolatrous action is not so obvious.

The Second Commandment says, "You shall not make for yourself an idol" (Exodus 20:4-6). Habakkuk 2:18 says: "What profit is the idol when its maker has carved it, or an image, a teacher of falsehood? For its maker trusts in his own handiwork when he fashions speechless idols." Isaiah described well the absurdity and futility of those who worship the very thing they create. In chapter 44, verses 9-19, Isaiah tells how a man planted and raised trees, then cut one down and burned part of it to warm himself and prepare his food. "But the rest of it he makes into a god, his graven image. He falls down before it and worships; he also prays to it and says, 'Deliver me, for thou art my god'" (Isaiah 44:17).

We would consider it stupid to worship the thing we create with our own hands. Modern western man would not think of making a golden calf, setting it up in his living room, and bowing down before it. What he does is much more subtle.

Humanists are sophisticated idol makers. They are like the guy who carves an idol and worships it — they trust in their own handiwork. They create their own laws, think up their own value systems, form their own governmental and educational systems, and worship them, trusting in them to be "god" (that which is right and true). They can do this, but at their own peril, for if their work is not based upon God's truth, it will lead to ruin. Such idol worship produces bondage, not liberty.

Isaiah speaks of those who worship what they create, ending by asking, "Shall I fall down before a block of wood?" (Isaiah 44:19). Americans must ask themselves, "Shall we as a nation fall down before a block of wood?" "Shall we worship the creation of our own hand?" Shall we look to civil government to be our provider, our comforter, our savior, our god? Jeremiah warns that those who do "are altogether stupid and foolish" (Jeremiah 10:8).

While civil government is a divine institution with an important purpose, it is very limited in what it is supposed to do — it basically is to protect the life, liberty, and property of its citizens (Romans 13:4; 1 Peter 2:14). But we have made it like Babel, thinking the state (something of our own creation) will do much more than God says it is to do. We allow it to take on the role of God, the family, the church, and business. Many people look to the state to meet their needs from cradle to grave, to bring peace and utopia on earth, to help them in times of trouble, to solve all their problems, to care for them when they are sick, and to control and regulate all things. We as a nation have given over to the state many of the responsibilities that God says belong to individuals, the family, or the church.

Separation of Church and State

In His teaching on tribute to Caesar in Matthew 22:15-21, Jesus used a coin with Caesar's image upon it to illustrate that civil government has certain jurisdictional authority, such as in the area of taxation. However, Christ went on to pronounce that the state's jurisdiction is limited when He said that we are to render "to God the things that are God's." The inference is that there is a sphere of life where civil government (i.e. Caesar) has no jurisdiction at all. That sphere is implied here as involving the soul and mind of men, being made, not in Caesar's image, but in the image of God. Jesus was affirming that religious worship and opinions, and any endeavor relating to thoughts or speech, must remain completely free from government control.

Jesus' teaching explains the biblical idea of the separation of church and state. It is not like the modern idea, which says we must remove God from public life. The principle of separation of church and state, the separation of school and state, and the separation of the press and speech from the control of the state, which are articulated in the First Amendment of the United States Constitution, are rooted in this historic political teaching of Christ. Before Christianity, the pagan world always included religion and education under the jurisdiction of the state. It was a radical political concept for Christ to declare that Caesar's power should be limited, and, therefore, was used against Jesus when He was convicted of treason and crucified under Roman law. The Founders of America incorporated Christ's teaching on church-state relations into our government. Unfortunately, we have more recently been replacing this with the old pagan view.

A denarius featuring Caesar.

Fruit of Statism

The fruit of statism or socialism — or the "Caesar mentality"— is loss of liberty, loss of prosperity, and loss of the ability for the church to disciple the nations. A statist government will suppress Christian involvement in government, education, and social life. It will seek to control not only what is taught in schools, but what is taught in homes and in churches. It will suppress Christian liberty.

Liberty is freedom to do God's will — freedom to do, not what I want to do, but to do what God wants me to do. The freedom of parents to educate their children is becoming more and more limited. We are not free to labor hard throughout life, and confidently save money that will have the same purchasing power it did when we earned it — this due to unbiblical action of the government (fiat money, fractional reserve banking, legal tender laws). We are becoming less free to provide for ourselves and our family because the state is taking more money from us and assuming control of more and more of our responsibilities.

Businesses are not free to operate based upon their moral convictions (like the photographers in New Mexico who were fined $6000 because they refused to photograph a homosexual union). In America, we are not free, in many ways, to govern the use of our property, especially upon death with inheritance taxes. We are experiencing a gradual loss of liberty to govern our children, live securely on our own property, freely worship, and freely speak.

If we turn over to the state control of the most important areas of education and property, we will have little positive long-term influence in reforming the nation. We must assume our responsibility to govern the education of our children and to place control of property in private hands if we hope to restore America.

War against Evil

While secularism was on the rise in America in the twentieth century, she still adhered to much biblical truth and was involved in the battle against evil –

in World War I and WWII; standing against Hitler and Nazism; resisting communism during the Cold War; and warring against Muslim terrorists. God raised up men for these battles, such as President Ronald Reagan who was instrumental in seeing communism collapse toward the end of the century.[505]

Even many secular thinking leaders, like President Franklin Roosevelt, understood the nature of evil and the source of liberty,

Franklin D. Roosevelt

declaring on November 1, 1940: "Those forces hate democracy and Christianity as two phases of the same civilization. They oppose democracy because it is Christian. They oppose Christianity because it preaches democracy."[506] In his State of the Union address, January 6, 1942, he said: "The world is too small...for both Hitler and God. ... Nazis have now announced their plan for enforcing their...pagan religion all over the world—a plan by which the Holy Bible and the Cross of Mercy would be displaced by Mein Kampf and the swastika."[507]

Our Forefathers and Founding Fathers both declared and lived the truth of the Christian faith. They understood that Christianity is the source of all liberty. More recent generations decla red this truth, even if they did not live it. Unfortunately, as the fruit of secularism has increased, the majority of Americans today neither live nor understand this vital idea, that, in the words of Jedidiah Morse, "To the kindly influence of Christianity we owe that degree of civil freedom, and political and social happiness which mankind now enjoys."[508]

This poster (showing a dagger thrust through a Bible by a Nazi) produced by the U.S. government to help sell war bonds during WWII reveals the Nazi's opposition to Biblical faith.

The American Decline and Remedy

To summarize, America was founded upon biblical principles which produced much godly fruit — freedom, prosperity, advancement, spreading of liberty and charity. Christianity produced liberty of all kinds — personal, civil, religious, economic. Personal, religious, and civil liberty made economic liberty possible. Freedom to work and invent, and benefit from the fruit of that labor, encouraged many advances leading to economic prosperity.

As the American republic grew, the influence of Christianity gradually diminished. How did this occur and what is the remedy for this?

Why the Influence of Christianity Has Eroded

Minister and "Father of American Geography," Dr. Jedidiah Morse, preached an insightful Election Sermon in 1799 from the biblical text, "If the foundations be destroyed, what can the righteous do?" (Psalm 11:3), stating:

To the kindly influence of Christianity we owe that degree of civil freedom, and political and social happiness which mankind now enjoys. In proportion as the genuine effects of Christianity are diminished in any nation, either through unbelief or the corruption of its doctrine, or the neglect of its institutions; in the same proportion will the people of that nation recede from the

Jedidiah Morse

blessings of genuine freedom, and approximate the miseries of complete despotism. I hold this to be a truth confirmed by experience. If so, it follows, that all efforts made to destroy the foundations of our holy religion, ultimately tend to the subversion also of our political freedom and happiness. Whenever the pillars of Christianity shall be overthrown, our present republican forms of government and all the blessings which flow from them, must fall with them.[509]

He identified three reasons why the "genuine effects of Christianity are diminished in any nation:" (1) unbelief, (2) corruption of its doctrine, and (3) neglect of its institutions.

Unbelief — Revival is the Remedy

"And how shall they believe in Him whom they have not heard? And how shall they hear without a preacher?" (Romans 10:14).

"The church of the living God, (is) the pillar and support of the truth" (1 Timothy 3:15).

Christianity cannot prevail in society without mature believers and strong vibrant churches. These cannot exist without dedicated godly ministers. Biblical revival is the remedy for unbelief. Many people think that a revival is largely a move of God where individuals are converted and the church grows. While this does occur, true biblical revival is much more.

Noah Webster defines *revival*: "1. Return, recall or recovery to life from death or apparent death. 2. Return or recall to activity from a state of languor… 4. An awakening of men to their spiritual concerns."[510] Arthur Wallis said that,

"Revival is necessary to counteract spiritual decline and to create spiritual momentum."[511] Revival is the inrush of the Spirit into a body that threatens to become a corpse. It is God bringing us to life that we might rejoice in Him (Psalm 85:6). According to Winkie Pratney, "revival makes the Church" – we His people – "whole and happy in God again."[512]

Revival begins by the recovery of life from death, where people who are dead spiritually are supernaturally brought to life. These Christians whose hearts have been renewed also need renewed minds (Romans 12:2). How they act is dependent upon how they think (Proverbs 23:7). Many Christians today are brain-dead. Lack of a biblical worldview among many believers has contributed to the secularization of America and many nations. Revival causes spiritual life to flood into a nation, but it also causes a rising tide of biblical thinking which transforms the laws and institutions of the society.

Revival is a divine attack on society. Revival is God tearing open the heavens, coming down to earth, and doing awesome things (Isaiah 64:1-3). We need the supernatural intervention of God in our lives and in our nation. We need to recover the life that flows from the living God (personal transformation), and return to activity from a state of languor. Our languor has enabled those who oppose God to infiltrate all spheres of life (education, law, media, science, arts, and economics). While we were sleeping the enemy came in (Matthew 13:25); while the watchmen were asleep the horde invaded the city.[513] When we are revived by Him, we will return to activity that will transform all society and all institutions – the family, church, civil government, schools, and businesses.

Methodist revival of 1839. Revival is needed to remedy the decline in America today.

Corruption of Doctrine — Restoration of the New Testament Church and Biblical Truth is the Remedy

Another important reason for a declining America is corruption of doctrine within the church (as both an institution and the entire body of individual believers). By corrupt doctrine Morse meant not merely theological doctrine (like the doctrine of the Word of God, the nature of God, the nature of man, redemption, etc.), which are very important and do affect society. He also meant the general doctrines that Paul refers to in Acts 17:24-28:

> The God who made the world and all things in it since He is Lord of heaven and earth does not dwell in temples made with hands; neither is He served by human hands, as though He needed anything, since He Himself gives to all life and breath and all things; and He made from one, every nation of mankind to live on all the face of the earth, having determined their appointed times, and the boundaries of their habitation, that they should seek God, if perhaps they might grope for Him and find Him, though He is not far from each one of us; for in Him we live and move and exist.

Four primary doctrines that have practical implications on how we view the world are mentioned in these verses. They are:

(1) Creation — "God made the world." The world and life did not just happen by chance. The doctrine of creation began to be neglected in our public schools in the late 1800's. It was no longer being taught in a reasonable way because Christians began to neglect the field of science. Therefore, it became an irrelevant "religious" dogma taught in the schools. This neglect left a void for a competing ideology—evolution. We mentioned previously how Charles Darwin's theory of evolution only gained prominence as Christian scientific thought diminished. Today, the tables are being turned as creation scientists are restoring solid reasoning for Christians to articulate rather than simply saying, "The Lord made the earth."

Charles Darwin

(2) Lordship — "He is Lord of Heaven and earth." This means He is absolute Master and final authority to whom all must give allegiance. As this doctrine has been neglected, so another competing ideology has gained ascendancy—humanism. Humanism teaches that man is the measure of all things and the one who determines right and wrong for himself. Since 1961, when the Supreme Court recognized humanism as a religion, it has been systematically replacing Christianity as the United States' unofficially established or recognized religion.

(3) Providence — "He Himself gives to all life and breath and all things; ... for in Him we live and move and exist." God is the source of every man's provisions and the One to Whom each man and woman should look. As the doctrine of Providence has been abandoned, the competing ideology of socialism has prospered. Karl Marx's communist ideology had little influence in America until we began to turn from Christian principles of economics and embrace greed and materialism. As prosperity grew, wealth was accumulated for private consumption instead of compassionately employed for the betterment of society, including meeting the needs of the deserving poor. Individual interests replaced the common good of the community.

Rising economic challenges began to be exploited by Marxist and socialist leaders. Marshall Foster writes that in 1905,

> in the loft above Peck's restaurant at 140 Fulton Street in lower Manhattan, a group of young men met to plan the overthrow of the predominantly Christian worldview that still pervaded America. At this first meeting five men were present: Upton Sinclair, 27, a writer and a socialist; Jack London, writer; Thomas Wentworth Higginson, a Unitarian minister; J. G. Phelps Stokes, husband of a socialist leader; and Clarence Darrow, a lawyer. Their organization was called the Intercollegiate Socialist Society. Their purpose was "promote an intelligent interest in socialism among college men and women." These men were ready to become the exponents of an idea passed on to them by an obscure writer named Karl Marx—a man who never tried to be self-supporting but was supported by a wealthy industrialist who, inexplicably, believed in his theory of "the dictatorship of the proletariat." Although a small group in the beginning, these adherents of socialism more than succeeded in their task.[514]

Foster explains that "by using the proven method of gradualism, taken from the Roman general, Quintus Fabius Maximus, these men and others who joined with them slowly infiltrated" the public schools of our nation. By 1912 there were chapters in 44 colleges. By 1917 there were 61 chapters of student study groups of the League of Industrial Democracy. "At that time John Dewey, the godfather of progressive education, was the vice-president of the league. By 1941 Dewey had become president and Reinhold Niebuhr, the liberal socialist theologian, was the treasurer."[515]

In 1907, Charles and Mary Beard began to popularize Marx's ideas in their revisionist history books. These false ideas gradually began to influence what was taught in public schools throughout the nation.

The loss of Christian character and responsibility led to the failure of many state banks in the early 1900's. In an effort to remedy this situation, power was granted to a centralized Federal Reserve Board in 1913. But this unbiblical economic structure, in conjunction with a diminishing Christian character of the citizens, produced even greater problems. Within 20 years the stock market had crashed and America was in the midst of the Great Depression. With the propagation of socialism, people were ready for the "New Deal" of Franklin Roosevelt. Programs such as Social Security, and other welfare agencies, set up the state as provider rather than God.

Another corrupting event that occurred in 1913 was the passing of a federal income tax amendment, which paved the way for deficit spending, inflation, and financing of ungodly nations and causes.

(4) Sovereignty — "He made...every nation...having determined their appointed times and the boundaries of their habitation." Our Founders and early generations of Americans were unified and motivated by this basic truth, but teaching on the sovereignty of God was gradually replaced by a new ideology — Existentialism. Existentialists believe history is meaningless and the future unpredictable, and therefore to plan and work for goals is hopeless. Instead their philosophy is "eat, drink, and be merry for tomorrow we die." It is totally present-oriented and hedonistic. Marshall Foster warns:

> Many Christians have subconsciously adopted the existential view of history. They de-emphasize their importance in a God-ordained historical chain of Christianity and see themselves simply as individuals God has plucked out of an evil world who are now just awaiting heaven. Their sense of responsibility for the past and their hope and planning for the building of the future are lost in the "now generation" where they are called to focus on self-improvement. This attitude covers the burden of guilt that lays heavily on the head of American Christians, but it does not

alleviate their responsibility for our nation's crisis. ... Until the Christian comes to grips with his historical duties denouncing his existential perspective and reaffirming the providential view of history, the renewal of our nation will be impossible.[516]

...In colonial America the God of the Bible was seen as sovereign over men and their property, reflecting the "Biblical worldview" of the Reformation. But in the past 100 years a disarming doctrine, which sees Satan as the sovereign of this world, has been accepted by many in Christian circles. Many Bible teachers today see Jesus as an absentee king who is concerned exclusively with building and maintaining His church until He returns to earth. They see Jesus as having the authority and right to rule, but as having given over powers to subjugate the world temporarily to Satan.

The worldview of the reformers was diametrically opposite to this view. Jesus Christ is the ruler of the earth (1 Timothy 6:16; Hebrews 2:14) and Satan, a defeated foe (Colossians 2:15).

One's attitude toward the sovereignty issue is of paramount importance, because it affects what is done in every area of life. Here is the contrast:

If you see God ruling the earth:

1. Your commission is to subdue the earth and build godly nations through evangelizing and discipleship.
2. You see Christian culture as leavening all areas of life, replenishing the earth, and blessing all mankind.
3. All of God's world is His and every activity, to be seen as a spiritual work of God.
4. Reformation is expected if a nation is obedient to God's word.

If you see Satan ruling the earth:

1. Your commission is just to concentrate on saving souls from this evil world.
2. You see Christian culture as a counter-culture, an isolated, persecuted minority in an evil world.
3. Church activity is primary and spiritual, while worldly pursuits are secular and to be dealt with only as a necessity.
4. Reformation is impossible since things must get worse because Satan is in control.

The above contrasts illustrate the importance of ideas in determining consequences, because to the degree Christians have abdicated their leadership role and denied the "crown rights to Jesus Christ," to that degree the humanists have filled the void.[517]

What is the remedy for the corruption and neglect of these vital doctrines? It is the **Restoration of the New Testament Church** in its practical theology and biblical reasoning and worldview. After the Civil War "liberal" churchmen of the North continued emphasizing social reform but without the Bible as the basis. This is sometimes called the "Social Gospel" today. The more "Fundamental" or Bible-based churchmen of the South, after the military defeat of the South, became fatalistic. They retreated to emphasizing only religious or church concerns and viewed most social movements with suspicion. Two new "Christian" positions developed among these "fundamentalists:" (1) an eschatology of defeat and escape, and (2) a "separation of church and state" concept that sanctioned their non-involvement in society.

Neglect of Our Institutions — Reformation of Society is the Remedy

A third reason for America's secularization is that Christians have neglected societal institutions – the family, schools, government, the economy, business, etc. Christians developed and governed these institutions for the first three centuries of America's history. Due to false thinking (corrupt doctrine) Christians retreated from government, media, education, and law because they saw these things as secular, dirty and non-spiritual. The vacuum they left was filled by secularists who controlled these spheres for most of the twentieth century and on to the present.

Christians not only neglected these "non-religious" institutions, but they also neglected many aspects of the institution of the church. For nearly three centuries the church fulfilled its civil duties by instructing its members in a biblical worldview. However, towards the end the 19th century, the clergy ceased preaching political sermons — like Election, Anniversary, Artillery, and Execution Sermons

The church also neglected the Sabbath. Deuteronomy 5:15 reveals that one purpose of the Sabbath was to remember God's hand in history. This once was a regular practice in Sunday Schools as well as Sabbath day traditions in the home. The parents and grandparents would tell stories to their children on Sunday about how God's hand was seen in their home, church, and nation. This is in serious neglect today.

Economic institutions are also in neglect. Marshall Foster writes:

> In the early days of our nation, the tithe supported not only churches, but church schools and colleges, and provided for a variety of other social needs. In Rushdoony's *Revolt Against Maturity* he discusses how one New England town coped with radical population changes wholly by the use of the tithe. Salem, Massachusetts, saw a population boom between 1795 and 1845, doubling its population several times over until it had grown from a village into a city. There was a flood of foreign immigrants and one would think that the town's character would have been completely changed and that the burden of such an influx of people would have caused a complete dislocation of its social fabric. But, as a matter of fact, the needs of the immigrants—as well as of the town's own citizens— were met through a variety of tithing agencies that cared for the poor, provided education, job-training, children's education, Bible courses, and taught the immigrants English. Salem shows what conscientious tithing Christians can accomplish in the field of social welfare. As Powell and Rushdoony point out: "Conscientious and intelligently administered tithing by even a small minority can do much to reconstruct a land."[518]

God commanded Israel to provide for the poor through their tithe (Deut. 14:27-29). Social needs were met in America through the tithe (and privately financed charitable organizations) for 300 years before the civil government began to assume that responsibility under FDR's "New Deal" policies. If Christians today would tithe and give special offerings for the poor, to distribute individually or pool together with other Christians in their church, great things could happen. This must be done if we are ever going to disestablish the unbiblical welfare system. Church-going Christians only give about 2% of their income to the church. In 1983, only 32% of Christians in America tithed. If every church in America took responsibility for just 3 families, there would be no need for welfare!

The remedy for our neglect of institutions is the **Reformation of Society.** Biblical revival and the recovery of truth will change the moral and social climate of a community. J. Edwin Orr writes, "The revived church by many or few is moved to engage in evangelism, teaching, and social action."[519] According to A.W. Tozer, "Revival must of necessity make an impact on the community and this is one means by which we may distinguish it from the more usual operations of the Holy Spirit."[520]

As mentioned above, revival results in the establishment of truth in man and society. Charles Finney defined revival as "nothing else than a new beginning of obedience to God."[521] Recovery of truth as revealed in the Bible is a central aspect of any revival. Pratney writes that, "Revival is not magical. It is not mystical. It is, as far as men are concerned, a heartfelt return to love and faith in the living and written Word."[522]

Revival is not merely the conversion of many people, though this does occur in revivals. Revival involves the conversion of men and institutions. Revival has not occurred until truth is encoded within a nation via changed laws and societal institutions. History shows us that the entire culture is transformed when true biblical revivals occur.[523]

True revival transforms all society, like in the First Great Awakening, which was sparked by the preaching of George Whitefield.

We must continually fight spiritual entropy, a decline to a lower spiritual state. We must constantly add fuel to the fire within us and keep the flames burning. We must keep alive the passion and life within us. We must labor to be salt and light in our society, for as we do corruption shall subside, "the righteous will be in authority," and the people will rejoice" (Proverbs 29:2). God understands the need for renewed life and mercifully has sent His Spirit to revive mankind. He has come down many times to bring people and nations to life and He desires to do this today. As a remedy for decline, we need revival, restoration of truth, and the reformation of all society.

Today, the American Christian Republic still stands by the grace of God, yet its foundations have seriously eroded away. If our nation's problems were the result of some conspiracy of men, the solution would be beyond the reach of most of us, and thus fatalism, apathy and despair would prevail. However, since God says the real problem began with our neglect, then the solution is within the grasp of the church. If we accept our responsibility and do our duty, we have grounds for hope.

Chapter 20

The Power for Reforming America

Our Problems Today

In Chapter 13 we explained the importance of keeping the government as close to the people as possible and why our founders limited the power of the national government by keeping most power in the hands of the states and the people.

Today, unfortunately, federalism and a limited or small national government has largely passed away. The pyramid is now inverted. The states have become in many ways mere administrative extensions of Washington, D.C. How has this happened?

One major cause of the problem is rooted in the 14th Amendment to the Constitution. After the Civil War, Congress desired to prevent such an evil as slavery from ever happening again. Though this was well-intentioned, the method of solving the problem was flawed. It stated in paragraph 1 that no state shall "deprive any person of life, liberty, or property, without due process of law." This was the guilt of the South before the war—they refused to recognize and protect the inalienable rights of blacks whom they had enslaved. Their state legislatures and state courts were immoral because they rebelled against God's higher law. But why could the legislatures and courts get away with it? Because of the backslidden, materialistic character of the people who had elected them. Many of the churches had compromised and the minority of those with moral integrity were too apathetic to try and change their legislatures by political action.

The problem was with the loss of the "spirit" of the Constitution: religion, morality and knowledge. The "letter" of the Constitution had left the power of solving social problems with the states; the national government would be too distant from the people to handle such problems. The "spirit" of the Constitution was strong enough in the northern states so that slavery was abolished there. As soon as the Civil War was over, the Congress, being controlled by the northern states, proposed two amendments — the 13th was to abolish slavery. It was ratified by three-quarters of the state legislatures in late 1865. Six

United States Capitol, Washington, D.C.

months later the 14th Amendment was proposed by Congress to protect the rights of all citizens. When it was examined by the state legislatures, many of them (even some in the North) rejected it on the grounds that it would undermine the Founders' idea of federalism or dual government. The problem was in paragraph 5: "The Congress shall have power to enforce, by appropriate legislation, the provisions of this article." The Southern States in particular were champions of the idea of strong state government and most therefore refused to ratify this amendment. The radical Reconstruction Congress made a serious mistake at this point. Instead of listening to the serious objections to the wording of the amendment, they declared the southern legislatures to be illegal governments due to their involvement in the Civil War and placed them under martial law. (If they were truly illegal, then the 13th Amendment ratified by them just six months earlier would also not be legal). Once new legislatures were elected that would ratify the 14th Amendment, then they could enjoy their freedom once again. The 14th Amendment, then, was passed at the point of a gun and has become a very significant cause in the growth of the national government today. The courts have increasingly struck down numerous state laws, and the powers of the states have been greatly usurped. In almost every amendment that followed this one, problem-solving or over-riding powers have been granted to the national government. The whole intention of the Bill of Rights, especially Amendment 10, has been completely undermined. The national government can now overrule **any** law passed by any state and is often done by Executive Orders from the President, or by the federal courts.

Two other amendments have also destroyed state powers and enlarged the national government. Passed in 1913, the 16th Amendment gave the Congress power to "collect taxes on incomes…without apportionment among the several States." Prior to this, the federal budget was entirely provided by import and federal sales taxes collected by the states and turned over to Congress. Now the national government could bypass any accountability to the states as to their spending. History shows that since this was passed, the federal deficit has soared and the federal bureaucracy grown to enormous proportions. Now the states get much of their money from the national government, but with strict guidelines as to its use, thus becoming administrative agents of the national government.

The 17th Amendment, also passed in 1913, changed how U.S. Senators are selected. They would no longer be appointed by the state legislatures to represent the states' interests as a whole, but would be "elected by the people thereof." Now, no one in Congress represents only their state. Both Senators and Congressmen represent many different special-interest groups who will help in their re-election. The day of the statesman, moved only by principle, has been eclipsed by the day of the mere politician.

These things have contributed to the demise of federalism. Thomas Jefferson warned long ago that "the true theory of our Constitution is surely the wisest and best…[for] when all government…shall be drawn to Washington as the centre of all power, it will render powerless the checks provided of one government on another, and will become as…oppressive as the government from which we separated."[524]

Unfortunately, the executive branch has grown in size and power unconstitutionally in many ways since the 14th Amendment. Now, the President makes more laws than Congress through what are known as "Executive Orders." They were originally only administrative instructions or policies that affected federal departments and agencies. Over time, however, the federal courts began to uphold these as legally binding as legislation by Congress. Before Teddy Roosevelt, no President issued more than 70 executive orders in their term of office, but Roosevelt felt he could do anything not specifically prohibited by the Constitution. Thus, in his term, he issued over 1000 orders! This trend continued, with Franklin Roosevelt far surpassing all presidents issuing over 3700. In 1935 Congress began requiring that these be published in the Federal Register. Today there are nearly 14,000 Executive Orders on the books. The Executive branch has usurped the power of Congress to make laws.

The branch responsible for guarding the Constitutional separation of powers is the nine member Supreme Court, 13 Circuit Courts of Appeals and about 100 other federal courts. The Judicial branch has as its primary purpose the interpretation of the laws of Congress in light of the Constitution and higher law. The Court has failed to check the President and the Congress in many of the areas mentioned previously, but, even worse, it has itself acted unconstitutionally. Our Founders never imagined that the Courts would become as powerful as they have. The Constitution reflects this: 255 lines of copy deal with the powers of Congress, 114 with the powers of the President, and only 44 with the Courts. They never imagined that the court needed extensive restraints. An exception to this was Thomas Jefferson who said:

> The germ of dissolution of our federal government is in the constitution of the federal judiciary; an irresponsible body, (for impeachment is scarcely a scarecrow,) working like gravity by night and by day, gaining a little today and a little tomorrow, and advancing its noiseless step like a thief, over the field of jurisdiction, until all shall be usurped from the States, and the government of all be consolidated into one. ...[525]

Thomas Jefferson

> [T]o consider the judges as the ultimate arbiters of all constitutional questions [is] a very dangerous doctrine indeed, and one which would place us under the despotism of an oligarchy. ... The Constitution has erected no such tribunal.[526]

The Court has evolved to this very state today. Edwin S. Corwin in *The Constitution of the United States* describes four distinct stages in the history of the Supreme Court. From 1800 to 1835, he calls the era of "National supremacy," then from 1835 to 1895 the era of "Constitutional supremacy." These were generally good. But then from 1895 to 1950 was the era of "Judicial supremacy" in which the decisions of the Court were no longer just the interpretation of the laws, but now considered "the law of the land," in place of the Constitution itself. In the words of Chief Justice Charles Evans Hughes in 1907: "the Constitution is what the judges say it is."[527] Finally, Corwin describes our present era as one of "Judicial Activism" or "Judicial Legislation."[528] Today the Court no longer limits itself to settling disputes between parties. It strikes down laws in all fifty states and issues restraining orders and decrees that usurp both legislative and executive powers. The Warren Court that struck down prayer and Bible reading in the schools in the early 1960's did not have any judges with any prior substantive judicial experience.[529] Most lawyers and judges today do not study the Constitution in law school, which is the very document they are supposed to defend; rather, they study past judicial decisions to prepare them for legal service.

Law not founded on absolutes is very dangerous. Without absolutes, the Supreme Court has reversed itself over 100 times. In 1973, the Court invented a new Constitutional right to abortion and has thereby denied the inalienable right to life to over 60 million unborn children to this date. A similar mistake was made in the Dred Scott decision of 1857, when the Supreme Court denied the personhood of blacks. This was finally overturned by the 13th Amendment as a result of the Civil War. Abraham Lincoln criticized the Supreme Court for its denial of the Law of God, which asserts the inalienable liberty of every individual. Lincoln believed that if that Court decision was the absolute law of the land, then "the people will have ceased to be their own rulers, having to that extent practically resigned their government into the hands of that eminent tribunal."

Neglecting Political Involvement

Today in America, only 50% of registered voters go to the polls, but no more than about 5% participate in the precinct level of politics where the selection or nomination of candidates actually takes place (no more than one-half of 1% attend caucuses or conventions). Christians also vote and participate in local party politics at about the same percentage. This is really the only place where the divine command for selecting godly leaders is able to be discharged, and it is where your vote and participation is 1000 times more significant than on Election

Day. A political party is simply an organization through which the people choose their representatives. If Christians wait until November to make their choices, they more often than not are forced to choose between "the lesser of two evils," where usually neither fulfill the biblical requirements in rulers.

Samuel, the prophet/statesman, was an example of God's people being active in public affairs. Like Israel, America's decline began when God's people neglected their political responsibilities.

This is a primary reason why our government has violated the rights of blacks in the past, the unborn in the present, and exhibited corruption to various degrees in every branch over the past 200 years. "Our Constitution," as John Adams wrote, "was made only for a moral and religious people. It is wholly inadequate for the government of any other."[530] In a Christian nation, the people make the laws, but the church makes the people. When the church fails to bring the necessary moral influence — the "spirit" of the Constitution — then the "letter" of the law will not work. A brief history of Latin America provides an example. Many of those nations have had a revolution or military coup and then wrote a piece of paper very similar to our Constitution. Then within a few years, a whole new revolution occurred to overthrow the oppression of the previous regime. Another

"Constitution" was written and the process is repeated. The "letter" is the same as ours but the "spirit" is not there to make it work.

In America, the problem with slavery was not in the letter of the Constitution. The Northern States were proof of that. The problem between 1830 and 1860 was a moral one and unfortunately led to corrupt legislatures and courts in the South that denied the rights of black citizens. If the problem was a moral one, then working for amendments to the "letter" of the Constitution, which simply gave power to a higher legal body to correct it, was really a dangerous mistake. Likewise, it would be dangerous today to attempt to solve problems through centralizing power. The centralized higher authority may have a right moral stance now, but what do you do when it is morally wrong on an issue? If the problem was a lack of virtue in some of the states, is it not possible for the same lack of virtue to occur in the national government?

Not only is this probable, but it is history. Today the rights of 60 million unborn children have been disregarded by rulers in the national government who are not "men of truth who rule in the fear of God." The problem, here again, is not with the Constitution, but it is with the men in public office.

Therefore, to put the focus of our efforts on amendments to change the Constitution is a mistake. The solution is in changing the men in office. However, this will never occur if godly Americans are not involved in party politics on the local level.

Changing the letter of the Constitution never solves a problem rooted in the spirit. This is not to say that the letter of the law is useless — only that it must have the spirit of the law to sustain it. This was the mistake of the liquor prohibition amendment in 1919. A lack of the spirit to sustain prohibition began creating more problems than it solved, and public reaction led to an amendment to repeal it in 1933. This unfortunately convinced those conservative Christians (who had worked for years to pass this mistaken amendment) that their involvement in politics was futile, and so they retreated into the four walls of their churches.

The same thing would happen with a pro-life amendment without virtue being restored to the people. The immoral lifestyle of the people and millions of unwanted pregnancies would lead to some undesired reaction against it. When the South was forced to outlaw slavery, the result was an entrenchment of bitterness and prejudice against the blacks that took longer to eradicate than if it had operated originally from the internal to the external. As awful as slavery was, and as grotesque as the slaughter of the unborn is today, the only lasting and permanent solutions to such social problems must come from the influence of the church on local politics and in building a godly conscience in the nation.

The Scriptural Duty of Every American Christian

James Madison articulated clearly that the real power for preserving a republic such as ours was placed in the hands of a people who governed themselves. In the Federalist #39 he wrote of "that honourable determination which animates every votary of freedom, to rest all our political experiments on the capacity of mankind for self-government."[531] The basis of the ability for man

to govern himself well is rooted in his being in subjection to a higher power—to "the Laws of Nature and of Nature's God," in the words of the Declaration of Independence. If men do not govern themselves under God, they will be governed externally by force. Speaker of the U.S. House of Representatives from 1847-49, Robert C. Winthrop declared:

> Men, in a word, must necessarily be controlled either by a power within them, of by a power without them; either by the Word of God, or the strong arm of man; either by the Bible or the bayonet.[532]

Robert C. Winthrop

One "essential ingredient in the happiness we enjoy as a nation," according to President of the Continental Congress (1782-83) Elias Boudinot, "is the right that every people have to govern themselves in such a manner as they judge best calculated for the common benefit."[533] The ability of the American people to govern themselves under God was the foundation for their ability to effectively govern their civil affairs. They understood the importance of choosing leaders who reflected their character and worldview.

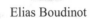

In the book of Exodus, Chapter 18, verses 19-23, Moses is advised by his father-in-law to be "the people's representative before God," but to also command the people themselves to "select out of all

Elias Boudinot

the people able men who fear God, men of truth, those who hate dishonest gain;

and you shall place these over them, as leaders of thousands, of hundreds, of fifties and of tens. ... If you do this thing and **God so commands you,** then you will be able to endure." Deuteronomy 1:13 states that the people were to "choose wise and discerning and experienced men." Therefore, it is a biblical command to choose leaders who fear God, display Christian character, and have a biblical worldview.

The freedom to choose one's representative is not an American invention, but a Divine plan for Godly government. John Jay, one of the authors of the *Federalist Papers* and first Chief Justice of the Supreme Court, said:

> Providence has given to our people the choice of their rulers, and it is the duty, as well as the privilege and interest of our Christian nation, to select and prefer Christians for their rulers.[534]

Noah Webster wrote:

John Jay

[L]et it be impressed on your mind that God commands you to choose for yourselves rulers, "just men who rule in the fear of God." The preservation of a republican government depends on the faithful discharge of this duty; if the citizens neglect their duty and place unprincipled men in office, the government will soon be corrupted; laws will be made, not for the public good, so much as for selfish or local purposes; corrupt or incompetent men will be appointed to execute the laws; the public revenues will be squandered on unworthy men; and the rights of the citizens will be violated or disregarded. If a republican government fails to secure public prosperity and happiness, it must be because the citizens neglect the divine commands, and elect bad men to make and administer the laws.[535]

Noah Webster

For most Americans, to neglect consistent involvement in local politics is to neglect a great privilege, but for Christians to do so is far worse. It is a failure to keep a biblical command. Scripture makes it clear that Christians who fail to use what God has given them will not only suffer in this life, but also give an account in the one to come (Matthew 25:14-30).

The qualifications of a candidate should not be issue-oriented as much as character-oriented. They should certainly be "able" and "experienced" men for the position which they seek. Beyond that, Scripture says they should be men who "fear God," that is, they should be Christians, as affirmed by John Jay. They should also be "men of truth" and "wise and discerning" men. This means that they should be Christians with a biblical worldview — men who reason from absolute truth, not human wisdom. Many candidates may claim to be Christians, but do not hold to a biblical worldview. Former President Jimmy Carter was an example of a Christian whose mind was un-renewed by Scripture and, thus, reasoned and governed from a "humanistic" worldview. Finally, Scripture says that our representatives must "hate dishonest gain." This means that beyond a correct worldview, they must have Christian character, a godly home life, and pure motives.

Only when you are involved in local politics on a consistent basis, regularly going to meetings with the party members, is it possible to know if a candidate meets these criteria. When a vacancy occurs in a public office, candidates are frequently chosen from among the regular members of the party, whom you would work with and know personally if you are involved. Over the course of various debates and party activities you will come to understand each person's worldview and character. Therefore, you can faithfully discharge your biblical duty and help to nominate a godly representative. If none is available to meet those qualifications, then you should be willing to run yourself.

The nomination of a candidate by a political party is usually determined by a very small percentage of Americans. Consequently, your vote is most influential on the local level, when candidates are chosen by the parties. If you get to know and work with candidates on the local level who later become state or national elected officials, as a friend you more readily have access to them for future issues. People who never are involved in local party politics but then desire to communicate with their congressman on an issue rarely get to do so. A letter, email, or phone call is usually received by an assistant who records your views and compiles it with others and passes it on to the congressman. The congressman really only sees numbers: so many for and against a certain piece of legislation. Even if Christians manage to outnumber others on an issue and we sway our congressman by sheer numbers, we end up in the dangerous promotion of democracy. We really do not want representatives who are swayed by majorities, but rather by correct principles. The education of our representative is only possible when we have been faithful to work with him on the local level in consistent party politics.

"We the People" — The Power for Changing America

If all the godly people who are presently involved in some special interest political or social group would focus their time, energy, and money on consistent local participation in the political party of their choice, then the very issues that they are interested in could be solved and much more. Two out of three of the political precincts (or neighborhoods of approximately 1000 homes) in this country are continually lacking leadership. If godly people would simply call the headquarters of any political party and ask how to get involved they would be welcomed.[536] Experience has shown that when godly people go consistently to the party meetings and seek to serve and contribute, they can become influential, if not official leaders of that party within two years. The apathy of other Americans can become a blessing and advantage to Christians who choose to get involved and fill the void of leadership.

Should Christians be involved in both of the current major parties in America? If everyone who claims to be a Christian participated regularly in the two parties, their number is large enough to exert a major influence in both. However, the growing number of secularists in America will mean, at least in the near future, that one party will likely be controlled by those who do not embrace biblical principles or policies. Hence, Christians in America will find they will have a greater united influence by participating in the party that comes closest to embracing biblical ideals.[537]

The ultimate goal is for there to be enough politically active Christians to control both major political parties. Were that to occur, there would be multiple candidates on the ballot in November who embrace biblical qualifications. That would be real choice.

There are only approximately 2.5 million people involved in each political party on the local level today in America. If Christians get involved nationwide, only 3 million in each party would be necessary to change them dramatically. This is much less than 10% of all Christians in America who claim to be "born again." If just 10% of all Christians in America today woke up (which would include adopting a biblical worldview) and got involved consistently for the long haul, it would not take long to bring immense change to America. How long? It could be done within ten years. Here's how:

If Christians in every locality became a controlling influence in a political party after two years of consistent service, then most representatives in most state legislatures and the national Congress could be replaced within six years. Godly governors and a President could also be chosen. Working together they could appoint new judges who would begin changing the unconstitutional influence of the courts within a few years. Even if *Roe v. Wade* was overturned by the Supreme Court today, abortion would still be legal until each state legislature passed new pro-life laws. If a Human Life Amendment was passed by Congress today, it would have to be ratified by three-quarters of the state legislatures. So why wait? Get involved on the local level to change your state legislature today. Even if the national Congress is not changed, if we select more godly representatives in two-thirds of the state legislatures then we can bypass Congress and call a new Constitutional Convention to clean up some of the mess we have made in the past 200 years. With godly state legislatures, the delegates appointed by them to a new Convention would likely be godly and wise as well.[538]

Consistent Party Politics — This is one part of the price of liberty we must pay today to maintain our free republic. (However, as we have stated before, this must be preceded by an internal transformation of many hearts and minds.) Our Founders paid a higher price. Of the fifty-six signers of the Declaration of Independence, nine died in war, five were captured or imprisoned, two lost their sons, the houses of twelve were burned to the ground, and 17 lost everything they owned. Thomas Jefferson wrote that the price of maintaining that liberty they sacrificed so much for is "eternal vigilance." James Monroe said:

> The establishment of our institutions forms the most important epoch that history hath recorded. ... To preserve and hand them down in their utmost purity to the remotest ages will require the existence and practice of the virtues and talents equal to those which were displayed in acquiring them.[539]

The power of our republic is "We the People." If we are virtuous then it will be good power; if not, then it will be dangerous. The trend toward secularism today

James Monroe

is making the possibility of virtuous people and rulers even more remote. Revivalist Charles Finney said:

> The Church must take right ground in regard to politics. ... The time has come that Christians must vote for honest men, and take consistent ground in politics, or the Lord will curse them. ... God cannot sustain this free and blessed country, which we love and pray for, unless the Church will take right ground. Politics are a part of a religion in such a country as this, and Christians must do their duty to the country as a part of their duty to God. ... He [God] will bless or curse this nation, according to the course they [Christians] take [in politics].[540]

Rev. Charles G. Finney

Hopefully, you have been inspired to do many things as a result of this book. One thing of great importance is for you to fulfill your biblical duty to choose godly representatives by getting involved in local party politics for the rest of your life. Edmund Burke once said, "All that is necessary for evil to triumph is for good men to do nothing."[541]

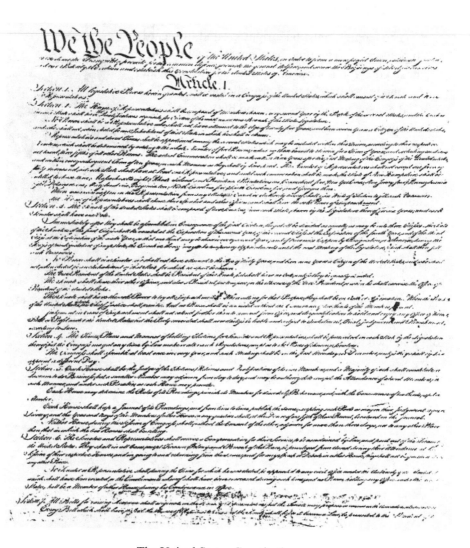

The United States Constitution

Conclusion

Seven Principles of Liberty

In this book we have learned seven basic principles that produce liberty when applied by individuals or nations. Miss Rosalie Slater identified these principles and recorded them in *Teaching & Learning America's Christian History*. In conclusion, we will briefly summarize these principles. While Miss Slater stated them historically, we will state them in general terms since they are applicable to all areas of life.

1) Principle of Power and Form

External forms always result from an internal power. This is true for civil governments, churches, homes, businesses, or associations. The power, which is internal, precedes the form, which is external.

Both a power and a form are needed for anything to function properly. The Bible speaks of certain men who hold to a form of godliness yet deny its power (2 Tim 3:5). Those that do are dead in their faith. The internal power, or Spirit, is the life or energizing force and is essential for any form to work as it should; yet, a form is absolutely necessary to channel the power properly.

For an analogy revealing the need for both power and form, let's consider a fireman fighting a fire. If he rushed to a fire with his hose (the form), but had not turned on the fire hydrant and, therefore, did not have water (the power) flowing through it, the fire would rage on. Similarly, if he just went and opened the hydrant without a hose attached, he would do little, if any, good in extinguishing the flames. Both a power and form are necessary.

We not only need power and form, but we also need a balance between the two. Too much form causes all involved to dry up, while too much power causes them to "blow up." Communism, for example, produces a form of civil government that relies almost totally on external pressure to keep everyone "in line." The internal creativity, life, and motivation of each individual is suppressed by these external constraints.

An over-emphasis on power with little form leads to anarchy and eventually bondage. Historically, this can be seen after many national revolutions, the French being an excellent example.

2) God's Principle of Individuality

This principle is stated by Rosalie Slater in *Teaching and Learning America's Christian History* as follows:

> Everything in God's universe is revelational of God's infinity, God's diversity, God's individuality. God creates distinct individualities. God maintains the identity and individuality of everything which He created.[542]

God does not create carbon-copy molds of anything — be they humans, animals, trees, minerals, mountains, rivers, planets, or stars. Everything He creates is unique and distinct, yet there is a unity among all things for God created them all.

God's Principle of Individuality reveals a unity with diversity for all creation. Take snowflakes for example. All snowflakes are alike in their material composition (frozen H_2O) and their structure (all have 60° between their axes), yet no two snowflakes are alike in their crystal growth pattern. Wilson Bentley, affectionately called "Snowflake" Bentley, was the first person to photograph and study snowflakes in depth. Around the beginning of the 20th century, this farmer,

Wilson Bentley with snowflakes he photographed. Snowflakes, like all of creation, reflect the unity and diversity of God. He makes all things unique.

with his wooden box camera, photographed over 5000 different snowflakes. No two of them were alike.

This individuality is seen in all creation for God Himself is a picture of individuality. God is One (a unity), yet He is also a triune Being (a diversity)— He is three in one.

3) Christian Principle of Self-Government

The Dutch political philosopher Hugo Grotius summarized this principle well, writing in the 17th century:

Hugo Grotius

He knows not how to rule a kingdom, that cannot manage a Province; nor can he wield a Province, that cannot order a City; nor he order a City, that knows not how to regulate a Village; nor he a Village, that cannot guide a Family; nor can that man Govern well a Family that knows not how to Govern himself; neither can any Govern himself unless his reason be Lord, Will and Appetite her Vassals; nor can Reason rule unless herself be ruled by God, and (wholly) be obedient to Him.[543]

Stated another way, you must rule yourself before you can rule others. The Bible says that a man who does not know how to manage his own household, cannot manage the church of God (1 Tim. 3:5) or any other area.

Today there are many civil government leaders who are attempting to govern our nation whose own lives and families are falling apart. It's no wonder that our nation is becoming more of a mess in many ways when we consider who is providing direction for it.

Effective government begins by an individual learning to govern himself. The more internal self-government a person possesses, the less external government he needs. Consequently, the more rules and laws required to keep people acting rightly is a revelation of a diminishing amount of self-government.

As Americans have become less self-governed, our civil government (especially the national government) has grown and grown, making more and more laws and spending more and more money. Lack of self-government leads to greater centralized external government.

4) Principle of Christian Character

Character literally means "to stamp and engrave through pressure." This sums up nicely what God is doing in our lives. God's plan is to make each person like Him. Romans 8:29 tells us that God has predestined that we are to be conformed into the image of Christ. He is building His character within us, or you might say, He is stamping and engraving upon us His image. In so doing, He often uses pressure.

The fifteenth chapter of the gospel of John tells us that Jesus is the vine, and we are the branches, and the Father is the vine-dresser. What happens to every branch that does not bear fruit? It is cut away, then dries up and is finally burned. What happens to every branch that bears fruit? He prunes it. Therefore, no matter what we do we are going to get cut.

Why are branches pruned? To produce fruit of greater quantity and quality. While much of God's pruning hurts, we should greatly rejoice in the pruning process because through this He is building His character within us.

Character has been defined as a convictional belief that results in consistent behavior. We can see that character begins internally (a convictional belief) and is expressed externally (consistent behavior). Our internal character will be seen in our external lifestyle.

God is stamping His image upon us so that we might be examples of him to the world, and be able to fulfill his purpose for our lives. We saw how the Pilgrims exemplified this principle so very well.

5) Principle of Christian Union

Only an internal unity of ideas and principles produces an external union among people. This is the basis of the Christian union of the United States of America. About two and a half centuries ago, thirteen independent states were able to join together in a permanent union because they all embraced the Christian idea of man and government. Our motto, E. Pluribus Unum ("From many one"), expresses this unity with union.

While the United States reveals a Christian Union, the former Soviet Union was an example of an unbiblical union. External force and fear were used to hold all the people groups together. It was an involuntary union which rapidly collapsed when the constraints were removed. In America, unity brings union; in Russia, union attempted to force unity.

Stronger internal bonds will produce a stronger union and action. If the original colonies had never formed a union, they would have never individually made the positive impact upon the world that corporately the United States has been able to make. In fact,

America's national motto, E Pluribus Unum, expresses the principle of Christian Union.

they might not ever have survived. Similarly, the church has made the greatest impact upon society as they have moved together in union.

As the internal unity breaks down within a family, church, or civil government, so does the external union. Therefore, in order to keep any union strong, common biblical ideas and principles must be sown in the hearts of the people. A union cannot be maintained long by only external means such as laws or force. Union must voluntarily flow from the hearts of an enlightened people.

6) Principle of Christian Education

Christian education can also be called the Principle of Sowing and Reaping because education "plants seeds" in people which will grow and produce results.

The Bible tells us that we will reap what we sow. In the birth of the United States, the first Christian nation in history, we see the fruit of seeds that had been planted for generations by parents, ministers, statesmen, teachers, and others.

The Bible tells us much about the "seed principle." It is extremely important for us to understand the parable of the sower and the soils (Mark 4), and that the kingdom of God (as well as faith) is like a seed. Although we are instantly converted when we repent and submit ourselves to Christ, the establishment of God's character and kingdom within us is a gradual process. It takes place like the growth of a plant or tree. A seed is planted; nourishment,

Education is like a seed. Its potential is great; after all, you can count how many seeds are in an apple, but you cannot count how many apples are in a seed.

care, and sunlight is provided; and then a mature plant comes forth bearing fruit (we must remember the pruning process, also).

This same principle applies in establishing God's truth in the nations of the world. It is a gradual process that must occur through Christian education.

7) Principle of Property

James Madison revealed much about the Principle of Property when he wrote:

James Madison

Property ... In the former sense, a man's land, or merchandise, or money, is called his property. In the latter sense, a man has a property in his opinions and the free communication of them. He has a property of peculiar value in his religious opinions, and in the profession and practice dictated by them. ... He has an equal property in the free use of his faculties, and free choice of the objects on which to employ them. In a word, as a man is said to have a right to his property, he may be equally said to have a property in his rights.[544]

God has created everything, including us, and given us the right to possess property, both internal (opinions, ideas, talents, etc.) and external (land, merchandise, money, etc.). In the United States this right is acknowledged to be endowed by God and is also secured by the law of the land, the Constitution.

God requires us to be good stewards of everything He puts into our hand, whether that be houses, land, and money or talents, abilities, and knowledge. The idea of stewardship is embodied in the Principle of Property.

How we take care of our external property reflects how we take care of our internal property. If our house is constantly in a disheveled state, we can be assured that our thoughts are just as disorderly.

—

These are liberating principles. To the extent that these seven principles become a part of the life and worldview of the American people is the extent to which we as a nation will be free, just, and prosperous.

A Checklist for Reforming America

Throughout this book we have seen that we must take action to assure that America is reestablished on a firm Christian base, and hence, secure our God-given liberties and provide a free and prosperous platform from which we can go and make disciples of all the nations. The following checklist will help remind you of certain areas where you can begin to take action:

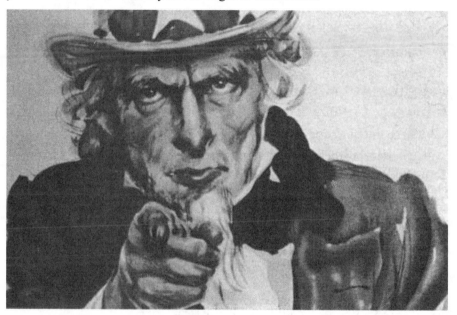

"Christians, America needs you!"

Personal and Family

☐ I will acknowledge the Lordship of Jesus in my life.

☐ I will remember God and His Providential hand in history.

☐ I purpose to implant the Principles of Liberty in my heart.

☐ I purpose to be self-governed in the use of the property God has given me by tithing and supporting ministries and those in need as God directs.

☐ I will take responsibility in educating my children in the biblical principles of liberty, effectively communicating the vision to them.

☐ I will seek to fulfill my godly calling and vocation, producing needed goods and/or services for the amelioration of mankind and the advancement of God's kingdom in the earth.

Church

☐ I will continually receive instruction from my pastor on applying God's Word to every aspect of life.

☐ I will support my church in fulfilling Christ's command to make disciples of all the nations.

Education

☐ Since the education of my children is my responsibility, I will carefully choose who I delegate that responsibility to, and to what schools my children go.

☐ I will become aware of who is on the school board in my community and will work to replace those who do not act in accordance with godly principles.

☐ I will work to educate my neighbor in biblical principles.

☐ I will work to see that our public schools and universities begin operating on the biblical base which was their foundation.

☐ I will work to establish a media with a biblical worldview.

Civil Government

☐ I will take responsibility for choosing and instructing those who stand in my place in every area of civil government.

☐ I will register to vote.

☐ I will participate regularly in a political party on the local level.

☐ I will keep informed on political issues affecting me, my community, my state, and my nation.

Bibliography

Adams, John and Abigail. *The Book of Abigail and John, Selected Letters of the Adams Family, 1762-1784,* Cambridge, Mass.: Harvard University Press, 1975.

Adams, John. *The Works of John Adams, Second President of the United States,* Boston: Little, Brown and Co., 1854.

Adams, Samuel. *The Writings of Samuel Adams*, Harry Alonzo Cushing, ed., New York: G.P. Putnam's Sons, 1905.

Adams, Moody. *America is Too Young to Die.* 1976.

Addresses and Speeches on *Various Occasions,* Boston: Little, Brown & Co., 1852.

Alexander, David, and Pat Alexander, editors. *Eerdmans' Handbook to the Bible.* Grand Rapids: William B. Eerdmans Publishing Co., 1973.

Alexander, Samuel Davies. *Princeton College During the Eighteenth Century,* New York: Anson D.F. Randolph & Co.

America, Great Crises in Our History Told by Its Makers, A Library of Original Sources. 12 volumes. Issued by Americanization Department, Veterans of Foreign Wars of the United States, Chicago, 1925.

American Vision, 360 Years Later, The (Cassette Study Guide). Atlanta: American Vision, 1980.

Amos, Gary T. *Defending the Declaration.* Brentwood, Tennessee: Wolgemuth & Hyatt, 1989.

Annals of America, The. Chicago: Encyclopaedia Britannica, 1968.

Anthony, Greg. *Biblical Economics.* Charlottesville, Virginia: Providence Foundation, 1988.

Appel, David H., editor. *An Album for Americans.* New York: Crown Publishers, Inc.

Appel, Joseph H. *The Business Biography of John Wanamaker, Founder and Builder*, New York: The Macmillan Company, 1930.

Baldwin, Alice. *The New England Clergy and the American Revolution.* Fredick Ungar Pub. Co., 1928.

Bancroft, George. *History of the United States.* 6 volumes. Boston: Little, Brown, and Co., 1878.

Bancroft, George. *History of the United States of America.* 10 volumes. D. Appleton and Co., 1891.

Banyard, Joseph. *Daniel Webster, His Life and Public Services*, Chicago: Werner Company, 1875.

Barret, David. *Cosmos, Chaos, and Gospel, a Chronology of World Evangelization from Creation to New Creation.* Birmingham, AL: New Hope, 1987.

Barlett, John. *Barlett's Familiar Quotations,* Boston: Little, Brown & Co., 1863, 1980.

Barton, David. *Original Intent.* Aledo, Texas: Wallbuilder Press, 1996.

Beliles, Mark, and Jerry Newcombe, *Doubting Thomas? The Religious Life and Legacy of Thomas Jefferson*, New York: Morgan James, 2015.

Bloom, Sol. *The Story of the Constitution*. Washington, D.C.: United States Constitution Sesquicentennial Commission, 1937.

Blumenfeld, Samuel L. *Is Public Education Necessary?* Boise, Idaho: The Paradigm Company, 1985.

Blumenfeld, Samuel L. *NEA: Trojan Horse in American Education*, Boise, Idaho: The Paradigm Company, 1985.

Bowen, Catherine Drinker. *Miracle at Philadelphia*. Boston: Little, Brown and Co., 1986.

Bradford, Gamaliel. *Lee the American.* Houghton and Mifflin Co., 1913.

Bradford, William. *Of Plimoth Plantation*. Boston: Wright & Potter Printing Co., 1901.

Brigham, Kay. *Christopher Columbus' Book of Prophecies*, Libros CLIE, 1992.

Bruce, Philip Alexander. *Robert E. Lee.* W.B. Jacobs and Co., 1907.

Brutus, Junius. *A Defense of Liberty Against Tyrants (Vindiciae Contra Tyrannos)*. Edmonton, AB Canada: Still Waters Revival Books, reprinted from the 1689 translation, 1989.

Cardozo, Benjamin. *The Growth of Law*, New Haven: Yale University Press, 1924.

Casson, Herbert N. *Cyrus Hall McCormick, His Life and Work*, Chicago: A.C. McClurg &Co., 1909.

Chilton, David. *Productive Christians in an Age of Guilt Manipulators: A Biblical Response to Ronald J. Sider*. Tyler, TX: Institute for Christian Economics, 1982.

Chilton, David. "Alfred the Great," *Equity*, the newsletter of the Christian Public Policy Council, January, 1989.

Christopher Columbus's *Book of Prophecies*, Reproduction of the Original Manuscript with English Translation by Kay Brigham. Quincentenary Edition. Barcelona, Spain: CLIE Publishers.

Coffin, Charles Carleton. *The Story of Liberty*. New York: Harper & Brothers, 1878.

Cole, Franklin, editor. *They Preached Liberty*. Indianapolis: Liberty Press.

Cooper, James F. *Knights of the Brush, The Hudson River School and the Moral Landscape*, New York: Hudson Hills Press, 1999.

Cord, Robert L. *Separation of Church and State*. New York: Lambeth Press, 1982.

Cousins, Norman. *"In God We Trust," The Religious Beliefs and Ideas of the American Founding Fathers*. New York: Harper & Brothers, 1958.

Dabney, R.L. *Life and Campaigns of Lieut-Gen. Thomas J. Jackson*. Original published in 1865. Republished by Sprinkle Publications, Harrisonburg, Virginia, 1983.

D'Aubigne, J.H. Merle. *History of the Reformation of the Sixteenth Century*. Translated by H. White. New York: Hurst & Company.

Demar, Gary. *God and Government, Vol. 1, A Biblical and Historical Study*. Atlanta: American Vision Press, 1982.

Demar, Gary. *God and Government, Vol. 2, Issues in Biblical Perspective*. Atlanta: American Vision Press, 1984.

Dolson, Hildegarde. *William Penn, Quaker Hero*. New York: Random House, 1961.

Dorchester, Daniel. *Christianity in the United States.* New York: Hunt & Eaton, 1895.

Douglass, Frederick. *The Frederick Douglas Papers*, John Blassingame, editor, New Haven: Yale University Press, 1982.

Dreisbach, Daniel L. *Real Threat and Mere Shadow, Religious Liberty and the First Amendment.* Westchester, Illinois: Crossway Books, 1987.

Dreisbach, Daniel L. *Religion and Politics in the Early Republic*, Lexington, Ken.: The University Press of Kentucky, 1996.

Edwards, Brian. *God's Outlaw.* Wheaton, Illinois: Tyndale House Publishers, Inc., 1981.

Eidsmoe, John. *Christianity and the Constitution.* Grand Rapids, Michigan: Baker Book House, 1987.

Eidsmoe, John. *Columbus & Cortez, Conquerors for Christ*, Green Forest, Ark.: New Leaf Press, 1992.

Federer, William J. *America's God and Country*, Coppell, Tex.: FAME Publishing, Inc., 1994.

Federer, William J., compiler. *The Faith of FDR, From President Franklin Delano Roosevelt's Public Papers*, 1933-1945, St. Louis: Amerisearch, 2006.

Findlay, Bruce Allyn, and Esther Blair Findlay. *Your Rugged Constitution.* Stanford, California: Stanford University Press, 1969.

Finney, Charles G. *Revivals of Religion.* Virginia Beach, VA: CBN University Press, 1978.

Fiske, John. *The Beginnings of New England.* New York: Houghton, Mifflin and Co., 1898.

Fiske, John. *The Critical Period of American History, 1783-1789.* New York: Houghton, Mifflin and Company, 1898.

Fitzpatrick, John C, editor. *Writings of George Washington.* United States Government Printing Office, 1930.

Flood, Robert. *Men Who Shaped America.* Chicago: Moody Press, 1976.

Folsom, Jr., Burton. *New Deal or Raw Deal, How FDR's Economic Legacy Has Damaged America*, New York: Threshold Editions (Simon & Schuster), 2008.

For the Colony in Virginea Britannia, Lawes Divine, Morall and Martiall, etc., compiled by William Strachey, edited by David H. Flaherty, Charlottesville: The University of Virginia, Charlottesville, 1969.

Foster, Marshall, and Mary-Elaine Swanson. *The American Covenant the Untold Story.* California: Mayflower Institute, 1983.

Franklin, Benjamin, The Autobiography of. Compiled and edited, with notes by John Bigelow. New York: Walter J. Black, Inc., 1932.

Franklin, Benjamin. Albert Henry Smyth, ed., *Writings of Benjamin Franklin*, Macmillan Co., 1905-7.

Frantz, Joe B. *Gail Borden, Dairyman to a Nation*, Norman: University of Oklahoma Press, 1951.

Frothingham, Richard. *The Rise of the Republic of the United States*. Boston: Little, Brown, and Co., 1895.

Gaustad, Edwin Scott. *A Religious History of America*. New York: Harper & Row, 1974.

Gifford, Carolyn. *Writing Out My Heart: Selections from the Journal of Frances E. Willard*, 1855-96, 1995.

Gould, Lewis L. *The Presidency of William McKinley*, Lawrence: University Press of Kansas, 1980.

Grady, Lee. "Can We Make a Deal for Peace?" *The Forerunner*, Vol. VIII, No. 8, December 1987.

Grant, George. *In the Shadow of Plenty*, Fort Worth, Texas: Dominion Press, 1986.

Grimsley, Mark. "Jackson: The Wrath of God," *Civil War Times*.

Guyot, Arnold. *The Earth and Man*. Boston: Gould and Lincoln, 1863.

Guyot, Arnold. *Physical Geography*. New York: Ivison, Blakeman and Co., 1885.

Hakluyt, Richard. *A Selection of the Principal Voyages, Traffiques and Discoveries of the English Nations*, compiled by Laurence Irving, New York: Alfred A. Knopf, 1926.

Hall, Mark David. *Did America Have a Christian Founding?* Nashville: Nelson Books, 2019.

Hall, Verna M., and Rosalie J. Slater. *The Bible and the Constitution of the United States of America*. San Francisco: Foundation for American Christian Education, 1983.

Hall, Verna M., compiler. *The Christian History of the American Revolution, Consider and Ponder*. San Francisco: Foundation for American Christian Education, 1976.

Hall, Verna M., compiler. *The Christian History of the Constitution of the United States of America, Christian Self-Government*. San Francisco: Foundation for American Christian Education, 1980.

Hall, Verna M., compiler. *The Christian History of the Constitution of the United States of America, Christian Self-Government with Union*. San Francisco: Foundation for American Christian Education, 1979.

Hamilton, Alexander, James Madison and John Jay. *The Federalist Papers*. First published in 1787-1788. New York: Bantam Books, 1988.

Hamilton, Alexander, James Madison and John Jay. *The Federalist,* edited by Michael Loyd Chadwick, Washington, DC: Global Affairs Publishing Company, 1987.

Hardinge, Leslie. *The Celtic Church in Britain*. London: Church Historical Society, 1973.

Hawthorne, Hidlegarde. *Matthew Fontaine Maury, Trail Maker of the Seas*, New York: Longmans, Green and Co., 1943.

Hill, David J. *Elements of Rhetoric and Composition*, Hills Rhetorical Series, 1884.

Holy Bible, The. As printed by Robert Aitken and Approved & Recommended by the Congress of the United States of America in 1782. Reprinted, New York: Arno Press, 1968.

Holt, Rackham. *George Washington Carver, An American Biography*, Garden City, NY: Doubleday, Doran, and Co., Inc., 1943.

Hosmer, William McAuley. "Divine Providence—God Himself in the Battle of Yorktown." Foundation for Christian Self-Government newsletter, Sept. 1981.

"How to Understand the Purpose Behind Humanism." Institute in Basic Youth Conflicts, 1983.

Hughes, Charles Evans. *The Autobiographical Notes of Charles Evans Hughes*, David J. Danelski and Joseph S. Tulchin, editors, Cambridge: Harvard University Press, 1973.

Hutson, James H. *Religion and the Founding of the American Republic,* Washington: Library of Congress, 1998.

Inaugural Addresses of the Presidents of the United States. Washington, D.C.: United States Government Printing Office, 1969.

Irving, Washington. *Life of Washington*. New York: The Cooperative Publication Society, Inc.

Jaspers, Glen A., and Ruth Jaspers Smith. *Restoring America's Heritage of Pastoral Leadership*. Granger, Indiana: Pilgrim Institute, 1982.

Jefferson, Thomas. *The Complete Jefferson,* Saul K. Padover, ed., Tudor Publishing Co. 1943.

Jefferson, Thomas. *The Writings of Thomas Jefferson*, Andrew A. Lipscomb and Albert Ellery Bergh, Editors, Washington, DC: The Thomas Jefferson Memorial Association, 1903.

Johnson, William J. *George Washington the Christian*. Reprinted by Mott Media, Milford, ML, 1976.

Johnson, William J. *Robert E. Lee the Christian*. Reprinted by Mott Media, 1976.

Johnson, William J. *Abraham Lincoln the Christian*. Reprinted by Mott Media, 1976.

Jones, J. William. *Christ in the Camp*. B.F. Johnson and Co., 1897.

Jones, J. William. *Personal Reminiscences, Anecdotes, and Letters of General Robert E. Lee*. D. Appleton and Co., 1874.

Journal of the Proceedings of Congress, 1774. A Facsimile of the Official Edition Printed in 1774. Philadelphia: Printed for the Library Company of Philadelphia, 1974.

Kengor, Paul. *The Crusader, Ronald Reagan and the Fall of Communism*, Regan (HarperCollins Publishers), 2006.

King, Jr, Martin Luther. *Strength to Love*, 1994.

King, Jr, Martin Luther and Coretta Scott King, et al, *A Gift of Love*, 2012.

Lancaster, Bruce. *The American Revolution*. Garden City, NY: Garden City Books, 1957.

Lewis, Charles Lee. *Matthew Fontaine Maury, The Pathfinder of the Seas*, New York: AMS Press, 1969 (reprinted from edition of 1927).

London, Joshua E. *Victory in Tripoli, How America's War with the Barbary Pirates Established the U.S. Navy and Built a Nation*, Hoboken, NJ: John Wiley & Sons, Inc., 2005.

Lossing, Benson J. *Our Country, A Household History*, Vol. 2, New York: Johnson & Miles, 1877.

Lossing, Benson J., *Mount Vernon and Its Associations*, New York: Townsend, 1859.

Lossing, Benson J., editor. *Recollections and Private Memoirs of the Life and Character of Washington by George Washington Parke Custis, with Memoir of George Washington Parke Custis by His Daughter: with the Epistolary Correspondence between Washington and Custis,* 1859.

Lossing, Benson J. *Seventeen Hundred and Seventy-Six, or the War of Independence; a History of the Anglo Americans.* New York: Edward Walker, 1847.

Love, Jr., W. DeLoss. *The Fast and Thanksgiving Days of New England*, Boston: Houghton, Mifflin and Company, 1895.

Lutz, Donald S. ed. *Colonial Origins of the American Constitution*, Indianapolis: Liberty Fund, 1998.

Lutz, Donald S. "The Relative Influence of European Writers on Late Eighteenth-Century American Political Thought," *American Political Science Review, Vol. 78,* 1984.

Mabee, Carleton. *The American Leonardo, A Life of Samuel F. B. Morse*, New York: Alfred A. Knopf, 1943.

Madison, James. *Journal of the Federal Convention.* Albert, Scott & Co., 1893.

Madison, James. *Notes of Debates in the Federal Convention of 1787 Reported by James Madison.* New York: W.W. Norton & Co., 1987.

Madison, James. *The Papers of James Madison*, Robert A. Rutland, ed., University of Chicago Press, 1962.

Magoon, E.L. *Orators of the American Revolution.* New York: C. Scribner, 1857. Reprinted by Sightext Publications, El Segundo, California, 1969.

Marshall, Peter, and David Manuel. *The Light and the Glory.* Old Tappan, New Jersey: Fleming H. Revell, 1977.

Marshall, Peter, and David Manuel. *From Sea to Shining Sea.* Old Tappan, New Jersey: Fleming H. Revell, 1986.

Mather, Cotton. *The Great Works of Christ in America, Magnalia Christi Americana*, Carlisle, Penn.: The Banner of Truth Trust, 1979 (reprint of 1852 edition).

Maury, Matthew Fontaine. *The Physical Geography of the Sea and its Meteorology*, New York: Harper & Brothers, 1856.

McDowell, Bart. *The Revolutionary War.* Washington, D.C.: National Geographic Society, 1970.

McDowell, Stephen. *Abraham Lincoln's Faith*, Charlottesville: Providence Foundation, 2012.

McDowell, Stephen. *America's Providential History, A Documentary Sourcebook*, Charlottesville: Providence Foundation, 2004.

McDowell, Stephen. *Apostle of Liberty, The World-Changing Leadership of George Washington.* Nashville: Cumberland House, 2007.

McDowell, Stephen. *Kingdom Missionaries Marcus and Narcissa Whitman, The Founding of the Oregon Territory*, Charlottesville: Providence Foundation, 2011.

McDowell, Stephen. *Monumental: Restoring America as the Land of Liberty.* Libertyman Studios, 2013.

McDowell, Stephen. *No Cross, No Crown, The Life Message of William Penn*, Charlottesville: Providence Foundation, 2017.

McDowell, Stephen. *Ruling Over the Earth, a Biblical View of Civil Government*. Charlottesville: Providence Foundation, 2020.

McDowell, Stephen and Jim Arcieri, *Teacher's Guide to America's Providential History*, Charlottesville: Providence Foundation, 2005.

McDowell, Stephen. *The American Dream, Jamestown and the Planting of the American Christian Republic*, Charlottesville: Providence Foundation, 2007.

McDowell, Stephen. *The Bible: America's Source of Law and Liberty*. Charlottesville: Providence Foundation, 2015.

McDowell, Stephen. *Transforming Nations through Biblical Work, Christians Have Led the Advancement in All Spheres of Life*, Charlottesville: Providence Foundation, 2018.

McLaughlin, Andrew C. Foundations *of American Constitutionalism*. Greenwich, Conn.: Fawcett Publications, Inc., 1966.

M'Guire, E.C. *The Religious Opinions and Character of Washington*, New York: Harper & Brothers, 1836.

Moore, Frank. *American Eloquence: A Collection of Speeches and Addresses,* New York: D. Appleton & Co., 1858.

Morris, B.F. *Christian Life and Character of the Civil Institutions of the United States*. Philadelphia: George W. Childs, 1864.

Morris, Richard B., editor. *Significant Documents in United States History, Volume 1, 1620-1896*, New York: Van Nostrand Reinhold Company, 1969.

Morse, Jedidiah. *Annals of the American Revolution*. First published in 1824. Reissued, Port Washington, N.Y.: Kennikat Press, 1968.

Mourt's Relation: A Journal of the Pilgrims of Plymouth, Plymouth, MA: Plymouth Rock Foundation, 1985.

Mowry, William A. *Marcus Whitman and the Early Days of Oregon*, New York: Silver, Burdett and Company, 1901.

Niles, Hezekiah. *Principles and Acts of the Revolution in America,* New York: A.S. Barnes & Co., 1876.

Noll, Mark A., Nathan O. Hatch and George M. Marsden. *The Search for Christian America*. Westchester, Illinois: Crossway Books, 1983.

North, Gary. *Healer of the Nations, Biblical Principles for International Relations*. Fort Worth, Texas: Dominion Press, 1987.

North, Gary. *Honest Money, Biblical Principles of Money and Banking*. Ft. Worth, Texas: Dominion Press, 1986.

North, Gary. *Inherit the Earth*, Ft. Forth: Dominion Press, 1987.

Olcott, Charles Sumner. *The Life of William McKinley, vol. 2*, New York: Houghton Mifflin, 1916.

Old South Leaflets. Published by The Old South Association, Old South Meeting-house, Boston, Mass.

Owen, G. Frederick. *Abraham Lincoln: The Man and His Faith*. Tyndale House Publishers, Inc., 1981.

Padover, Saul K., editor. *The Complete Jefferson*. Tudor Publishing Co., 1943.

Parks, Rosa with Gregory J. Reed. *Quiet Strength: The Faith, the Hope, and the Heart of a Woman Who Changed a Nation*, 1994.

Peck, Jesse T. *The History of the Great Republic, Considered from a Christian Standpoint*. New York: Broughton and Wyman, 1868.

Perry, Richard L, editor. *Sources of Our Liberties*, New York: American Bar Foundation, 1952.

Phillips, Kevin. *William McKinley*, part of *The American Presidents*, Arthur M. Schlesinger, Jr., General Editor, New York: Henry Holt and Company, 2003.

Pope, Norman V. "Educator, Minister, Patriot," in *Nation Under God*, Frances Brentano, editor. Great Neck, New York: Channel Press, 1957.

Pound, Roscoe. *The Spirit of the Common Law*, New York: The Legal Classics Library.

Powell, Edward A., and Rousas John Rushdoony. *Tithing and Dominion*. Vallecito, CA: Ross House Books, 1982.

Pratney, Winkie. *Revival, Principles to Change the World*, Springdale, Penn.: Whitaker House, 1983.

"Proceedings of the Virginia Convention in the Town of Richmond on the 23rd of March, 1775." Richmond: Saint John's Church, original publication copyrighted in 1927.

"Providential Discovery of the Treason of Benedict Arnold-September 25th, 1780." San Francisco: Foundation for American Christian Education.

Rebirth of America, The. Arthur S. DeMoss Foundation, 1986.

Remember William Penn, 1644-1944, a Tercentenary Memorial. Compiled by the William Penn Tercentenary Committee. Harrisburg, PA: Commonwealth of Pennsylvania, 1945.

Richardson, James D. *A Compilation of the Messages and Papers of the Presidents*, Philadelphia: Lippincott, 1857.

Rollin, Charles. *The Ancient History of the Egyptians, Carthaginians, Assyrians, Babylonians, Medes and Persians, Grecians, and Macedonians; including a History of the Arts and Sciences of the Ancients. 2 volumes*. New York: George Dearborn, 1836.

Rose, James B. *A Guide to American Christian Education for the Home and School, the Principle Approach*. Palo Cedro, CA: American Christian History Institute.

Rowland, Kate Mason. *Life and Correspondence of Charles Carroll of Carrollton*, New York & London: G.P. Putnam's Sons, 1898.

Rush, Benjamin. *Essays, Literary, Moral and Philosophical*, Philadelphia: Printed by Thomas and William Bradford, 1806.

Rushdoony, Rousas John. *The Institutes of Biblical Law*. The Presbyterian and Reformed Publishing Company, 1973.

Rutherford, Samuel. *Lex Rex, or The Law and the Prince*. First published in 1644. Reprint, Harrisonburg, Vir.: Sprinkle Publications, 1982.

Rutland, Robert A., editor. *The Papers of James Madison.* University of Chicago Press, 1962.

Sandoz, Ellis, editor. *Political Sermons of the American Founding Era, 1730-1805.* Indianapolis: Liberty Press, 1991.

Schaeffer, Francis A. *How Should We Then Live?* Old Tappan, New Jersey: Fleming H. Revell Company, 1976.

Schaeffer, Francis A. *A Christian Manifesto.* Westchester, Illinois: Crossway Books, 1982.

Sidney, Algernon. *Discourses Concerning Government.* Edited by Thomas G. West. Indianapolis: Liberty Classics, 1990.

Skousen, W. Cleon. *The Making of America.* Washington, D.C.: The National Center for Constitutional Studies, 1985.

Skousen, W. Cleon. *Study Guide to the Making of America.* Washington, D.C.: The National Center for Constitutional Studies.

Slater, Rosalie J. *Teaching and Learning America's Christian History, the Principle Approach.* San Francisco: Foundation for American Christian Education, 1980.

Slater, Rosalie J. An essay on Noah Webster in the preface to a reprint of *An American Dictionary of the English Language* by Noah Webster, 1828. San Francisco: Foundation for American Christian Education, 1980.

Smyth, Albert Henry, editor. *Writings of Benjamin Franklin.* Macmillan Co., 1905-7.

Stedman, W. David, and LaVaughn G. Lewis, editors. *Our Ageless Constitution.* Asheboro, NC: W. David Stedman Associates, 1987.

Stoel, Caroline P., and Ann B. Clarke. *Magna Carta, Liberty Under the Law.* Portland, Oregon: published jointly by Magna Carta in America and Graphic Arts Center Publishing Co., 1986.

Story of the Seal, The. Merrimac, Mass.: Destiny Publishers.

Taylor, John M. *Garfield of Ohio: The Available Man*, New York: W.W. Norton & Co., Inc., 1970.

Thornton, John Wingate. *The Pulpit of the American Revolution.* Boston: Gould & Lincoln, 1860.

Titus, Herbert W. *God, Man, and Law: The Biblical Principles*, Oak Brook, Ill.: Institute of Basic Life Principles, 1994.

Tocqueville, Alexis de. *Democracy in America.* Edited by J.P. Mayer. Garden City, NY: Doubleday & Co., Inc., 1969.

Townsend, Col. G.W. *Memorial Life of William McKinley, Our Martyred President*, D.Z. Howell publisher, 1902.

Walton, Rus. *One Nation Under God.* Nashville: Thomas Nelson, 1987.

Walton, Rus. *Biblical Solutions to Contemporary Problems.* Brentwood, Tennessee: Wolgemuth & Hyatt, 1988.

Warfel, Harry R. editor. *Letters of Noah Webster*, New York: Library Publishers, 1953.

Washington, Booker T. *Up From Slavery*, New York: Airmont Publishing Company, 1967.

Washington, George. *George Washington: A Collection*, ed. W.B. Allen, Indianapolis: Liberty Fund, 1988.

Washington, George. *The Writings of George Washington from the Original Manuscript Sources, 1745-1799*, John C. Fitzpatrick, Editor, Washington: United States Government Printing Office, 1931.

Watson, Henry B. *George Washington, Architect of the Constitution*. Alexandria, Virginia: Patriotic Education, Inc., 1983.

Wayland, John W. *The Pathfinder of the Seas, The Life of Matthew Fontaine Maury*, Richmond: Garret & Massie, Inc., 1930.

Weaver, Robert B. *Our Flag and Other Symbols of Americanism*. Alexandria, Virginia: Patriotic Education, Inc., 1972.

Webster, Daniel. *The Works of Daniel Webster*, Boston: Little, Brown, and Co., 1853.

Webster, Daniel. *The Writings and Speeches of Daniel Webster Hitherto Uncollected,* Boston: Little, Brown, and Company, 1903.

Webster, Noah. *An American Dictionary of the English Language*, A Facsimile Edition of 1828 version, reprinted by Foundation for American Christian Education.

Webster, Noah. *History of the United States*. New Haven: Durrie & Peck, 1833.

Wells, William V. *The Life and Public Services of Samuel Adams*. 3 volumes. Boston: Little, Brown, and Company, 1865.

Westerhoff III, John H. *McGuffey and His Readers*. Milford, Michigan: Mott Media, 1982.

Whitehead, John W. *The Second American Revolution*. Elgin, Illinois: David C. Cook Publishing Co., 1982.

Wilbur, William. *The Making of George Washington*. Alexandria, Virginia: Patriotic Education, Inc., 1973.

Willard, Emma. *A System of Universal History in Perspective*. Hartford: F. J. Huntington, 1835.

Willard, Emma. *History of the United States, or Republic of America*. New York: A.S. Barnes & Co., 1849.

William Wirt, *Sketches of the Life and Character of Patrick Henry*, Philadelphia: James Webster, 1818.

About the Authors

Dr. **Mark A. Beliles** is president of the Global Transformation Network and its USA branch called the America Transformation Company. Beliles is a popular speaker and cultural leadership coach who has traveled to over 60 countries and addressed parliaments and high-level leaders of nations on the topic of faith and freedom. He founded an educational ministry called the Providence Foundation in 1983, and co-authored books for popular audiences including *America's Providential History* and *Contending for the Constitution: Recalling the Christian Influence on the Writing of the Constitution and the Biblical Basis of American Law and Liberty*. He also authored *National Transformation* and several other books for international audiences.

Beliles, an ordained minister since 1977, has served as pastor of various non-denominational churches for over 35 years and was the founder of Grace Covenant Church in Charlottesville, Virginia. He has provided apostolic oversight to dozens of churches in the U.S. and abroad.

Beliles earned his Ph.D. from Whitefield Theological Seminary. He has organized, with sponsorship of the Virginia Foundation for the Humanities, several scholarly symposiums held at the University of Virginia on Jefferson and religion that each featured dozens of nationally-known Jefferson scholars and church and state historians. Beliles' most recent scholarly books on Thomas Jefferson are *Doubting Thomas? — The Religious Life and Legacy of Thomas Jefferson* and *The Selected Religious Letters and Papers of Thomas Jefferson*. (www.AmericaPublications.com)

He has served for many years as Chairman of the Charlottesville Historic Resources Committee and co-chairman of the city's 250th Anniversary observed in 2012. He and his wife Nancy homeschooled their three children and now are blessed with eight grandchildren.

Stephen McDowell is co-founder and President of the Providence Foundation, a nonprofit Christian educational organization whose mission is to train and network leaders of education, business, and politics to transform their culture for Christ. After obtaining a B.S. Degree in physics at the University of North Carolina at Chapel Hill and a M.S. Degree in geology at the University of Memphis, he was ordained for the ministry in 1978, working in the pastorate until 1984 when he assisted in establishing the Providence Foundation.

McDowell is the editor of the *Providential Perspective* and has authored or co-authored over 40 books, videos, and training courses, including *America's Providential History, Liberating the Nations, Building Godly Nations, In God We Trust Tour Guide, Transforming Nations through Biblical Work*, and *Apostle of Liberty: The World-Changing Leadership of George Washington*. His study, *Monumental: Restoring America as the Land of Liberty*, was done in conjunction with Kirk Cameron as a follow-up course to Cameron's Monumental film. *The Bible: America's Source of Law and Liberty* has been distributed to members of state legislators in 20 states with the goal of reaching all 50. Stephen's books and writings have been translated into 18 languages and distributed to over one million people.

He has traveled throughout the United States and to 40 nations in six continents, teaching tens of thousands of people from more than 100 different countries. He has consulted with numerous government officials, assisted in writing political documents and starting political parties, established classes on godly reformation in numerous churches, and helped start a number of Christian schools.

McDowell has been an Adjunct Professor at Regent University, has written scores of articles for various publications, appeared on numerous TV and radio programs (including the Glenn Beck show and Fox & Friends), contributed articles to *The Founders' Bible*, appeared in the *Monumental* film, and spoken to many different religious, educational, civic, and political organizations. He also periodically does historic portrayals of Thomas Jefferson. He and his wife Beth live in Charlottesville, Virginia, and have four children and six grandchildren.

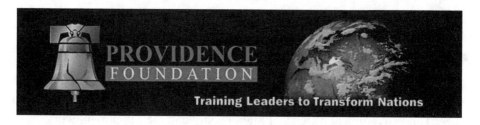

Discipling the Nations ♦ Restoring America as the Land of Liberty

The Providence Foundation is a Christian educational organization whose mission is to train leaders to transform their culture for Christ, and to teach all citizens how to disciple nations. We have been working since our founding in 1984 to fulfill Christ's commission to "make disciples of all nations." Such nations will have transformed people, but also transformed institutions – family, church, and state.

We have focused on training in a principled, biblical education that has historically produced liberty, justice, prosperity, virtue, and knowledge in people and nations.

The Providence Foundation provides training and produces resources necessary for pastors, teachers, government leaders, businessmen, parents, and students to live and think Biblically, and to equip others to disciple the nations.

- We have produced scores of different books, audios, videos, and courses in 18 different languages with over 2 million being distributed around the world.
- We have trained tens of thousands of people from over 100 countries.
- We have consulted with leaders who have started political parties, Christian schools, organizations, and reformational groups.
- We have representatives throughout the USA and around the world who are educating others and working to bring godly reform.
- We offer over 50 different seminars, presentations, and talks, with staff and representatives speaking to thousands of churches, schools, home-school groups, social and political organizations, radio and TV outlets.

To arrange a speaker or for more information contact:

Providence Foundation, PO Box 6759, Charlottesville, VA 22906
Website: **providencefoundation.com**   Phone: 434-978-4535
Email: info@providencefoundation.com

What Others Have Said

"America as well as nations across the world have benefited from the principles of Godly government that the Providence Foundation teaches both to citizens and government officials. I highly commend their important work."
David Barton, President, WallBuilders

"I am SOOO thankful for you and the Providence Foundation's ministry. Your booklets are tremendous and my favorite educational tools. I feel desperate to get their principles into the hands of the nation. Keep up the great work!" –
Kirk Cameron, Actor

"*America's Providential History* had a life changing effect on me. God has spoken to my heart to share this book at our conferences and make it available to other Christians so that they may obtain knowledge and become aware of their Christian heritage and experience the effect of it in their lives."
Dave Meyer, Life in the Word / Joyce Meyer Ministries

"I just finished studying your booklet, *The Threat of Islam to liberty and Christianity*. It is a fine piece of scholarship that merits the widest distribution possible. It is a first rate summary of the history and interaction of Christianity and Islam. Your handling of the Crusades is the most succinct I have read anywhere. Congratulations, very well done." – **General Jerry Curry** (Ret.)

"This latest book by Stephen McDowell is a great resource for anyone who desires to know the true source of law and liberty in America. For decades, American Family Association has worked to restore biblical values in our culture and this book by Stephen is a great tool to do just that."
Tim Wildmon, President, American Family Association

"If you are a leader, Stephen McDowell's book, *The Bible: America's Source of Law and Liberty*, is absolutely essential knowledge. On our shoulders rests the future of the greatness of our nation. Read this! Finish it. Read it again. Retain it. Teach it until it is retained!"
Kevin Jones, Kansas State Representative, 5th District, Former US Army Green Beret

Training & Networking Local Teams to Develop Long-Term 7-Sphere Strategic Plans to Transform America for Christ.

400 years ago when Europe became corrupt, Christians journeyed to America to build a godly nation from the ground up. In 1620 a strategic group of believers in the Plymouth Company sent "Pilgrims" with a comprehensive, multi-generational strategy for raising up Biblical leaders and institutions in all the key spheres of influence (i.e. 7 "mountains"). Their strategy worked. America emerged as a nation that God could bless and also use to bless the world. Although it has now greatly fallen away, thankfully today, new strategic "companies" of godly leaders are meeting in local cities nationwide. These local community action councils do 5 things:

1. Provide *general education* in **5 signs transformation vision (see books below)**
2. Identify and provide *advanced training* for **5 signs leaders**
3. Connect trained **5 signs leaders** into *networked teams*
4. Execute long-term *strategic 5 signs action plans*
5. Develop *funding* for permanent **5 signs** *institutions*

Christ's Strategy to Disciple Nations is a series of books that gives historically-proven best practices for the church to transform society. The five titles in the series are:

How Nations Cast Out their Demons (i.e. spiritual transformation)
How Nations Speak their New Tongues (i.e. intellectual transformation)
How Nations Take up their Serpents (i.e. political transformation)
How Nations Drink their Deadly Things (i.e. financial transformation)
How Nations Lay Hands on their Sick (i.e. social transformation)

Contact us to find out how to join or start a "company" in your area.
Find us at **www.AmericaTransformationCompany.com**
Phone: 434-249-4032   Email: nationaltransformation@gmail.com

PROVIDENCE FOUNDATION

P.O. Box 6759, Charlottesville, VA 22906 ♦ 434-978-4535
info@providencefoundation.com ♦ providencefoundation.com

Thank You for Your Support!

☐ I would like to support the Providence Foundation and their mission to bring biblical transformation.

☐ $15   ☐ $25   ☐ $50   ☐ $100   ☐ $250   ☐ $500 ☐ Other: $_____

I want to join the Providence Foundation:

☐ **Basic Member:** Those who contribute $120 per year (or $10/month) or more receive our newsletters, a 30% discount on books and materials, access to a free online course and *Perspectives*.

☐ **Premium Member:** Those who contribute $500 (or $42/month) or more per year receive Basic Member benefits plus vouchers for free BWU courses, electronic copies of most of our books, and much more (see website).

For Membership: I request my bank or credit card company to transfer funds in the amount of $_____ per month / quarter / year (circle one) until further notice. I prefer a transfer date of the ☐ 5th or the ☐ 20th starting _____ (month). I have enclosed an initial gift of $____.

America's Providential History

Explores God's hand in American history. Regular price: $24.95 (members save 30%)

Special Offer

Make a donation to the Providence Foundation of any amount and receive a 50% discount on ordering 1-10 copies of *America's Providential History* (one-time only offer). Use the order/donor form on the next page or call our offices.

America's Providential History, A Documentary Sourcebook

A compilation of over 25 primary source readings expanding ideas mentioned in *America's Providential History*. Contains early sermons, political writings, speeches, and more revealing the biblical worldview of the Founders. Price: $17.95.

Receive articles and updates via Facebook. Like Providence Foundation today.

☐ I would like to subscribe to your email newsletter.

www.providencefoundation.com

Quan	Resource Name	Regular Price	Total
	America's Providential History	$24.95	
	America's Prov. History (with donation)	$12.50	
	Donation		
	APH, A Documentary Sourcebook	$17.95	
	Member donation		
Total for products			
Member discount (30%)			
Subtotal			
(Tax: Virginia residents 5.25%)			
Shipping/handling (12%, $4.50 min.)			
Donation			
Total Amount			

☐ Check   ☐ Checking/Savings (attach a voided check/deposit ticket for recurring giving)

☐ VISA   ☐ Mastercard   ☐ AmEx   ☐ Discover

Acc. # _____

Exp. Date _____ Security Code _____

Name _____

Address_____

City/State/Zip _____

Phone _____Email_____

Date _____ Signature _____

☐ I would like to subscribe to your email newsletter.

If paying by check, make payable to Providence Foundation. Mail to Providence Foundation, PO Box 6759, Charlottesville, VA 22906. You can also place an order by calling our office (434-978-4535). Donations and orders can also be made online at **providencefoundation.com**

End Notes

Introduction

[1] B.F. Morris, *Christian Life and Character of the Civil Institutions of the United States*, Philadelphia: George W. Childs, 1864, p. 270.

Chapter 1

[2] M. Mallet Du Pan, *Considerations on the Nature of the French Revolution, and on the Causes Which Prolong Its Duration*, Translated from the French, London: J. Owen, 1793, p. 31. Also in, George Bancroft, *History of the United States*, in 10 vols., Boston: Little, Brown, and Co., 1874, 9:492.

[3] http://www.globalissues.org/article/26/poverty-facts-and-stats

[4] http://www.nmci.org/news/news_items/trafficking.html;
http://www.dreamcenter.org/new/images/outreach/RescueProject/stats.pdf

[5]http://www.guttmacher.org/pubs/FB-ATSRH.html;
http://www.4parents.gov/sexrisky/teen_preg/teen_preg.html#72b;
http://www.cdc.gov/std/stats08/trends.htm;   http://www.usatoday.com/news/health/2008-03-11-std_n.htm

[6] http://www.guttmacher.org/pubs/fb_induced_abortion.html
http://www.guttmacher.org/media/nr/abortww_nr.html

[7]http://www.washingtonpost.com/wp-dyn/content/story/2008/02/28/ST2008022803016.html;
http://www.ojp.usdoj.gov/bjs/glance/tables/exptyptab.htm

[8] http://www.unhcr.org/cgi-bin/texis/vtx/news/opendoc.htm?tbl=NEWS&id=448915214>

[9] http://www.globalissues.org/article/75/world-military-spending

[10] David Barret, Chaos, Cosmos, and Gospel.

[11] Matthew Henry, *Commentary on the Whole Bible*, complete and unabridged in one volume, Henrickson Publishers, 1991, p. 1775.

[12] Verna M. Hall and Rosalie J. Slater, *The Bible and the Constitution of the United States of America*, San Francisco, 1983, p. 18.

[13] *The Christian History of the American Revolution, Consider and Ponder*, compiled by Verna M. Hall, San Francisco: Foundation for American Christian Education, 1976, p. 47 (designated *Consider and Ponder* in future references).

[14] *A Facsimile Edition of Noah Webster's 1828 Edition of An American Dictionary of the English Language,* San Francisco: Foundation for American Christian Education, 1980, definition of providence.

[15] William Bradford, *Of Plimoth Plantation*, quoted in *The Christian History of the Constitution of the United States of America*, compiled by Verna M. Hall, San Francisco, 1980, p. 186.

[16] James Madison, *Journal of the Federal Convention*, Albert, Scott & Co., 1893, pp. 259-260.

[17] B.F. Morris, *Christian Life and Character of the Civil Institutions of the United States,* 1864, pp. 327-328.

[18] *A Compilation of the Messages and Papers of the Presidents*, James D. Richardson, Philadelphia: Lippincott, 1857, 1:56.

[19] *Consider and Ponder*, p. 46.

Chapter 2

[20] Arnold Guyot, *The Earth and Man: Lectures on Comparative Physical Geography, in its Relation to the History of Mankind, Boston: Gould and Lincoln*, 1852, quoted in Rosalie J. Slater, *Teaching and Learning America's Christian History,* San Francisco, 1980, p. 142.

[21] Arnold Guyot, *Physical Geography*, New York: Ivison, Blakeman & Co., 1885, quoted in Slater, p. 149.

[22] Guyot, *The Earth and Man*, quoted in Slater, pp. 145-146.

[23] Arnold Guyot, *Physical Geography*, quoted in *The Christian History of the Constitution*, p. 4.

[24] Guyot, *The Earth and Man*, quoted in Slater, p. 148.

[25] Ibid., p. 149.

[26] Ibid., p. 147.

[27] Guyot, *Physical Geography*, quoted in *The Christian History of the Constitution*, p. 3.

[28] Ibid., pp. 3-4.

[29] Ibid., p. 4.

[30] Emma Willard, *History of the United States, or Republic of America*, New York: A.S. Barnes & Co., quoted in Slater, p. 153.

[31] Alexis de Tocqueville, *American Institutions and their Influence*, New York: A.S. Barnes & Co., quoted in Slater, p. 153.

[32] Guyot, *Physical Geography*, quoted in *The Christian History of the Constitution*, pp. 4-5.

Chapter 3

[33] For a deeper look at the government of ancient Israel see, Stephen McDowell, *Ruling Over the Earth, a Biblical View of Civil Government*, Charlottesville: Providence Foundation, 2020.

[34] Richard Frothingham, *The Rise of the Republic of the United States*, Little, Brown & Co., 1890, quoted in *The Christian History of the Constitution,* p. 1.

[35] Ibid., p. 2.

[36] Dr. Augustus Neander, *General History of the Christian Religion and Church*, Boston: Houghton, Mifflin & Co., 1871, quoted in Slater, p. 213.

[37] Ibid., p. 214.

[38] Norman Cousins, editor, *"In God We Trust," The Religious Beliefs and Ideas of the American Founding Fathers,* New York: Harper & Brothers, 1958, p. 369.

Chapter 4

[39] *Eerdmans' Handbook to the Bible*, Edited by David Alexander and Pat Alexander, Grand Rapids, 1973, p. 588.

[40] David Chilton, "Alfred the Great", in *Equity*, the newsletter of the Christian Public Policy Council, Jan. 1989, p. 3.

[41] W. Cleon Skousen, *The Making of America,* Washington, D.C., 1985, p. 32.

[42] Rousas John Rushdoony, *The Institutes of Biblical Law*, The Presbyterian and Reformed Publishing Company, 1980, p. 1.

[43] Prof. Gotthard Victor Lechler, *John Wycliffe and His English Precursors*, London: The Religious Tract Society, 1904, quoted in Slater, p. 167.

[44] Ibid.

[45] Ibid., p. 168.

[46] Charles Carleton Coffin, *The Story of Liberty,* New York: Harper & Brothers, 1878, p.79.

[47] John Eidsmoe, *Columbus & Cortez, Conquerors for Christ*, Green Forest, Ark.: New Leaf Press, 1992, pp. 90-91. The American Vision, 360 Years Later (Cassette Study Guide), 1980, p. 2-

3. This quote is an excerpt from Columbus' *Book of Prophecies*. The complete work of *Christopher Columbus' Book of Prophecies* was translated into English by Kay Brigham and published by Libros CLIE in 1992.

[48] The Vikings had sailed to North America in the 11th century (which was around the same time many of them were embracing Christianity), and of course there were many natives who had lived there for many centuries before this. Therefore, Columbus did not technically discover the Americas, but his action sparked the beginning of its colonization by Western Europe.

[49] Daniel Dorchester, *Christianity in the United States,* New York: Hunt & Eaton, 1895, p. 24.

[50] Morris, pp. 41-42.

[51] Henry C. Sheldon, *History of the Christian Church*, 1894, quoted in Slater, p. 169.

[52] Sheldon, *History of the Christian Church*, quoted in Slater, p. 171.

[53] J. H. Merle D'Aubigne, *History of the Reformation in Europe*, New York: Robert Carter and Bros., 1867, quoted in Slater, pp. 170-171.

[54] D'Aubigne, *History of the Reformation in Europe,* quoted in Slater, p. 172.

[55] Ibid.

Chapter 5

[56] D'Aubigne, *History of the Reformation in Europe,* quoted in Slater, p. 334.

[57] Ibid., p. 336.

[58] Ibid.

[59] Ibid.

[60] Ibid., p. 337.

[61] John Overton Choules, August 12, 1843, Preface to the 1844 reprint of Daniel Neal, The *History of the Puritans*, 1731, published by Harper Bros. in 2 Vol., 1844, quoted in *The Christian History of the Constitution*, p. 183.

[62] Richard Hakluyt, *A Selection of the Principal Voyages, Traffiques and Discoveries of the English Nations*, compiled by Laurence Irving, New York: Alfred A. Knopf, 1926, p. 260.

[63] To learn about the providence of God in Richard Hakluyt's life see, Stephen McDowell, *The American Dream, Jamestown and the Planting of the American Christian Republic*, Charlottesville: Providence Foundation, 2007, Chapter 3.

[64] *Ibid.*, p. 285.

[65] *Ibid., p.* 291.

[66] *Ibid.*, p. 287.

[67] *Ibid.*, p. 291.

[68] *Ibid.*, p. 292.

[69] *Ibid.*, p. 292.

Chapter 6

[70] Marshall Foster and Mary-Elaine Swanson, *The American Covenant the Untold Story*, California: Mayflower Institute, 1983, p. 71.

[71] Ibid., p. 72.

[72] Ibid.

[73] John Brown, *The Pilgrim Fathers of New England and Their Puritan Successors*, Pasadena, Tex.: Pilgrim Publications, 1970, p. 93, quoted in Foster and Swanson, p. 72.

[74] Ibid.

[75] Cotton Mather, *Life of William Bradford* in *The Story of the Pilgrim Fathers*, London: Ward and Downey, 1897, p. 40, quoted in Foster and Swanson, p. 72.

[76] *Bradford's History "Of Plimoth Plantation" From the Original Manuscript*, printed by order of the General Court of Massachusetts, Boston: Wright & Potter Printing Co., State Printers, 1898, the excerpts are from pages 11-121. The spelling has been modernized.

[77] Ibid., p. 116.

[78] Peter Marshall and David Manuel, *The Light and the Glory,* Old Tappon, NJ: Fleming H. Revell Co., 1977, pp. 130-132. See also, Bradford, pp. 116-117; and *Mourt's Relation: A Journal of the Pilgrims of Plymouth,* Plymouth, MA: Plymouth Rock Foundation, 1985, p. 48.

[79] *Mourt's Relation,* pp. 72-73; Marshall and Manuel, pp. 135-136; see also, *The Pilgrims and Plymouth Colony,* by the editors of American Heritage, New York: American Heritage Publishing Co., 1961, pp. 102-103.

Chapter 7

[80] Rushdoony, *The Institutes of Biblical Law,* p. 1.

[81] "The First Charter of Virginia," *Sources of Our Liberties*, Richard L. Perry, editor, New York: American Bar Foundation, 1952, pp. 39-40.

[82] *For the Colony in Virginea Britannia, Lawes Divine, Morall and Martiall, etc.,* compiled by William Strachey, edited by David H. Flaherty, Charlottesville: The University of Virginia, Charlottesville, 1969.

[83] For more on the founding of Virginia see, Stephen McDowell, *The American Dream, Jamestown and the Planting of the American Christian Republic*, Providence Foundation, 2007.

[84] Morris, pp. 98-101.

[85] B.F. Morris, pp. 96-98. See also *Narratives of Early Carolina, 1650-1708,* edited by Alexander S. Salley, Jr., New York: Charles Scribner's Sons, 1911, pp. 230-232.

[86] Edwin Scott Gaustad, *A Religious History of America,* New York, 1974, p. 104.

[87] Morris, pp. 101-104.

[88] Foster and Swanson, p. 90.

[89] John Winthrop, "A Modell of Christian Charity, 1630," Old South Leaflets, No. 207, Boston: Old South Assoc., p. 20.

[90] Ibid.

[91] John Fiske, *Beginnings of New England*, 1889, quoted in *The Christian History of the Constitution*, p. 252.

[92] Ibid.

[93] "Charter of Rhode Island and Providence Plantations," July 8, 1663, *Sources of Our Liberties*, Richard L. Perry, ed., pp. 169-170.

For resources on the founding of the colonies see: *Colonial Origins of the American Constitution*, Donald S. Lutz, ed., Indianapolis: Liberty Fund, 1998; B.F. Morris, Chapters 7, 8; Gaustad, *A Religious History of America*; James H. Hutson, *Religion and the Founding of the American Republic,* Washington: Library of Congress, 1998.

[94] Agreement of the Settlers at Exeter in New Hampshire, July 5, 1639, *Colonial Origins of the American Constitution, A Documentary History*, Donald S. Lutz, editor, Indianapolis: Liberty Fund, 1998, pp. 3-4. Spelling has been modernized.

[95] B.F. Morris, pp 70-71.

[96] B.F. Morris, p. 95.

[97] Ibid.

[98] B.F. Morris p. 90.

[99] Ibid., p. 91.

[100] Memoirs of the Historical Society of Pennsylvania, Philadelphia, 1826, quoted in *Remember William Penn,* compiled by the William Penn Tercentenary Committee, Harrisburg, Penn.: Commonwealth of Pennsylvania, 1945, p. 74.

[101] *Remember William Penn,* pp, 85-86.

[102] "Frame of Government of Pennsylvania," April 25, 1682, *Sources of Our Liberties,* p. 210-211.

[103] William Penn, "To the Czar of Muscov, April 18, 1698," *Writings of Penn,* Vol. 3, Editors Richard Dunn and Mary Dunn, University of Pennsylvania Press, 1986, pp. 540-541.

[104] Stephen McDowell, *No Cross, No Crown, The Life Message of William Penn,* Charlottesville: Providence Foundation, 2017, p. 16.

[105] The New England Confederation, 1643, *Colonial Origins of the American Constitution, A Documentary History,* p. 365-366.

[106] While the Southern colonies had governors appointed by the king of England, they also had elected representatives that exercised significant power.

Chapter 8

[107] Slater, pp. 278-279.

[108] Gary Demar, *God and Government,* Vol. 2, Atlanta: American Vision, 1984, p. 12.

[109] Greg Anthony, *Biblical Economics,* 1988, p. i.

[110] Slater, p. 88-89.

[111] A Facsimile Edition of Noah Webster's 1828 Edition of *An American Dictionary of the English Language,* reprinted by Foundation for American Christian Education, definition of education.

[112] For many examples see Stephen McDowell, *Transforming Nations through Biblical Work, Christians Have Led the Advancement in All Spheres of Life,* Charlottesville: Providence Foundation, 2018.

[113] Slater, p. 88.

[114] *Consider and Ponder,* pp. 605-606.

[115] Cotton Mather, *The Great Works of Christ in America, Magnalia Christi Americana,* Carlisle, Penn.: The Banner of Truth Trust, 1979 (reprint of 1852 edition).

[116] Fiske, quoted in *Christian History of the Constitution,* p. 273. The "Old Deluder Law" can be found in *The Laws and Liberties of Massachusetts,* reprinted from the copy of the 1648 edition in The Henry E. Huntington Library, Birmingham: The Legal Classics Library, 1982, p. 47.

[117] Samuel Blumenfeld, *Is Public Education Necessary?* Boise: The Paradigm Company, 1985, pp. 19-20.

[118] Samuel Blumenfeld, *N.E.A.—Trojan Horse in American Education,* Boise: The Paradigm Company, 1985.

[119] Letter to David McClure, October 25, 1836, *Letters of Noah Webster,* Harry R. Warfel editor, New York: Library Publishers, 1953, p, 453.

[120] Noah Webster, *An American Speller,* Preface.

[121] Webster, *An American Speller.* There were many different versions of the Speller published. While the Christian content varied over the years, it remained ubiquitous in the various editions.

[122] Noah Webster, *An American Dictionary of the English Language,* Facsimile edition of 1828 Dictionary, San Francisco: Foundation for American Christian Education, 1980, p. 27.

[123] William McGuffey, *The Eclectic Fourth Reader,* originally printed in 1838, republished by Mott Media, 1982, p. x.

[124] John H. Westerhoff III, *McGuffey and His Readers,* Milford, Mi.: Mott Media, 1982.

[125] "America's Universities," an unpublished paper by Mark Beliles.

[126] Morris, pp. 74-75.

[127] *The Pageant of America*, Ralph Henry Gabriel, editor, New Haven: Yale University Press, Vol.10, 1928, p. 256. See also Richard Morris, editor, *Significant Documents in United States History, Vol. 1*, p. 19.

[128] "New England's First Fruits in Respect to the Progress of Learning in the College at Cambridge, in Massachusetts Bay," *America, Great Crises In Our History Told by Its Makers, A Library of Original Sources, Vol. 2*, Chicago: Americanization Department, 1925, pp. 155-156.

[129] Francis Simkins et al, *Virginia: History, Government, Geography*, New York: Charles Scribner's Sons, 1964, pp.48-49. See also Gaustad, p. 45.

[130] B.F. Morris, *Christian Life and Character of the Civil Institutions of the United States of America*, p. 239.

[131] Daniel Dorchester, *Christianity in the United States*, New York: Hunt & Eaton, 1895, p. 244.

[132] Ibid., p. 245.

[133] Gaustad, p. 90.

[134] *Sources of Our Liberties*, p. 396.

[135] Morris, p. 72.

[136] Noah Webster, "Education of Youth in America," *American Magazine* (March 1788):212, quoted in Alan Snyder, *Defining Noah Webster, Mind and Morals in the Early Republic*, New York: University Press of America, 1990, p. 114. See also Webster's 1828, p. 12.

[137] Samuel Adams, October 4, 1790, in *Christian History of the Constitution*, p. XIV.

Chapter 9

[138] David Gregg, *Makers of the American Republic*, quoted in Slater, p. 40.

[139] Skousen, p. 678.

[140] Skousen, p. 679.

[141] Nathaniel Appleton, *The Great Blessing of Good Rulers, Depends upon God's Giving His Judgments and His Righteousness to Them, A Sermon Preached before His Excellency William Shirley,...Of the Province of Massachusetts Bay, May 26, 1742*, quoted in Slater, p. 38-39.

[142] For excerpts of Williams' "The Essential Rights and Liberties of Protestants," see Stephen McDowell, *America's Providential History, A Documentary Sourcebook*, Charlottesville: Providence Foundation, 2004, p. 32 ff.

[143] E. L. Magoon, *Orators of the American Revolution*, New York: C. Scribner, 1857, reprinted by Sightext Publications, 1969, pp. 207-208.

[144] Jonathan Mayhew, "A Discourse Concerning Unlimited Submission and Non-Resistance to the Higher Powers," a Sermon Preached January 30, 1749/50, quoted in John Wingate Thornton, *The Pulpit of the American Revolution*, Boston: Gould and Lincoln, 1860, pp. 53-54.

[145] Quoted in Morris, p. 339. See also George Bancroft, *History of the United States*, 1874, 6:12-13.

[146] Norman V. Pope, "Educator, Minister, Patriot," in *Nation Under God*, ed. Frances Brentano, Great Neck, New York, 1957, pp. 41-42. See also Mary-Elaine Swanson, *The Education of James Madison, A Model for Today*, Montgomery: The Hoffman Center, 1992, p. 53.

[147] Slater, p. 249.

[148] John Wingate Thornton, *The Pulpit of the American Revolution*, Boston, 1860, pp. xxii, xxiii, xxvi.

[149] Thornton, p. xxvi.

[150] *American Political Science Review*, Vol. 78, 1984.

[151] Morris, pp. 377-380. Also in J.T. Headley, *The Chaplains and Clergy of the Revolution*, 1864.

[152] Alice Baldwin, *The New England Clergy and the American Revolution*.

Chapter 10

[153] *The Autobiography of Benjamin Franklin*, edited by John Bigelow, New York: Walter J. Black, Inc., 1932, p. 217.

[154] George Bancroft, quoted in Slater, p. 251-252.

[155] Slater, p. 257.

[156] Richard Frothingham, *The Rise of the Republic*, 1890, quoted in *The Christian History of the Constitution*, p. 322.

[157] Samuel Adams, "Rights of the Colonists," November, 1772, from William V. Wells, *The Life and Public Services of Samuel Adams*, Boston: Little, Brown, and Company, 1865, 1:502-507.

[158] Richard Frothingham, *The Rise of the Republic*, quoted in *The Christian History of the Constitution*, p. 332.

[159] Resolution for a Day of Fasting and Prayer, Issued Tuesday, the 24th of May, 1774, by the Virginia House of Burgesses, Facsimile copy printed by Colonial Williamsburg.

[160] Richard Frothingham, *The Rise of the Republic*, quoted in *The Christian History of the Constitution*, p. 337.

[161] Ibid., p. 338.

[162] Ibid., p. 339.

[163] John Adams, quoted in Jedidiah Morse, *Annals of the American Revolution*, first published in 1824, reissued in 1968 by Kennikat Press, p. 218.

[164] Slater, p. 263.

[165] B.F. Morris, pp. 209-213.

[166] *Journal of the Proceedings of the Congress Held at Philadelphia September 5, 1774, A Facsimile of the Official Edition Printed in 1774*, Philadelphia: printed for the Library Company of Philadelphia, 1974, pp. 214-215.

[167] John Adams letter to Abigail Adams, Sept. 16, 1774, *The Book of Abigail and John, Selected Letters of the Adams Family, 1762-1784*, Cambridge, Mass.: Harvard University Press, 1975, p. 76.

[168] Printed in Thatcher's Military Biography (1777), in B.F. Morris, p. 213.

[169] John Adams letter to Abigail Adams, Sept. 16, 1774, *The Book of Abigail and John, Selected Letters of the Adams Family, 1762-1784*, p. 76. Dr. Cooper was John Adams' pastor.

[170] Silas Deane, *The Deane Papers: Collections of the New York Historical Society for the Year 1886*, New York: Printed for the Society, 1887, Vol. 1, p. 20, Wednesday, September 7, 1774, quoted in David Barton, *Original Intent*, Aledo, TX: WallBuilder Press, 1996, p. 93.

[171] Jedidiah Morse, *Annals of the American Revolution*.

[172] *Consider and Ponder*, p. 402. See also Thornton, p. xxxvii. The proclamation can be seen on page 140 in this book.

[173] Alice Baldwin, *The New England Clergy and the American Revolution*, Fredick Ungar Pub. Co., 1928.

[174] Richard Frothingham, *The Rise of the Republic*, quoted in *The Christian History of the Constitution*, p. 343.

[175] A copy of the Proclamation can be seen in *The Christian History of the Constitution*, p. Id.

[176] Franklin Cole, ed., *They Preached Liberty,* Indianapolis: Liberty Press, p. 39.

[177] William V. Wells, *The Life and Public Service of Samuel Adams*, Boston: Little, Brown, and Company, 1865, Vol. 2, pp. 291-294.

[178] Cole, p. 39.

[179] Governor Jonathan Trumbull, A Proclamation for a Day of Fasting and Prayer, to Be Observed April 19, 1775. A copy of the Proclamation is on page 202.

[180] Quoted in Morris, p. 432.

[181] *America, Great Crises in Our History Told by Its Makers, a Library of Original Sources,* Chicago: Veterans of Foreign Wars, 1925, Vol. III, pp. 184-185.

[182] Copy of the Proclamation in *Consider and Ponder,* p. 510a.

[183] "A Sermon, Preached on the Day of the Continental Fast, at Tredyffryn, in Chester County, by the Rev. David Jones, A.M., Philadelphia, 1775," in Evans Microprint Collection, American Antiquarian Society, #14133, in Stephen McDowell, editor, *America's Providential History, A Documentary Sourcebook,* pp. 46-53.

[184] *The Proceedings of the Virginia Convention in the Town of Richmond on the 23rd of March, 1775,* Saint John's Church, 1927, pp. 12-13. Also in William Wirt, *The Life and Character of Patrick Henry,* pp. 137-142.

[185] Morris, pp. 346-347.

[186] Morris, p. 349.

[187] Benson J. Lossing, *Washington and the American Republic,* quoted in Slater, p. 248.

[188] Thorton, p. xxxviii.

[189] Broadside printed in Salem, Massachusetts-Bay by E. Russell by Order of the Council, R. Derby, President. (see p. 176)

[190] Thorton, p. xxix. This is likely a paraphrase of Adams' words from a July 4th, 1837, oration. See Stephen McDowell, *Building Godly Nations,* Charlottesville: Providence Foundation, 2003, p. 167.

Chapter 11

[191] Samuel Davies Alexander, *Princeton College During the Eighteenth Century,* New York: Anson D.F. Randolph & Co., p. ix.

[192] Robert Flood, *Men Who Shaped America,* Chicago, 1976, p. 45.

[193] *The Annals of America, Vol. 2,* Chicago, 1968, p. 276.

[194] George Bancroft, *History of the United States, Vol. VI,* Boston, 1878, p. 355.

[195] William V. Wells, *The Life and Public Services of Samuel Adams,* 3:408. Also in, Frank Moore, *American Eloquence: A Collection of Speeches and Addresses,* New York: D. Appleton & Co., 1858, Vol. 1, p. 324.

[196] *The Book of Abigail and John, Selected Letters of the Adams Family, 1762-1784,* pp. 139-140. See also Bancroft, Vol. VI, p. 321.

[197] John Hancock, "Oration, Delivered at Boston, March 5, 1774," in Hezekiah Niles, *Principles and Acts of the Revolution in America,* New York: A.S. Barnes & Co., 1876, p. 42.

[198] Foster and Swanson, p. 126. See also Julian P. Boyd, *The Declaration of Independence, the Evolution of the Text,* Washington: The Library of Congress, 1999.

[199] Skousen, p. 32.

[200] Mark David Hall, *Did America Have a Christian Founding?* Nashville: Nelson Books, 2019, p. 78.

[201] Robert B. Weaver, *Our Flag and Other Symbols of Americanism,* Alexandria, Vir., 1972, p. 9.

[202] *The Story of the Seal,* Merrimac, Mass., p. 19.

[203] W. DeLoss Love, Jr., *The Fast and Thanksgiving Days of New England,* Boston: Houghton, Mifflin and Company, 1895. Love lists over 1400 times governments declared official Days of Prayer between 1620 and 1815.

[204] Robert Dearden and Douglas Watson, *The Bible of the Revolution,* San Francisco: Edwin & Robert Grabhorn, 1930, quoted in Slater, p. 339.

[205] Letter to John Banister, April 21, 1778, *The Writings of George Washington from the Original Manuscript Sources, 1745-1799,* John C. Fitzpatrick, Editor, Washington: United States Government Printing Office, 1931, 11:291.

[206] *The Writings of George Washington*, 10:195.

[207] Henry Armit Brown, "Centennial Oration of Valley Forge," in *Consider and Ponder*, Verna Hall, compiler, p. 61.

[208] Bart McDowell, *The Revolutionary War,* Washington, D.C.: National Geographic Society, 1970, p. 128.

[209] William Wilbur, *The Making of George Washington,* DeLand, Florida: Patriotic Education, 1973, p. 196.

[210] Brown, "Centennial Oration of Valley Forge," in *Consider and Ponder*, p. 61.

[211] Wilbur, p. 195.

[212] *The Writings of George Washington*, 11:291-292.

[213] Bart McDowell, p. 131.

[214] George Bancroft, *History of the United States,* Vol. 6, Boston: Little, Brown, and Co., 1878, p. 41.

[215] Letter to the President of Congress, December 23, 1777, *The Writings of George Washington*, 10:196.

[216] Brown, "Centennial Oration of Valley Forge," in *Consider and Ponder*, p. 66.

[217] Ibid., p. 68.

[218] William J. Johnson, *George Washington the Christian*, reprinted by Mott Media, 1976, pp. 120-121.

[219] E. C. M'Guire, *The Religious Opinions and Character of Washington*, New York: Harper & Brothers, 1836, p. 159.

[220] *Recollections and Private Memoirs of the Life and Character of Washington by George Washington Parke Custis, with Memoir of George Washington Parke Custis by His Daughter: with the Epistolary Correspondence between Washington and Custis,* Benson J. Lossing, editor, 1859, 275. See also M'Guire, 159, and Johnson, 104.

[221] Bruce Lancaster, *The American Revolution,* Garden City, NY: Garden City Books, 1957, 42.

[222] *The Writings of George Washington*, 11:354. For how they celebrated the day of Thanksgiving see Jared Sparks, *The Life of George Washington,* Boston: Little, Brown, and Company, 1860, p. 267.

[223] George Washington, *The Writings of George Washington*, 12:343.

[224] Letter to Rev. Samuel Langdon on September 28, 1789, *The Writings of George Washington*, 30:416.

[225] The American Vision, 360 Years Later.

[226] Bancroft, Vol. V, p. 387. And Washington Irving, *Life of George Washington,* New York: G.P. Putnam's Sons, 1857, 2:310-17.

[227] Irving, *Life of Washington*, 2:317.

[228] Marshall, *The Light and the Glory*, pp. 317-318.

[229] Ibid.

[230] Washington to John A. Washington, October 18, 1777, *The Writings of George Washington,* 9:399. Johnson, *George Washington the Christian*, p. 100.

[231] B. F. Morris, pp. 530-531.

[232] "The Providential Discovery of the Treason of Benedict Arnold — September 25th, 1780," booklet published by Foundation for American Christian Education. For details of this incident from the writings of Washington see: Letter of September 26, 1780, 20:88-89. Letter to the President of Congress, September 26, 1780, 20:92; Letter of October 13, 1780, 20:173; 20:95; in *The Writings of George Washington*.

[233] *America*, Vol. III, pp. 284-285.

[234] Morris, p. 537.

[235] Foster and Swanson, pp. 165-166.

[236] William McAuley Hosmer, "Divine Providence — God Himself in the Battle of Yorktown," Foundation for Christian Self-Government Newsletter, Sept. 1981.

[237] Ibid.

[238] George Washington, General Orders, October 20, 1781, *The Writings of George Washington*, 23:245, 247.

Chapter 12

[239] John Fiske, *The Critical Period of American History*, 1783-1789, New York: Houghton, Mifflin and Company, 1894, p. 231.

[240] Ibid.

[241] Albert Henry Smyth, ed., *Writings of Benjamin Franklin*, Macmillan Co., 1905-7, Vol. 9, p. 702.

[242] Robert A. Rutland, ed., *The Papers of James Madison*, University of Chicago Press, 1962, Vol. 10, p. 208.

[243] Skousen, p. 5.

[244] *Writings of George Washington*, 29:525.

[245] James Madison's *Notes of Debates in the Federal Convention of 1787*, New York: W.W. Norton & Co., 1987, pp. 209-210.

[246] B.F. Morris, p. 252.

[247] B.F. Morris, p. 253. See also Max Farrand, *The Records of the Federal Convention of 1787*, New Haven: Yale University Press, 1911, 3:467-473. Hamilton opposed the resolution, saying such an action at that time might communicate to the populace (who knew nothing of the events in the closed convention) they were having troubles and, hence, undermine the people's support. Mr. Sherman from Connecticut pointed out they would have greater troubles if they neglected this important duty. It was also proposed to have a sermon preached on July 4th at the request of the convention. Dayton records the motion appointing a chaplain was seconded and carried. Madison records they did not vote on the issue. If this were so, it was because they had no funds to officially invite a chaplain, as pointed out by Delegate Williamson. (See Madison, 210-211.) However, chaplains were certainly obtained in some manner as they opened future daily sessions with prayer. See Farrand, p. 472.

[248] B.F. Morris, pp. 252-253.

[249] *The Writings of George Washington*.

[250] George Bancroft, *History of the United States of America*, D. Appleton and Co., 1891, Vol. 6, p. 420.

[251] Bancroft, p. 414.

[252] See Benson J. Lossing, *Mount Vernon and Its Associations*, New York: Townsend, 1859, p. 202.

[253] Morris, p. 271.

[254] *The Writings of George Washington*, 30:291 ff.

[255] Northwest Ordinance, July 13, 1787, *Sources of Our Liberties*, pp. 395-396.

[256] Morris, p. 274.

[257] *A Compilation of the Messages and Papers of the Presidents,* Bureau of National Literature, 1897, Vol. 1, p. 56. See also Morris, p. 275.

[258] B. F. Morris, pp. 530-531.

[259] Morris, p. 537.

[260] *The Holy Bible*, As printed by Robert Aitken and Approved & Recommended by the Congress of the United States of America in 1782. Facsimile edition reprinted, New York: Arno Press, 1968.

[261] Morris, p. 543. See Morris, Chapter 22, for the text of many Days of Prayer proclaimed by government in early America.

[262] Some secularists today claim the originally worded Treaty with Tripoli (1797) shows we were not a Christian nation due to this wording. However, the context of this treaty shows the intent was to bring peace with an Islamic power who had only dealt with so-called "Christian" nations in Europe who had warred against them. Following the quoted statement, the treaty states: "as it has in itself no character of enmity against the laws, religion or tranquility of Musselmen." European "Christian" nations had state-established churches. Unique to all nations, the United States had no officially established religion (in this sense it was not founded upon the Christian religion), yet it was founded upon Christian principles as this book clearly reveals; and these principles recognized religious freedom and encouraged peace, not war. Even so, later versions of the treaty removed the language that America was not founded upon the Christian religion. For a fuller explanation of the Treaty of Tripoli, see Barton, *Original Intent*, pp. 126-130.

[263] Morris, p. 328.

[264] Runkel v. Winemiller, 4 Harris & McHenry 256, 259 (Sup. Ct. Md. 1799).

[265] Church of the Holy Trinity v. United States; 143 U. S. 457, 471 (1892).

[266] "A Letter to the Officers of the First Brigade of the Third Division of the Militia of Massachusetts, Oct. 11, 1798," in *The Works of John Adams, Second President of the United States*, Boston: Little, Brown and Co., 1854, 9:228-229.

[267] Daniel Webster, *The Writings and Speeches of Daniel Webster Hitherto Uncollected*, Boston: Little, Brown, and Company, 1903, Vol. IV, pp. 656-657, to Professor Pease on June 15, 1852.

[268] James Madison, "Letter to Frederick Beasley, Nov. 20, 1825."

[269] George Washington, "Circular to the Governors of the States," June 8, 1783, *Writings of George Washington*, 26:496.

[270] *A Compilation of the Messages and Papers of the Presidents*, James D. Richardson, Philadelphia: Lippincott, 1857, 1:205 ff. Also in *America's Providential History, A Documentary Sourcebook*, pp. 88-95.

[271] "Washington to the Philadelphia clergy, March 3, 1797," *Writings of George Washington*, 35:416.

[272] Samuel Adams, *The Writings of Samuel Adams*, Harry Alonzo Cushing, ed., New York: G.P. Putnam's Sons, 1905, Vol. IV, p. 124.

[273] Benjamin Rush, *Essays, Literary, Moral and Philosophical*, Philadelphia: Printed by Thomas and William Bradford, 1806, p. 93.

[274] B.F. Morris, p. 239.

[275] Skousen, p. 664.

[276] Sol Bloom, *The Story of the Constitution*, Washington, D.C., 1937, p. 183.

[277] Morris, p. 326.

[278] Morris, p. 234.

[279] Morris, p. 235.

[280] Morris, p. 231.

[281] Morris, p. 239.

[282] Robert L. Cord, *Separation of Church and State*, New York: Lambeth Press, 1982, pp. 12-13.

[283] Kentucky Resolutions, November 16, 1798, *Significant Documents in United States History, Volume 1, 1620-1896*, edited by Richard B. Morris, New York: Van Nostrand Reinhold Company, 1969, p. 187.

[284] Saul K. Padover, ed. *The Complete Jefferson*, Tudor Publishing Co. 1943, p. 412.

[285] See Mark Beliles and Jerry Newcombe, *Doubting Thomas? The Religious Life and Legacy of Thomas Jefferson*, New York: Morgan James, 2015.

[286] Zorach v. Clauson, 343 U.S. 306 at 313.

[287] Lynch v. Donelly, 465 U.S. at 673.

[288] Daniel L. Dreisbach, *Religion and Politics in the Early Republic*, Lexington, Ken.: The University Press of Kentucky, 1996, p. 113.

Chapter 13

[289] *The Christian History of the Constitution of the United States of America, Self-Government with Union*, Verna Hall, compiler, San Francisco: Foundation for American Christian Education, 1979, p. 34.

[290] Madison's *Notes of Debates*, p. 210.

[291] Donald Lutz, "The Relative Influence of European Writers on Late 18th Century American Political Thought," *American Political Science Review*, LXXVIII (1984) 189-197. See Stephen McDowell, *Building Godly Nations,* Charlottesville: Providence Foundation, 2003, pp. 185-90, for Christian views of these writers.

[292] *Newsweek*, Dec. 26, 1982.

[293] *The Federalist, A Collection of Essays, Written in Favor of the Constitution of the United States, as Agreed Upon by the Federal Convention, September 17, 1787*, by Alexander Hamilton, John Jay, and James Madison, Jr., edited by Michael Loyd Chadwick, Washington, DC: Global Affairs Publishing Company, p. 1987, No. 51.6, p. 281.

[294] *The Federalist*, No. 45.12, p. 252.

[295] *Our Ageless Constitution*, edited by W. David Stedman and LaVaughn G. Lewis, Asheboro, NC, 1987, p. 32.

[296] Skousen, p. 177.

[297] *Our Ageless Constitution*, p. 33.

[298] *The Federalist*, No. 47.4. and 47.5, p. 261.

[299] Hamilton, Madison and Jay, *The Federalist Papers,* New York, 1982, p. 244.

[300] *The Federalist Papers.*

[301] Noah Webster, *History of the United States,* New Haven: Durrie & Peck, 1833, pp. 273-74.

Chapter 14

[302] Charles Hull Wolfe, "The Principle Approach to American Christian Economics," in *A Guide to American Christian Education for the Home and School, the Principle Approach*, by James B. Rose, Palo Cedro, CA: American Christian History Institute, p. 415.

[303] Ibid.

[304] Ibid., p. 402.

[305] Ibid.

[306] Ibid.

[307] Ibid.

[308] Ibid., pp. 402-403.

[309] Ibid., p. 398.

[310] Greg Anthony, *Biblical Economics*, 1988, p. 13

[311] Wolfe, p. 398.

[312] Ibid., p. 403.

[313] Ibid.

[314] *How to Understand the Purpose behind Humanism*, booklet published by Institute in Basic Youth Conflicts, 1983, p. 7.

[315] Wolfe, p. 403.

[316] Cleon Skousen, *Study Guide to the Making of America*.

[317] William Bradford, *Of Plimoth Plantation*, Boston, 1901, p. 162.

[318] Ibid., p. 163.

[319] Wolfe, p. 405.

[320] Ibid.

[321] Ibid.

[322] *The Christian History of the Constitution of the United States of America*, p. 64.

[323] Slater, p. 234.

[324] Slater, p. 228-229.

[325] Wolfe, p. 406.

[326] George Grant, *In the Shadow of Plenty*, Fort Worth, Texas: Dominion Press, 1986, p. 4.

[327] Wolfe, p. 406.

[328] David Chilton, *Productive Christians in an Age of Guilt Manipulators: A Biblical Response to Ronald J. Sider*, quoted in Anthony, p. 27.

[329] Anthony, p. 28.

[330] Ibid., pp. 28-29.

[331] For more on money, inflation, and banking see Stephen McDowell, *Honest Money and Banking*, Charlottesville: Providence Foundation, 2009.

[332] Verna Hall and Rosalie Slater, *The Bible and the Constitution of the United States of America*, San Francisco, 1983, p. 35.

[333] John Locke, "Of the State of Nature," *Of Civil Government*, in *Christian History of the Constitution*, p. 58.

[334] Locke, "Of Property," *Of Civil Government*, in *Christian History of the Constitution*, p. 64.

[335] Wolfe, p. 406.

[336] *Our Ageless Constitution*, p. 30.

[337] James Madison's *Notes of Debates in the Federal Convention of 1787*, pp. 470-471.

[338] Andrew Jackson, 8th Annual Message to Congress, in *Our Ageless Constitution*, p. 37.

[339] Gary DeMar, *God and Government, Vol. 2*, pp. 131, 121.

[340] Anthony, p. 34.

[341] Chilton, quoted in Anthony, p. 34.

[342] Anthony, p. 34.

[343] For more on economics and the role of government, see Stephen McDowell, *The Economy from a Biblical Perspective*, Charlottesville: Providence Foundation, 2009.

Chapter 15

[344] *Our Ageless Constitution*, p. 39.

[345] Ibid.

[346] Ibid.

[347] George Washington, Farewell Address, 1796, in *America's Providential History, A Documentary Sourcebook*, pp. 88-95.

[348] Ibid.

[349] Ibid.

[350] Gary North, *Healer of the Nations, Biblical Principles for International Relations*, Fort Worth, TX, 1987, p. 11.

[351] Thomas Jefferson. First Inaugural, 1801, in Morris, *Significant Documents in United States History*, p. 196.

[352] The Monroe Doctrine, 1823, in Morris, *Significant Documents in United States History*, pp. 228-229.

[353] John Eidsmoe, *Christianity and the Constitution*, Grand Rapids, Mich.: Baker Book House, 1987, p. 364.

[354] Foster and Swanson, pp. 145-146.

[355] Lee Grady, "Can We Make a Deal for Peace?" *The Forerunner*, Vol. VIII, No. 8, December 1987, pp. 15-17.

[356] Ibid.

Chapter 16

[357] For a listing of biblical ideas contained in the Declaration see Stephen McDowell and Jim Arcieri, *Teacher's Guide to America's Providential History*, Charlottesville: Providence Foundation, 2005, pp. 80-81.

[358] George Washington, *The Writings of George Washington*, 12:343.

[359] John Quincy Adams, *An Oration Delivered before the Inhabitants of the Town of Newburyport on the Sixty-First Anniversary of the Declaration of Independence, July 4th, 1837*, Charles Whipple, Newburyport, 1837, pp. 5-6.

[360] For more on the framework of the Constitution and Godly government, see *America's Providential History*, Chapter 13, *Liberating the Nations*, Chapter 11, and Mark Beliles and Doug Anderson, *Contending for the Constitution*, Charlottesville: Providence Foundation, 2005.

[361] Robert A. Rutland, ed., *The Papers of James Madison*, University of Chicago Press, 1962, Vol. 10, p. 208.

[362] W. Cleon Skousen, *The Making of America*, Washington, DC: The National Center for Constitutional Studies, p. 5.

[363] Washington to Jonathan Trumbull, July 20, 1788, *The Writings of George Washington*, Vol. 30, p. 22.

[364] *Cyrus Hall McCormick, His Life and Work*, Herbert N. Casson, Chicago: A.C. McClurg &Co., 1909, p. 202. For more on McCormick see Stephen McDowell, *Biblical Principles of Business, Exemplified in the Life of Cyrus Hall McCormick*, Charlottesville: Providence Foundation, 2018.

[365] Ibid., p. 40.

[366] Ibid., p. 47.

[367] Ibid., p. 53.

[368] Ibid., p. 54.

[369] Ibid., p. 58.

[370] Ibid., p. 79. To learn how McCormick applied biblical principles (that are used today by successful businesses) in founding his new business, see McDowell, *Biblical Principles of Business, Exemplified in the Life of Cyrus Hall McCormick*.

[371] Carleton Mabee, *The American Leonardo, A Life of Samuel F. B. Morse*, New York: Alfred A. Knopf, 1943, p. 279.

[372] Ibid., p. 275.

[373] Ibid., p. 276.

[374] Ibid., p. 280.

[375] Ibid.

[376] Ibid., p. 369.

[377] Charles Lee Lewis, *Matthew Fontaine Maury, The Pathfinder of the Seas*, New York: AMS Press, 1969 (reprinted from edition of 1927), p. 82.

[378] Other accounts say his wife read the Bible to him.

[379] Lewis, pp. 251-252.

[380] Ibid., pp. 240a-240b.

[381] Matthew Fontaine Maury, *The Physical Geography of the Sea and its Meteorology*, New York: Harper & Brothers, 1856, p. 80.

[382] John W. Wayland, *The Pathfinder of the Seas, The Life of Matthew Fontaine Maury*, Richmond: Garret & Massie, Inc., 1930, pp. 60-61.

[383] Lewis, p. xiv.

[384] Maury to Frank Minor, July 25, 1855, in Lewis, p. xiv.

[385] Wayland, p. 131.

[386] Lewis, p. 96.

[387] Lewis, pp. 98-99.

[388] Hidlegarde Hawthorne, *Matthew Fontaine Maury, Trail Maker of the Seas*, New York: Longmans, Green and Co., 1943, pp. 154-155.

[389] For stories of more of these people see Stephen McDowell, *Transforming Nations Through Biblical Work, Christians Have Led the Advancement of Mankind in All Spheres of Life*, Charlottesville: Providence Foundation, 2018.

[390] *The Pageant of America*, Vol. 10, p. 315.

[391] Joe B. Frantz, *Gail Borden, Dairyman to a Nation*, Norman: University of Oklahoma Press, 1951, p. 166.

[392] See Stephen McDowell, *Kingdom Missionaries Marcus and Narcissa Whitman, The Founding of the Oregon Territory*, Charlottesville: Providence Foundation, 2011. A little more information is given about Whitman later in this chapter.

[393] *The Writings of Thomas Jefferson*, Andrew A. Lipscomb and Albert Ellery Bergh, Editors, Washington, DC: The Thomas Jefferson Memorial Association, 1903, 5:364.

[394] Ibid., 5:366.

[395] Joshua E. London, *Victory in Tripoli, How America's War with the Barbary Pirates Established the U.S. Navy and Built a Nation*, Hoboken, NJ: John Wiley & Sons, Inc., 2005, p. 23-24.

[396] Ibid., p. 25.

[397] Ibid., p. 11.

[398] Benson J. Lossing, *Our Country, A Household History*, Vol. 2, New York: Johnson & Miles, 1877, p. 1179. For more on historic relations between America and Islamic nations see, Stephen McDowell, *The Threat of Islam to Liberty and Christianity*, Charlottesville: Providence Foundation, 2015.

[399] See Stephen McDowell, *Abraham Lincoln's Faith*, Charlottesville: Providence Foundation, 2012.

[400] Joseph Banyard, *Daniel Webster, His Life and Public Services*, Chicago: Werner Company, 1875, pp. 131-133.

[401] Daniel Webster, *The Works of Daniel Webster*, Boston: Little, Brown, and Co., 1853, Vol.1, p. 49, from "A Discourse Delivered at Plymouth, on the 22nd of December, 1820."

[402] B.F. Morris, p. 270.

[403] David J. Hill, *Elements of Rhetoric and Composition*, Hills Rhetorical Series, 1884, p. 3.

[404] James F. Cooper, *Knights of the Brush, The Hudson River School and the Moral Landscape*, New York: Hudson Hills Press, 1999, p. 17, Description on inside jacket cover.

[405] Ibid., Forward.

[406] Ibid.

[407] Ibid., p. 23.

[408] Ibid.

[409] Ibid., pp. 23-24.

[410] For more on the Hudson River painters, including dozens of their paintings, see Cooper, *Knights of the Brush*. For a summary of Cooper's book, see the article by Stephen McDowell on the Providence Foundation's website: https://providencefoundation.com/knights-of-the-brush-famous-painters/

[411] To learn about American literature from a Christian perspective see Rosalie June Slater, *The Noah Plan, Literature Curriculum Guide*, published by Foundation for American Christian Education, and Rosalie June Slater, "The Christian History Literature Program," in James B. Rose, *A Guide to American Christian Education, The Principle Approach*, Camarillo, Cal.: American Christian History Institute, 1987.

[412] William A. Mowry, *Marcus Whitman and the Early Days of Oregon*, New York: Silver, Burdett and Company, 1901, p. vi.

[413] To learn this fascinating story see Stephen McDowell, *Kingdom Missionaries Marcus and Narcissa Whitman, The Founding of the Oregon Territory*. (This can be ordered from providencefoundation.com)

[414] Mowry, p. 72.

[415] Mabee, p. 294.

[416] With the reduction of taxes and removal of excessive regulations during President Trump's administration, many businesses started returning to the United States. But if taxes and regulations increase again, businesses will flee again.

[417] For more on Unitarianism see David Barton, *Original Intent*, pp. 314-316.

Chapter 17

[418] "Washington's Farewell Address, 1796," in *America's Providential History, A Documentary Sourcebook*, Stephen McDowell, ed., pp. 88-95.

[419] Ibid.

[420] Ibid.

[421] Kate Mason Rowland, *Life and Correspondence of Charles Carroll of Carrollton*, New York & London: G.P. Putnam's Sons, 1898, Vol. II, p. 321, to Robert Goodloe Harper, April 23, 1820. To learn more about the Founders and slavery see McDowell, "The Bible, Slavery, and America's Founders," in *Building Godly Nations*.

[422] Letter to Robert Morris, April 12, 1786, in *George Washington: A Collection*, ed. W.B. Allen, Indianapolis: Liberty Fund, 1988, p. 319.

[423] Quoted in Marshall Foster and Mary-Elaine Swanson, *The American Covenant, the Untold Story*, California: Mayflower Institute, 1983, p. 142.

[424] Frederick Douglass, *The Frederick Douglas Papers*, John Blassingame, editor, New Haven: Yale University Press, 1982, pp. 385-386, from "What to the Slave is the Fourth of July?", July 5, 1852.

[425] G. Frederick Owen, *Abraham Lincoln: The Man and His Faith*, Wheaton, IL, 1981, p. 86-87, 91.

[426] Daniel Dorchester, p. 454.

[427] *Old South Leaflets*

[428] Recognizing the sinful nature of man and his potential for evil behavior, the Bible does allow for divorce in certain limited cases (adultery and abandonment).

[429] Abraham Lincoln, Second Inaugural, 1865, in Morris, *Significant Documents in United States History*, p. 319.

[430] William J. Johnson, *Abraham Lincoln the Christian*, Milford, Mich.: Mott Media, 1976, p. 106.

[431] See B.F. Morris, Chapter 26.

[432] Dorchester, p. 473.

[433] Dorchester, p. 460.

[434] J. William Jones, *Personal Reminiscences, Anecdotes, and Letters of General Robert E. Lee*, D. Appleton and Co., 1874, p. 138.

[435] Gamaliel Bradford, *Lee the American*, Houghton and Mifflin Co., 1913, p. 92.

[436] Bradford, p. 242.

[437] Mark Grimsley, "Jackson: The Wrath of God," *Civil War Times*, pp. 15-19.

[438] Proclamation Issued on March 30th, 1863, *A Compilation of the Messages and Papers of the Presidents*, James D. Richardson, 8:3365-3366.

[439] Grimsley, p. 18.

[440] Johnson, pp. 112-114.

[441] Philip Alexander Bruce, *Robert E. Lee*, W.B. Jacobs and Co., 1907, p. 359.

[442] Robert E. Lee, Jr. *Recollections and Letters of General Robert E. Lee*, Doubleday, Page and Co., 1904, p. 105.

[443] J. William Jones, *Christ in the Camp*, B.F. Johnson and Co, 1887, (reprinted by Sprinkle Publications, 1986), p. 56-57.

[444] Jones, *Christ in the Camp*, p. 51.

[445] Abraham Lincoln, Gettysburg Address, 1863, in Morris, *Significant Documents in United States History*, p. 313.

[446] Johnson, p. 172.

[447] Johnson, pp. 178-179.

Chapter 18

[448] William J. Federer, *America's God and Country*, Coppell, Tex: FAME Publishing, Inc., 1994, p. 98.

[449] Rackham Holt, *George Washington Carver, An American Biography*, Garden City, NY: Doubleday, Doran, and Co., Inc., 1943, pp. 226-227.

[450] Ibid., p. 227.

[451] Ibid., p. 229.

[452] Charles E. Jones, *The Books You Read*, Harrisburg, PA: Executive Books, 1985, 132. Quoted in Federer, p. 96.

[453] Holt, p. 220.

[454] Federer, p. 97.

[455] James Manship, "George Washington Carver," notes of speech, 1998.

[456] Joseph H. Appel, *The Business Biography of John Wanamaker, Founder and Builder*, New York: The Macmillan Company, 1930, p. 205.

[457] Ibid., p. 206.

[458] Ibid., p. 208.

[459] Ibid., p. 55.

[460] Ibid., p. xv.

[461] Ibid.

[462] Ibid., p. viii.

[463] Ibid., p. xvi.

[464] Ibid., p. 197.

[465] Ibid., p. 291. For more on Wanamaker see, Stephen McDowell, *Transforming Medicine and Business with Biblical Principles, Examples of Joseph Lister and John Wanamaker*, Charlottesville: Providence Foundation, 2010.

[466] John M. Taylor, *Garfield of Ohio: The Available Man*, New York: W.W. Norton & Co., Inc., 1970, p. 180. Quoted from "A Century of Congress," by James A. Garfield, Atlantic, July 1877.

[467] Col. G.W. Townsend, *Memorial Life of William McKinley, Our Martyred President*, D.Z. Howell publisher, 1902, p. 406.

[468] Townsend, *Memorial Life of William McKinley, Our Martyred President*, pp. 351, 381, 392, 394, 418, 419.

[469] Kevin Phillips, *William McKinley*, part of *The American Presidents*, Arthur M. Schlesinger, Jr., General Editor, New York: Henry Holt and Company, 2003, p. 16.

[470] Ibid.

[471] William McKinley, March 4, 1897, First Inaugural Address.

[472] Lewis L. Gould, *The Presidency of William McKinley*, Lawrence: University Press of Kansas, 1980, p. 242.

[473] Charles Sumner Olcott, *The Life of William McKinley, vol. 2*, New York: Houghton Mifflin, 1916, p. 368.

[474] Townsend, p. 351.

[475] Townsend, p. 250-251, 266.

[476] Frederick Douglass, *The Frederick Douglass Papers*, John Blassingame, editor, New Haven: Yale University Press, 1982, Vol. 2, p. 397, from a speech delivered at Ithaca, New York, October 14th, 1852.

[477] Lynchings were more politically motivated than racially. Between 1882 and 1964, 4743 individuals were lynched – 3446 blacks and 1297 whites. Almost all of those lynched were Republicans. Republicans led the attempt to pass federal anti-lynching laws; Democrats blocked those bills. (David Barton, *Setting the Record Straight: American History in Black and White*, Aledo, Tex.: WallBuilders, 2004, p. 115.).

[478] Booker T. Washington, *Up From Slavery*, New York: Airmont Publishing Company, 1967, p. 120.

[479] Mary Bethune's Last Will and Testament, https://www.cookman.edu/about_bcu/history/lastwill_testament.html

[480] Rosa Parks, with Gregory J. Reed, *Quiet Strength: The Faith, the Hope, and the Heart of a Woman Who Changed a Nation*, 1994, p. 42.

[481] Martin Luther King, Jr, *Strength To Love*, 1994, p. 16.

482 Martin Luther King, Jr, Coretta Scott King, et al, *A Gift of Love*, 2012, p. 143.

483 Martin Luther King, Jr, Coretta Scott King, et al, *A Gift of Love*, 2012, p. 18.

484 Although women could not vote, this did not mean they did not have a voice in government. The biblically minded Americans saw that the family as an institution was to be represented in civil government by the husband/father (representing the family) choosing via his vote officials to representative the family regarding public affairs.

485 Carolyn Gifford, *Writing Out My Heart: Selections from the Journal of Frances E. Willard*, 1855-96, 1995, p. 47.

486 For population statistics see:
https://userpages.umbc.edu/~bouton/History407/SlaveStats.htm and
https://en.wikipedia.org/wiki/Demographic_history_of_the_United_States

487 Californios are Hispanic people native to the U.S. state of California, who are culturally or genetically descended from the Spanish-speaking community that has resided there since 1683, of varying Criollo Spaniard, Mestizo, and Indigenous Californian origins. (https://en.wikipedia.org/wiki/Californios)

488 From 1820 to 1996 over 61 million people immigrated to America. For immigrants to U.S. by Country of Origin see: https://www.infoplease.com/us/race-population/immigrants-us-country-origin

Chapter 19

489 Slater, p. 54.

490 Quoted in Slater, p. 251.

491 Slater, pp. 52-53.

492 See McDowell, "Education and the Kingdom of God," in *Building Godly Nations*, pp. 267 ff.

493 See Herbert W. Titus, *God, Man, and Law: The Biblical Principles*, Oak Brook, Ill.: Institute of Basic Life Principles, 1994, pp. 3-6.

494 Roscoe Pound, *The Spirit of the Common Law*, New York: The Legal Classics Library.

495 Benjamin Cardozo, *The Growth of Law*, New Haven: Yale University Press, 1924, p. 49.

496 Charles Evans Hughes, *The Autobiographical Notes of Charles Evans Hughes*, David J. Danelski and Joseph S. Tulchin, editors, Cambridge: Harvard University Press, 1973, p. 144, speech at Elmira on May 3, 1907.

497 Barna Poll conducted in the Spring of 2002.

498 Gary North, *Inherit the Earth*, Ft. Forth: Dominion Press, 1987, p. 34.

499 Some of the ideas that follow in this section are from North, p. 41 ff.

500 In ancient Israel, and in much of Christendom throughout history, the first born received a larger inheritance because it was his responsibility to care for his parents in their old age. In modern socialist states, the government is attempting to provide this (in the USA via social security), which adds to the destruction of the family, while greatly increasing the power of government.

501 For more see Stephen McDowell, *Honest Money and Banking* and *The Economy from a Biblical Perspective*, both published by the Providence Foundation, 2009. Also see *Foundations of Biblical Economics, Business, and the Marketplace*, a Providence Foundation Biblical Worldview University course.

502 See Burton Folsom, Jr., *New Deal or Raw Deal, How FDR's Economic Legacy Has Damaged America*, New York: Threshold Editions (Simon & Schuster), 2008.

503 See McDowell, *Honest Money and Banking*, for more on fiat money.

[504] In the spring of 2020, the government shut down much of the economy of the United States in response to the Coronavirus pandemic. To provide financial assistant to those who were forced to stop their economic activities, Congress appropriated over 2.5 trillion dollars in relief money to individuals and businesses. The cause of the national economic coronavirus pandemic problems was different than the recession of 2008 (and earlier recessions), and since governmental decrees stopped individual productivity, the money given to people could be seen as reparations, rather than handouts. Nonetheless, this creation of money by decree (fiat money) will result in the same type of problems that any deficit spending produces.

[505] See Paul Kengor, *The Crusader, Ronald Reagan and the Fall of Communism*, Regan (HarperCollins Publishers), 2006.

[506] *The Faith of FDR, From President Franklin Delano* Roosevelt's *Public Papers*, 1933-1945, compiled by William J. Federer, St. Louis: Amerisearch, 2006, p. 1.

[507] Ibid., p. 2.

[508] Verna Hall, *Christian History of the Constitution*, p. iv.

[509] Verna Hall, *Christian History of the Constitution*, p. iv.

[510] Noah Webster, *An American Dictionary of the English Language*, definition of *revival*.

[511] Wallis, *In the Day of Thy Power*, p. 45, quoted in Winkie Pratney, *Revival, Principles to Change the World*, Springdale, Penn.: Whitaker House, 1983, p. 15.

[512] Pratney, *Revival, Principles to Change the World*, p. 15.

[513] See Bruce Anderson, Mark Beliles, and Stephen McDowell, *Watchmen on the Walls*, Charlottesville, Vir.: Providence Foundation, 1995.

[514] Foster and Swanson, p. xvii.

[515] Foster and Swanson, p. xviii.

[516] Foster and Swanson, p. 37.

[517] Foster and Swanson. p. 106-107.

[518] Foster and Swanson, p. 125.

[519] Quoted in Pratney, p. 18.

[520] Quoted in Pratney, p. 18.

[521] Charles G. Finney, *Revivals of Religion*, 1978, p. 7.

[522] Pratney, p. 20.

[523] To learn more see Stephen McDowell, *Biblical Revival and the Transformation of Nations*, Charlottesville: Providence Foundation, 2013.

Chapter 20

[524] Thomas Jefferson, Letter to Charles Hammond , August 18, 1821, *The Writings of Thomas Jefferson*, Andew Lipscomb and Albert Bergh, editors, Washington, DC: The Thomas Jefferson Memorial Association, 1903, 15:332

[525] Thomas Jefferson, Letter to Charles Hammond , August 18, 1821, *The Writings of Thomas Jefferson,* 15:331-332.

[526] Thomas Jefferson, Letter to Charles Jarvis , September 28, 1820, *The Writings of Thomas Jefferson,* 15:277.

[527] Charles Evans Hughes, *The Autobiographical Notes of Charles Evans Hughes*, David J. Danelski and Joseph S. Tulchin, editors, Cambridge: Harvard University Press, 1973, p. 144, speech at Elmira on May 3, 1907.

[528] Some people present three eras of the court: (1) 1800-1895: Constitutional supremacy, (2) 1895-1950: Judicial supremacy, (3) 1950-present: Judicial activism. (See Robert K. Dornan and